Berkeley: Critical and Interpretive Essays

Berkeley
Critical and
Interpretive Essays

Colin M. Turbayne
editor

University of Minnesota Press
Minneapolis

Library of Congress Cataloging in Publication Data
Main entry under title:

Berkeley: critical and interpretive essays.

"Some of the papers delivered at the Berkeley
Commemorative Conference held at Newport, Rhode
Island, from September 27 to 30, 1979" —
    "A bibliography of George Berkeley, 1963-
1979": p.
    Includes index.
    1. Berkeley, George, 1685-1753 — Addresses,
essays, lectures.   I. Turbayne, Colin Murray.
B1348.B44   192   82-1967
ISBN 0-8166-1065-7   AACR2
ISBN 0-8166-1066-5 (pbk.)

Illustration on p. xi reproduced from the drawing by Alexander Nesbitt
with permission of The National Society of the Colonial Dames of America
in the State of Rhode Island and Providence Plantations.

To
the Guardians of Whitehall,
the Colonial Dames of
Rhode Island and
Providence Plantations

Contents

Contributors

Edwin B. Allaire
University of Texas
Austin, Texas

Geneviève Brykman
70 Rue du Javelot
75645 Paris 13, France

Phillip Cummins
University of Iowa
Iowa City, Iowa

Georges Dicker
State University of New York
at Brockport
Brockport, New York

Willis Doney
Dartmouth College
Hanover, New Hampshire

E. J. Furlong
Trinity College
Dublin, Ireland

Daniel Garber
University of Chicago
Chicago, Illinois

Michael Hooker
Johns Hopkins University
Baltimore, Maryland

Richard T. Lambert
Carrol College
Helena, Montana

William McGowan
California State University
Long Beach, California

Joseph Margolis
Temple University
Philadelphia, Pennsylvania

Nancy L. Maull
100 Walter Street
Cambridge, Massachusetts

Theodore Messenger
  University of North Dakota
  Grand Forks, North Dakota

Lawrence A. Mirarchi
  Hartwick College
  Oneonta, New York

George Pappas
  Ohio State University
  Columbus, Ohio

Désirée Park
  2 South Parks Road
  Oxford OX1 34B England

Gary Thrane
  2031 W. Farragut Ave.
  Chicago, Illinois

I. C. Tipton
  University College of Wales
  Aberystwyth
  Great Britain

Colin M. Turbayne
  University of Rochester
  Rochester, New York

Margaret D. Wilson
  Princeton University
  Princeton, New Jersey

Whitehall on Berkeley Avenue, Middletown, R.I., home of George Berkeley from 1729 to 1731, now open as a memorial to Berkeley's American sojourn.

Preface

Most of the following essays, appearing here for the first time, are revised versions of some of the papers delivered at the Berkeley Commemorative Conference held at Newport, Rhode Island, from September 27 to 30, 1979. The Conference, organized by the International Berkeley Society, celebrated Berkeley's arrival in Newport in 1729. Much planning and work in years prior to the Conference were done by Dr. Raymond W. Houghton, President of the Society, by members of the Department of Philosophy of Rhode Island College, and by the Colonial Dames of Rhode Island and Providence Plantations who care for Whitehall, Berkeley's American home.

But if the Commemorative Conference was the occasional cause for this collection of essays, then the underlying cause has been the increased scholarly attention given to Berkeley's philosophy in recent years. Berkeley is alive and well and a citizen of the world. The bibliographies show that, while fewer than three hundred works on Berkeley's philosophy appeared between 1709 and 1932, there have been nearly a thousand items in various languages since that time. The increased interest, it seems, began in the 1930s, and was reflected in A. J. Ayer's remark in the preface to his *Language, Truth, and Logic* (1936), to the effect that modern "analytical" philosophy was "the logical outcome" of the empiricism of Berkeley and Hume. Interest in Berkeley quickened in the decade after World War II, the main event being the magnificent nine-volume edition of the *Works*, edited by A. A. Luce and T. E. Jessop, published by Thomas Nelson of Edinburgh (1948-1957). The bibliography attached to the present volume reflects a steadily grown interest, especially in America.

Why is there so much attention paid to Berkeley today? The answer, I believe, is that he is astonishingly contemporary. He tackled most of the problems that concern present-day philosophers, such as the problems of perception, the distinction between primary and secondary qualities, the problem of universals, the nature of explanation, the importance of language, and the nature, existence, and knowledge of ourselves and others, and of God. Moreover, he writes so well. In our time, in which all the emphasis is placed upon argument, his works are widely recognized as paradigms of argumentative discourse. Perhaps, however, this has been in part a hindrance. He writes so lucidly that we tend to think prematurely that we understand him well.

Since the Editor invited scholars of Berkeley to present papers on aspects of Berkeley according to their choice, the character of this book has been determined entirely by the interests of the contributors. The topics discussed in the following essays give some idea of the problems that are important in Berkeleyan scholarship today. These problems are much the same as those just mentioned. In addition, there are articles on Berkeley's influence on philosophical method, on Berkeley's accounts of or attitudes toward such concepts as common sense, relativism, space, time, aether, and corpuscles.

Since the 1950s, commentators have shown growing dissatisfaction with the traditional view of Berkeley as the middle man between Locke and Hume in the argument of British Empiricism. The traditional view has diverted critical attention from richer areas in Berkeley's thought, including his philosophy of science, his theory of language, and his account of the nature of mind. Now, at long last, as some of the essays that follow indicate, these other areas are being increasingly explored.

I wish to record my gratitude to Lynne McCoy, Joseph Anesi, and Anna Harrison for secretarial and editorial assistance. I appreciate Daniel Garber's suggestion of including the drawing of Whitehall.

Colin M. Turbayne
University of Rochester

I Common Sense and Relativism

1

Berkeley, Perception, and Common Sense

George Pappas

Berkeley elaborated an idealist metaphysics, which, when coupled with his nominalism, yields the thesis of Berkeleyan idealism, viz., that the only existing individuals are infinite and finite spirits or perceivers, and nonactive, nonperceiving ideas and collections of them. Ideas are themselves construed as nonmaterial mental entities each of which exists when and only when it is perceived. Yet Berkeley also claimed that his philosophy is consistent with common sense. Indeed, he repeatedly claims that he was a defender or champion of the views of common sense. But it is most difficult to see how Berkeleyan idealism is to be reconciled with common sense, let alone how Berkeley's views support common sense. For Berkeleyan idealism implies that either

(a) There are no physical objects.

or that

(b) Each physical object is nothing but a collection of ideas.

and neither of these claims, it would seem, is consistent with common sense.

Moreover, given the thesis that each idea exists when and only when it is perceived, and the claim that (b) holds, we get

Earlier versions of this paper were read at Ohio State University; the University of Nebraska; the Canadian Philosophical Association meetings in Saskatoon, Saskatchewan, in June 1979; and the meetings of the International Berkeley Society, Newport, Rhode Island, in September 1979. I have benefited from comments and criticisms from Robert Audi, James Cornman, Philip Cummins, Alan Hausman, Mark Pastin, and Nelson Potter.

(c) Each physical object exists when and only when it is perceived.

Statement (c), though, seems no more consistent with common sense than are (a) and (b).

A related problem is that there are certain views that are indisputably commonsensical, and that Berkeley either explicitly accepts or is committed to accepting given some of his remarks; but these very views seem to be ones that Berkeleyan idealism cannot accommodate. The views I have in mind are four in number: Berkeley holds that (d) physical objects are immediately perceived; and that (e) physical objects are public in the sense that more than one perceiver can often immediately perceive the same physical object; and that (f) people often have immediate knowledge of physical objects; and that (g) people often have *certain* knowledge of physical objects. Of course, if Berkeley really can consistently and perhaps plausibly hold these views, then he will have gone a long way toward making his philosophy comport with common sense. But it is normally held, I think, that Berkeley's philosophy can accommodate none of the views listed in (d) through (g). So, although Berkeley would certainly like to defend common sense, he really fails in the attempt to do so.

We thus have two problems: first, can Berkeleyan idealism, to the extent that it is represented in statements (a), (b), and (c), be made consistent with common sense? and, second, is Berkeleyan idealism consistent with the four claims noted in (d) through (g)?

In what follows I will argue that Berkeley can consistently and perhaps even plausibly claim that (b) and (c) are compatible with common sense and also that there is nothing in his philosophy that logically excludes any one of the claims (d) through (g). I will ignore statement (a), since I take it as obvious, Samuel Johnson to the contrary notwithstanding, that (a) does not express a view that Berkeley was either committed to or endorsed.

It is worth noting that the two problems I propose to discuss are distinct. We can see this by letting common sense consist of a set of statements, K. Then the first problem concerns whether the set formed with (b), (c), and K as members is consistent. Statements (d) through (g) are commonsensical, and so are members of K. The second problem, then, concerns whether that subset of K formed by (d) through (g) is consistent with Berkeleyan idealism as expressed in (b) and (c). Of course, if the first problem is solved, so is the second; however, the converse does not hold.

Three further preliminary points deserve mention. First, Berkeleyan idealism includes more than (b) and (c) since it also incorporates a claim about infinite and finite perceivers. I am not considering this latter claim in this paper in any detail; however, I will indicate at appropriate places why this omission does not threaten my arguments or their conclusions. Second, it is assumed that common sense, as Berkeley would construe it, includes much more than the statements (d) through (g) singled out for discussion. I focus on these because they have been and are of philosophical importance. It should also be observed, third, that I do not attempt to cover all the aspects of Berkeley's defense of common sense. Ultimately that would involve comparing how his philosophy fares in relation to competing philosophies with regard to common sense, and that issue is beyond the scope of the present paper.[1]

I will begin with the second of the two problems noted above. Within that context, statement (d) will be taken up first.

I

To help us see that Berkeley actually endorses statement (d), let us consider the following passage:[2]

> Wood, stones, fire, water, flesh, iron, and the like things which I name and discourse of are things that I know. And, I should not have known them but that I perceived them by my senses; and the things perceived by the senses are immediately perceived.

Moreover, for Berkeley physical objects are *sensible* objects, that is, objects that are perceived by means of the senses (as opposed to being "perceived" by means of a reasoned inference), and, he maintains, everything perceived by means of the senses is immediately perceived.[3] Further, we know that Berkeley accepts (b), and he plainly tells us that some of those combinations of ideas that are physical objects are immediately perceived. For instance, at one point he says that we should mean by 'body' (and in this context the term designates physical objects)

> . . . what every plain, ordinary person means by that word, to wit, that which is immediately seen and felt, which is only a combination of sensible qualities or ideas. . . . (*Works*, II, p. 82)

Consider also this passage from Berkeley's early notebooks:

> There is a Philosopher who says we can get an idea of substance by no way of Sensation or Reflection. & seems to imagine that we want a sense proper

for it. Truly if we had a new sense it could only give us a new idea. now I suppose he will not say substance according to him is an Idea. for my part I own I have no Idea can stand for substance in his or ye Schoolmen's sense of that word. But take it in the common vulgar sense & then we see & feel substance (*Philosophical Commentaries*, sect. 724)[4]

What is the vulgar sense of 'substance'? Among other places, this question is answered in the *Principles*, for instance at 37:

It will be argued that thus much at least is true, to wit, that we take away all corporeal substances. To this my answer is, that if the word *substance* be taken in the vulgar sense, for a combination of sensible qualities, such as extension, solidity, weight, and the like; this we cannot be accused of taking away. But if it be taken in a philosophic sense, for the support of accidents or qualities without the mind: then indeed I acknowledge that we take it away, if one may be said to take away that which never had any existence, not even in the imagination. (*Works*, II, p. 56)

Combinations of sensible qualities, for Berkeley, are physical objects. These several passages, together with the Berkeleyan claim that everything perceived by sense is immediately perceived, yield again the thesis that physical objects are immediately perceived (= (d)). There is little question, then, that Berkeley accepts (d); the issue is whether he is consistent in doing so.

To help see that he is, we need to clarify Berkeley's notion of immediate perception. Early in the *Dialogues*, Philonous asks Hylas:

Are those things only perceived by the senses which are perceived immediately? Or may those things properly be said to be "sensible" which are perceived mediately, or not without the intervention of others? (*Works*, II, p. 174)

As this passage makes clear, immediate perception for Berkeley is that perception which occurs and which is not dependent on the occurrence of some other perception. It is this notion of immediate perception that Berkeley uses in the *Essay Towards a New Theory of Vision* when he argues that since distance is not immediately seen, then the visual perception of distance must be dependent on some other perception. And, indeed, he argues that the visual perception of distance *is* so dependent, the other perception being sensations received from movement of and pressure on the eyes. Moreover, in the same place Berkeley uses this notion of immediate perception to refute the received view of how we see distance; the visual perception of distance is not dependent on the *perception* of the lines and angles formed by light rays as, Berkeley claims, the received view must hold. Those lines and angles are not perceived at all, he maintains, and so the received view must be incorrect.[5]

As characterized in these places, Berkeley's notion of immediate perception is a purely factual relation; as we might say, for Berkeley 'immediate perceive' is a term that describes a factual perceptual relationship holding between an observer and some object.[6] Berkeley's term 'immediately perceives' is nonpropositional and extensional, taking a grammatical direct object rather than a propositional clause as complement. Immediate perception, for Berkeley, is not a species of perceiving *that* something is or is not the case, nor is it a species of perceiving something *as* something else.

Now, often and ordinarily, if an observer sees some constituents of an object, then he also sees the object in question. For example, in the normal case, if someone sees the attached fenders, tires, doors, windows, and trim on the driver's side of a car, then he also sees the car. And this is unquestionably so even though the observer does not see (or otherwise perceive) all the constituents of the car; indeed, one is seldom in a position to perceive all the constituents of a thing at one time. It is similar in Berkeley's case. We know that Berkeley accepts (b) and (d); we also know that Berkeley allows that ideas of various sorts are immediately perceived, usually in clusters or combinations. In order to maintain that *physical objects* are immediately perceived, then, Berkeley needs to hold only that on many occasions some ideas are immediately perceived, and that these ideas are constituents of physical objects, so that *by* immediately perceiving these constituents, one immediately perceives the physical object in question. Just as one need not see all the attached parts of a car in order to see a car, so one need not immediately perceive all the constituents of a physical object in order immediately to perceive that physical object. With 'immediately perceive' construed as above, this is no more problematic for Berkeley than is the case of seeing the car with the ordinary extensional direct-object use of 'see'. So, given that he accepts (b), and given the above construal of 'immediately perceives', it is perfectly consistent for Berkeley to maintain, as he does, that physical objects are often enough immediately perceived. Indeed, it is *reasonable*, on these assumptions, for Berkeley to accept (d).

The car analogy we have used is not completely appropriate, since it relies on the relation of part to whole, and the latter is not applicable in Berkeley's case. I think the analogy is close enough, however. We can also utilize another example. Imagine that the general is on the reviewing stand watching the passing troops and armaments. By seeing some proportion of the division of troops at a time, the general thereby sees the division at that time. Of course, the division must be organized in some fashion, rather than milling about all over the grounds. An analogous point holds for parts of the car: they must be (appropriately) attached if the example is to work. Moreover, the general must see some sizable portion of the total division. Seeing one soldier in an organized parade will not suffice, just as seeing one part of the car will not typically suffice for the person to see the car.[7] The parade of troops case is somewhat more analogous to Berkeley's situation. For troops in the parading division are not parts of the division; rather, they are members of a group, just as individual sensible ideas are members of the collections that make up physical objects. And the needed inference works just as well in the troop case as it does in the car case.

Another problem for my account of (d) concerns the term 'immediately perceives'. It might be maintained that the crucial element in the concept of immediate perception is the lack of any *suggestion*, a point Berkeley himself brings up in several places.[8] I believe that my argument regarding the consistency of (d) would go through, however, even if we utilized this "no-suggestion" notion of immediate perception used earlier. To see this we need only note that if some perception *does* include an element of suggestion, then it occurs (as mediate perception) only if some other perception occurs. Thus, the "no-suggestion" notion of immediate perception implies, and may be reduced to, the notion used earlier in the argument concerning (d). And this fact shows, of course, that what I have said about (d) would hold no matter which of these two notions of immediate perception was used.

It is plain that whether perceivers are spirits or not raises no problems for (d); nor does the claim expressed in statement (c). Hence, since the foregoing argument make clear that (b) and (d) are consistent, we can conclude not only that Berkeley accepts the claim that physical objects are often immediately perceived, but also that this is consistent with Berkeleyan idealism.[9]

We turn now to (e), which is the claim that different perceivers immediately perceive the same physical object. There are few places where Berkeley says anything directly bearing on (e), but in one such place he says this:

> Sensible objects may likewise be said to be "without the mind" in another sense, namely, when they exist in some other mind; thus, when I shut my eyes, the things I saw may still exist, but it must be in some other mind.[10]

If we recall that Berkeley claims that everything perceived *by sense* is immediately perceived, then this passage can be plausibly taken as acceptance of (e). Moreover, the *Dialogues* are filled with passages in which Berkeley, through Philonous, makes reference to the view of common folk, which Berkeley accepts, that the things they see, feel, and otherwise perceive are real objects, that is, physical objects.[11] Such passages would scarcely make sense if these physical objects were not publicly perceivable, that is, immediately perceived by more than one percipient at the same time, as well as at different times. Certainly common people take physical objects to be public in this sense. So there is textual evidence that Berkeley accepts (e).

However, it seems to some commentators that Berkeley just cannot consistently accept (e). This is because ideas are allegedly private in the sense that any idea, or group of them, immediately perceived by one individual, is not (and perhaps cannot be) immediately perceived by anyone else. So it is concluded that no two percipients ever do (can) immediately perceive the same physical object. Hence, Berkeley must reject (e) if he is to be consistent,[12] and along with a rejection of (e) goes a rejection of common sense.

The foregoing argument can be refuted. First, there is no place in Berkeley's writings where he actually *says* that each idea is private in the way just described. At one point, when Hylas brings up this issue in the *Dialogues*, Berkeley explicitly waffles on the point, and he notes that he cannot make up his mind with regard to it because the (philosophic) notion of identity is too unclear for him to be able to say one way or the other.[13] Second, I know of no reason to think that Berkeley is committed to holding that each idea is private in the sense described. After all, any idea immediately perceived by a finite perceiver is also immediately perceived by God. So, Berkeley is committed to the contrary line, viz., that ideas are publicly perceivable entities.[14] Third, and perhaps most important, there is a premise missing in the argument. Even if it is true that no two perceivers ever do (can) immediately perceive the same ideas, it will not follow that no two perceivers immediately perceive the same physical object unless we add the further premise that if two perceivers cannot (do not) immediately perceive the same constituents of an object, then they cannot (do not) immediately perceive the same physical object. This premise is surely not a necessary truth, so Berkeley would not be inconsistent in denying it even if ideas were private in the described sense. Hence, the alleged privacy of ideas does not, in conjunction with (b), entail the privacy of physical objects and the rejection of (e).

To give some rough intuitive plausibility to the point concerning (e), notice that we do not balk at all at allowing that two people see the same physical object even when they do not see the same parts of the object. If I see the driver's side of the car, and another observer sees the opposite side, then we each still see the same car even though we see no common parts of the car. It is similar (though, of course, not *quite* the same) in Berkeley's case. Two people immediately perceive the same physical object even though they do not (perhaps cannot) immediately perceive the same constituents of that object. There is nothing logically incongruous about this at all.

It is important to notice that it is *not* being claimed here that no two people ever immediately perceive the same parts of a physical object at the same time. Berkeley would reject such a claim, and would do so consistently even if no individual constituent of a physical object is ever immediately perceived by more than one percipient. Such constituents of physical objects are not *parts* of them.

We have shown that (e) is consistent with (b). But this is enough. For (e) is plainly in no conflict either with Berkeley's claim about the nature of perceivers or with his claim about the nature of physical objects. Hence, (e), the thesis about the public character of physical objects, is logically consistent with Berkeleyan idealism.

What about (f), the claim that we have immediate knowledge of physical objects? Berkeley apparently held that we have such knowledge, since he wrote:

> I am the farthest from Scepticism of any man. I know with an intuitive knowledge the existence of other things as well as my own Soul. this is w^t Locke nor scarce any other Thinking Philosopher will pretend to. (*Commentaries*, sect. 563)

as well as:

> We have intuitive Knowlege of the Existence of other things besides our selves & even praecedaneous to the Knowlege of our own Existence. in that we must have Ideas or else we cannot think. (sect. 547)

By 'intuitive knowledge' Berkeley means 'immediate knowledge' (as do many other eighteenth-century writers). Since the other things he refers to are physical objects, in these passages it certainly appears that Berkeley is accepting (f). Moreover, at *Principles,* sect. 18, Berkeley contrasts *knowing by sense* and *knowing by reason,* where the latter is inferential or derivative knowledge, based on what is immediately perceived. Since, as we have seen, Berkeley maintains that physical objects are often immediately perceived, *Principles,* sect. 18, gives us some additional reason to think that he accepts (f); physical objects are among the things known *by sense*, without inference.[15]

To see if Berkeley is consistent in accepting (f), we need to explicate what he means by 'immediate knowledge' ('intuitive knowledge'). Berkeley himself provided no definition of this term. But if we make the reasonable assumption that he follows Locke in his use of the term, we can make some headway. Locke said:

> . . . if we will reflect on our own ways of thinking, we shall find that sometimes the mind perceives the agreement or disagreement of two ideas *immediately by themselves,* without the intervention of any other; and this I think we may call *intuitive knowledge.*[16]

Here the notion of intuitive knowledge is similar to Berkeley's notion of immediate perception. The latter is roughly that perception which is not dependent on some other perception; the former is that knowing that is not dependent on some other knowing or knowledge. We can try unpacking Locke's notion in different ways, for instance as

(1)   A person *S* immediately (intuitively) knows some proposition, *h,* at a time *t* if and only if: (i) *S* knows that *h* at *t;* and, (ii) *S* has no evidence at *t* for *h.*

or perhaps as

(2)   A person *S* immediately (intuitively) knows some proposition *h* at a time *t* if and only if: (i) *S* knows that *h* at *t;* and, (ii) *S* would know that *h* at *t* even if he were to lack evidence for *h* at *t.*

The root idea behind Locke's notion of intuitive knowledge is that such knowledge is not dependent on something else, perhaps on knowing or other knowledge. I have tried to capture the point about this lack of dependence in clauses (ii) of definitions (1) and (2), respectively. In each, however, I have broadened Locke's notion somewhat by speaking of a lack of dependence on evidence, rather than on other knowledge or knowing. Knowledge not dependent on some other piece of knowledge might well qualify as inferential, and so as not immediate or intuitive, if it happened to be dependent on some background evidence that was thoroughly justified but not known.

It is not difficult to see that definition (1) is too broad. A person might have evidence for something he knows immediately if, for example, the evidence he actually has is completely inoperative.[17] Moreover, definition (2), though closer to what is needed, is also too broad. We can see this by considering a case of what some have plausibly claimed is one of immediate knowing. Imagine — to adapt a case made famous by Austin—that S has visual, olfactory, and auditory experiences of a "piglike" sort; S's perceptual and discriminative abilities are not in any way impaired; S has all the relevant concepts (he knows what pigs are, for example); S is duly attentive to his surroundings; and there is nothing wrong with the conditions under which S makes his observations (the lighting is normal, for instance). Imagine further that S owns a pig, that he frequently and regularly observes this pig of his at this time of day in this place. Two things seem uncontroversial in this case: first, that S is fully justified in believing that there is a pig before him; and, second, that S knows that there is a pig before him. Moreover, it is quite reasonable to hold that S knows immediately or intuitively that there is a pig before him. After all, what with all his background knowledge and experience, S qualifies as an expert with respect to whether his pig stands before him or not. But notice that definition (2) is not satisfied, because its clause (ii) is not met. S would not know that there is a pig before him if he lacked his extensive background knowledge or evidence.

It is important to see that this example does not trade on the fact that S is, supposedly, immediately knowing something about a physical object. Thus, consider what many have reckoned paradigm cases of immediate knowledge, such as the case of a person immediately knowing that he then feels a pain. Even in such cases the person would not have that knowledge if he lacked appropriate background evidence, such as the knowledge or at least justified belief that pains feel a certain way, and that the concept *pain* is applicable to the way he then feels. Yet, were we to make use of definition (2), such cases would have to be regarded as instances of inferential knowledge.

We can better capture what Locke had in mind, and thus what Berkeley means in his endorsement of (f), with the following:

(3)   A person S immediately (intuitively) knows that h at a time t if and only if: (i) S knows that h at time t; and, (ii) S would know that h at t even if his knowledge that h at t were not based on any evidence S has at t.

The key idea behind this definition comes in clause (ii); we can understand it by considering its opposite, namely, a case in which a person does know something on the basis of some evidence. In such a situation, the person's belief is justified on the basis of the evidence he has; that is, that evidence makes up or constitutes his justification for belief. Thus, clause (ii) of (3) amounts to the claim that S would be justified in his belief that h at the time t even if his justification for this belief were not made up of, were not constituted by, his having some evidence at that time for h.[18]

We can best grasp the idea behind (3) by going back to our example. In that case, S would *not* know that there is a pig before him if he were to lack relevant background knowledge or evidence. But his knowledge does not thereby count as mediate or inferential in such a situation, for it is not that background evidence which currently makes up, or constitutes, his justification for his belief that there is a pig before him. What does justify his belief, instead, is the experience he is then having of the pig. It is precisely because S has had such extensive experiences of this pig in this place that he has such extensive background knowledge or evidence. And it is precisely because he has such extensive background evidence that he does not need to fall back on it for purposes of current justification of his belief. Put another way, we could say that it is because S has such extensive background evidence that he can make do, epistemically, without it in the sense that it is not an element of what justifies his present belief that there is a pig before him. And, this is so despite the fact that he would not be justified in this belief if he were to lack this background evidence.

How does this excursion into epistemology bear on Berkeley and common sense? First, we may note that definition (3) is self-consistent. Moreover, it is surely consistent to maintain, with Austin and many others, that people often have immediate knowledge of physical object propositions, where the notion of immediate knowledge is spelled out along the lines of (3). There is nothing in Berkeley's philosophy to prevent him from from taking this same line with respect to (f). More specifically, Berkeley's phenomenalist account of physical objects, represented in (b), is perfectly consistent with (f), given the notion of immediate knowledge stated in (3). A person might still have the extensive background knowledge or evidence discussed above in connection with the pig example. It would amount to knowledge of relationships between specific olfactory, auditory, and visual ideas. And a person such as S would not know that there was a pig before him if he lacked this background evidence. But this background evidence need not make up his current justification for his belief. Rather, given his extensive background knowledge of relationships between specific sorts of sensible ideas, his immediate knowledge that there is a pig before him is based on the immediate perception of different sensible ideas then occurring. That is, to utilize the terminology introduced above, his current justification for his belief that there is a pig before him is made up of, or constituted by, his current immediate perception of various "piglike" ideas. His background evidence, as before, is indispensable; it is just not an element in his current justification. Thus, immediate knowledge of physical objects, as claimed in (f), is consistent with a phenomenalist account of such objects, as claimed in (b). And, for reasons cited earlier in connection with (d) and (e), we may also conclude that (f) is consistent with Berkeleyan idealism.[19]

There is an important and powerful objection facing this last conclusion, however. Intuitive or immediate knowledge is often regarded as *certain* knowledge. Furthermore, Locke himself endorsed this latter claim,[20] and it is reasonable to think that Berkeley would endorse it, as well, since (in various passages in which he describes how far removed his views are from scepticism) he often brings up intuitive knowledge and certainty together. However, the objection goes, no propositions concerning physical objects are certain for any person, in which case the support for the claims that (f) and (g) as well are consistent with Berkeleyan idealism is swept away.

This way of stating the objection can be easily dealt with, however. The mere fact that (g) is false, if it is, does not show that (g) is inconsistent with (b). Similarly, the mere falsity of (f) would not show that (f) and (b) were inconsistent. To get some bite into the objection, we need to restate it to claim that the phenomenalist account of physical objects expressed in (b) implies that (g) is false. Then, if it is also correct that (f) implies (g), or at least that Berkeley thought as much, then we would also have to conclude that (b) and (f) are inconsistent, contrary to what was concluded earlier.[21]

Whether this objection succeeds depends on how the crucial notion of certainty is analyzed. If a proposition h is certain for a person only if the person logically cannot be mistaken in the belief that h, then there is some plausibility to the claim that (b) entails the falsity of (g). Let us, in any case, grant this point. I doubt if this is what Berkeley meant by 'certain', however. At one point in the *Dialogues,* Berkeley says (through Philonous):

> Let me be represented as one who trusts his senses, who thinks he knows the things he sees and feels, and entertains no doubts of their existence . . . . (*Works*, II, p. 237)

Philonous says shortly thereafter that

> I do therefore assert that I am as certain as of my own being that there are bodies or corporeal substances (meaning the things I perceive by my senses) . . . (p. 238)

Elsewhere, Berkeley says:

> I might as well doubt of my own being as of the being of those things I actually see and feel. (p. 230)

These passages, and the many others in which Berkeley speaks of the trust he places in the senses,[22] make clear, I think, that Berkeley links certainty not only with propositions that are not at all doubtful, but also with propositions that it would be ludicrous actually to doubt since there are no grounds for doubting them. Moreover, there is reason to think that Berkeley was sensitive to his own meaning of 'certain', since he claimed:

> I am certain there is a God, tho I do not perceive him have no intuition of him, this not difficult if we rightly understand w^t is meant by certainty. (*Commentaries*, sect. 813)

If we construe certainty in this manner, then it is obviously plausible for Berkeley to maintain that we are often, indeed frequently, certain that physical object propositions are true. The example used earlier about the pig may serve here as an illustration; it is just one example among many of physical object propositions that are certain. Furthermore, this relatively weak account of certainty shows that (b) does not entail the falsity of (g). As Berkeley says in the *Principles:*

> We may, from the experience we have had of the train and succession of ideas in our minds, often make, I will not say uncertain conjectures, but sure and well-founded predictions concerning the ideas we shall be affected with, pursuant to a great train of actions, and be enabled to pass a right judgment of what would have appeared to us, in case we were placed in circumstances very different from those we are in at present. Herein consists the knowledge of Nature, which may preserve its use and certainty very consistently with what has been said. (*Principles*, sect. 59, in *Works,* II, p. 66)

Put succinctly, a phenomenalist account of physical objects will require that knowledge of such entities consist in part of what ideas one would immediately perceive in various circumstances. There is no reason why beliefs about what one would immediately perceive in specific circumstances would not qualify as certain given Berkeley's use of the term. Hence, (b) and (g) are consistent. With this result, we also undercut the objection designed to show that (b) and (f) are inconsistent.

As with (d), (e), and (f), there is no reason to suppose that the existence of certain knowledge of physical object propositions is inconsistent with Berkeley's thesis concerning infinite and finite perceivers or with (c). So we may conclude that (g), too, is perfectly consistent logically with Berkeleyan idealism.

This solution of the second of the two problems I have proposed may be taken as some support for the well-known, and widely rejected, Luce-Jessop interpretation of Berkeley as a "common sense realist." This is not to say that Berkeley is a *realist*, since after all he accepts both (b) and (c). Rather, it is to say that four claims that are essential to common sense realism, namely those stated as (d) through (g), are consistent with Berkeley's idealism. This latter claim, I think, makes up a major part of the Luce-Jessop interpretation, and if so then it seems to me that it has been shown here that their interpretation is quite plausible. Of course, whether other elements in their construal of Berkeley as common sense realist are also plausible is another question altogether.

II

It is difficult to think of anything less in line with common sense than (b) and (c). If this is right, then it is unlikely that we will solve the first of the two problems proposed, and Berkeleyan idealism will be shown after all to be inconsistent with common sense. At best we will have shown that Berkeleyan idealism is consistent with that sub-part of common sense consisting of (d) through (f). We begin our examination of this issue with another look at (b).

Statement (b) has some close cousins in Berkeley's writings. One is this:

(h)   Physical objects are just those things that are immediately seen and felt and otherwise immediately perceived.

This claim finds expression, for instance, in this passage:

. . . if by "material substance" is meant only sensible body, that which is seem and felt (and the unphilosophical part of the world, I dare say, mean no more), than I am more certain of matter's existence than you or any other philosopher pretend to be.[23]

Another important relative of (b) is this:

(i)   Physical objects are nothing but combinations of sensible qualities.

This statement finds expression in this passage:

. . . if the word *substance* be taken in the vulgar sense, for a combination of sensible qualities, such as extension, solidity, weight, and the like; this we cannot be accused of taking away. (*Principles*, sect. 37, in *Works*, II, p. 56)

It is also clear that Berkeley regards (h) and (i) as pretty much equivalent, for he says in the *Principles:*

> Take away this *material substance,* about the identity whereof all the dispute is, and mean by *body* what every plain, ordinary person means by that word, to wit, that which is immediately seen and felt, which is only a combination of sensible qualities or ideas, and then their most unanswerable objections come to nothing. (*Principles*, sect. 95, in *Works*, II, p. 82)

Moreover, as all of these quoted passages indicate, Berkeley regards (h) and (i) as the views of common sense. On this point, I think, no critic or commentator would demur; (h) and (i) *do* express common sense views or beliefs.

We know, however, that Berkeley collapses these commonsensical claims into a third, namely (b):

> (b)   Each physical object is nothing but a collection of ideas.

and (b) is anything but commonsensical.[24] It is tempting to think that Berkeley has indulged in a little philosophical sleight of hand here, or perhaps that he was guilty of considerable self-deception about the matter. At best, it would seem, Berkeley has made a serious error, and his much-touted defense of common sense breaks down.

Two Berkeleyan responses to these important objections come to mind. The first would be to "brazen it out" and simply insist that (b) *is* what common people or the vulgar believe. This line is suggested by the last two lines of the last-quoted passage. A somewhat different response would be to argue that commonsensical beliefs are *topic-neutral* in the sense that they imply no idealist thesis about the nature of physical objects nor any realist thesis about the nature of such objects. Hence, common sense beliefs such as those expressed by (h) and (i) are perfectly consistent with the idealist (phenomenalist) thesis about physical objects expressed by (b).

I suspect that Berkeley was tempted by this second response; nevertheless, it will not withstand criticism. For it would mean that a claim such as

> (j)   Each physical object is nothing but a material substance in which sensible qualities inhere.

is likewise compatible with common sense. However, Berkeley uses the fact that (j) is *in*consistent with common sense as a weapon against the materialists. So we should avoid any interpretation that requires Berkeley to hold that (j) is consistent with common sense. Moreover, (j) implies

(k)   Physical objects have a real, absolute existence, i.e., physical objects would exist even if they and their inherent qualities were
not perceived.

But, as we see below in connection with (c), Berkeley is in no position to allow that (k) is consistent with common sense.

We are left with the first of the two responses noted above. In this
regard, consider this exchange between Hylas and Philonous:

> Hyl. But still, Philonous, you hold there is nothing in the world but
> spirits and ideas. And this you must needs acknowledge sounds very oddly.
>
> Phil. I own the word "idea," not being commonly used for "thing,"
> sounds something out of the way. My reason for using it was because a
> necessary relation to the mind is understood to be implied by the term;
> and it is now commonly used by philosophers to denote the immediate
> objects of the understanding. But however oddly the proposition may
> sound in words, yet it includes nothing so very strange or shocking in its
> sense, which in effect amounts to no more than this, to wit, that there
> are only things perceiving and things perceived. . . . [25]

This passage indicates that there is a clear sense in which the vulgar do not believe (b), namely, they would not *express* their belief(s)
concerning physical objects by asserting (b). Nonetheless, properly
understood, Berkeley claims, all that (b) comes to is something that
the vulgar *do* believe. Thus, all that (b) comes to is what is expressed
by (h) and (i), and so in a sense the vulgar do believe (b) even though
they would not use those words to express what they believe.

Is it true, though, that *all* that (b) amounts to is what is expressed
in (h) and (i), as Berkeley maintains? After all, in many places Berkeley uses the terms 'sensible ideas' and 'sensations' interchangeably;
but the common person does not believe that physical objects are
nothing but collections of *sensations.* Moreover, even waiving problems arising from identifying sensible ideas with sensations, we know
that each sensible idea is an entity that exists when and only when it
is perceived, and this leads to trouble. For claiming that (b) amounts
to no more than what is expressed by (h) and (i) requires us to say
that immediately perceived sensible qualities exist when and only
when they are perceived *and* that this is acceptable to common sense.
Thus, the foregoing strategy of Berkeley's would ultimately fail.

Both these problems can be handled satisfactorily. The first problem can be dealt with in the same manner in which the issue of
whether the vulgar believe (b) was treated. That is, Berkeley's likely
reply would simply be that although a claim such as

(l)   Each physical object is nothing but a collection of sensations.

would never be used to express what the vulgar believe—at least not by the vulgar, at any rate—nevertheless, all that (l) comes to is all that (b) comes to, viz., the conjunction of (h) and (i). It is true that the words 'ideas' and 'sensations', as used in philosophy during the seventeenth and eighteenth centuries, connote such features as that of being states of mind. Berkeley's point regarding these two terms, and thus about both (b) and (l), is that, as he uses the terms, all they come to is captured by (h) and (i).

This response, however, immediately raises the second problem noted above. As Berkeley uses the term 'idea', it denotes an entity that exists when and only when it is perceived. Thus, the foregoing remarks have Berkeley saying that all that (b) and (l) come to can be expressed by

(m)   Each physical object is nothing but a collection of immediately perceived sensible qualities each of which exists when and only when it is perceived.

The problem is not that Berkeley does not hold (m); rather, the problem is that (m) is not acceptable to common sense. Thus, we could say that although the above-described strategy for dealing with whether the vulgar actually believe (b) wins the battle, it loses the war. For it leads to the conclusion that (m) is commonsensical, and that conclusion is false.

Berkeley thinks that (m) *is* commonsensical, as is something it implies, namely (c):

(c)   Each physical object exists when and only when it is perceived.

It is clear that (c) is the final statement on the list of those proposed for investigation in the opening pages of this paper.

Berkeley notes, first, that (c) is to be understood in a certain broad sense, namely, as meaning something like,[26]

(c_1)   No physical object exists when not perceived at all, by any percipient; i.e., no physical object has an absolute real existence.

When so understood, we have a statement that is clearly at odds with (k), since the latter alleges an absolute real existence for physical objects. According to Berkeley, we also have a statement that is part and parcel of common sense. The common person, he claims, *means* by 'exist' when applied to physical objects just that they are perceived. As Berkeley has Philonous say in regard to the real existence of sensible (physical) objects:

I am content, Hylas, to appeal to the common sense of the world for the truth of my notion. Ask the gardener why he thinks yonder cherry tree exists in the garden, and he shall tell you, because he sees and feels it; in a word because he perceives it by his senses. Ask him why he thinks an orange tree not to be there, and he shall tell you because he does not perceive it. What he perceives by sense, that he terms a real being, and says it "is" or "exists"; but that which is not perceiveable, the same, he says, has no being. (*Works*, II, p. 234)

Given that this *is* what the common person means when he says that there are (are not) physical objects, it should be obvious that there is no conflict whatever between common sense and (c). Nor is (m) in conflict with common sense, and for the same reason: the common person, Berkeley argues, does believe (m). According to Berkeley, when properly understood as (c_1), statement (c) expresses exactly what the common person believes with respect to physical objects. Hence, Berkeley's strategy for dealing with (b), outlined earlier, does not lead to the predicted trouble with respect to (c) and (m).

Whether Berkeley is ultimately correct in thinking that (c) and (m) are commonsensical is a matter we will not examine here. It is enough that his contention is not altogether implausible, and I would urge that this much at least can be reasonably claimed for it. Thus, the first of the two problems proposed in opening this paper has been resolved in Berkeley's behalf. We may therefore conclude, contrary to what many commentators have maintained, that Berkeleyan idealism and common sense are consistent.[27]

Of course, Berkeley claimed that not only are his idealist views compatible with common sense, but also that he is a defender of, or champion of, common sense. In order to establish this larger thesis, we would need to show that Berkeley attributes the right claims to common sense *and* that his views fare better with respect to common sense than do competing philosophies. That is a much larger undertaking, for which the present paper is a relatively modest beginning.

Notes

The matter is discussed rather fully in Ian C. Tipton, *Berkeley: The Philosophy of Immaterialism,* (London: Methuen, 1974). I should add that I will not try to explicate the notion of common sense here, though in a fuller treatment of this issue the notion would have to be carefully analyzed.

2. From *Three Dialogues Between Hylas and Philonous,* in A. A. Luce and T. E. Jessop, eds., *The Works of George Berkeley, Bishop of Cloyne,* 9 vols. (London: Thomas Nelson and Sons, 1948-57), vol. II, p. 230.

3. *Works,* II, p. 183.

4. *Philosophical Commentaries*, sect. 724. In *Works*, I, p. 88.

5. This paragraph summarizes one of Berkeley's main arguments against the geometrical method of visually estimating distance. Berkeley gives the argument, along with others, in the *Essay Towards a New Theory of Vision,* in *Works*, I, pp. 171-74. The relevant notion of immediate perception is clearly discernible in Berkeley's characterization of what *mediate* (or indirect) perception is, namely that perception which occurs only if some other perception occurs. See especially sections, 9, 10, and 18 of the *New Theory of Vision.*

6. See James Cornman, *Materialism and Sensations,* (New Haven: Yale University Press, 1971), p. 223, for this claim about Berkeley's notion of immediate perception. See also his paper, "On Direct Perception," *Review of Metaphysics,* XVI (September, 1971).

7. For an interesting discussion of this question, see Peter Alexander, "Inferences About Seeing," in *Knowledge and Necessity,* Royal Institute of Philosophy Lectures, vol. 3 (London: Macmillan, 1970).

8. For example, in *Works,* II, p. 174.

9. There are other serious problems confronting ascription of (d) to Berkeley that I cannot take up here. They include the question of whether acceptance of (d) would be incompatible with the argument of the *New Theory of Vision;* whether acceptance of (d) can be brought into line with Berkeley's oft-made claim that, e.g., nothing can be immediately seen but light and colors; and the problem of how one can immediately perceive a physical object by immediately perceiving sensible ideas that are *not* constituents of that object. I discuss these matters in "Berkeley and Immediate Perception" (unpublished).

10. *Treatise Concerning the Principles of Human Knowledge,* sect. 90, in *Works,* II, p. 80.

11. *Works,* II, pp. 234, 261, and 262, for example.

12. This is the line taken by R. van Iten in "Berkeley's Alleged Solipsism," *Revue Internationale de Philosophie* XVI, 61-62 (1962), repr. in C. M. Turbayne, ed., *Berkeley: Principles, Texts and Critical Essays* (Indianapolis: Bobbs-Merrill, 1970), pp. 47-56.

13. See *Works,* II, pp. 247-48.

14. I am indebted to Robert Audi for this point.

15. The same argument can be used to show that a passage in the *Dialogues* results in endorsement of (f). See *Works,* II, p. 230.

16. John Locke, *Essay Concerning Human Understanding,* bk. IV, chap. 2, quoted from an abridged edition edited by A. Woozley (Cleveland: World Publishing Co., 1964), p. 325.

17. See my "Non-Inferential Knowledge," *Philosophia* (forthcoming), for further discussion of this point concerning definition (1).

18. I have proposed and defended definition (3) in "Non-Inferential Knowledge." Compare James Cornman, "Materialism and Some Myths About Some Givens," *The Monist* 56 (1972): 222. For definitions along the same lines of related notions, see M. Pastin, "Modest Foundationalism and Self-Warrant," in G. Pappas and M. Swain, eds., *Essays on Knowledge and Justification* (Ithaca: Cornell University Press, 1978); and W. Alston, "Self-Warrant: A Neglected Form of Privileged Access," *American Philosophical Quarterly* 13 (1976).

19. This conclusion rests to some extent on my reconstruction of Locke and Berkeley's notion of intuitive (immediate) knowledge along the lines of definition (3). I would argue, however, that the same conclusion would be apposite if a different notion of immediate knowledge were utilized, e.g., that proposed by David Armstrong, *Belief, Truth and Knowledge* (New York: Cambridge University Press, 1973), pt. 3. My definition, (3), however, is more in line with what Locke actually says.

20. Locke, *Essay,* IV, 2, in Woozley, ed., *Essay,* p. 326.

21. These two objections derive from my reading of Harry Bracken, "Berkeley's Realisms," in his *Early Reception of Berkeley's Immaterialism,* rev. ed. (The Hague: Martinus Nijhoff, 1965). I am unclear about which of these two objections he advances, though I would think it is the second.

22. For instance, *Commentaries,* sects. 517a, 686a, and 740.

23. See *Works,* II, p. 237, as well as pp. 229-30.

24. Compare David Givner, "Berkeley's Ambiguity," *Dialogue* VIII (1971), esp. pp. 660-62, as well as Tipton, *Berkeley,* passim.

25. See *Works,* II, pp. 235-36.

26. Ibid., p. 61.

27. I am here assuming, perhaps overly optimistically, that Berkeley's thesis regarding finite and infinite perceivers (spirits) and his nominalism are individually and jointly consistent with common sense.

2

Berkeley's Commitment to Relativism

Richard T. Lambert

George Berkeley's *Principles* and *Dialogues* contain many allusions to the "relativity" of sensible qualities, by which perceived features of objects vary for different observers. Commentators have differed, however, on the significance of these references. Berkeley's editors Luce and Jessop, for instance, dismiss his relativity arguments as mere *ad hominems* and the perceptual differences he cites as "accidental"; they point to Berkeley's apparent claims that public and continuous sensible objects exist independently of their varying perceptions by this or that finite mind.[1]

Other scholars have considered the relativity factor in Berkeley more serious and have made lengthy analyses of the logic and historical background of the relativity argument.[2] Some have interpreted Berkeley as a "relativist" who believed that variability extended to all perceptions whatever.[3] Because of necessary variations in the distance, spatial position, and physiological condition of perceivers, each single sense content must be unique, able to exist in only one perceiver at only one moment of time.

My paper will attempt to resolve this severe disagreement among intelligent reporters of Berkeley. Since this can only be done with a close exegesis of Berkeley's actual texts, I shall begin by considering the pertinent passages, some of which support the position that he was a relativist and some of which do not. On the basis of these texts I shall claim that Berkeley's commitment to the concept of relativity grew from the *Principles* to the *Dialogues*. Finally, I shall clarify how he could have asserted, along with that of relativity, the apparently incompatible claim that objects continue identically through many perceptions.

I. Relativity in the *Principles* and *Dialogues*

A. The Relativity Argument

Berkeley devotes a few numbers of the *Principles* to argumentation based on the changing appearance of sensible qualities in different situations.[4] But he concludes that the relativity argument can establish at most a skepticism of the senses. It "does not so much prove that there is no extension or color in an outward object as that we do not know by sense which is the true extension or color of the object" (Sect. 15). He restricts the relativity argument to an *ad hominem* attack on those who already believe in the subjectivity of secondary qualities, and to mere confirmation of the genuinely conclusive arguments for immaterialism, which reason *a priori* from the meanings of "existence" and "idea."[5]

The *Dialogues* manifests a complete change in attitude toward the relativity argument. This argument appears early in the work, long before any *a priori* demonstrations. It is much more extensive there, covering some ten pages on the entire spectrum of sensible qualities.[6] Most impressively, the *Dialogues* regards the relativity argument as "a good argument" (I, p. 129), "conclusive" (I, p. 134), proving materialism to be "false" (I, p. 117), and immaterialism to be "past all doubt" (I, p. 124). Clearly, Berkeley had determined in constructing the *Dialogues* to give relativity considerations a very significant role in the work's argumentation.

B. The Extent to Which Perceptions Are Relative

Many of the relativity arguments that Berkeley presents in both books conform to Warnock's objections that the argument concentrates on abnormal, even pathological, situations.[7] Jaundice, microscopes, and prisms alter the apparent color of an object; a fevered palate tastes flavors differently than a healthy one; a cold hand feels a vat of water to be warmer than a hot hand does. Arguments restricted to this evidence could yield only the very weak conclusion that "not all perceptions are uniform."

Yet Berkeley seems to have had something more than unusual exceptions in mind when he offered the relativity arguments. He suggested, and sometimes came close to saying explicitly, that *all* perceptions vary, perhaps not as obviously as in jaundice or fever, but with enough difference that any one perception could be distinguished from any other in principle.

The *Principles* nods mildly in this direction:

> Again, *great* and *small, swift* and *slow* are allowed to exist nowhere without the mind, being entirely relative, and changing as the frame or position of the organs of sense varies. (Sect. 11)

> Now, why may we not as well argue that figure or extension are not patterns or resemblances of qualities existing in matter, because to the same eye at different stations, or eyes of a different texture at the same station, they appear various and cannot, therefore, be the images of anything settled and determinate without the mind? (Sect. 14)

Despite the suggestiveness of these claims, no subsequent texts in the *Principles* confirm or employ their promise. Indeed, as we have seen, Berkeley distrusts the whole concept of relativity at this time; he will not ascribe the above arguments to himself, only to other philosophers.

The *Dialogues* also contains several suggestions of a universal relativity, but these are more frequent and emphatic than in the *Principles*. In the case of colors, is it not evident that

> upon the use of microscopes, upon a change happening in the humors of the eye, or a variation of distance, without any manner of real alteration in the thing itself, the colors of any object are either changed or totally disappear? Nay, all other circumstances remaining the same, change but the situation of some objects and they shall present different colors to the eye. The same thing happens upon viewing an object in various degrees of light. (I, pp. 124-125)

The same implication of an indefinitely varying range of sensations appears in the following remark on extension: "But, as we approach to or recede from an object, the visible extension varies, being at one distance ten or a hundred times greater than at another" (I, p. 128). The *First Dialogue* closes with an impassioned denial of any proportion between relative ideas and absolute objects:

> How then is it possible that things perpetually fleeting and variable as our ideas should be copies or images of anything fixed and constant? Or, in other words, since all sensible qualities, as size, figure, color, etc., that is, our ideas, are continually changing upon every alteration in the distance, medium, or instruments or sensation—how can any determinate material objects be properly represented or painted forth by several distinct things each of which is so different from and unlike the rest? (I, p. 147)

If consistently applied, Berkeley's suggestions would immunize his relativity argument to the Warnock objection mentioned earlier. For the argument would no longer be restricted to predictable perceptual abnormalities but would include all perceptions whatever, which we now know must vary in some small degree; variant ideas could not all represent an independent object correctly and thus would nearly all be incorrect. Berkeley knew his realistic audience would sympathize with sense knowledge; so (he thought) they could only draw the conclusion that there are no independent objects that could invalidate our perception.

C. Issues Entailed by Relativity

The *Principles* does not forthrightly confront any implications of the concept of relativity. Berkeley does mention the objection that under his doctrine "things are every moment annihilated and created anew" because they exist "only when they are perceived" (Sect. 45); but his answer (Sects. 46-48), which at one juncture affirms and at another denies the objection's point, scarcely represents a clear decision on the matter.[8]

The *Dialogues*, in contrast, presents several serious discussions of relativity issues, all of which give qualified support to relativism. At III, p. 245, Hylas (the antagonist in the *Dialogues*) asks Philonous (who represents Berkeley) whether the variability of perceptions would not be inconsistent with Philonous' trust in the deliverances of the senses. Philonous' answer is that variable ideas are not threats to knowledge at all, unless one also subscribes to independent objects, which, of course, Philonous has been attacking all along. He reiterates this answer later when he says that upon the supposition of external objects "the objections from the change of colors in a pigeon's neck, or the appearance of the broken oar in the water, must be allowed to have weight. But these and the like objections vanish if we do not maintain the being of absolute external originals but place the reality of things in ideas, fleeting, indeed, and changeable" (III, p. 206). This confirms a dramatic change in Berkeley's attitude from the time he wrote the *Principles*, when he could only attach the relativity arguments to skepticism.

Hylas also poses the question of the effect of relativity upon the "publicity" of objects: "But the same idea which is in my mind cannot be in yours or in any other mind. Does it not, therefore, follow from your principles that no two can see the same thing?" (III, p. 193) Philonous answers that, under the common meaning of "same," which is "where no distinction or variety is perceived," many could be said to perceive the "same" thing; but if we are interested in relativity and concentrate on "the diversity of persons who perceived," we would say that many perceived "different" things (III, pp. 193-94).

Thus the pattern of the *Principles* and the *Dialogues* emerges. The former downgraded the potential of relativity for proving immaterialism and ignored or evaded the hard issues of the diversity and momentariness of perceptions. The *Dialogues* represented at least a significant growth in the appreciation of relativity; it granted demonstrative power to the relativity argument, admitted that different minds receive their experiences differently, and explicitly discussed the impact of relativity upon the validity of sense perception and upon the belief that many can perceive the same thing.

II. Explanation for the Change in Berkeley's Attitude

Why did the *Dialogues'* magnified assessment and use of relativity differ so from the role given that concept in the *Principles?* I contend that the major reason for this change was a rhetorical one. The *Principles* had failed to command the attention or admiration of its audience, and Berkeley determined to change the mode of expression of his concepts to secure for them an improved response. This program for the *Dialogues* resulted in many rhetorical improvements, among them the adoption of the dialogue form, the avoidance of suspicious terms like "ideas,"[9] and the resurrection of the relativity argument. The latter had enjoyed a proven success in the skeptical tradition and employed a very concrete terminology, which lent it accessibility and plausibility.

This by itself, of course, would have made the *Dialogues* only better literature, not better philosophy. Berkeley himself now believed that the relativity argument was better philosophy; it was logically conclusive, not just psychologically persuasive. Yet he came to this realization probably because of his rhetorical reconstruction.

The composition of a dialogue confronted Berkeley with a concrete, if imaginary, antagonist in the person of Hylas, whom he had to convince of the truth of immaterialism. Hylas came already equipped with typical materialist prejudices, which his author had to dissolve; but in searching Hylas' mind to prepare his attack, Berkeley discovered that at least one of those prejudices could actually aid his assault. Since Hylas was a common-sense materialist, he believed that things were as he, and everyone else, perceived them to be;[10] thus he would reject anything that contradicted his trust in the senses. Berkeley knew that the materialist tenet of independently existing objects was a contradiction of naive common sense; and he could show Hylas this by presenting, among other things, the relativity argument. Since, according to common sense, things exist as they are perceived, and because, according to the relativity argument, perceptions vary from perceiver to perceiver, there cannot be objects outside of perceptions. For then one object would possess all manner of contrary qualities at once.

Because the *Principles* had involved no concrete audience with whom to argue, it had not inspired Berkeley to see the potential of the relativity argument for affecting that audience; so he had ignored it as weak and given little thought to the whole matter of the variability of ideas. Once he decided to exploit the advantage of that argument in the *Dialogues*, however, he had to face the issues implied by its premises. He had to suggest, at least, that all perceptions were relative, and to explain what relativity implied for the traditional identity and publicity of objects.

III. Limitations of Berkeley's Commitment to Relativity

From what has been presented thus far, one might think that all the textual evidence from the *Dialogues* supported the notion that Berkeley held a universal relativity there. If the evidence really were this preponderant, one might wonder about the attentiveness or rationality of those, like Luce and Jessop, who have not subscribed to this interpretation of Berkeley.[11]

Yet there are several features of the *Dialogues* that lend some plausibility to the Luce-Jessop reading. First of all, there is no definite "proof text" stating explicitly and unequivocally that each and every perception is unique to its individual perceiver. Some passages may insinuate this doctrine, but they do not *say* it to be a philosophical truth. That being the case, the relativistic reading of Berkeley can never be more than a circumstantial interpretation of him.

Not only do definitive claims of relativism not appear in the *Dialogues*, but some passages do appear that seem to militate against relativism. Berkeley claims that the ideas perceived by a particular mind may or do exist independently of that mind; sensible things "depend not on my thought and have an existence distinct from being perceived by me" (II, p. 153). Again, "these ideas or things by me perceived, either themselves or their archetypes, exist independently of my mind . . . [and] must therefore exist in some other mind, whose will it is they should be exhibited to me" (II, p. 156). One text even states that a sensible object continues in existence when a particular subject is unaware of it: "Now it is plain [that sensible things] have an existence exterior to my mind, since I find them by experience to be independent of it. There is therefore some other mind wherein they exist during the intervals between the times of my perceiving them, as likewise they did before my birth, and would do after my supposed annihilation" (III, p. 175). The relativistic doctrine that every object is intrinsically ordered to the individual experiencing it certainly cannot be true if several minds can perceive the same thing or if perceived qualities may continue to exist through time.

IV. Resolving the Tension

Two very different strains of thought have been uncovered in Berkeley's *Dialogues.* Let us first recapitulate and amplify them, so that we can then compare them.

One theme relativizes perceptions to the point that each one is separable from every other; no single idea may be repeated through time or space, and none is perceivable by more than one person. God produces sensations in us singly, but in a regular order. He coordinates the private sensations of many spirits so that they perceive similar ideas at similar times; this engenders the belief that there is a literally public and continuous world.

If Berkeley's whole presentation had contained essentially this position, it would have been, if somewhat eccentric, still unproblematically consistent. But the *Dialogues* did not stop here, of course; it also included a nonrelativistic element that affirmed, or assumed, that objects do continue in existence independently of human perceptions and are publicly available.

There is no evidence that Berkeley conceived one of these strains before the other or thought one was more basic; indeed, they exist side by side at *Dialogues,* III, p. 191 (and *Principles,* sects. 14, 45-58). But their reconciliation is an obvious problem; how could Berkeley have held both these positions without gross contradiction?

A. The Theological Solution

It is very widely believed that Berkeley's appeal to "divine archetypes" or "ideas in the mind of God" was intended to safeguard the permanence and publicity of the experienced world. Under this interpretation, God "continues to perceive" a sensible thing even if no finite perceiver is aware of it. God's eternal perception grants the desired substantiality to sensible things, without introducing material substrata unperceived by any mind.[12]

In actuality, however, the "divine archetypes" cannot explain or guarantee continuity in the world, because eternity has no necessary relation with continuity. Insofar as objects exist archetypally in the divine mind, they are all equally eternal;[13] but from our viewpoint objects may vary in their temporal status. There are many things that God perceives eternally to which we would not attribute continuous existence. Among these are momentary sensations, which by definition are not continuous, and more substantial entities like dinosaurs and the Colossus of Rhodes, which do not continue to exist in our time. It is true that God is "now" perceiving enduring objects that exist in our present; so God might be said to provide some type of metaphysical explanation for continuous objects. But what is said to be "continuous" and what "momentary" is a distinction that the divine ideas cannot help us with.

The simultaneous availability of one idea to many minds presents a similar situation. All of God's objects are "public" because of their equal presence to him and equal integration into his system of ideas, wherein all ideas are known from all possible perspectives at once. But again, only some human experiences represent objects accessible to many perceivers; some, like pain, are private. Yet my pain is known to God in the same way that he would know trees and books; so, as in the case of continuity, the divine ideas cannot tell us which objects of human experience are public and which are not.

B. The Linguistic Solution

Philonous' remark that disagreement about the sameness or difference of experiences was only *verbal* suggests the way in which "relativistic" difference and "absolutistic" sameness could be reconciled: experiences could be "different" under strict criteria for a "philosophical" vocabulary and "the same" under the looser criteria that govern popular usage.[14] The opposition between the relativity of ideas and the identity of objects, both of which Berkeley espouses, would then be primarily linguistic and could be resolved by clarifying the conditions under which "strict" and "loose" rules are to be in operation.[15]

Berkeley dismisses out of hand the usage of "same" that supposedly refers to an abstract idea of material identity,[16] but he finds other functions of the word useful for ordinary discourse. "But in case every variation was thought sufficient to constitute a new kind or individual, the endless number or confusion of names would render language *impracticable*. Therefore, to avoid this as well as other *inconveniences* which are obvious upon a little thought, men combine together several ideas. . . . all which they refer to one name and *consider as* one thing" (*Dialogues,* III, p. 191). Philosophers are prejudiced in favor of the abstract idea of material substances "from not rightly understanding the *common language* of men speaking of several distinct ideas as united into one thing *by the mind*" (III, p. 192). The italicized phrases make it clear that Berkeley has here interpreted the concept of identity only as a pragmatically successful notion and not as a "true" one. The truth in this matter remains that "every variation [is] sufficient to constitute a new kind or individual"; but this particular truth is not immediately useful, so it is replaced by a more practical construct.

Nevertheless, this pragmatic sameness is hardly enough to solve the philosophical problem of relativism; that things are unified and public must be not only useful, but in some way true and philosophically respectable. Conveniently, one means of achieving a practical language is by loosening the rules governing "same" so that it can be applied to perceptions *without falsity.* Berkeley realizes this at *Dialogues,* III, p. 194: "Words are of arbitrary imposition; and since men are used to apply the word 'same' where no distinction or variety is perceived, and I do not pretend to alter their perceptions, it follows that, as men have said before, *several saw the same thing,* so they may, upon like occasions, still continue to use the same phrase without any deviation either from propriety of language or the truth of things." While *Dialogues,* III, pp. 191-92 emphasized that variety could be neglected for the sake of a practicable language, the present text asserts that, given sufficiently loose criteria, the designation "same" accurately states the way things are. The perceptions given to us really are similar and coherent, and to talk of "the same thing" is to describe that coherence in an informal and condensed way.

Thus the disagreement between philosophy and the common language is not over the reality being described; the dispute is verbal, directed at the propriety of applying one set of perfectly respectable linguistic rules as opposed to another set. With this, the problem of Berkeley's incompatible positions is dissolved; he can speak in strict truth about irreducibly private and fleeting perceptions, yet he can also turn to the familiar framework of permanent and public objects when ordinary usage is appropriate and advantageous for him.

V. Conclusion: The Relativity Language

It is ironic that an element of Berkeley's program of rhetorical improvement, the extended relativity argument, should have created a specifically rhetorical problem for the *Dialogues.* He knew that there were ways of speaking that his audience would ridicule, among them being the relativist "language" of unique perceptions; its nominalistic restriction to singular perceptual contents would have been tedious, to say the least. Since he felt there was no good reason to bait his readers on this point, his solution was (as the *Principles* had stated in another context) to "think with the learned and speak with the vulgar" (sect. 51). He would accede to common linguistic habits while retaining his relativism as one massive reservation on those habits. He would speak as if permanent and public objects existed, even in discussions that indicated relativity.[17]

Berkeley's deference on relativism contrasts with the manner in which he managed to express idealism. Although occasionally he employed an object-language to secure irony and to speak the "realistic" language of his opponents, as on the opening page of the *Dialogues,* most of his dialect was consistently "idealistic," free of blatant concessions or unconscious slips into materialism. He made few concessions in response to specific idioms of ordinary usage or values, and made some with obvious reluctance.[18]

Speaking an idealist language was comparatively easy, however, since Berkeley's immaterialism was careful to leave common perceptions as it found them. The relativist language, in contrast, could not avoid contradicting the popular beliefs in continuity and publicity; thus he was forced to speak in loose ways. But Berkeley could do so without damaging the integrity of his relativism because, as we have seen, speaking loosely need not be speaking falsely; under criteria that are both generous and reasonable, perceptions really are public and continuous.

Notes

1. A. A. Luce, *Berkeley's Immaterialism* (1945; repr. New York: Russell and Russell, 1968), p. 124; A. A. Luce and T. E. Jessop, eds., *The Works of George Berkeley, Bishop of Cloyne,* 9 vols., (London: Thomas Nelson and Sons, 1948-57), vol. I, p. 118n; II, pp. 9, 12, 44n, 192n.

2. I. C. Tipton, *Berkeley: The Philosophy of Immaterialism* (London: Methuen, 1974), pp. 36-41, 236-48; Harry M. Bracken, *Berkeley* (London: Macmillan, 1974), chap. 6; Phillip Cummins, "Perceptual Relativity and Ideas in the Mind," *Philosophy and Phenomenological Research* 24 (1963-64): 202-14.

3. Russell A. Lascola, "Ideas and Archetypes: Appearance and Reality in Berkeley's Philosophy," *The Personalist* 54 (1973): 42-49; C. D. Broad, "Berkeley's Denial of Material Substance," in C. B. Martin and D. M. Armstrong, eds., *Locke and Berkeley: A Collection of Critical Essays* (Notre Dame: University of Notre Dame Press, 1968), p. 263; S. A. Grave, "The Mind and Its Ideas: Some Problems in the Interpretation of Berkeley," in Martin and Armstrong, eds., *Locke and Berkeley,* pp. 297-306.

4. *A Treatise Concerning the Principles of Human Knowledge,* sects. 11-15. In Colin M. Turbayne, ed., *Principles, Dialogues, and Philosophical Correspondence* (Indianapolis: Bobbs-Merrill, 1965).

5. Berkeley delivered a similar judgment on the relativity argument in his earlier notebooks for the *Principles,* the *Philosophical Commentaries* (*Works,* I). He toyed with some instances of relativity (sects. 87, 104), then questioned visual relativity (sects. 218, 257), and ended by forsaking the whole approach (sect. 265).

6. *Three Dialogues Between Hylas and Philonous,* I, pp. 116-17, 119, 124-25, 128-30. In Turbayne, ed., *Principles, Dialogues, Correspondence.*

7. G. J. Warnock, *Berkeley* (1953; repr. London: Penguin, 1969), p. 152.

8. *Principles,* sect. 46, reiterates that sensible things exist solely when perceived, implying that the objects an individual perceives *are* reduced to nothing when he shuts his eyes. Sects. 46-47 attempts to make "continual creation" more plausible by ascribing that doctrine to other philosophers, too, such as the Scholastics. But sect. 48 seems to turn in a different direction by claiming that, while sensible objects cannot exist out of all minds whatever, they may exist when not perceived by this or that spirit.

9. "Idea" does not begin to appear with regularity until p. 129, well into the *First Dialogue.*

10. "Whatever degree of heat we perceive by sense, we may be sure the same exists in the object that occasions it" (*Dialogues,* I, p. 113): "Each visible object has that color which we see in it" (I, p. 122).

11. Russell Lascola finds Luce's reading to be "incredible"; "The Role of Relativity in Berkeley's Philosophy" (Diss. University of Southern California, 1970), p. 177.

12. G. A. Johnston, *The Development of Berkeley's Philosophy* (1923; repr. New York: Russell and Russell, 1965), p. 185; G. Dawes Hicks, *Berkeley* (London: Oxford University Press, 1932), pp. 153-54.

13. *Dialogues,* III, p. 199: "When things are said to begin or end their existence, we do not mean this with regard to God, but his creatures. All objects are eternally known by God, or, which is the same thing, have an eternal existence in his mind"; III, p. 200: " . . . nothing is new, or begins to be, in respect of the mind of God."

14. Prominent writings that have analyzed the "two languages" include: A. D. Ritchie, *George Berkeley: A Reappraisal* (New York: Barnes and Noble, 1967), p. 97; Jonathan Bennett, *Locke Berkeley Hume* (Oxford: Clarendon Press, 1971), pp. 153ff.; S. A. Grave, in Martin and Armstrong, eds., *Locke and Berkeley,* pp. 301, 306; Konrad Marc-Wogau, "The Argument from Illusion and Berkeley's Idealism," in ibid., pp. 350-52.

15. Berkeley often distinguished strict and loose usages of terms: see *Principles,* sect. 142, and *Dialogues,* III, p. 176 on having an "idea" of God; *Dialogues,* I, p. 112 on "feeling" the cause of heat or weight; *Dialogues,* I, p. 145 on "hearing" objects rather than sounds.

16. *Principles,* sect. 95; *Dialogues,* III, p. 194.

17. In *Principles,* sect. 14, Berkeley talked of "the same eye at different stations, or eyes of a different texture at the same station," although there can strictly be no "same" entities; *Dialogues,* III, p. 191 cites "the same sense at different times or in different circumstances."

18. *Principles,* sect. 38, debated whether to call sensible objects "ideas" or "things," and sect. 142 distinguished "idea" from "notion"; *Dialogues,* III, p. 181 repeats the latter distinction; and III, p. 190 admits that he may "be obliged to use some ambages and ways of speech not common."

II Ideas and Perception

3

On Taking Ideas Seriously

Désirée Park

If one proposes, as I do, to give serious attention to Berkeley's term *idea,* sooner or later his dictum *'esse* is *percipi'* must be dealt with satisfactorily. This requires the sorting out of his several uses of the word 'idea' as it appears in the works that he published and in the manuscript remains.

The ordinary uses of the word 'idea' are easily detected. Berkeley, like most English speakers, not infrequently means by 'idea' any thought that he might be entertaining. Again he sometimes means a relatively complex object which he has in mind, such as a tree or a seagull. Sometimes too he writes 'idea' when, on his own evidence, he ought to have written 'concept' or 'notion'. Nevertheless, it is clear that Berkeley's strict use of the word 'idea', to mean a sensation or sensory image or mental picture, occurs when his distinctive usage is important to his argument.[1] This indeed is hardly surprising when only this restricted meaning conforms with his consistently held claim that for an *idea,* "to be is to be perceived."

Several consequences of this rule repay examination. For instance, an idea of this required and austere type is an idea precisely as and when it is perceived. It is wholly present, has no hidden features, and is clearly just the idea that it is. If such an idea is informally said to be hazy or indistinct, as the appearance of a ship in a fog may be hazy to an observer, then the idea present to the perceiver is clearly a hazy idea. Moreover, an idea of this strictly interpreted sort has neither past nor future, and even the present in which it occurs is properly attributed to the perceiver, not to the idea.

35

One further peculiarity of such ideas is of special interest for our present purposes. The assertion that, "an idea can be like nothing but an idea" is comparatively well known.[2] A less widely appreciated corollary of this same rule is the consequence that the identity of any two ideas consists in "perfect likeness."[3]

Few notions could separate ideas from any other sort of object or thing more sharply than this condition. The *perfect likeness* requirement, which alone establishes the identity of two ideas, literally prescribes that identical ideas as ideas be indiscernible. The identity is of course qualitative, but the point is that an idea has just one quality.[4]

These several conditions enjoy the historical advantage of conforming to Berkeley's stated requirements for ideas. The more general philosophical interest of these rules is to be found in Berkeley's consequent articulation of the external world, and for one very good reason. As I have argued elsewhere,[5] in addressing himself to that which can be known, Berkeley was right to insist on a fundamental distinction between *the essentially perceived* and *the inherently imperceptible*; between, that is, *ideas* and *notions*, respectively.

In the following discussion it will be my purpose to draw attention to ideas and to show that the correct analysis of the Berkeleyan idea provides for distinctions which are crucial in solving a notably recalcitrant problem about perception. It will be seen that the argument turns on the clear difference between the irreducible sensory evidence which grounds a perceptual claim and any description which may be given of that evidence.

The advantages of attending to ideas are nicely illustrated when examining the contemporary puzzle of the color continuum. The problem usually is presented by hypothesizing a continuum of colors in which some colors are perceptibly indistinguishable from their neighbors or, as we should say, identical with their neighbors. The interest is said to focus on the fact that whereas, among the colors of the continuum, A, B and C, it is seen that A = B and B = C, it is also seen that A ≠ C.[6] What then is to become of identity and of the transitivity of identity statements?

In developing the problem, it is sometimes the case that the pairs of indistinguishable colors are said to form part of a continuous color spectrum proper, and at other times these pairs of colors are referred to as "color patches."[7] In either case, the difficulty is essentially the same.

Imagine then the aforementioned colors A, B and C as color patches, side by side and from left to right. The colors are said to be separated at the outset by the spaces between each patch. Let us further say that each intervening space is white so that the sequence A, B and C which progresses from more-like-red to more-like-orange, is easily seen against the background. The problem now can be stated fully. The sequence of colors, A, B and C perceptibly begins by being more like red and ends by being more like orange. Perceptibly, A = B, B = C and A ≠ C. But if this is so; Either two colors are not properly said to be identical just because they look alike; or the identity of colors has the peculiar feature of being non-transitive, and therefore is unlike any other notion of identity. If the latter alternative is true, then it follows that the description of colors is fundamentally incoherent.

I shall argue that both of these consequences are to be rejected; as well as the further consequence that the visible spectrum can be proved to be of only one color, if the identity of colors depends on perception. My objections are based on the fact that all of these puzzling results rely on a misdescription of perceived colors, which themselves are of course ideas *par excellence*. The temporally continuous color patch and its fellow, the temporally continuous middle color in the color continuum, are the particular culprits to be exposed.

Before entering on a strictly Berkeleyan analysis of the color continuum, it may be useful to notice some of the consequences of accepting the terms of the problem.[8] Crispin Wright offers an account of it which has influenced discussion for some time.[9] In his essay entitled "Language-Mastery and the Sorites Paradox," we are told:

> If colour predicates are observational, any pair of patches indistinguishable in colour must satisfy the condition that any colour predicate applicable to either is applicable to both. Suppose, then, that we build up the series of colour patches of the third example, [which provided a sequence of patches from red to orange in which "each patch is *just* discriminable in colour from those immediately next to it . . . ," p. 228] interposing new patches to the point where every patch in the resultant series is indiscriminable in colour from those immediately adjacent to it. The possibility of doing so, of course, depends upon the non-transitivity of our colour discriminations.[10]

It follows that, if the first colored patch is seen to be red, then the next patch in the sequence, which must be indistinguishable from the first patch, also is seen to be red. When this process is suitably repeated, in due course the result is that the whole constructed red/orange spectrum must be conceded to be red.

Now, even if there are many occasions on which it is not important to distinguish between some reds and some oranges, Wright points out that it is not necessary to tolerate a one-color spectrum of this sort. The solution is to devise a color chart, which in this case would show a color continuum from red to orange. A slice of the continuum near the apparent border between red and orange would then be called 'red', and any color to the left of that slice would also be called 'red', leaving any color to the right to be called 'orange'.[11] A candidate colored object could then be compared with the chart so as to determine the object's exactly matching place in the continuum and be given a name accordingly. The advantage of these operations is to preserve the use of color predicates for most of our ordinary and undemanding purposes, and also to limit those cases which might require more accuracy. In fact accuracy is not so easily achieved, but this does not especially interest Wright because his purpose here is to identify the tolerance of color predicates.

In effect, then, we do not have to accept a one-color spectrum because color charts can always be constructed, and in the great majority of cases the question of our matching colors perfectly does not even arise. Nevertheless, it is instructive to notice the conditions under which perfect accuracy in matching colors can be achieved.

To decide whether one color patch is indistinguishable from another, it will always be necessary to view them together, and the only way in which such a comparison can reliably be repeated is to examine the same patches under the same conditions. Again, it is true that we do not often make this sort of demand on our color schemes, but it can be done—and it regularly is done in the theatre. An effect such as changing the time of day onstage by obliterating part of the scenery frequently consists in causing formerly unlike color patches to match each other. A special case is the abrupt appearance of Hamlet's father's ghost and then his vanishing again. These kinds of transformations are possible precisely because the relationships between colors and lighting can be controlled, noted and reproduced. In practice therefore a color patch can be systematically matched with another color patch, once the conditions of the matching are known and available for use.

The example of a theatrical set is admitted to be unusual, but its elements are essential features of our observations, to which we shall return.[12] For now, however, let us acknowledge that this result is somewhat beside the point of Wright's inquiry, since he is not in any case much concerned with the enterprise of matching colors. The 'non-transitive indiscriminability' of color patches remains for him the important fact, and his interest is to show that this state of affairs does not interfere unduly with our use of color predicates.

Although there are clearly differences of emphasis in inquiring about the color continuum, some points can be agreed. For instance there is no dispute that questions about the colors in the color continuum must be about how the colors *look*. This is not a discussion based on wavelengths, nor is it addressed to the place of a color in the visible spectrum as determined by refraction. Moreover it seems too that the introduction of color charts would help in teaching the standard uses of color words. Where only colors differ, it might be supposed that the learner's attention would most easily be fixed on the parts of a colored surface exhibited one after another. Still, the fact that color discrimination is tolerant in practice ought not to be read as a straightforward acknowledgment of the claim that color predicates are fundamentally tolerant. Even less should it be assumed that this practice is fortunate because of the unreliable behavior of color patches in the color continuum.

In the first place, our practical tolerance in the use of color predicates is justified by our usual sheer lack of interest in the precise colors of colored objects. This is hardly surprising, since our language on the whole tends to pick out objects rather than seizing on their more decorative and transient features. Objects are, after all, endowed with the advantage that they can be consulted under varying conditions, whereas the colors of their surfaces have been observed to change merely with the passing of a cloud overhead, or with the fading of the evening light. For reasons such as these, our rather casual practice in noticing colors and naming them might have been anticipated.

Second, and more important, the chief objection to the problem of the color continuum is that the questions which it is understood to raise are misconceived. The problem is not about color predicates, at least not in the first instance, but about colors as they are observed and the best account that can be given of them. Consequently, to begin by assuming that the question is concerned with the non-transitive indiscriminability of color patches is effectively to conceal the fact that some telling distinctions can be drawn between observed colors and observed colored objects, or color patches.

To sum up, it is a fundamental mistake to accept the terms on which the problem of the color continuum depends. In order to make this plain, the analysis which follows will bring to light several features which mark off colors from any kinds of colored objects. In this manner, I shall undertake to provide a distinction where there has always been a difference.

It is not my intention to deny that a sequence of observations of the sort described in the original problem can be made at all. This would be a misreading of the objection. The criticism rather is that the original problem is at fault because it mixes two different kinds of color descriptions and represents them as being of one kind only.

Specifically, it assumes that perceived colors and perceived colored shapes are amenable to essentially the same type of sequential ordering. The difficulty with this assumption is that there are features of shapes which can coherently be held to endure from moment to moment, whereas perceived colors, which are ideas in the strictest sense, are confined to the present. The objection therefore is that important differences between perceived colors and perceived colored shapes are concealed in the statement of the original problem, and that when these differences are recognized, the problem itself is dissolved.

The chief differences can be shown by inquiring into some details of the original claim. Thus briefly, a selection of shapes, like colored rectangles, may be assumed to fit a description in which rectangle 1 is indistinguishable in color from rectangle 2, and 2 likewise is indistinguishable in color from rectangle 3, and yet rectangles 1 and 3 are distinguishable by color from each other. For the sake of convenience, let it be said also that the rectangles here mentioned are ordinary-issue two-color postage stamps in the reddish-orange part of the spectrum, and that they have the usual white borders, but the figure and lettering have been replaced by the color of the ground. There ought to be no reservations about this choice of modified postage stamps since the whole question is supposed to be about perceived colors and, if the stamps are perceived, it is common ground that they must be some color or other. There is the further advantage that the colors in the original problem plainly are supposed to have some continuous shape since, as color patches, they are freely shifted about as the necessary comparisons are made between selected pairs of them. A final advantage is that by the explicit selection of a regular and familiar shape like a postage stamp, we are enabled both to avoid the ambiguities customarily associated with the phrase 'color patch', and to prepare the way for drawing the necessary distinction between perceived colored shapes and perceived colors.

The original sequence can now be restated, so that the color A of stamp 1 is perceptibly indistinguishable from the color B of stamp 2; that, similarly, stamp 2 is indistinguishable in color from stamp 3 whose color is C; and that, by the same type of comparison, the respective colors of stamps 1 and 3 are nevertheless distinguishable from each other.

On the analysis of ideas, which states that the identity of any two ideas consists in perfect likeness, this result would require us to assert that the perceived colors A and B are identical, and that the perceived colors B and C are also identical. This in turn invites the objection that it must then follow either that B is not identical with itself, if A and C are distinguishable as required, and that consequently there are no logical relations, including that of transitivity, which hold between perceived colors; or that the identity of two perceived colors is not ensured by their being perceptibly indistinguishable. The latter course is usually preferred, but both these conclusions miss the point.

Emphasis properly is given to the judgments which are made sequentially when the stamps 1, 2 and 3 are compared in respect of their colors. In the first instance of judgment, stamp 1 is perceived together with stamp 2, and the two stamps are pronounced indistinguishable with regard to their colors A and B, respectively. Perceptibly stamp 1 is identical in color with stamp 2.

In the second instance, stamp 2 is perceived together with stamp 3, and again the two respective colors, B and C, are judged to be indistinguishable from each other. It follows that stamp 2 is identical in color with stamp 3 as well.

So far, in comparing the colors of stamps 1, 2 and 3, we have addressed ourselves to the perceived colors of perceived colored shapes. We are thereby easily led to suppose that the color of stamp 2, the stamp mentioned in both judgments, is the same color on the two occasions because it is the color of the same stamp. And so the color B comes to be called perceptibly the same, and therefore identical in the two instances, because stamp 2 occurs in both instances. The inference fails, however, because—while it is true to say that postage stamp 2 continues to be the same postage stamp during the two distinct perceptual moments which we have described—the perceived color B, like any perceived color, is restricted to the single moment of its perception. A perceived color is an idea, hence a putative second instance of the same perceived color is a second idea.

To sum up so far, the color B is said, though mistakenly, to be the same B in both observations, because postage stamp 2 is a continuous colored shape whose color is judged to be B. This is the way in which we ordinarily assign colors to objects; that is, in most cases we suppose that an object keeps its color unless the color is changed by some known method.[13] Given this assumption, it is readily inferred that the color B of stamp 2 is the same color in the two instances, and no great difficulties ensue from this practical approach, so long as it is directed to practical questions. Nevertheless, a careful analysis of perceived colors is a different exercise and requires more accurate discriminations. In particular, the easy assumption that a single color is temporally continuous and therefore can be perceived at different moments is open to challenge.

The point to insist on is that the color B of the second instance of comparison is a new idea. Consequently it is as entirely separate from the color B of the first instance as from any other idea at all. For unlike stamps, no idea is available for a second look, and every idea is logically independent of every other idea.

When the third comparison is made—that is, the one between A and C—it is manifest to all that color A is perceptibly distinguishable from color C. At that moment, it may also be supposed that color B is not attended to, and so plays no part whatever in the dissimilarity recognized between colors A and C. This is worth noticing because habitual usage makes it tempting to think of a single perceived color B as enjoying a more or less prominent place in the relationships established sequentially between the above-mentioned A and B, then between the succeeding B and C, and their successors A and C. But again, this assumption of a temporally continuous B would be a conflation of perceived colors, which are ideas and cannot literally recur, with perceived colored shapes which characteristically are endowed with repeatable relationships.

Given that a perceived color is, as an idea, confined to its moment of perception, it is obvious that the comparison of any two such colors must be made at the same moment. In the case of the postage stamps, this may be managed easily by placing them against a suitably contrasting background and arranging them in a line from left to right, beginning with stamp 1. This shows stamps 1, 2 and 3 with their customary borders, exhibiting respectively the colors A, B and C.[14] Let the white borders now be eliminated so that the stamps 1, 2 and 3 form an unbroken rectangle of a reddish-orange color.[15]

The result is that the perceptible difference between colors A and C can be noted by attending to the extreme vertical edges of the rectangle. Alternatively, and to remove all doubt, the rectangle may be curved, with its upper edge shortened so as to form a flattened ring, and the edges displaying colors A and C joined together. In this case, the colors A and C show a line where they meet.[16] The color B however, which was formerly the color of stamp 2, is no longer to be seen. On one interpretation this latter result is not surprising, since *ex hypothesi* the color B is not perceptibly distinguishable from either A or C. Nevertheless, we are presented with the fact that the perceived color B does not survive the loss of stamp 2; from which we may infer that the supposedly *middle color* was all along the *middle figure*. Put differently, it now seems clear that the original problem was addressed to a middle perceived colored shape, not to a middle perceived color, of which there evidently is none.

This is not to say that the former relationship cannot be restored, so that there are again stamps 1, 2 and 3 displaying respectively colors A, B and C. A stamp 2 of a perceived color B can easily be extracted from the new rectangle by dividing the reddish-orange continuum into three equal parts and removing the middle section. This, however, is obviously a division of the continuum based not on perceptible differences of color but, in this case, on the remembered positions of colored shapes.

In summary, the proper context in which to test the distinctions among perceived colors is by juxtaposing them and then viewing them at the same moment. When a colored rectangle such as that composed of stamps 1, 2 and 3 is examined closely, it is clear that the color continuum which is formed has no perceptible color B distinct from A and C. This is in accordance with the concept of a color continuum, and there is no objection about this part of the account. The disputed claim is the conclusion that the perceived color B can and does figure in contradictory propositions about identity and transitivity when, as a matter of record, it is not perceived as B at all. But if it is not so perceived, it is not a perceived color to the purpose of the original problem. We may conclude therefore that the color B is not a self-contradictory element as was at first supposed, but rather that the statement of the original problem trades in ambiguities. For provided that perceived colors are properly distinguished from perceived colored shapes, the identity of two colors consists precisely in their perfect likeness at just the single moment they are perceived.

There is a further point about continuous shapes and the spacing of colors which brings the subdivisions of the visible spectrum into shaper relief. An assortment of colored threads such as one sees in some department stores and which range from red to orange to yellow, provides a good example of a practical color continuum. Very likely there is no one who can distinguish between the perceived colors of each thread and its immediate neighbors when a full complement of the manufacturer's stock is suitably displayed. At any rate there is no doubt about the principle that any pair of adjacent threads could be perceptibly indistinguishable by color, and one member of that pair and the next adjacent thread also be indistinguishable by color. It could be true, in fact, that every adjacent pair of threads in the entire continuum similarly is indistinguishable by color. Yet it does not follow from this that one is thereby committed to calling all threads in the continuum 'red' if one begins with the red part of the assortment.

There is a fundamental difference between saying that two threads are perceptibly indistinguishable by color and therefore their respective perceived colors are at that moment identical; and saying that any two threads which have once been pronounced indistinguishable from their respective neighbors and therefore of identical colors with their neighbors, are now indistinguishable from each other. The second inference does not follow for two related reasons.

First, the threads are continuous perceived colored shapes, even if somewhat attenuated ones. It is indeed this fact which permits them to be distinguished in the color continuum on some ground other than a perceptible difference of color.

Second, it is because the threads are continuous colored shapes that they are to be carefully distinguished from momentary colors. For only when this difference is recognized does it make sense to require that the colors of any two threads be compared *as colors*; that is, perceived at the same time.

As in the case of the stamps, the proper approach to the comparison of the colors of any pair of threads is to place them together and view them at the same moment. Seen in this way, there will be some threads which are indistinguishable, which are therefore judged to be identical in color. Other pairs will be perceptibly different. For instance, if one begins with the red thread at one extremity of the continuum and compares its color with that of its neighboring thread, the colors are indistinguishable as mentioned. If one then compares the first thread with the third thread, and continues in this manner, so that each pair is formed with the first thread as one member of the pair and judged in respect of its perceived colors, sooner or later, the first thread, which is perceptibly red, will be compared with a perceptibly orangeish-red thread and the two colors will be judged to be perceptibly different. There is therefore no reason to assert that the color continuum must nevertheless be composed of one color only because identity and transitivity require it. When the colors are accurately distinguished from the threads, the demands of logic cease to be counter-intuitive. Perceptible differences between red and orange emerge in the continuum after all; not thread for thread, which is the order of *colored shapes,* but in the order of momentary *colors* which literally are perceived.

Although individual perceived colors are confined to their respective moments, the sequences in which they appear may be said to recur. Transitivity is consequently a relationship which holds between reports of the repeatable sequences of unrepeatable perceived colors. The principle is clear enough, even granted that it is not often stated or deliberately applied.

First, any color which can be picked out because it is perceptibly distinguishable from the adjacent colors can, under *essentially the same conditions,* be picked out on subsequent occasions.

Second, each color which is so selected on one occasion can in principle replace that chosen by the same method on a second and third occasion, without thereby altering a true report of the colors perceived.

Third, so long as each color is selected by the same method, the color of any one occasion can be substituted for that of any other occasion. It follows that the transitivity of indistinguishable, and therefore identical, perceived colors is ensured by repeatable sequences, and that transitivity is described with no reference whatever to perceived colored shapes.

An illustration is provided by the reddish-orange color continuum constructed from the postage stamps mentioned earlier. The rectangle formed by placing stamps 1, 2 and 3 in a line, removing their borders and closing the gaps between them, will under the same conditions continue to show colors A and C, but not color B. Hence identical perceived As can be picked out on successive occasions, as can identical perceived Cs, and any chosen A or C can be substituted for any other A or C, respectively. In these conditions, the true reports of the perceived colors continue undisturbed, and colors A and C can be selected as often as one pleases. The rules of transitivity require only that for each selection the appropriate sequence of observations should be made.

In principle then, we can find a color by attending to a sequence of observations that precedes its momentary appearance, and we can find its like by repeating the essential conditions of the sequence.

For practical reasons, including our much greater interest in continuous colored shapes than in colors, we do not often seek to select perceived colors in this way.[17] Still, it is important to recognize that momentary perceived colors can be picked out sequentially, and that this is done quite independently of any shape that may be attributed to them under another description.

In conclusion, I have tried to show that when the Berkeleyan idea is taken seriously it reveals a genuine division between sensory information and the ways in which such information has come to be interpreted. The color continuum is not the only contemporary puzzle which yields to this sort of analysis, but the solution does illustrate one fruitful method of dealing with the consequences of unexamined, ordinary usage. When it is necessary to draw distinctions which are not commonly made, it is evident that a detailed approach is the only one which will serve. But then we have been told that " . . . he who is short-sighted will be obliged to draw the object nearer, and may, perhaps, by a close and narrow survey discern that which has escaped far better eyes." Accordingly I conclude that this creeping method of examination can hardly be faulted in its company, whatever may be its shortcomings in dramatic effect.

Notes

1. A. A. Luce and T. E. Jessop, eds., *The Works of George Berkeley, Bishop of Cloyne,* 9 vols. (London: Thomas Nelson and Sons, 1948-57). See *Works,* I. p. 93, entry 775; II, pp. 79, 78. See also the related manuscript notes: Add. MS 39305 fol. 75^r; Add. MS 39304 fols. 38^r and 37^r, respectively. (These manuscript notes are discussed in my *Complementary Notions: A Critical Study of Berkeley's Theory of Concepts* [The Hague: Martinus Nijhoff, 1972], in chap. II.)

2. *Works,* II, p. 44, and I, p. 80, entry 657.

3. *Works,* I, p. 25, entry 192.

4. Or it may be said that an idea is a quality. In either case, there is no sort of resemblance between two ideas *qua* ideas, other than perfect likeness.

5. *Complementary Notions,* see esp. chap. I and II.

6. See, for example, Crispin Wright, "Language-Mastery and the Sorites Paradox," in Gareth Evans and John McDowell, eds., *Truth and Meaning: Essays in Semantics* (Oxford: Oxford University Press, 1976), pp. 223-47.

7. Ibid, p. 233 ff.

8. This section of ten paragraphs has been added to the paper which I originally delivered at the Meeting of the International Berkeley Society in September 1979.

9. The problem of the color continuum was presented by Crispin Wright in a paper delivered to the Philosophical Society in Oxford a few years before the published version quoted in the following paragraph.

10. Wright, "Language-Mastery," p. 233.

11. Ibid., p. 242.

12. See discussion on transitivity to follow.

13. Elsewhere I have discussed the balance to be struck between the attribution of perceived colors and the continuity of perceived objects. See my *Persons: Theories and Perceptions* (The Hague: Martinus Nijhoff, 1973), chaps. I and III.

14. Figure 1.

15. Figure 2.

16. Figure 3.

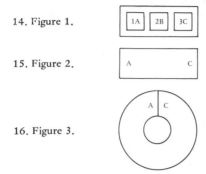

17. An exception is the habitual expectation that the colors of the rainbow or of a white light divided by a prism will continue to appear in the same order and, under the same conditions, be of a like intensity. The technique is much more commonly applied to perceived sounds, as in tuning a musical instrument.

4

The Concept of Immediate Perception in Berkeley's Immaterialism

Georges Dicker

At the outset of Berkeley's *Three Dialogues Between Hylas and Philonous*, Hylas says:

> . . . [B]y "sensible things" I mean those only which are perceived by sense, and . . . in truth the senses perceive nothing which they do not perceive immediately, for they make no inferences.[1]

Berkeley is here putting forward a general principle that Philonous frequently invokes in the ensuing arguments; namely, that

> (P) Whatever is perceived by the senses is immediately perceived.

The import of (P) depends, of course, upon the meaning given to Berkeley's ubiquitous technical term, "immediately perceived." This term can be interpreted in such a way that (P) allows us to say that we perceive pretty much the things that we commonly take ourselves to see, touch, hear, taste, and smell; or it can be interpreted in ways that make (P) significantly restrict the range of possible objects of perception. Thus, to take a trivial example, interpreting "immediately perceived" to mean, "perceived in January 1983," would make

A shorter version of this paper, entitled "Berkeley on Immediate Perception," was read at the 1980 meeting of the Western Division of the American Philosophical Association and at the Spring 1980 meeting of the Creighton Club (New York State Philosophical Association), as well as at the International Berkeley Society's Commemorative Conference in September 1979. I am grateful to the commentators at the two former meetings, Professor Gary Thrane and Professor Elizabeth Ring, respectively, for stimulating discussions of the issues raised in the paper.

(P) imply that *nothing* is ever perceived by the senses before or after January 1983. In this paper, I wish to show that although the meaning Berkeley gives to "immediately perceived" when he introduces (P) renders that principle true and innocuous, the meaning he gives to the term when he subsequently invokes (P) allows him to use the principle as a premiss that leads readily to many of his more paradoxical doctrines. In section I, I shall expose the shift in meaning and show that it turns on conflating a psychological notion of immediate perception with an epistemological one. In section II, I shall show how this conflation contributes to Berkeley's case for immaterialism, and sketch how it has led to certain serious errors in the philosophy of perception.

I

How should we interpret "perceive immediately" in the passage quoted above? Well, Hylas is supposed to be a fairly unsophisticated thinker, who must certainly not be assumed to be familiar with the fine points of Berkeley's theory of perception at the beginning of the *Dialogues*. So his statement should be understood straightforwardly, as making an obvious psychological (phenomenological) point. Hylas means that perceiving has a characteristic immediacy that sets it off from inferring or reasoning. Thus the notion of immediate perception he has in mind may be defined as follows, where the subscript "p" indicates that the notion is a psychological one:

> D1   X is immediately perceived$_p$ = $_{df}$X is perceived without (the perceiver's) performing any (conscious) inference.

Note that if "immediately perceived" in principle (P) means "immediately perceived$_p$," then Hylas is certainly right to endorse the resulting principle—let us call it (P_p)—that whatever is perceived by the senses is immediately perceived$_p$. For in sense perception as such there is no experienced movement from data to conclusion, or conscious transition from sign to signified.[2]

Consider now the following *epistemological* notion of immediate perception:

> D2   X is immediately perceived$_e$ = $_{df}$X is perceived in such a way that its existence and nature can be known solely on the basis of one's present perceptual experience.

This definition invites many questions, such as: do the words "known *solely* on the basis of one's present perceptual experience" imply that the knowledge in question is somehow prior to any conceptualization? Or do they merely imply (more plausibly) that this knowledge requires no corroboration from experiences occurring before or after the present experience? And does the reference to knowledge of X's "nature" mean that all, or only some, of X's properties must be so knowable? For present purposes, however, we need not settle these or other questions about how exactly to interpret D2's *definiens*. The important point, rather, is that no matter how such questions are answered, if "immediately perceived" in principle (P) is taken to mean "immediately perceived$_e$," then the resulting principle—call it (P_e)—that whatever is perceived by the senses is immediately perceived$_e$, will have a drastically restrictive effect on the range of objects that we can be said to "perceive by sense." For example, if (P_e) were true, then it would also be true that (*i*) we never perceive any material thing; for the indistinguishability of some (actual or possible) hallucinatory perceptual experiences from nonhallucinatory ones does show that no material thing is ever immediately perceived$_e$. Again, it would follow that (*ii*) we never perceive any of the causes of our perceptual experiences; for the fact that any perceptual experience can be caused in a number of alternative possible ways (e.g., by direct stimulation of the brain as well as by stimulation of a sense receptor) does show that we cannot immediately perceive$_e$ any causes of our perceptual experiences. And from (*i*) and (*ii*), the road is smooth to the further conclusions that (*iii*) all we ever perceive is our own sensations or ideas, and (*iv*) the objects of perception (such as "houses, mountains, rivers, and, in a word, all sensible objects"[3]) are not *causes* of sensations or ideas but merely *collections* of sensations or ideas.

Although implications such as (*i*) through (*iv*) may reasonably be seen as constituting a *reductio ad absurdum* of (P_e), Berkeleyans cannot reasonably be expected to see them in that light. Indeed, Berkeley himself *accepts* (P_e). Moreover, as I shall show, he accepts it because he conflates "immediately perceived$_e$" with "immediately perceived$_p$." The conflation takes the form of assuming that psychological immediacy is a *sufficient* condition for epistemic immediacy, i.e., of assuming that:

(Q)   For any x, if x is immediately perceived$_p$, then x is immediately perceived$_e$.

Given (Q) as a premiss, the paradox-generating (P_e) follows from the innocuously true (P_p). I shall now undertake to show, accordingly, that Berkeley accepts (Q).

I shall proceed by concentrating on a single passage occurring near the end of the *First Dialogue*, where Philonous says:

> . . . [W]hen I hear a coach drive along the streets, immediately I perceive only the sound; but from the experience I have had that such a sound is connected with a coach, I am said to hear the coach. It is nevertheless evident that, in truth and strictness, nothing can be *heard* but *sound*; and that the coach is not then properly perceived by sense, but suggested from experience. . . . [T]hose things alone are actually and strictly perceived by any sense which would have been perceived in case that same sense had then been first conferred on us. As for other things, it is plain that they are only suggested to the mind by experience grounded on former perceptions.[4]

This difficult passage, as Jonathan Bennett notes, "subtly mixes shrewd truth with serious error."[5] The error is, of course, Berkeley's claim that we do not really hear the coach.[6] To hear the sound of a coach driving along the street *is* to hear a coach. Why, then, does Berkeley deny that we hear the coach?

His reasoning, presumably, is that (*i*) whatever is perceived by sense is immediately perceived, but (*ii*) the coach is not immediately perceived; therefore (*iii*) the coach is not perceived by sense. Now, (*i*) is true provided that "immediately perceived" means "immediately perceived$_p$." Therefore, "immediately perceived" in (*ii*) must also have this sense; otherwise the inference to (*iii*) commits the fallacy of equivocation. Accordingly, by (*ii*) Berkeley must mean to assert that the coach has to be (very rapidly but consciously) inferred from the sound; much as rain may be inferred from thunderclouds, or fire from smoke. But (*ii*), taken in this sense, is simply *false*; it is just false that the coach has to be (though in certain circumstances it might be) inferred, however rapidly, from the sound. Upon hearing the sound of an airplane (to modernize Berkeley's example), we do not *infer* that it is the sound of an airplane. We immediately take it to be the sound of an airplane—with no inference or reasoning in any ordinary sense involved. If we stick to the definition of "immediately perceived$_p$," then the airplane (the coach) is perceived (heard) just as immediately as the sound.

Nevertheless, under the cover of his mistake, Berkeley has certainly said something true.[7] This is that in order to *recognize* the sound as the sound of a coach, we must associate the sound with certain experiences that would be obtained under different conditions; such as the sight of wheels, horses, people being transported, etc. This is not to say that these or any other expectations concerning the experiences we could obtain under different conditions must be consciously entertained or imaginatively rehearsed when we hear the sound, but only that we would be prepared to retract or revise our claim (belief) that it was the sound of a coach if under suitable conditions such experiences turned out not to be obtainable. In this sense, these experiences must be, in Berkeley's language, "suggested" to the mind. This is a valuable insight of Berkeley's. What Berkeley seems not to have recognized, however, is that "suggestion" is a matter of unconscious and automatic association; it must not be confused with the conscious reasoning or inferring ruled out by "immediately perceived$_p$." One can immediately perceive$_p$ a coach *and* be, in the relevant sense, associating the sound one hears with other experiences: for one does not thereby *infer* those experiences from the sound.

These remarks suggest that Berkeley is confusing some sense in which it is true that the coach is not immediately perceived with "immediately perceived$_p$" — yielding, *via* (P$_p$), the paradoxical result that the coach is not perceived by sense at all! In line with our remarks about "suggestion," consider the following *genetic* notion of immediate perception:

D3   *X* is immediately perceived$_g$ $=_{df}$ *X* is perceived in such a way that
it would still be perceived even if one had not learned to associate
one's present perceptual experience with any other experiences
that would be obtained under different conditions.

This definition seems to capture what Berkeley means by something's being perceived without any element of "suggestion." It also harmonizes with his remark that "those things alone are actually and strictly perceived by any sense which would have been perceived in case that same sense had then been first conferred upon us." For the things that would have been perceived by a given sense had it just been conferred upon us are presumably those that we would still perceive even if we had never had the chance to learn to associate the perceptual experiences yielded by that sense with any other experiences.[8]

D3, as it stands, however, still does not succeed in excluding the coach as an object of immediate perception. For one could make the following objection: "Why should the associations that we have or have not learned to make be thought to affect which objects we perceive? The objects we perceive are simply those that cause us to have perceptual experiences by stimulating our sense receptors in a certain way; and those objects are the same regardless of the associations we make or fail to make. Thus, for example, so long as one's auditory experience is caused by a coach stimulating one's ears in a certain way, one hears a coach; regardless of whether one has learned to associate this experience with the sight of wheels, horses, etc."

It will be justifiably felt that this objection is a verbal quibble, calling only for an explicit mention of something left implicit in D3. Of course, the associations we are able or unable to make do not affect which objects we perceive, if "perceive" is taken in a non-epistemic sense. But suppose we take "perceive," as Berkeley clearly intends in his discussion of "hearing a coach," to imply some knowledge of the object perceived. Then, given the kind of beings we are, it is true that we must have learned to make certain associations before we can "perceive" certain objects. For example, given the kind of beings we are, it is true that we must have learned to associate the sound of a coach with appropriate visual or tactual experiences before we can "hear the coach" in such a way as to *know* that it is a coach we are hearing. Otherwise, we would not "hear a coach" but only a noise.

Accordingly, D3 should be interpreted as containing a suppressed clause to the effect that X is so perceived that its existence and nature can thereby be known. Then the full definition reads:

> D3a X is immediately perceived$_g$ = $_{df}X$ is perceived in such a way that one would still thereby be able to know its existence and nature even if one had not learned to associate one's present perceptual experience with any other experiences that would be obtained under different conditions.[9]

Given this definition, and given the kind of beings we are, it is true that we do not immediately perceive$_g$ the coach. For we do not perceive the coach in such a way that we thereby know it to be a coach (or to have any other property), unless we have learned to make associations of the sort in question. It is a serious error to conclude from this, however, that we do not hear the coach. For it is certainly false that whatever is perceived by the senses is immediately perceived$_g$. On the contrary, we ordinarily perceive things in such a way that we thereby come to know their existence and (some of their) properties, just because we have learned to make associations of the type in question. Berkeley is inclined to deny this because he fails to see that not perceiving a thing immediately$_g$ is perfectly compatible with perceiving it immediately$_p$.

The main point I wish to make about D3*a*, however, is that it still does not adequately reflect the fundamental reason for denying that the coach is immediately perceived. For it excludes the coach as an object of immediate perception only *on the condition* that the perceiver is so constituted that (s)he cannot make certain associations unless (s)he has *learned* to do so. To see this, suppose that a person, S, undergoes a brain operation shortly after birth. The brain surgeons, whom we may suppose to be very advanced in their art, do things that will cause S to make certain associations *before* experiencing the items to be associated. Among other things, they cause it to be the case that whenever S has an auditory experience as of hearing a coach, this triggers certain expectations in S concerning other obtainable experiences: S expects visual experiences as of seeing horses, wheels, passengers, etc. Now, according to D3*a*, the coach could be immediately perceived by S; for S could perceptually know it to be a coach even though S had never *learned* to associate the auditory experience with other, obtainable experiences. But in order to grasp the basic, conceptual point embedded in Berkeley's example, we must see why the coach is *categorically* excluded as an object of immediate perception. Why is it that, despite the genetic difference between them, neither an ordinary perceiver nor our preprogrammed perceiver can immediately perceive the coach?

The answer is that perceiving a coach, in the sense of perceptually knowing it to be a coach, requires having certain correct expectations concerning what other experiences would be obtained under different conditions. How these correct conditional expectations were acquired, however, is not crucial. It is logically possible, though in fact not the case, that my brain could have been so constituted that, regardless of my previous experience, whenever I heard the sound of a coach I would consistently expect (under suitable conditions) visual experiences of horses, wheels, and passengers. That I would then have never *learned* to associate my auditory experience with the visual ones would not prevent my perceptually knowing that what I heard was a coach. The reason why the coach is categorically excluded as an immediate object of perception, then, is that it is not perceived in such a way that one could know it to be a coach even if one had no correct expectations of the sort just indicated.[10] So let us modify once again the definition of immediate perception that we are seeking to elicit from Berkeley's example:

D4 X is immediately perceived$_k$ = $_{df}$ X is perceived in such a way that
its existence and nature can be known on the basis of one's present

perceptual experience independently of any correct expectations concerning what other experiences would be obtained under different conditions.

We are now in a position to see that the notion of immediate perception that Berkeley invokes in the coach example closely approximates "immediately perceived$_e$." For the proposition that

(A)   If X is immediately perceived$_e$, then X is immediately perceived$_k$

is a logical truth: to say that X's existence and nature can be known *solely* on the basis of one's present perceptual experience obviously entails that it can be known on the basis of that experience whether or not one has any correct conditional expectations about other experiences. And although the converse entailment does not hold — it is possible that requirements for knowing X's existence and nature other than having correct conditional expectations might prevent it from being knowable solely on the basis of a present perceptual experience — it seems clear that Berkeley intends his notion of immediate perception to rule out such additional requirements (whatever they might be). His reason for ruling them out, I believe, is that he quite plausibly assumes that there are no objects whose existence and nature can be perceptually known independently of correct conditional expectations, which cannot also be known *solely* on the basis of a present perceptual experience. (Such objects would be neither ideas/sensations, which Berkeley holds to be immediately perceived$_e$, nor material things, which are not immediately perceived$_k$: what then would they be?) In other words, Berkeley accepts the proposition that

(B)   If X is immediately perceived$_k$, then X is immediately perceived$_e$

as being true, though unlike (A) it is not a logical truth. Thus, since he holds that "immediately perceived$_k$" and "immediately perceived$_e$" are extensionally equivalent, it is natural for him to construe the intension of his notion of immediate perception to comprise not merely "immediately perceived$_k$" but also the stronger "immediately perceived$_e$." The upshot is that the notion of immediate perception embedded in the coach passage is virtually identical in meaning to "immediately perceived$_e$."[11]

It can now be seen, at last, that Berkeley conflates "immediately perceived$_e$" with "immediately perceived$_p$." For our analysis of the coach passage has shown that there are two different distinctions that he does not make clearly. First, he does not clearly distinguish the habitual and unconscious association of sign and signified, which he calls "suggestion," from the performance of rapid albeit conscious inferences from sign to signified.[12] In effect, then, he accepts the false proposition that:

(1)   If X is immediately perceived$_p$, then X is immediately perceived$_g$.

This proposition is false because, as we have seen, one can perceive a coach without performing any inferences *and* still be making the learned associations of sign and signified that enable perceivers constituted like ourselves perceptually to know it to be a coach. Second, Berkeley does not clearly distinguish the partly genetic point that perceptually knowing something to be a coach requires perceivers constituted like ourselves to make certain learned associations, from the purely conceptual point that perceptually knowing something to be a coach requires any kind of perceiver whatever to have certain correct conditional expectations. In effect, then, he also accepts the false proposition that:

(2)   If X is immediately perceived$_g$, then X is immediately perceived$_k$.

This proposition is false because our hypothetical perceiver, who is programmed from birth to expect the sight of horses, wheels, etc. (under suitable conditions), whenever he hears the sound of a coach, immediately perceives$_g$ the coach, but does not immediately perceive$_k$ the coach. Moreoever, as we have seen, Berkeley employs the notion of "immediately perceived$_k$" as one part of the meaning of a stronger notion whose meaning also includes "immediately perceived$_e$." Thus, his confusion of "immediately perceived$_g$" with "immediately perceived$_k$" is actually part of his confusion of the former with a notion that entails not just "immediately perceived$_k$," but also the somewhat stronger "immediately perceived$_e$." Accordingly, we are justified in ascribing to Berkeley not just (2), but also the somewhat stronger principle that:

(2′)   If X is immediately perceived$_g$, then X is immediately perceived$_e$.[13]

It follows from (1) and (2′), however, that:

(3)   If X is immediately perceived$_p$, then X is immediately perceived$_e$.

which is just the assumption (labeled (Q) on p. 50) that psychological immediacy implies epistemic immediacy.

It is (3) that allows Berkeley to infer, from his valuable insight that one does not perceptually know something to be a coach unless one has certain correct conditional expectations, the false proposition that one does not perceive the coach. Berkeley sees that

(4)   The coach is not immediately perceived$_k$

and infers from (4), (A), and (3) that

    (5)   The coach is not immediately perceived$_p$

from which he draws, via (P_p), the erroneous conclusion that the coach is not "perceived by sense" at all.[14]

II

I shall now discuss the role played by Berkeley's conflation of psychological and epistemic immediacy in the overall strategy of the *First Dialogue*. I shall show that an important argument (one that, so far as I know, has not been noticed by commentators) used by Berkeley to support his main thesis turns on this conflation.

Throughout the *First Dialogue*, Philonous tries to demonstrate to Hylas that sensible qualities are nothing but sensations. In attempting to resist this identification, Hylas tries repeatedly to make a certain distinction. This is the distinction between what I have elsewhere called the dispositional and the manifest aspects of a sensible quality.[15] The quality red, for example, can be viewed in two ways: as a disposition or capacity of certain objects to look red to a normal perceiver in normal light (dispositional aspect of the quality), or as the event, occurrence, or episode, involving consciousness, that constitutes the manifestation of this disposition (manifest aspect of the quality). Sweetness, likewise, can be viewed either as a disposition of certain objects to taste sweet to normal perceivers, or as the enjoyed, qualitative event or episode that constitutes the manifestation of this disposition. I have argued elsewhere that this distinction is essential to an adequate account of the nature of sensible qualities and that it provides the key for elucidating the difference between primary and secondary qualities.[16] Here, however, I wish only to note Hylas' attempt to make the distinction, and to show that Berkeley's argument against the distinction turns on conflating the psychological and epistemic senses of "immediately perceived." For present purposes, I shall also assume that the dispositional aspect can be equated with what Locke calls "the power to produce a certain sensation (idea) in our mind," and that the manifest aspect can accordingly be equated with the sensation or idea produced when the power manifests itself. In fact, I believe that this assumption is mistaken and detracts from the plausibility of Locke's view, and that it can be rejected, by dropping the act-object analysis of perceptual experience that Locke and Berkeley accepted in favor of an adverbial analysis of the sort pioneered by Thomas Reid and defended more recently by

C. J. Ducasse and R. M. Chisholm.[17] Since it is in its Lockean formulation that Berkeley attacks the distinction between the manifest and dispositional aspects, however, I shall here allow myself to speak as if the phrases "disposition to look red (taste sweet, etc.) to a perceiver" and "power to produce a sensation of red (of sweetness, etc.) in a perceiver" were interchangeable.

Directly after Philonous has appealed to the familiar argument from the relativity of perception in order to show that colors are nothing but sensations, Hylas says:

> Light and colors, as immediately perceived by us, I grant cannot exist without the mind. But in themselves they are only the motions and configurations of certain insensible particles of matter.[18]

In effect, Hylas is here conceding that the *manifest* aspect of a color exists only when the color is being perceived, i.e., only when the disposition is manifesting itself, but denying that this is true of the dispositional aspect. At best, therefore, Philonous' argument has shown that the manifest aspect of a color is only a sensation. But the dispositional aspect is not a sensation; it exists objectively in a material object. A little earlier in the *Dialogue*, Hylas attempts to make the same distinction for sounds:

> You must distinguish, Philonous, between sound as it is perceived by us, and as it is in itself; or (which is the same thing) between the sound we immediately perceive and that which exists without us. The former, indeed, is a particular kind of sensation, but the latter is merely a vibrative or undulatory motion in the air.[19]

Unfortunately, in both of these passages (and throughout the *Dialogue*), Hylas mischaracterizes the dispositional aspect. Instead of saying that colors, as they exist unperceived, are only the powers of individually imperceptible particles collectively to produce sensations of color, he says that they are only "configurations of insensible particles of matter." Instead of saying that a sound, as it exists unperceived, is only the power of certain vibrations in the air (now called "sound waves") to produce a sensation of sound, he says that it is only the sound waves themselves ("merely a vibrative or undulatory motion in the air"). In thus confusing a disposition or Lockean "power" with (the factors that provide) its scientific explanation, Hylas exposes himself to Philonous' *ad hominem* retort that if colors are just configurations of invisible particles, then colors are invisible; that if sounds are just certain motions in the air, then sounds may be seen or felt but not heard, etc.[20]

Berkeley, however, is not content merely to exploit the confusion between a disposition and its scientific explanation: his main objecttion to Hylas' distinction is an argument, always presented enthymematically, that turns directly on the notion of immediate perception. Hylas first attempts to distinguish between the dispositional and manifest aspects in order to meet Philonous' pleasure/pain argument concerning temperatures and tastes:

> You asked whether heat and cold, sweetness and bitterness, were not particular sorts of pleasure and pain; to which I answered simply that they were. Whereas I should have thus distinguished: those qualities as perceived by us are pleasures or pains, but not as existing in the external objects. We must not therefore conclude absolutely that there is no heat in the fire or sweetness in the sugar, but only that heat or sweetness, as perceived by us, are not in the fire or sugar. What say you to this?[21]

Philonous' response, which he repeats on each subsequent occasion that Hylas tries to make the same distinction, is this:

> I say it is nothing to the purpose. Our discourse proceeded altogether concerning sensible things, which you defined to be "the things we immediately perceive by our senses." Whatever other qualities, therefore, you speak of, as distinct from these, I know nothing of them, nor do they at all belong to the point in dispute.[22]

Why does Philonous here confidently assume that the definition of sensible qualities as those that are *immediately perceived* by the senses precludes their having a dispositional aspect? The answer is revealed by the following remark of Philonous', made later in the *Dialogue*: "But the causes of our sensations are not things immediately perceived, and therefore not sensible. This point I thought had been already determined."[23] Philonous' enthymemes may be completed in the following, unified argument:

(1) Whatever is perceived by the senses is immediately perceived.
(2) All sensible qualities are perceived by the senses.

∴ (3) All sensible qualities are immediately perceived.
(4) No causes of sensations are immediately perceived.

∴ (5) No sensible qualities are causes of sensations.

Premiss (1), as we have seen, is true provided that "immediately perceived" is taken in the purely psychological sense of "immediately perceived$_p$." And aside from premiss (4), to which I return in a moment, the rest of the argument is sound: (2) is a matter of definition, (3) follows from (1) and (2), and (5) follows from (3) and (4). But by adding one further premiss, the argument can be turned into a direct disproof of the view that sensible qualities have a dispositional aspect. The additional premiss is:

(6) All powers to cause sensations are causes of sensations.

This premiss, in conjunction with (5), allows us to deduce the conclusion that

(7) No sensible qualities are powers to cause sensations.

In other words, sensible qualities have *no* dispositional aspect but only a manifest aspect. The upshot is that if Hylas concedes that Philonous' arguments prove that the manifest aspect of a sensible quality is merely a sensation, then he cannot escape the conclusion that sensible qualities are nothing but sensations.

Premiss (6) is admittedly debatable. It may be questioned whether the power to cause a certain sensation is, strictly speaking, a cause of the sensation. This difficulty becomes clearer when one speaks (more correctly, as I would argue) of a disposition to look red, taste sweet, etc., to a perceiver rather than of a "power to cause a sensation of red, sweetness, etc., in a perceiver." It is questionable whether a disposition to X is strictly speaking a cause of X (or of something's X-ing), and it seems odd to speak of dispositions as causes of their manifestations.[24] Nevertheless, let us grant premiss (6), for the sake of the argument. For in a broad and perhaps loose sense, dispositions are causes: "the cause of the explosion was the volatility of the jet fuel" and "the acid's corrosiveness caused the metal to give way" are not deviant utterances. Hence, if Berkeley's argument really proves that sensible qualities cannot be any sort of cause of our sensations, then it is at least doubtful that they can be dispositions. So a maximally effective criticism of the argument should show that it fails to establish even (5). I shall now show that the argument does fail to establish (5), because its premisses equivocate on the notion of immediate perception.

Let us examine premiss (4). In order for that premiss to connect with premiss (1), "immediately perceived" in (4) must mean "immediately perceived$_p$." At the outset of the *Dialogue*, Philonous deftly introduces (4) in such a way as to suggest that the premiss can indeed be so understood.

Does it not follow from this [i.e., from the definition of "sensible things" as "those (things) only which can be perceived *immediately* by sense"] that, though I see one part of the sky red, and another blue, and that my reason does thence evidently conclude there must be some cause of that diversity of colors, yet that cause cannot be said to be a sensible thing or perceived by the sense of seeing? . . . In like manner, though I hear a variety of sounds, yet I cannot be said to hear the causes of those sounds. . . .[25]

Although this passage wins Hylas' assent that the causes of our sensations are never immediately perceived (and hence never perceived by sense at all), it hardly supports Berkeley's position. For Philonous' attempt to generalize from the case of seeing different colors in the sky is fallacious. When I see part of the sky red and part of it blue, normally just after sunset, I may be said to *infer* that the cause of this diversity is the sun, because I can no longer *see* the sun, which is now below the horizon. One cannot conclude from this case that awareness of the causes of one's sensations is always inferential. Suppose that you are having salty, crispy sensations, which you rightly take to-be caused by a potato chip in your mouth. Must you then *infer* that the cause of these sensations is a potato chip? Plainly not. You can just immediately take them to be produced by a potato chip. This is not to say, of course, that you could not have been mistaken about the cause: a similar sensation could, after all, have been produced by a french fry or in some other way. But what that shows is that you do not immediately perceive$_e$ the cause of your gustatory sensations. It does not show that you do not perceive it with *psychological* immediacy. There is, therefore, no objection to saying that you immediately perceive$_p$ (one of) the cause(s) of your gustatory sensations. So if "immediately perceived" means "immediately perceived$_p$," this case is a counterexample to premiss (4) of Berkeley's argument. It is easy to give further counterexamples.[26] Berkeley's own example of the coach is a case in point: it is a case where I immediately perceive$_p$ (one of) the cause(s) of my auditory sensations, i.e., the coach. The upshot is that if "immediately perceived" means "immediately perceived$_p$," then premiss (1) is true but premiss (4) is false.

Let us suppose, on the other hand, that "immediately perceived" means "immediately perceived$_e$." Then premiss (4) becomes true. For we cannot immediately perceive$_e$ the causes of our sensations. The basic reason for this, as previously mentioned, is that any sensation that is caused in a given way is subjectively indistinguishable from one that could be caused in some different way. For example, the auditory sensation caused by Berkeley's coach can be duplicated in other ways, e.g., by an open carriage, a recording, a disturbance in the subject's nervous system, or (more radically) by directly stimulating the subject's brain. Thus, in order to know the cause of any given sensation, other sensations must be brought into the picture for corroboration, e.g., those that occurred for some time before and some time after the sensation in question.

Since these other sensations can each also be caused in a variety of different ways, however, there is an epistemological problem here, concerning how we are able to know that our sensations are caused by physical objects stimulating our sense receptors rather than in some other way. Some philosophers, e.g., Descartes and Locke, have maintained that this problem can be satisfactorily solved (though it is true that Descartes thought it could be solved only by appealing to the veracity of God). Berkeley, however, believed that the problem is insoluble. Accordingly, he sought to avoid scepticism by proving that physical objects are not *causes* of sensations but merely *collections* of sensations. One way in which he tries to demonstrate this reductionism is by conflating the psychological sense of "immediately perceived" on which premiss (1) of his argument is true but premiss (4) false, with the epistemological sense on which premiss (4) is true but premiss (1) false. I am not suggesting that Berkeley deliberately conflated two discernibly different notions, but rather that it was probably, at least in part, the pressure of the epistemological problem of perception that drove him to conflate them. What then seemed to follow is that (5) is true, i.e., that sensible qualities cannot be any sort of cause of our sensations. In particular, they cannot be "powers to cause sensations" or disposition to appear in certain ways to perceivers. Instead, sensible qualities can only be the sensations themselves. And since physical things are simply collections of coexisting sensible qualities (Locke's occult substratum having been discarded), it follows that physical things can be nothing but collections of "sensations or ideas." Scepticism with regard to the senses is avoided by reducing physical objects to concatenations of elements whose existence and nature can be known solely by inspecting one's present sensory experience.

It can be shown, though there is not space to marshall the evidence here, that other philosophers have followed Berkeley in conflating psychological with epistemic immediacy, i.e., in assuming that

(Q)   For any x, if x is immediately perceived$_p$, then x is immediately perceived$_e$.

It can also be shown, I believe, that (Q) has led to serious errors in the philosophy of perception—errors that distort and aggravate the epistemological problem of perception (difficult as it is).[27] I shall conclude by showing schematically how (Q) leads to the doctrines that (*i*) physical things are unperceivable, (*ii*) only sense-data (to use the modern term for Berkeley's "sensations or ideas") are perceivable, and (*iii*) a causal analysis of perceiving implies the unperceivability of physical things.

(*i*) to see how (Q) leads to the idea that physical things are unperceivable, consider the following pair of syllogisms (in which (Q) is formulated as a categorical proposition):

(P$_p$) Whatever is perceived by the senses is immediately perceived$_p$.
(Q)   Whatever is immediately perceived$_p$ is immediately perceived$_e$.

∴ (P$_e$) Whatever is perceived by the senses is immediately perceived$_e$.
(4)   No physical things are immediately perceived$_e$.

∴ (5)   No physical things are perceived by the senses.

(*ii*) The argument can easily be modified to yield the conclusion that only sense-data are perceivable, by substituting for (4) the premiss that

(4') Only sense-data are immediately perceived$_e$.

The conjunction of (P$_e$) and (4'), or alternatively, the conjunction of (P$_p$), (Q), and (4'), then entails that

(5') Only sense-data are perceived by the senses.

(*iii*) The argument can also be modified to yield the doctrine that a causal analysis of perceiving implies that physical things are unperceivable. This may be done in two steps. The first is to substitute for (4) the premiss that

(4'') No causes of any perceptual experiences are immediately perceived$_e$.

It then follows from (P$_e$) and (4''), or, alternatively, from (P$_p$), (Q), and (4''), that

(5'') No causes of any perceptual experiences are perceived by the senses.

The second step is to add the premiss that

(6) If some physical things are perceived by the senses, then some causes of some perceptual experiences are perceived by the senses.

This premiss is a corollary of a causal analysis of perceiving, i.e., of an analysis of the form, "S perceives *M* if and only if *M* causes

S's present perceptual experience in manner R." But now it follows from (5″) and (6), again, that no physical things are perceived by the senses. Thus, the argument leads from a causal analysis of perception (invoked in (6)), *via* the Berkeleyan premises about immediate perception, to the conclusion that physical things are unperceivable—thereby seeming to show that this paradoxical proposition is implied by such an analysis.

I believe that Locke had (4), (4′), and (4″) in mind when he insisted that the only *immediate* objects of perception are ideas. I know of no evidence, however, that indicates that he was committed to Berkeley's premiss, (Q), or its consequence, (P_e). And I do not think that anything else in the logic of Locke's position commits him to the paradoxical conclusions (5) and (5′), which he accepts only waveringly, but which Berkeley evidently supposed must follow from a causal realism like Locke's.[28]

Notes

1. *Three Dialogues Between Hylas and Philonous*, p. 112. In C. M. Turbayne, ed., *Principles, Dialogues, and Philosophical Correspondence* (Indianapolis: Bobbs-Merrill, 1965). All page references to the *Dialogues* will be to this volume.

2. I assume that this point is familiar and uncontroversial. Cf. R. M. Chisholm, *Perceiving: A Philosophical Study* (Ithaca: Cornell University Press, 1957), pp. 158-59. In "Dicker on Berkeley on Immediate Perception" (comments delivered at the Spring 1980 meeting of the Creighton Club), however, Elizabeth Ring has shown that, on *some* interpretations, principle (P_p) is false. She suggests, as the most plausible interpretation of (P_p), "For any x, if S perceives x by the senses, then S perceives x and no conscious inference of S is necessary for S to perceive x." If what I shall say in the body of this paper is correct, it will turn out that (P_p) (suitably interpreted, as Ring suggests) is the *only* interpretation of principle (P) on which that principle is true.

3. *Principles of Human Knowledge*, sect. 4.

4. *Dialogues*, I, p. 145.

5. *Locke, Berkeley, Hume: Central Themes* (Oxford: Clarendon Press, 1971), p. 142.

6. Cf. D. M. Armstrong, *Perception and the Physical World* (New York: Humanities Press, 1961), p. 19.

7. Cf. ibid., p. 20.

8. No doubt Berkeley would add to this: "and if we had not learned to integrate (colligate) the perceptual experiences yielded by that sense with those of other senses." I omit this point from D3 for the sake of simplicity. Note, however, that the point would help to explain Berkeley's doctrine that only the "proper objects" of each sense are immediately perceived, and so perceived by sense (though, for the reason given in the text immediately following, such an addition to D3 would still not fully explain this doctrine).

9. The point of this definition is to rule out, as a necessary condition of perceptually knowing X, one's having learned to make certain associations. So the *definiens* is compatible with whatever *other* necessary conditions there might be for perceptually knowing X.

10. In a helpful discussion of the coach passage, Jonathan Bennett writes: "The vital point is that my belief that I 'hear a coach' is answerable to facts about what I shall or should

experience under different conditions, and that it could be defended by . . . a disciplined appeal to the ways in which, in the past, certain visual or tactual 'ideas' have been associated with auditory states like my present one. This is what Berkeley needs for this part of his argument—an analytic thesis about the meaning of 'hears a coach,' not a genetic one about how he or anyone comes to believe that he hears a coach" (*Locke, Berkeley, Hume*, pp. 142-3). Except for the slightly misleading way in which Bennett lumps together the conceptual point about what a perceptual belief is "answerable to" and the epistemological point about how such a belief "could be defended," this is exactly the point I have been making.

11. The notion of "immediately perceived$_e$" is not *exactly* the same as the Berkeleyan notion of immediate perception, however, because its definition fails to bring out the fact that Berkeley wished to restrict the possible values of "X" to what can be immediately perceived$_e$ by any *single sense*—i.e., to the "proper objects" of each sense (see n. 8, above). The important point for present purposes, however, is that Berkeley's perceptual vocabulary is designed to restrict the extension of "immediate object of perception" *at least* to objects whose existence and nature can be known solely on the basis of a present perceptual experience.

12. That Berkeley does not clearly distinguish (conscious) inference from (unconscious) association can also be seen in his *Essay Towards a New Theory of Vision*. There he describes the relationship between visual cues such as faintness and the awareness of distance with such phrases as "I thence form a judgment or conclusion that the object I see is . . . at a great distance" (sect. 3); "I do, upon perceiving these ideas of sight, forthwith conclude what tangible ideas are like . . . to follow" (sect. 45); and he speaks of the "sudden judgments men make of distance" (sects. 20, 24)—as if automatic association amounted to a conscious inference or deliberative judgment performed very rapidly. The same confusion occurs in the much later work, "*Theory of Vision, or Visual Language Vindicated and Explained*," where Berkeley complains that "men . . . mistake inferences of reason for perceptions of sense" (sect. 16), and warns that "throughout this whole affair, the mind is wonderfully apt to be deluded by the sudden suggestions of fancy which it confounds with the perceptions of sense . . ." (sect. 52). It should be noted, however, that there are *also* passages where Berkeley seems to be aware of the difference between "suggestion" and conscious inference: "We cannot open our eyes but the ideas of distance, bodies, and tangible figures are suggested by them. So swift, and sudden, and *unperceived* [my emphasis] is the transition from visible to tangible ideas that we can scarce forbear thinking them both the immediate [i.e., perceived without unconscious association] object of vision" (*New Theory of Vision*, sect. 145). The most explicit such passage that I have found is this: "To perceive is one thing; to judge another. So, likewise *to be suggested is one thing*, and *to be inferred another*. Things are *suggested and perceived* by sense [my emphasis] . We make judgments and inferences by the understanding" (*Theory of Vision . . . Vindicated*, sect. 42). It appears, then, that sometimes Berkeley connects "suggestion" with perception and distinguishes it from inference; while at other times he equates "suggestion" with inference or with "judgment" and contrasts it with perception. He seems not to have noticed any ambiguity or inconsistency in his treatment of these notions. The works from which I have here quoted are collected in George Berkeley, *Works on Vision*, ed. C. M. Turbayne (Indianapolis: Bobbs-Merrill, 1963).

13. If (2') were not intended as a necessary truth, it would follow from (2) and the contingently true proposition, (B).

14. It may be noted that (5) also follows from (4), (1), and (2). However, since Berkeley treats "immediately perceived$_k$" as an element in a stronger notion of immediate perception that also entails "immediately perceived$_e$", the inference of (5) from (4), (A), and (3) more faithfully reflects his line of thought.

15. Georges Dicker, "Primary and Secondary Qualities: A Proposed Modification of the Lockean Account," *The Southern Journal of Philosophy*, XV, 4 (Winter, 1977): 457-71.

16. Ibid.

17. Ibid., esp. sects. 2 and 4. I discuss the adverbial analysis of perceptual experience in my *Perceptual Knowledge: An Analytical and Historical Study* (Dordrecht, Boston, and London: Reidel Publishing Company, 1980), pp. 158-67.

18. *Dialogues*, I, p. 126.

19. Ibid., p. 120.

20. Ibid., pp. 126, 121. I do not mean to suggest that Philonous' objections are successful even against Hylas' defective characterization of the dispositional aspect. The point about colors, for example, obviously commits a fallacy of composition.

21. Ibid., p. 118.

22. Ibid. Cf. also pp. 120, 126.

23. Ibid., p. 130.

24. For a helpful discussion of dispositions and causes, see Robert Cummins, "Dispositions, States, and Causes," *Analysis*, (June 1974).

25. *Dialogues*, I, p. 112.

26. Indeed, since I accept a causal analysis of perceiving of the sort proposed by Grice, I would contend that *every* case of normal perception constitutes a counterexample to (4) if "immediately perceived" means "immediately perceived$_p$." For a discussion of causal analyses of perceiving, see my *Perceptual Knowledge* (n. 17), pp. 80-87.

27. For a fuller discussion of these errors, see ibid., pp. 59-65, 91-95.

28. This matter is also discussed in ibid., pp. 88-95.

III Method and Mathematics

5

Microscopes and Philosophical Method in Berkeley

Geneviève Brykman

As early as 1728, Chambers noticed that Berkeley had gone a long way toward setting philosophy on a new footing.[1] More recently, A. J. Ayer stated that Berkeley was essentially not a metaphysician and that, if what Berkeley discovered was that material things must be definable in terms of sense contents, then the doctrines of Russell and Wittgenstein might be considered as the "logical outcome" of Berkeley's philosophy.[2] Along these lines, I shall assume the analysts' distinction between philosophy and metaphysics in order to display how the philosophical method referred to in the title was initially drawn from the "minute inspection of external objects" by microscopes. In the second part of this paper, I shall raise the question of whether there is a genuine microscope metaphor in Berkeley and I shall suggest some questions regarding this metaphor and its possible relation to the familiar Berkeleyan language model.[3]

It is generally agreed that the whole of Berkeley's work is in the service of one single truth: We are in a state of direct and constant dependence with regard to God. But it is not yet so well accepted that Berkeley sets a quite limited place to philosophy within his works. Immaterialism was a means for the vindication of Holy Scripture. We have to remember that the end does not justify the means and that the latter must not be thought identical with the former. Berkeley says this explicitly as early as 1713, in his *Essays* in the *Guardian*.[4]

As a microscope is an instrument of a rather limited use, with which it would not be easy to manage in everyday life, so, according to Berkeley, philosophy is a tool that should be cautiously and parsimoniously used. Today, logicians acknowledge that the artificial languages they work out are confined to definite purposes, and analysts regard the "microscope metaphor" as a dead one. There is a trace of Berkeley's philosophy in the way Frege presented his new calculus. Frege said that the clearest way to settle the relation between his ideography and ordinary language was to compare it to the relation between the microscope and the eye:

> The eye is much better as far as broadness of possible uses and diversity of adaptations to the ever-changing circumstances are concerned. Yet, as an optical instrument, it shows many imperfections which, because of the close link between eyes and mental life, usually remain unperceived. But as soon as scientific purposes require a high separative power, the eye reveals its inadequacy. In the same way, my ideography is a means, invented for peculiar purposes, and should not be condemned for not being suited to other ends. . . . And if it is the task of philosophy to break the domination of words upon the human mind . . . by freeing thought from the mask of the existing means of expression, then my ideography, which has been thought out for these very ends, would become a useful instrument in the hands of philosophers.[5]

Such was immaterialism according to Berkeley: a detour, which, pursued to a certain point, should bring men back to common sense and ordinary language (*Dialogues*, III).[6]

To think of analysis as an activity of dissection may in some way be misleading, as may be any representation of facts *as if* they belong to one sort, when they actually belong to another.[7] Keeping this in mind, the following points should be stressed: (1) the breaking up of objects seen through microscopes gave rise to peculiar speculations in the second half of the seventeenth century; (2) the traditional and loose analogy between knowledge and sight then was brought into a new focus with the more precise metaphor of "close vision"; (3) Berkeley's interest in both microscopes and "close vision" is highly original, making his philosophy an important step toward critical and analytical philosophy; (4) the transposition from the "minute inspection of external objects" to intellectual analysis is not, in Berkeley, metaphorical in the ordinary sense of this particular metaphor; so that the metaphor from microscopes to analysis does not conflict with, but strengthens, Berkeley's conceptually more decisive language model.

Two representations of speculative activity can be located in Berkeley's writings. They are quite different, almost opposite, but nevertheless are often blended, on the received view, under the word "philosophy." The first representation refers to what we now should want to denote strictly as "philosophy": analysis of ideas and language. The second refers to what we are used to call "metaphysics," which is more properly "apologetics" in Berkeley. Thus are described two attitudes toward the universe, which, in Berkeley's opinion, are literally two different ways to see: *shortsightedness* and *longsightedness*. In the first case is meant the "minute inspection" of a definite object; in the second, the contemplation of the whole universe from the standpoint of Providence.

One must remember that the scientific revolution of the seventeenth century was above all an optical discovery of the universe, in which the new theoretical use of eyeglasses was a determining cause. In *The Concept of Mind*, G. Ryle stressed how the epistemologists' concepts of consciousness first came from a transformed application of the Protestant notion of conscience: the Protestant had to hold that a man could know his soul and the wishes of God without the aid of confessors and scholars. Therefore, the Protestant spoke of the God-given "light" of private conscience. Ryle insisted that because "Galileo's and Descartes' representations of the mechanical world seemed to require that minds should be salved from mechanism . . . the metaphor of 'light' seemed peculiarly appropriate since Galilean science dealt so largely with the optical discovery of the world."[8] Ryle's remark is not altogether correct. More exactly, the meaning of the already overused analogy between knowledge and sight changed with the use of eyeglasses. Previously, the analogy suggested the immediacy of intuitive knowledge, but an immediacy that allowed us to speak of intuition in terms of "union" or "contact" as well. From Kepler's and Galileo's discoveries, the visual metaphor became more exactly an optical metaphor, relating much more to optic sciences than to mystic experiences.

Descartes established the new status of the optical metaphor in the *Regulae*. Here he explicitly states that the meaning he will give to the word "intuition" is not the one that is usually accepted:

> By intuition I understand not the fluctuating testimony of the senses, nor the misleading judgment that proceeds from the blundering constructions of imagination, but the conception which an unclouded and attentive mind gives us so readily and distinctly that we are wholly freed from doubt about that which we understand. . . . But in case anyone may be put out by this new use of the term "intuition," and of other terms which in the following pages I am similarly compelled to dissever from

their current meaning, I here make the general announcement that I pay no attention to the way in which particular terms have of late been employed in the Schools, because it would have been difficult to employ the same terminology while my theory was wholly different. (*Regulae*, III)[9]

Later on, explaining what he means by "intuition," Descartes explicitly states that the way to use "intuition" would be better illustrated by a comparison with the way we employ our eyes. For "he who attempts to view a multitude of objects with one and the same glance, sees none of them distinctly; similarly the man who is wont to attend to many things at the same time by means of a single act of thought is confused in mind" (*Regulae*, IX). Comparing intuition and sight, Descartes does not explicitly state that "the resemblance on this occasion is only one of analogy," as he strongly does concerning the passive side of our cognitive power when compared to wax receiving impressions from the seal (*Regulae*, XII). We may observe the strong parellelism between the advice Descartes gives for using intuition as a warrant for deduction and the means he details in his *Dioptrica* (VII) to achieve the best sensible vision. Thus, emanating from optical sciences, a genuine metaphorical network is to be found throughout Descartes' works; this network will be used to some extent by all his successors.

Unlike the traditional analogy, which seems to be assumed by Ryle in the passage quoted above, the new formulation now stresses the variations of the visual field that *glasses* had made possible, and brings out a distinction between seeing a great number of things at once and seeing one thing distinctly. If we go back to M. Black's comment on metaphor,[10] we may observe that the traditional metaphor had *light* rather than *vision* as its focus, and religion rather than positive knowledge as its frame. The object of the familiar metaphor was to stress the immediacy of some kind of knowledge. Nevertheless, till the end of the sixteenth century, hearing remained (even among the learned) the accepted best medium for knowledge, whereas sight was much suspected as the womb of many illusions.[11] Then, at the beginning of the seventeenth century, the visual metaphor became an optical metaphor, bred by the use of optical instruments. Sight was concurrently accepted as the "most noble and comprehensive of the senses."

Once again: Descartes insisted upon the *distinction* between ideas, without which there would be no knowledge. To return to his comparison between intuition and sight, attention might be drawn to an auxiliary comparison that is highly significant to this point. "Just as workmen, who are employed in very fine and delicate operations and are accustomed to directing their eyesight attentively to separate points, and by practice have acquired a capacity for distinguishing objects of extreme minuteness and subtlety; so likewise do people who do not allow their thought to be distracted by various objects at the same time, but always concentrate it in attending to the simplest and easiest particulars, are clear-headed" (*Regulae*, IX). Indeed, the traditional distinction between the supra- and sublunary worlds had been strongly shaken by the discoveries that Galileo made with his telescope, but the realm of ordinary experience remained unaffected. On the other hand, the microscope was to sever completely the connections that we spontaneously make between visual and tactual data; so that it was peculiarly astonishing for the "virtuosi" to see familiar objects as quite different from how they ordinarily look. *First*, the microscope, by its power to disclose the minuteness of things, was able to make us realize the weakness of human vision. *Second*, the microscope made manifest the great part played by mediate elaborations in normal perception.

As a result, the topic of "close vision" or "narrow inspection" of objects became quite popular in the second half of the seventeenth century; and the interest in microscopes reached its peak with the publication of Hooke's *Micrographia* (1664). The *Journal des Scavans* spoke highly of this book, saying that "Mr. Hooke had in a few years discovered with his microscope many more things than the Ancients had made for centuries with their arguments." The topic of "close vision" was soon raised to the level of a methodological principle. In the Preface to his *Micrographia*, Hooke himself insists that the narrow inspection of material objects should be a model of a narrow inspection of theoretical objects; he says that the microscope is a means toward a "universal cure of the mind"[12]—that is, a model of the examination everyone must practice to improve the power of his own mind. There are numerous traces of this advice in Locke's small tract, *Of the Conduct of the Understanding*. Locke observes that human beings are all naturally shortsighted, so that they always have only a partial view of things. Above all, Locke insists that shortsightedness makes men have a confused sight of remote objects; out of that confusion they imagine remote objects to be dangerous and hideous ghosts that they dare not approach, though a critical inspection would make these imaginary objects vanish. This is the very thing Berkeley will do: make a narrow scrutiny of so remote an object, or imaginary ghost, as "material substance."

More precisely, one finds in Berkeley: *first*, a consideration of the real use of microscopes, which displays the complete heterogeneity of sight and touch (all this included more especially in *Notebook B* and the first two thirds of the *New Theory of Vision*); *second*, in *Notebook A*, an analogy between the close inspection of sensible objects and the examination of one's mind and ideas. Berkeley himself acknowledges his debt to Locke in numerous notes of *Notebook A* (492, 567, 678, 682, 717). Obviously, following the great discovery of the eye as a camera, it was Locke who invented the notion that the whole understanding is a camera,[13] receiving external resemblances ("ideas") from things without (*Essay Concerning Human Understanding*, bk. II, chap. xi, sect. 17). By a further extension of the metaphor, Locke suggested an auxiliary thesis, which is presented as an "extravagant supposition" and is concerned with the epistemological import of microscopes. This last idea was to become crucial in Berkeley. "If that most instructive of our senses, seeing, were in any man 1,000 or 100,000 times more acute than it is now by the best microscope . . . then [this man] would be in quite a different world" (*Essay*, II, iv, 11). If we suppose a man furnished with microscopic eyes, so that he could penetrate further than ordinary men into the secret composition of bodies, his acute sight would still not serve to conduct him to the market or communicate with other people. For instance, Locke says, this man would be able to perceive the minutest particles and springs of his clock without at the same time being able to see the clock as a whole and know what time it is (*Essay*, II, iv, 11). In his world, there would be no connection between visual data and tactile data, a connection Locke observed to be fitted by God for the convenience of human life and well being.

In the *New Theory of Vision*, Berkeley agrees that, although they may be useful in science, microscopes destroy the ordinary connections that we are used to make between visible and tangible objects; they are not to be considered as an improvement of sight, however, since we do not see more visible points with a microscope than with the naked eye.

> A microscope brings us, as it were, into a new world. It presents us with a new scene of visible objects, quite different from what we behold with the naked eye. But herein consists the most remarkable difference, to wit, that whereas the objects perceived by the eye alone have a certain connexion with tangible objects, whereby we are taught to foresee what will ensue upon the approach or application of distant objects to the parts of our own body, which much conduceth to its preservation, there

is not the like connexion between things tangible and those visible objects that are perceived by the help of a fine microscope. (*New Theory of Vision*, sect. 85)

Then Berkeley insists, exactly as Locke did, that ". . . were our eyes turned into the nature of microscopes, we should not be much benefited by the change. We should be deprived of the forementioned advantage we at present receive by the visive faculty, and have left us only the empty amusement of seeing . . ." (*New Theory of Vision*, sects. 86, 105. Cf. *Principles*, sects. 47, 60; *Dialogues*, II, in *Works*, II, p. 185).

On the one hand, Berkeley agrees with Locke on four points:

(1)   that there is an heterogeneity between tactile data and visual data,

(2)   that the ideas we get by using a microscope represent for us a completely new world,

(3)   that a man with microscopic eyes could not communicate with other people,

(4)   that connections between visual and tactile data are fitted by a providential God for our well being. (See *New Theory of Vision*, sect. 87. Cf. *Essay*, II, xxiii, 12)

On the other hand, there is a radical difference between Berkeley and Locke as to the nature of the connection between sight and touch. Locke maintains that besides ideas of sight and touch proper to each sense, there are simple ideas that are common to sight and touch—such as ideas of space or extension (*Essay*, II, v). On the contrary, Berkeley wrote his *New Theory of Vision* in order to show that there is not such an idea as "extension" common to several senses (sect. 127).[14] Just as the written letter "w" and the spoken sound "w" have no intrinsic characteristic in common and yet are both called "double-you," so a visual datum and a tactual datum are both called "table," for instance, because of familiar experience only. Whoever will look narrowly into his own thoughts and examine what he means by a table perceived, will agree that collections of different ideas are only *spoken* of as one; and Berkeley says that he is able to make the supposition of ideas common to several senses vanish (sects. 46, 140, 143, 147):

I am apt to think that when men speak of extension as being an idea common to two senses it is *with the secret supposition that we can single out extension from all other tangible and visible qualities and form thereof an abstract idea*, which idea they will have common both to sight and touch. (*New Theory of Vision*, sect. 122 [my emphasis])

Thus, the Introduction to the *Principles* will go to the very origin of philosophers' prejudice concerning the so-called "material substance": the belief that general words stand for abstract ideas. He who is shortsighted will see that he never finds in his mind ideas that cannot exist separately. Here we find an apparent metaphorical transposition: a purblind eye changes places with the microscope to picture the "philosophical eye," as distinct from the view of plain common sense and from trivial sight. The purblind eye will make words for particular sense data seem empty, as the microscope makes polished and homogeneous objects disappear, revealing heterogeneous particles and wrinkles. Minute scrutiny of the so-called "abstract idea" signified by the words "matter" and "material substance" leads to the conclusion that such words are either used inconsistently or are void of meaning. Here is the remote ghost that has to vanish, according to Berkeley. "How difficult and discouraging soever [my] attempt may seem," he confesses at the beginning of the Introduction to the *Principles*, "yet I am not without some hopes, upon the consideration that the largest views are not always the clearest, and that he who is shortsighted will be obliged to draw the object nearer, and may, perhaps, by a close and narrow survey, discern that which had escaped far better eyes"

The *Notebooks* obviously paved the way for this methodological attitude. Here Berkeley confessed that he was (*B* 266) distrustful (skeptical) at eight years old. He wrote: "A man of slow parts may overtake truth. . . . Even my shortsightedness might perhaps be aiding me in this matter; it will make me bring the object nearer to my thoughts. A purblind person etc. Introd:" (*A*, 742). On the other hand, myopia may be considered as a weapon to be used as the occasion requires. That is the reason why Berkeley, much later on, states (*Defence of Free-thinking in Mathematics*, 16), that "a purblind eye, in a close and narrow view, may discern more of a thing than a much better eye in a more extensive prospect."

There is a seeming paradox in Berkeley concerning the philosopher's publind eye. On the one hand, the "philosophical eye" is a metaphor and is rooted rather in the will than in any actual eye. Like Cartesian doubt, myopia is considered as an instrument to be used sporadically. On the other hand, as Berkeley describes it in the *Notebooks*, the philosopher seems to be congenitally shortsighted (*A*, 742), and Euphranor will say that he has naturally weak eyes (*Alciphron*, dial. VI, sect. 7). From this paradox a new look at the trite question of Berkeley's development is made possible. Indeed, one may observe an important shift of opinion concerning shortsightedness after 1713. Because of the cold reception that im-materialism first received,[15] Berkeley insisted (*Essays* in the *Guardian*) that shortsightedness may be not only an *instrument*, but a kind of *natural disorder* or illness: the latter characteristic of some-body who takes the part for the whole, the words for the things, or the means for the end.

Whereas Locke suggests (*Essay* II, xxiii, 13) the "extravagant supposition" of a man (or an angel) who would have the faculty to alter the structure of his eyes so as to make them capable of all the several degrees of vision that the assistance of glasses has taught us to conceive (so as to fit his eyes to all sorts of objects), Berkeley changes the "extravagant supposition" into a method-ological attitude. Hence, when at the beginning of the *Principles* he advises us to look closely into things and ideas, this does not con-tradict the texts where Berkeley says that (1) our prospects are "too narrow" and that we must "enlarge our views" so as to com-prehend the various ends and connections and dependencies of things (*Principles*, sects. 153-54); and that (2) the main difference between natural philosophers and other men consists not so much in an exacter knowledge of the cause of phenomena as in a "greater largeness of comprehension" (sect. 105). Myopia is most necessary as a preliminary to knowledge and as a constant vigil—*only* to prevent a danger that Kant will insist on, and that Berkeley already perceived when he said that a sort of endeavor toward omniscience is much affected by the mind (sect. 105), an endeavor that has to be permanently supervised and restrained (Introduction to *Principles*, sects. 2-3).[16]

Thus, at the very time when "microscopic eyes" and the eyes of insects were for many a kind of ideal and model for acute sight, Berkeley, in an essay in the *Guardian* in 1713, purposely suggested an imaginary fly, clinched to a pillar of St. Paul's Cathedral, as a good representation of the freethinker: "It require[s] some com-prehension in the eye of the spectator to take in at one view the various parts of the building in order to observe their symmetry and design. But to the fly, whose prospect was confined to a little part of one of the stones of a single pillar, the joint beauty of the whole or the distinct use of its parts were inconspicuous." In the same way, the mind of a freethinker is employed only on certain minute par-ticularities of religion or difficulties in a single text "without com-prehending the scope and design of Christianity." Both see only the wrinkles and small inequalities of the surface, missing completely the cohesion and beauty of the whole. Thus the advice now given

by Berkeley is to improve one's "*largeness of mind*." Christian religion "enlarges the mind beyond any other profession." But all
parts and branches of philosophy are useful to enlarge the mind;
and Berkeley now insists that "*astronomy is peculiarly adapted to
remedy a little and narrow spirit*." There is something in the immen-
sity of the distance between the stars that "shocks and overwhelms
the imagination . . . that dilates and expands the mind" and is
able to show us usefully (according to Berkeley) how minute we are
in the universe. Indeed, the significance of the minute philosophers
in Berkeley's *Alciphron* (I, 10) is to be understood in the same way
as that of the freethinkers in the *Guardian* essay.[17]

From Alciphron's point of view, the minute philosophers are
no more to blame for whatever defect they discover than a faith-
ful mirror is to blame for making the wrinkles that it only discloses.
"May be we are called minute philosophers," Alciphron suggests,
"because we are considering things minutely and not swallowing
them in the gross as other men do. Besides, we all know the best eyes
are necessary to discern the minutest objects; it seems therefore
that minute philosophers might have been so called for their distinguished perspicacity." Conversely, from Crito's and Euphranor's
point of view, the minute philosophers are a sect "which diminish
the most valuable things" and assign us "a small pittance of time
instead of immortality" (*Alciphron*, I, 10). Crito and Euphranor
speak of freethinking in the same way as Berkeley regards the use of
microscopes in the passages given previously. While it apparently
improves sight, a microscope—or a critical view—may leave us only
"the empty amusement of seeing," without conferring any benefit
for our daily life. Alciphron insists that, on the contrary, acute
sight is necessary in order to free people from the illusions they
live in and are fed on by princes and priests (cf. *Alciphron*, I, 6-7;
III, 10-13).

Alciphron sounds conspicuously like the young Berkeley, saying,
as Berkeley did earlier, that philosophers have "to think with the
learned and speak with the vulgar." That is not so odd as it may
seem at first. The whole of Berkeley's work may be considered from
the standpoint of the new metaphor based on the use of optical
instruments: telescopes and microscopes allowed Berkeley to imagine
the ways to knowledge and faith, to discovery and teaching, as a
metaphorical coming and going between close vision and remote
vision. Thus, as the microscope was a dangerous and impious instrument to be used with restraint, so immaterialism was too fine a
means for the vindication of Christianity. Similarly, as Crito suggests

to Alciphron that he go far away to teach his ideas and extrava-
gancies (II, 22), immaterialism would better be tried among a few
people in some remote corner of the world.

So far we have taken mainly an historical point of view. The
seventeenth century gave birth, among the learned, to *a new system
of associated commonplaces* concerning knowledge as vision. In this
context Berkeley was truly original. If to draw an object nearer in
the visual field can be only a metaphorical way of speaking, according to Berkeley, it is not merely because of the common transference
from the sensible (visual) realm to the realm of knowledge; it is because of the seemingly odd thesis that distance is never an object
of sight. How may it be said (as in the Introduction to the *Principles*,
sect. 5) that whoever will draw an object nearer will discern more
details than men usually do, whereas in Berkeley's works on vision
we read on several occasions (*New Theory of Vision*, 44-50) that
distance is not at all an object of sight?

As a matter of fact, throughout the *New Theory of Vision*,
Berkeley propounds the complete heterogeneity between sight
and touch, stating that the blind man, made to see, could not have
the least-idea of distance by sight alone:

> To show that the immediate objects of sight are not so much as the ideas
> or resemblances of things placed at a distance, it is requisite that we look
> nearer into the matter and carefully observe what is meant in common
> discourse, when one says that which he sees is at a distance from him.
> Suppose, for example, that looking at the moon I should say it were
> fifty or sixty semidiameters of the earth distant from me. *Let us see
> what moon this is spoken of*: it is plain it cannot be the visible moon . . .
> which is only a round luminous plane of about thirty visible points in
> diameter. (*New Theory of Vision*, sect. 44)

> Looking at an object I perceive a certain visible figure and colour, with
> some degree of faintness and other circumstances, which from what I
> have formerly observed, determine me to think that if I advance forward
> so many paces or miles, I shall be affected with such and such ideas of
> touch: so that in truth and strictness of speech I neither see distance
> itself, nor anything that I take to be at a distance. . . . And I believe
> whoever will look narrowly into his own thoughts and examine what
> he means by saying he sees this or that thing at a distance, will agree with
> me that what he sees only suggests to his understanding that, after having
> passed a certain distance, to be measure by the motion of his body, which
> is perceivable by touch, he shall come to perceive such and such visible
> ideas. (sect. 45)

Whenever we say an object is at a distance, whenever we say it draws near, or goes farther off, we must always mean it of the [tangible] sort, which properly belong to the touch, and are not so truly perceived as suggested by the eye in the like manner as thoughts by the ear. (sect. 50)

Now to return to the definition of metaphor as expressed by C. M. Turbayne — a peculiar sort-crossing that involves the pretense that something is the case when it is not — we may certainly assume that there is a metaphor in Berkeley's description of the purblind philosophical eye. We do not speak of ideas and words *as if* they were at a visible distance from us. Nevertheless, Berkeley's metaphor is an "extravagant" one when compared to Descartes', Locke's, Frege's, or Russell's optical metaphors. Sort-crossing in Berkeley is using idioms that come from tangible ideas to speak of a set of visible ideas. Indeed, we almost always speak of visible objects as if they were felt. As Berkeley says about the moon, that with the help of the quick and sudden suggestions of the imagination we fancy ourselves as being tangibly elsewhere; thus is phenomenalism rooted in these pretended trips that secure the links between actual visible data and past or possible tangible experiences. Without the steadiness of tangible data, there would be nothing steady in nature, and nothing free of ambiguity in speech (*New Theory of Vision*, sect. 55). The way we correlate sight and touch, by making the former the sign of the latter, is the model of any language. Therefore, whoever uses a microscope is lost in a new world: he has an experience analogous to that of the blind man made to see. A philosopher may be baffled by our usual way of swallowing things and words as a whole: he lives in a world that is not the familiar one, a world in which there are no connections between what is seen and what is felt.

We are again faced, however, with the puzzling question of the natural shortsightedness of men. The "sorts" in Berkeley are the ontologically different sets of ideas that constitute the truly Berkeleyan dualism between the *visible* and the *tangible*. The Cartesian dualism between *body* and *soul* is not so clearly stated in Berkeley and is not required by the sort-crossing involved in the microscope metaphor. But one may still ask: How can a methodological rule be given, assuming that we can willingly draw the object nearer, if men are naturally gifted with a steady visual sphere and are only dreaming of "microscopic eyes"? Is there any activity of the human mind that makes it different from a set of visible ideas? Are the two sentences (*New Theory of Vision*, sect. 41; *Alciphron*, IV, 9), which seem to assimilate the eye and the mind, only two slips of the pen? These questions have not yet been solved, though, fortunately, they have of late been raised.[18]

Attention to the microscope metaphor may elicit an aristocratic view of minds and a hierarchy of creatures in Berkeley, making some beings more similar to angels and others more similar to brutes. Berkeley strongly stated that no power to abstract one's ideas would make some men better than others. We would say that a power (whose name is *spirit* rather than *mind*) to question the ordinary connections between sight and touch would make some privileged people realize that there is a universal language of nature, of which human languages are only particular appendages.

Notes

1. Ephraim Chambers, *Cyclopaedia or an Universal Dictionary of the Arts and Sciences*, (London, 1728), x.v, "Abstraction."

2. *Language, Truth and Logic* (1936; repr. New York: Dover, 1946), preface to the first edition, and p. 53. By "Berkeley's philosophy," let us mean "immaterialism," which, strictly speaking, is the attempt to show that matter does not exist by way of a main double argument: (A) the word "matter" is meaningless; (B) the notion of matter (presuming it is meaningful) entails contradictions.

3. About the use of metaphors in talking about metaphor: Max Black, *Models and Metaphors* (Ithaca: Cornell University Press, 1962). About the life and death of metaphors: C. M. Turbayne, *The Myth of Metaphor* (New Haven: Yale University Press, 1962; rev. ed. Columbia: University of South Carolina Press, 1970), chap. I. For a conceptual settlement of similarities and differences between "model" and "metaphor": Rolf Eberle, "Models, Metaphors, and Formal Interpretations," in Turbayne, *Myth of Metaphor*, Appendix. The metaphor with which we are presently concerned in Berkeley will be read afterward from the traditional dualism between *body* and *soul*, though Berkeley's dualism was the "extravagant" one between *touch* and *sight*. Nevertheless, amazing similarities remain with (for instance) Russell's contemporary uses of the metaphor: "Just as the easiest bodies to see are those that are neither very near, nor very far, neither very small nor very great, so the easiest conceptions to grasp are those that are neither very complex nor very simple. . . . And as we need two sorts of instruments, the telescope and the microscope for the enlargement of our visual powers, so we need two sorts of instruments for the enlargement of our logical powers, one to take us forward to the higher mathematics, the other to take us backward to the logical foundation of the things that we are inclined to take for granted [in mathematics]" (*Introduction to Mathematical Philosophy* [London: George Allen & Unwin, 1919], chap. I). On the other hand, we read in Berkeley (*Notebook A*, 556) that "men have been very industrious in travelling forward; they have gone a great way. But few or none have gone backward beyond the principles. On that side there lies much *terra incognita* to be travel'd over and discovered by me. A vast field of invention." Invention needs to be audacious; but ordinary life requires wisdom or discretion; thus we read in *Alciphron*, VI, 7: "I beg leave to observe that sometimes men, looking deeper and higher than they need for a profound and remote sense, overlook the natural obvious sense, lying (if I may say so) at their feet."

4. In A. A. Luce and T. E. Jessop, eds., *The Works of George Berkeley, Bishop of Cloyne*, 9 vols. (London: Thomas Nelson and Sons, 1948-57), vol. VII.

5. Gottlob Frege, *Begriffschrift, eine der arithmetischen nachgebildete Formelspräche des reinen Denkens* (Halle: L. Nebert, 1879), Vorwort.

6. In *Works*, II, p. 263.

7. Turbayne, *Myth of Metaphor*, pp. 12-13.

8. Gilbert Ryle, *The Concept of Mind* (London: Hutchinson's University Library, 1949; 6th ed., 1973), pp. 152-53.

9. Citations to works of Descartes refer to the standard editions: Charles Adam and Paul Tannery, eds., *Oeuvres* (Paris: L. Cerf, 1879-1913); and Elizabeth F. Haldane and R. G. T. Ross, eds., *Philosophical Works* (London: Cambridge University Press, 1973-74). The *Regulae* may be found in Adam-Tannery, X, and in Haldane-Ross, I.

10. *Models and Metaphors*, chap. III, p. 28.

11. Lucien Febvre, *Le problème de l'incroyance au 16ème siècle* (Paris: Albin Michel, 1968), II, chap. IV. R. Bloch Olivier, *La philosophie de Gassendi* (La Haye: Martinus Nijhoff, 1971), pp. 24-25.

12. Robert Hooke, *Micrographia* (London, 1664), Preface.

13. C. M. Turbayne, "Commentary," in *Berkeley: Works on Vision* (Indianapolis: Bobbs-Merrill, 1963), p. xvi. Cf. his *Myth of Metaphor*, pp. 204ff.

14. Cf. *New Theory of Vision*, sects. 49-50, 59, 77, 82, 94-96, 102, 108, 111, 115; *Theory of Vision . . . Vindicated*, sect. 41. That visible ideas and tangible ideas are entirely different and heterogeneous is established in the *New Theory of Vision*, and is called "this main part and pillar thereof."

15. H. M. Bracken, *The Early Reception of Berkeley's Immaterialism (1710-1733)* (The Hague: Martinus Nijhoff, 1965).

16. Cf. Immanuel Kant, *Critique of Pure Reason*, Preface to the Second Edition. *Essays*

17. *Essays* in the *Guardian*, in *Works*, VII, pp. 206-07.

18. D. M. Armstrong, *Berkeley's Theory of Vision* (Melbourne: Melbourne University Press, 1961); G. Pitcher, "Minds and Ideas in Berkeley," in *American Philosophical Quarterly* 6 (July 1969), repr. in his *Berkeley* (London: Routledge & Kegan Paul, 1977), chap. XI.

6

Berkeley and Tymoczko
on Mystery in Mathematics

Theodore Messenger

> *Qu.* 44 Whether the difference between a mere computer and a man
> of science be not, that the one computes on principles clearly conceived,
> and by rules evidently demonstrated, whereas the other doth not?
>
> George Berkeley,
> *The Analyst*

Not all philosophical questions are equally relevant to all times and
places. In George Berkeley we have a philosopher many of whose
interests coincide with our own (partly, of course, because his
interests helped to shape ours). But in addition we find, as I shall
show, that some of Berkeley's inquiries, which at first glance seem
only to relate to issues of his own day, turn out on closer inspection to address some of our most current philosophical perplexities.
The work of Berkeley's that I have chosen for this demonstration is
The Analyst,[1] and the theme I have selected is "mystery in mathematics."

Let us begin in the bicentenary of Berkeley's death, 1953. In May
of that year, the world learned that Edmund Hillary and Tenzing
Norkhay had scaled Mount Everest: a "high point"—if ever there
was one—in the history of mountaineering.[2] The world also learned
that, in order to reach the summit, Hillary and Tenzing had been
compelled to take along their own oxygen supplies; and this precipi-
tated some discussion as to whether supplementing the mountain
climber's traditional equipment with oxygen tank and mask might
not be "changing the rules of the sport." On the other hand, it was

generally acknowledged that the conquest of Everest would have been impossible without the use of oxygen. Borrowing some categories from the formal logician, we might say that skill in traditional mountain-climbing techniques and skill in the use of certain new "hardware" (oxygen equipment) were both *necessary conditions* for the conquest of Everest; and that, since Everest was in fact scaled by the application of these skills, they almost seemed to be a *sufficient condition* for the accomplishment of that feat.

Ninety-nine years elapsed between the inception of mountaineering in 1854 and the conquest of Everest. This period coincides with much of the time during which efforts were being made to gain a more abstract summit—in the realm of mathematics. I refer to the solution of the so-called Four-Color Problem. This is the problem of proving that any "planar" map can be colored with only four colors in such a way that no two contiguous countries have the same color. This problem was first noticed in 1852 by Francis Guthrie; and, while the general lines of its solution were sketched in 1879 by Alfred Kempe, the problem was not definitively solved until 1976.[3] The work was done by Kenneth Appel and Wolfgang Haken, assisted by John Koch, and their results were published in 1977.[4] Like the final assault on Everest, proof of the Four-Color Theorem was a team effort. Also as in that assault, success involved using both traditional skills (some computations were done "by hand") and skill in the use of new hardware, in this case high-speed computers. There is, as with Everest, a sense in which the combination of traditional skills and skill in the use of new hardware can be said to have *sufficed* to gain the desired result. But, unlike Everest, there is a question as to whether this combination was *necessary*. That is, could the Four-Color Theorem have been proved without the use of computers?

The philosophical dimensions of this situation are perceptively explored by Thomas Tymoczko in a recent issue of *The Journal of Philosophy*.[5] Tymoczko asserts that the current proof of the Four-Color Theorem (4CT) "is no traditional proof, no a priori deduction of a statement from premises. It is a "traditional proof with a lacuna, or gap, which is filled by the results of a well-thought-out experiment" (p. 58). Traditional proofs are *convincing* ("to an arbitrary mathematician"), *surveyable* (in the sense that "they can be definitively checked by members of the mathematical community"), and *formalizable* (that is, representable as finite chains of deductions from the axioms of some theory) (pp. 59-63). But while the proof of the 4CT may be judged convincing (p. 69), it is not surveyable (p. 70). And although most mathematicians "would concur that there is a formal proof of the 4CT in an appropriate graph theory . . . our only evidence for the existence of that formal proof presupposes the reliability of computers" (p. 72).

A nice embellishment in Tymoczko's discussion, and one that is important for our present purpose, is the story of Simon the mythical Martian mathematician (pp. 71-72). At the beginning of his career, this genius "proved many new results by more or less traditional methods, but after a while he began justifying new results with such phrases as 'Proof is too long to include here, but I have verified it myself.'" Initially, Simon used this appeal only for basically combinatorial lemmas. But, in his later work, the appeal began to spread to more abstract lemmas and even to theorems. Simon's colleagues on Mars were often able to find proofs for his results—but not always. Yet, so great was his prestige that all his results were accepted and were incorporated into the body of Martian mathematics under the rubric "Simon says." Using "by computer" to justify a mathematical result bears a strong analogy to justifying it by using "Simon says," Tymoczko says.

Various aspects of the Four-Color-Proof Problem should have interested Berkeley, as we shall see. One of these is the fact that the proof seems to depend on the fulfillment of incompatible conditions. "Traditional" is admittedly a vague term. But Tymoczko does seem to be correct in making surveyability a feature of traditional mathematical proofs. It was this feature that Descartes had in mind when, in Part Two of his *Discourse*, he adopted the rules ". . . never to accept anything as true, unless [he] recognized it to be evidently such, . . . to include nothing in [his] conclusions unless it presented itself so clearly and distinctly to [his] mind that there was no occasion to doubt it," and "always to make enumerations so complete, and reviews so general, that [he] would be certain that nothing was omitted."[6] Since, in the Four-Color Proof, it is precisely at the point at which surveyability becomes humanly impossible that computer assistance becomes necessary, it's clear that this proof is (in Tymoczko's words) "no traditional proof." If we could invite him to comment on this awkward situation, Berkeley might observe, as he does in *The Analyst*:

> Nothing is plainer than that no just conclusion can be directly drawn from two inconsistent suppositions. You may indeed suppose any thing possible: But afterwards you may not suppose any thing that destroys what you first supposed: or, if you do, you must begin *de novo*. (sect. 15)

Perhaps before I look further at *The Analyst*, I may be permitted a final comment on the Four-Color impasse. Mr. Tymoczko's view is that traditional proofs are surveyable and a priori, whereas computer proofs are nonsurveyable and a posteriori. But it could be argued, I think, (1) that, insofar as a traditional proof is surveyable, it is not a priori, and (2) that grounds exist for considering a computer proof both a priori and surveyable. (1) By "proof" we mean, in part, a concatenation of legitimate steps; and by the "surveyability" of a proof we understand the certifiability of such legitimacy. A surveyable proof suggests by its length that the legitimacy of its steps is open to inspection. Having deemed a proof surveyable, an expert might feel compelled to *survey* it, that is, to check it "by hand." By publishing a proof, its author(s) and editor(s) are serving notice that they have checked it. *This* doesn't sound like an a priori matter. They are also indicating their willingness to have other persons with as much expertise as themselves check the proof, the prediction being that it will withstand such scrutiny. Neither does *this* sound like the communication of a priori knowledge. (2) On the other hand, a computer has the legitimacy of its routines built into it in advance. Its results are indifferent to time, place, or application. This *does* sound like a priori knowledge. As for the surveyability of the computer's tasks, the large number of these tasks and the rapidity with which the computer performs them are apparent obstacles. But it would be possible to organize teams of, let us say, accountants to perform various blocks of these tasks; so that at the end of a project each step would have been certified by some, though not by the same, human being. Perhaps the more serious obstacles here are actually the triviality and monotony of the computer's tasks.

It does not seem to me that we are faced with the total abandonment of traditional methods of proof. Rather, sophistication may consist in the ability to recognize which problems cannot be solved by conventional means. (That a problem is simple to state is virtually no criterion. The goal of visiting the moon is simply stated. But for a person to think of getting there without help from anyone else is fantastic.) It seems to me not impossible that some future historian of mathematics will be able to say of the computer what Alexandre Koyré says of the telescope. After its invention,

the whole subsequent development of astronomical science . . . became so closely linked together with that of its instruments that every progress of the one implied and involved a progress of the other. One could even say that . . . science as such . . . began a new phase of its development. . . .[7]

Berkeley explains his purpose in writing *The Analyst* in *A Defense of Free-Thinking in Mathematics:*[8]

> . . . it is very well known that several persons who deride Faith and Mysteries in Religion admit the doctrine of Fluxions for true and certain. Now if it be shown that fluxions are really most incomprehensible Mysteries, and that those who believe them to be clear and scientific do entertain an implicit faith in the author of that method; will this not furnish a fair *argumentum ad hominem* against men who reject that very thing in religion which they admit in human learning? And is it not a proper way to abate the pride, and discredit the pretensions of those who insist upon clear ideas in points of faith if it be shewn that they do without them even in science? (sect. 3)

By this account we could say, in terms of Tymoczko's parable, that in *The Analyst* Berkeley is "blowing the whistle on Simon." But the matter is not *quite* so simple.

> I do not say that mathematicians, as such are infidels. . . . But I say there are certain mathematicians who are known to be so; and that there are others who are not mathematicians who are influenced by a regard for their authority. (sect. 5)

Thus, *The Analyst* explicitly involves two parties, "the great author" of the method of fluxions (Sir Isaac Newton) and "an infidel mathematician" (apparently Edmund Halley—remembered for his comet).[9] The great author has committed some mathematical *gaucheries* and used a method that implies a metaphysical position regarded by Berkeley as theologically dangerous. The infidel has ignored the *gaucheries* and become one of those who, in the words of the *Defence*, "yield that faith to a mere mortal which they deny to Jesus Christ, whose religion they make it their study and business to discredit" (sect. 5). So in *The Analyst* Berkeley has in mind not only—nor, in fact, chiefly—this mathematical infidel, but ultimately those "men of less leisure"[10] who could easily be turned into infidels through their innocent respect for men of science.

Assuming that George Berkeley's thought has more than an antiquarian attraction for philosophers, what in *The Analyst* retains interest even after two and a half centuries? (Please note that I am not asking, "What in it resonates with the latest philosophic fashions?" but, "In our judgment, what can be expected to remain of interest?") The answer is not likely to involve the number of impressionable laymen Berkeley was able to save from infidelity. Neither are we likely to care very much whether Edmund Halley repented of his ways. Nor, in my opinion, does the treatise's main interest lie in how competent a mathematician it shows Berkeley to have been. The really intriguing topic, I think, and the one most likely to be of enduring significance, is Berkeley's appraisal of Newton, his preparedness to accept or reject Sir Isaac's system. Berkeley's technical objections to Newton's treatment of infinitesimals were timely and cogent,[11] and are generally considered to have been salutary for the development of mathematics.[12] But these objections are only symptomatic of some deeper difficulties that Berkeley had long been having with "the great author." These would not include, of course, Newton's religious zeal. Rather they would relate to those metaphysical views mentioned above.

Berkeley had long objected to Newton's application of the notions of infinitely great and infinitely small extension. According to Newton, infinitely great extension existed outside finite minds, and could even be regarded as an actual attribute of God.[13] Both views troubled Berkeley, who, in the *Philosophical Commentaries*[14] had complained of

> The great danger of making extension exist without the mind. in that if it does it must be acknowledg'd infinite immutable eternal &c. which will be either to make God extended (which I think dangerous) or an eternal, immutable, infinite, increate being beside God. (*Commentaries*, sect. 290)

An infinite being "beside God" would, of course, compromise God's omnipotence, which Berkeley would not want to do. But what is so "dangerous" about making God extended? While there is a hint in the *Commentaries* that to do so involves idolatry,[15] Berkeley also has definite technical objections: "I am certain there is a God," he says, "tho I do not perceive him[,] have no intuition of him. . ." (sect. 813). Again, ". . . we have no idea of God. tis impossible!" (sect. 782) That is, there can be no sensuous apprehension of a spiritual being. Nor could there be a Berkeleyan "idea" isomorphic with an infinite being:

> You ask me whether there can be an infinite idea? I answer . . . if by infinite idea you mean an idea too great to be comprehended or perceiv'd all at once. you must pardon me, I think such an infinite is no less than a contradiction. (sect. 475)

Finally, in the *Commentaries* we find Berkeley assimilating the infinitely small to the infinitely great: "Evident that which has infinite number of parts must be infinite" (sects. 352, 416.) Hence, although "infinitesimals" involve their own difficulties for Berkeley,[16] they also share those raised by the infinitely great. Insofar as Newton's method of fluxions involves infinitesimals,[17] that method incurs Berkeley's distrust.

These themes recur in the *Principles*,[18] supplemented by some interesting new arguments:

> Every particular finite extension which may possibly be the object of our thought is an *idea* existing only in the mind, and consequently each part thereof must be perceived. If, therefore, I cannot perceive innumerable parts in any finite extension that I consider, it is certain they are not contained in it . . . (*Principles*, sect. 124)

> There is no such thing as the ten-thousandth part of an inch; but there is of a mile or diameter of the earth . . . (sect. 127)

> [W]hen we say a line is infinitely divisible, we must mean a line which is infinitely great. (sect. 128)

Such considerations induce Berkeley to take the position that in the philosophy of mathematics of our own time has come to be called "intuitionism." [19]

> [T]here is in effect no such thing as parts infinitely small, or an infinite number of parts contained in any finite quantity[.] But you will say that if this doctrine obtains it will follow the very foundations of geometry are destroyed . . . To this it may be replied that what ever is useful in geometry . . . does still remain firm and unshaken on our principles. . . . But . . . some of the more intricate and subtle parts of *speculative mathematics* may be pared off without any prejudice to truth. . . . (sect. 131)

Like a latter-day intuitionist, Berkeley would prefer parting company with certain "parts of *speculative mathematics*" to abandoning our old friend "Sir Vey Ability."

In the light of these passages from the *Philosophical Commentaries* and the *Principles*, I think we can readily recognize Berkeley's intentions in the various Queries he appends to *The Analyst*. Thus, he asks:

> Whether . . . there be any need of considering quantities either infinitely great or infinitely small? (*qu.* 1)

> Whether extension can be supposed an attribute of a Being immutable and eternal? (*qu.* 14)

Whether all arguments for the infinite divisibility of finite extension do not suppose and imply, either general abstract ideas or absolute external extension to be the object of geometry?

And, therefore, whether, along with those suppositions such arguments do not cease and vanish? (*qu.* 20)

And, inevitably:

Whether those philomathematical physicians, anatomists, and dealers in the animal oeconomy, who admit the doctrine of fluxions with an implicit faith, can with a good grace insult other men for believing what they do not comprehend? (*qu.* 55)

It is Berkeley's position, of course, that the doctrine of fluxions is incomprehensible.

Notes

1. All textual references to Berkeley in this paper are to A. A. Luce and T. E. Jessop, eds., *The Works of George Berkeley, Bishop of Cloyne*, 9 vols. (London: Thomas Nelson and Sons, 1948-57)—hereinafter called *Works. The Analyst* is found in *Works*, vol. IV (1951), pp. 53-102.

2. Norris McWhirter and Ross McWhirter, *Guinness Book of World Records*, 12th ed. (New York: Bantam Books, 1973) pp. 585-86.

3. Kenneth Appel and Wolfgang Haken, "The Solution of the Four-Color-Map Problem," *Scientific American* CXXXVII, 8 (October 1977): 108-21.

4. Kenneth Appel, Wolfgang Haken, and John Koch, "Every Planar Map is Four Colorable," *Illinois Journal of Mathematics* XXI, 84 (September 1977): 429-567.

5. "The Four-Color Problem and Its Philosophical Significance," *The Journal of Philosophy* LXXVII, 2 (February 1979): 57-83.

6. *Discourse on Method*, tr. Laurence J. Lafleur (Indianapolis: Bobbs-Merrill, 1956), p. 12 (in the Adam, Tannery edition, pp. 18-19).

7. *From the Closed World to the Infinite Universe* (New York: Harper, 1958) p. 90.

8. In *Works*, IV (1951), pp. 103-42.

9. See Luce's introduction to *The Analyst*, pp. 56-57 (cited in n. 1).

10. Actually, the phrase is used by Hylas at the beginning of his first conversation with Philonous. But I think the passage should be considered an expression of a continuing concern of Berkeley's See Berkeley, *Three Dialogues Between Hylas and Philonous* in *Works*, II (1949), p. 172.

11. J. O. Wisdom, "The *Analyst* Controversy: Berkeley as a Mathematician," *Hermathena* LIX (1942): 111-28.

12. Florian Cajori, *A History of the Conceptions of Limits and Fluxions in Great Britain from Newton to Woodhouse* (Chicago and London: Open Court, 1919)— cited by Luce.

13. See Koyré, *From the Closed World*, chaps. vii-x.

14. In *Works*, I (1948), pp. 7-49. I have followed the transcription and edition of the *Commentaries* published by George H. Thomas (Alliance, Ohio: Mount Union College, 1976), but I have spelled out Berkeley's contractions.

15. *Commentaries*, sects. 17, 411.

16. Ibid., sects. 308, etc.

17. See Wisdom, "The *Analyst* Controversy," p. 117.

18. Berkeley, *A Treatise Concerning the Principles of Human Knowledge* in *Works*, II (1949), pp. 1-144.

19. This is Tobias Dantzig's interpretation of Berkeley, though he does not explicitly call him an "intuitionist." See Dantzig, *Number: The Language of Science*, 4th ed. (New York: The Free Press, 1967), chap. vii.

IV Primary and Secondary Qualities

7

Berkeley on the Limits of Mechanistic Explanation

Nancy L. Maull

An emerging consensus among recent commentators is that many of Berkeley's criticisms of the distinction between primary and secondary qualities were misdirected.[1] It turns out, for example, that Locke never intended to justify his assertion that secondary quality ideas do not resemble bodies with a claim that only the secondary quality ideas (and not the primary quality ideas) are relative to the perceiver. Berkeley, in offering his "counter-argument" (that the shapes and distances of things *also* vary with the observer's state and with perceptual conditions) misleads us, and perhaps even knowingly. Neither Locke nor, in fact, any other early modern proponent of the distinction intended that the primary quality doctrine rest on appeals to prescientific or "ordinary" experience. Rather, Locke and the others assumed that its fate hinged on the ultimate success or failure of quite specific mechanistic hypotheses about the interactions of minute particles.

However, there is one Berkeleyan criticism that appears flatly incontestable. It deserves, I think, more sustained attention than it has hitherto received. In a straightforward challenge to both the Cartesian and the corpuscularian programs, Berkeley pointed out a fundamental and seemingly fatal defect in mechanistic explanation. The explanatory lapse he detected was news to few. It had already been acknowledged (but as a limitation, rather than as a flaw) by Descartes, by Locke, and by the young Newton. Berkeley, however, thought that the problem was deep and fundamental. When viewed in terms of the compelling logic of his assertion, at any rate, it seems that Berkeley's criticism *should* certainly have made a difference for the future prospects of mechanical explanation. Yet it seems to have fallen on deaf ears. This next-to-universal disregard of Berkeley's well-formulated and convincing case, or so I want to argue, is what really calls for explanation. To preempt my own conclusion, the basic suggestion I have to offer is this: for the specific purposes of *scientific* theorizing, Berkeley's *philosophical* trump card was safely and rightly ignored. Needless to say, Berkeley's philosophical worry itself was not thereby put to rest. In fact, it has been resuscitated in present-day philosophies of perception as well as in the philosophy of science. However, as I shall go on to suggest, we are in a position to learn something new about Berkeley's problem from structurally similar problems that have *not* persisted.

I

What, then, was Berkeley's protest? Recall that both Descartes and Locke subscribed to two central claims: first, that all our sensations can be explained as the effects of causal interactions between minute bodies; and second, that those minute bodies can in turn be fully characterized by reference to their primary qualities. (Each expressed certain reservations or modifications of this two-part claim, some of which I shall discuss later in this paper.) Locke, as is well known, defended this reductionist claim and its corpuscularian elaborations with a measure of restraint, as the best available explanation of perception. (See, for example, Locke, *Essay Concerning Human Understanding*, bk. IV, chap. iii, sect. 16.) To this Berkeley responded that Locke actually offered no explanation at all, for Locke and his fellow materialists failed to show or even suggest precisely how a body can produce a sensation:

> But, though we might possibly have all our sensations without them [bodies], yet perhaps it may be thought easier to conceive and explain the manner of their production supposing external bodies in their likeness rather than otherwise; and so it might be at least probable there are such things as bodies that excite their ideas in our minds. But neither can this be said; *for though we give the materialists their external bodies, they by their own confession are never the nearer knowing how our ideas are produced, since they own themselves unable to comprehend in what manner body can act upon spirit, or how it is possible it should imprint any idea in the mind.* (*Principles*, sect. 19 [italics mine])[2]

As Berkeley said, Locke had acknowledged the problem (as well as the difficulty of conceiving how mind acts on body) in the *Essay*: "How any thought should produce a motion in body is as remote from the nature of our ideas, as how a body should produce any thought in the mind." Since "the ideas of sensible secondary qualities, which we have in our minds, can by us be in no way deduced from bodily causes nor any correspondence or connexion be found between them and those primary qualities which (experience shows us) produce them in us," Locke went on to conclude that "we can attribute their connexions to nothing else but the arbitrary determination of that all-wise Agent who made them to be and to operate as they do, in a way wholly above our weak understanding to conceive" (*Essay*, IV, iii, 28). Earlier in the *Essay* (II, viii, 13), Locke wrote that God *annexes* these ideas to motions "with which they have no similitude."

Thus, Locke's "answer" to Berkeley acknowledged default on the question as to how bodies could produce sensation (and how thought might move a body). Locke agreed, in other words, that mechanical philosophy gave an incomplete accounting in response to the question "Why do we have any sensations at all?" Nevertheless, Locke was quite lucid in proclaiming what *would* count as an adequate explanation: a "deduction" from the primary qualities of minute bodies to the particular secondary quality sensations with which they are coordinated or connected. Locke left open the possibility, I think, that such deductions might eventually be the products of human understanding. The contrastingly vague claim that God annexes sensations to motions might have been intended as a temporary solution.

II

As it turns out, Locke's annexation idea probably came from Newton.[3] The historical connection is worth pursuing, for while Locke was either casual or guarded about the annexation theory — it is difficult to say which — the young Newton was neither. Newton speculated in his early anti-Cartesian tract, "De Gravitatione" (dated between 1664 and 1668), that bodies are "*determined quantities of extension which omnipresent God endows with certain conditions*": "(1) that they be mobile; (2) . . . that they be impenetrable, and hence that when their motions cause them to meet they stop and are reflected in accord with certain laws"; and

(3)   *that they can excite various perceptions of the senses and the fancy in created minds, and conversely be moved by them, nor is it surprising since the description of the origin [of things] is founded in this.*[4]

God "decided," or so Newton seems to be saying, to associate certain sensations with certain regularly occurring patterns of motion. Happily enough, we can then suppose that sensations are physical effects (although second-order physical effects), since God causes them *through* the interactions of bodies (which he also causes). A God who can "stimulate our perception by his own will," wrote Newton, can surely "apply such power to the effects of his will," namely, to bodies.[5] God creates bodies which, *by definition*, can cause sensations. The underlying analogy here — alluded to by Locke in Book IV of the *Essay*[6] — is between our ability to move our bodies and God's ability to make space impenetrable, tangible, and visible.[7] Newton's God is continuously present in the world; in "De Gravitatione" (and even later, in the *Principia* and in the *Opticks*) Newton insisted that

> No being exists or can exist which is not related to space in some way. God is everywhere, created minds are somewhere, and body is in the space that it occupies; and whatever is neither everywhere nor anywhere does not exist. And hence it follows that space is an effect arising from the first existence of being, because when any being is postulated, space is postulated.[8]

Although Newton's God is ever-present in the natural world, Newton did *not* declare that the endowment of space with "conditions" (motion, impenetrability and perceptibility) requires God's ongoing causal intervention after the creation, for God then gave bodies these permanent causal "powers."

By contrast, Descartes' God exercises his power in the created universe at every instant. Descartes' God, unlike Newton's, is not located in space or in time.[9] But God, wrote Descartes, "is the cause of created things, *not only in respect of their coming into existence*, but also in respect of their continuing to exist, and must always expend His activity on the effect in some way in order to make it say the same thing."[10] God not only creates and conserves bodies in time, but He also conserves the quantity of motion in the universe.[11] In some way then, God recreates (and therefore conserves) mind, body, and motion. Presumably, God is by that same power the author of our sensations, too, In fact, Descartes was never very explicit about God's role in sensation, although his implicit suggestion was taken up by Malebranche; God must somehow coordinate "innate" sensations with bodies in motion.[12] This occasionalist solution, of course, places a permanent explanatory barrier between mind and body in a way that Newton's (and Locke's) annexation theory does not.

Berkeley, one recalls, argued in the following way: because materialists have no explanation of how a body can imprint an idea in the mind, they have no explanation of perception at all. Perhaps Berkeley's criticism rests on the assumption that all plausible explanation has no inherent limitations, but to that principle Berkeley's own practice never conformed.[13] On the face of it, at least, there is nothing *wrong* with supposing that there are limits to any sort of explanation. And, as we have learned, sensation was not the only limit to mechanistic explanation. The quantity of motion in the world (for Descartes), the conservation and creation of individual bodies and minds (again, for Descartes), and the mobility and impenetrability of bodies (for Newton) were "explained" only by reference to God's agency.[14]

No, the problem of sensation (and specifically the difficulty with sensation's full explanation in terms of the primary qualities of insensible bodies) presents more than just another limit to mechanistic explanation. Its solution seems to be a condition for the very possibility of mechanistic explanation, or, as Berkeley would have it, of materialism. The conundrum can be viewed this way:

1.   In mechanistic explanation, "observed" regularities are to be understood as the effects of causal interactions between bodies that are fully characterized by their primary qualities.

2.   However, the very distinction between primary and secondary qualities itself rests on the (mechanistic) claim that secondary quality sensations can be explained as the effects of causal interactions between (minute) bodies, those bodies, in turn, being fully characterized only by reference to their primary qualities.

3.   This circularity (mechanistic explanation rests on a primary-secondary quality distinction which itself depends on mechanistic explanation) is not vicious, provided that the promisory note of (2) is satisfactorily cashed. But if (2) fails (and Berkeley claims that for dualism, it is a principled failure) then mechanistic explanation fails.

Perhaps, however, Locke's own agnosticism with regard to the eventual fulfillment of a mechanistic explanation (and perhaps even with regard to dualism) was better founded than it seems at first glance. Certainly the annexation theory does not, in principle, rule out the eventual mechanistic understanding of sensation as Descartes' meddlesome God and firm dualism seem to. It remains a tantalizing speculation that Newton developed his annexation idea in explicit and reasoned response to the explanatory barriers that Descartes had built into the mechanical philosophy. In point of fact, the physical and psychological theories of the day (even the Cartesian examples that I shall presently use) rather successfully managed to step around any true chasm between mind and body. In scientific practice sensations were treated either as the physical outcome of mechanistic processes (in physiological optics, for example) or as experiential givens (in the psychology of judgment). Rarely, as we shall see, was there a pressing need or specific reason to ask about the agency between the physical and the mental or to invoke God's intervention to bridge the gap.[15]

IV

Let me briefly describe how a prominent scientific theory of the day treated sensation.[16] And the question we are now pursuing is this: was Berkeley right when he claimed that materialists failed to explain how a body "should imprint any idea in the mind"?

1. *Geometrical optics and the physiology of visual perception.* Descartes' theory is straightforwardly mechanistic. The geometrical lines of vision are reinterpreted physically as lines of pressure (light rays) propagated through a medium. (The medium is really a type of space—matter of the second kind—but this need not concern us here.) The eye, moreover, is treated as a mere mechanical device— as a *camera obscura*. The transferral of information contained in the retinal image to the pineal gland is accomplished by way of a baroquely conceived optical plumbing: a kinematics of fluids. The "content" of the sensation is treated as equivalent to that of the retinal image with appropriate physiological explanations of the differences. In this manner, sensations are discussed as if they were physical effects. The mental is simply treated as if it were physical. Berkeley understood, by the way, that the way to argue against this rather powerful (for the time) explanation was to pick apart the *empirical* theory. For example, in his *Essay Towards a New Theory of Vision*, he questions the very possibility of giving geometrical optics a physical interpretation.

2. *A psychological theory of judgment.* Here Descartes took sensation as a starting point, basic given, or surd, neither representing nor resembling. Introspection, it was thought, discerns no mental

activity accompanying sensation. And why develop a theory of mental activity to account for sensation, when sensation seems so obviously to be a starting point, basis, or datum for thought? Illusion, after all, could be explained as an error in perceptual *judgment*, following receipt of a sensation in itself neither illusory nor veridical. Or, when the "same" sensation was reported differently at different times or by different subjects, the discrepancy could be ascribed to the various past experiences ("associations") that influenced judgment formation.[17] With a few deviations, Berkeley himself adhered to the general outlines of this psychological program. He could do so, of course, just as long as the question of the origin of sensation did not come up.

We now come upon circumstances in which it might seem absolutely necessary to treat sensations in *both* of the ways I have discussed, as both physical effect and mental given. And here we might expect Berkeley's criticisms to come down with full force and to point out the explanatory gap between the mental and the physical. I shall discuss two such circumstances. Remember that, for the purposes of argument, we grant (along with Berkeley) the physical world of the materialists.

3.   *The account of correct perceptual judgment*. Descartes and Locke both claimed that ideas of primary qualities resemble what they represent. This assertion, as I have argued elsewhere, rests on a highly complex account of the visual perception of primary qualities.[18] Briefly, the account requires that we treat visual sensation as a physical effect insofar as it conveys information about the flat figures of objects (as they are projected on the retina) and as a mental given insofar as sensation is a starting point for reckoning the arrangements of objects in a three-dimensional space.

It is hard to see, however, how Berkeley's criticism has any force here. Descartes' strategy was simply to treat sensation as a physical effect and then to claim that we can reason about that physical effects as a physical explanandum like any other. (Similarly, we can take free fall, the rainbow, or the tides as phenomena to be explained.)

So far, the basic question, "What goes on *in between* the physical and the mental?" has not even been raised. Nevertheless, I may be accused of postponing the inevitable, for I have up to this point ignored colors, sounds, tastes, and the like.

4.   *The account of color sensation*. Descartes proposed to explain color differences mechanistically, in terms of differences. in the rotary motions of second-element particles. More precisely, since

second-element particles exhibit two tendencies, one to rectilinear motion and another to rotary motion, differences between colors are differences in the ratios of rectilinear to rotary motion, "so that those which have a much stronger tendency to rotate cause the color red and those which have only a slightly stronger tendency cause yellow."[19] Small fibers of the optic nerve were said to be sensitive to these various ratios and to cause, in turn, different movements in the nerve fibers of the brain.[20]

I said that for Descartes colors were differences in the ratios of motion. And to this Berkeley well might have object. For Descartes could not explain why a given ratio should appear *red*. Why not violet? Or why a color at all? Why not as the sound of middle C? Or, as D. M. Armstrong more recently put it, with reference to sounds, "Sound cannot be reduced to the properties of sound waves which physicists take professional notice of. The sound waves have an extra irreducible property: the property of sounding."[21] Here perhaps is the reason why Descartes claimed that sensations are innate and why Locke and Newton supposed that God originally annexes sensations to bodily movements.

Today, the usual next step is a discussion of micro-reduction, or emergent properties or permissable forms of property identity. Since my space is limited, I shall simply point out that we are in a far better position than Berkeley, Descartes, Locke, or Newton to evaluate the seriousness of what has been dubbed the problem of "dangling" (that is, irreducible) properties. I want now to draw an analogy between that dangling-property problem and another problem.

V

At the same time that Berkeley asked, "How can a body produce a thought?" physiologists and natural historians asked (although it was not a new question) "How can inert matter produce living things?" Organisms, it was stipulated, exhibit the distinctive properties of irritability, animal heat, and the reproduction of their kind. Could these distinctive features, it was queried, be explained solely in terms of physical causation, or must we suppose that all or some of these properties are irreducible? Need we invoke some agency other than physical causation? Descartes, on this issue at least, clung firmly to mechanism. But Von Helmont (1662) proposed a life principle. And even later, Liebig (who carried on the well-known debate with Pasteur about the causes of fermentation) proposed a living force, capable of overcoming physical forces.

I am suggesting, of course, a comparison of the irreducible life properties with the irreducible mental properties. And appeals to God's agency in the production of sensations should be compared to explanations in terms of life principles and living force. We might reformulate Armstrong's assertion this way: "Life cannot be reduced to the properties of the physical elements which physicists take professional notice of. Some matter has an extra irreducible property: the property of being alive."

I shall pursue the analogy (or *reductio*) only one step further. Vitalistic questions were fueled by an insistence on very strict distinctions between the living and the nonliving. It is an insistence that we have now learned to avoid. We have found that the demarcation between living and nonliving, while it can still be drawn, is not as clear-cut or as intuitive as it once seemed. For example, as Pasteur showed, fermentation (with its associated heat) is not a life-specific process. In biology the vocabulary of life processes has been supplemented by terms appropriate to talk of complex systems, biochemical pathways, self-replicating molecules, and even self-reproducing automata.

VI

It is a lingering and pervasive philosopher's error to require for scientific explanation precise and exacting definitions of explanatory terms or even unambiguous descriptions of the phenomena to be explained. Of course, it is possible that science works towards such terminological precision as a goal. (But this is not to say that the goal can always be attained.) Remember that such terms as 'element', 'gene', 'temperature', 'force', and 'life' have revealingly resisted attempts at precise definition. So too "the mental" even now resists unambiguous characterization.[22] My point in bringing forward the analogy with vitalistic theories is this: if we have learned anything at all from the history of past failure and success in science, it is that a price must be paid for dogged insistence on properties that are "strictly vital," or "strictly physical," or "strictly hereditary," or "strictly mental."

What is surprising, and what I have been trying to point out all along, is the extent to which Berkeley's problem, although it is unavoidable when we hold fast to a strict demarcation between the mental and the physical, goes by the board in seventeenth- and eighteenth-century theories of perception. In the reigning scientific theories, canonical philosophical differences between body and soul, between physical and mental, are largely ignored. Where we might well expect to see developing two discrete and nonoverlapping domains (each with distinctive goals, with domain-specific problems, techniques, vocabularies, and so forth), we do not. Instead, we discover not only several of the differences that we now recognize between the psychological and the physical. We also encounter (what still seems convincing today) a considerable overlap in investigatory domains, problems, techniques, and terms.

Indeed, Descartes himself explicitly (and in the face of his own dualism) recognized that sensations and imaginings are a hybrid of the mental and the physical.[23] For him, however, this recognition was not an illumination but an admission of defeat. The tension shows up again and again in the philosophical underpinnings that he proposes for science. For example, every invocation of the representational function of ideas is a symptom of the tension, since 'representation' only names one way in which ideas escape his own pre-established categories of mind and body.

VII

Berkeley, then, correctly charged that mechanistic theories of perception were foredoomed when judged according to a philosophical standard demanding precise demarcation between the mental and the physical. What he did not understand, I think, was the important wisdom that allowed mechanistic theorists *as* scientists to set aside and ignore those very same governing standards. Berkeley's "problem" (and so the lame "solutions" of Lockean annexation and Cartesian innateness) was shrewdly confined to secondary-quality sensations. Accounts of the physiology of visual perception, by contrast, sidestepped the problem by treating perception as a physical process. The psychology of judgment, employing another tactic, simply set aside questions about the originating physical processes of sentience and treated sensations as givens. Finally, the theory of correct perceptual judgment combined both strategies as if a firm distinction between mental and physical processes had never been drawn.

I want to avoid leaving the opposite impression, namely, that early modern science was just philosophically offhand, or, worse, that it advanced (or *had* to advance) in the absence of governing standards. Standards giving direction to this scientific work existed. My point is only that they were not always the canonical standards. What is more, the pragmatic and unstated criteria were in some ways better than the official ones. At the very least, this scenario begins to make some sense of the fact that Berkeley, who saw so plainly the inherent limitations of the new approach, put forward a criticism that was sound and right and yet ultimately ineffectual and irrelevant.[24]

Notes

1. See, for example, Peter Alexander, "Boyle and Locke on Primary and Secondary Qualities," in I. C. Tipton, ed., *Locke on Human Understanding* (Oxford: Oxford University Press, 1977), pp. 62-76; Maurice Mandelbaum, *Philosophy, Science and Sense Perception* (Baltimore: Johns Hopkins University Press, 1964); and John W. Yolton, *Locke and the Compass of Human Understanding* (Cambridge: Cambridge University Press, 1970).

2. References to Berkeley's work are to A. A. Luce and T. E. Jessop, eds., *The Works of George Berkeley, Bishop of Cloyne*, 9 vols. (London: Thomas Nelson and Sons, 1948-57); hereafter *Works*. References to the *Principles* are by section numbers.

3. See Martin Tamny, "Newton, Creation, and Perception," *Isis* 70 (1979): 48-59. The relevant conversation between Newton and Locke on annexation and conservation is mentioned by Pierre Coste in the third edition of his translation of Locke's *Essay* into French. In the *Essay* see IV, iii, 28-29. Margaret Wilson discusses some of these passages in "Superadded Properties: The Limits of Mechanism in Locke," *American Philosophical Quarterly* 16 (1979): 143-50.

4. "De Gravitatione et Aequipondio Fluidorum" in A. Rupert Hall and Marie Boas Hall, eds., *Unpublished Scientific Papers of Isaac Newton* (Cambridge: Cambridge University Press, 1962), p. 140; final italics are mine.

5. Ibid., p. 139.

6. . . . My right hand writes whilst my left hand is still. What causes rest in one and motion in the other? Nothing but my will, a thought of my mind; my thought is often changing, the right hand rests, and the left hand moves. This is a matter of fact which cannot be denied. Explain this and make it intelligible, and then the next step will be to understand creation. (*Essay*, IV, x, 19)

7. "De Gravitatione," pp. 138-39.

8. See also Isaac Newton, *Principia Mathematica*, vol. 2, bk. III, p. 543 in the 1934 revision by Florian Cajori of Andrew Motte's 1729 English translation (2 vols., Berkeley: University of California Press, 1966); and also Newton, *Opticks*, query 31, p. 403 (New York: Dover, 1952).

9. For the foundational discussion of Descartes' and Newton's view of space see Alexander Koyré, *Newtonian Studies* (Chicago: University of Chicago Press, 1965). On Descartes' rarely discussed view of the relation of God to time, see John Abbink, "Descartes on Time and God's Conservation," unpublished manuscript.

10. Reply to Objections V, 9, in E. S. Haldane and G. R. T. Ross, eds., *The Philosophical Works of Descartes* (Cambridge: Cambridge University Press, 1931), II, p. 219.

11. See *The World*, in Ralph M. Eaton, ed., *Descartes: Selections* (New York: Chas. Scribner's, 1927) p. 326. For the view that Descartes denies causal agency to moving matter (restricting agency to immaterial substance—minds and God), see Peter Machamer, "Causality and Explanation in Descartes' Natural Philosophy," in Machamer and Robert G. Turnbull, eds., *Motion and Time, Space and Matter*, (Columbus: Ohio State University Press, 1976), chap. 7; Richard J. Blackwell, "Descartes' Laws of Motion," *Isis* 57 (1966):

220-34; and Gary C. Hatfield, "Force (God) in Descartes' Physics," *Studies in History and Philosophy of Science* 10 (1979): 113-40.

12. Malebranche's further development of Descartes' hints about God's agency in his *Recherche de la vérité* are particularly interesting because Locke issued a devastatingly critical response to Malebranche's view that we "see all things in God," (See "An Examination of P. Malebranche's Opinion," *Works*, IX.)

13. See *Principles*, sect. 61, where Berkeley holds it as a *virtue* that his philosophy comes up against the limits of explanation (God) long before the materialists have exhausted their mechanistic ploys.

14. So, too, for Locke (as for Newton), gravity and the coherence of "the solid parts of matter" *may* not be explicable in mechanistic terms. I have emphasized the openness of their annexation theory to the possibility of mechanistic explanation. For a different view, see Margaret Wilson's discussion in "Superadded Properties: The Limits of Mechanism in Locke," *American Philosophical Quarterly* 16 (1979): 148-49. The relevant passages in Locke are in "Some Thoughts Concerning Education," *Works*, IX, p. 184; Letter to Stillingfleet, *Works*, IV, pp. 467-68; *Essay*, II, xxiii, 24, and IV, iii, 29.

15. Wilfrid Sellars ("Berkeley and Descartes: Reflections on the 'New Way of Ideas,'" in P. K. Machamer and R. G. Turnbull, eds., *Studies in Perception* [Columbus: Ohio State University Press, 1978]) considers why Descartes and others failed to ask, "Is there no *via media* between being physically triangular and being a conceptual representation of a physical triangle?" Sellars helpfully traces this failure to the conceptual limitations of the "way of ideas."

16. For a more detailed account, see my "Cartesian Optics and the Geometrization of Nature," *Review of Metaphysics* 32 (1978): 263-73.

17. See, for example, Descartes' discussions of the apparent and real size of the sun (*Meditations* III and IV).

18. See my "Perception and Primary Qualities," *P.S.A. 1978; Proceedings of the 1978 Biennial Meeting of the Philosophy of Science Association*, P. D. Asquith and I. Hacking, eds., pp. 3-17.

19. *Meteors*, Eighth Discourse, in Descartes' *Discourse on Method, Optics, Geometry and Meteorology*, P. Olscamp, ed. (Indianapolis: Bobbs Merrill, 1965), p. 337.

20. *Dioptrics*, Sixth Discourse.

21. "The Secondary Qualities," *Australasian Journal of Philosophy* 46 (1968): 228.

22. See, for example, Richard Rorty's suggestion in "Incorrigibility as the Mark of the Mental," *Journal of Philosophy* 67 (1970): 399-425; and K. V. Wilkes, *Physicalism* (Atlantic Highlands, N.J.: Humanities Press 1978), chap. 1 and 2.

23. In the 1643 exchange of letters with Princess Elizabeth, Descartes concentrated his attention not on the agency of interaction between body and mind, but on the notion that sensations are themselves psychophysical hybrids.

24. Margaret Wilson (in "Did Berkeley Completely Misunderstand the Basis of the Primary-Secondary Quality Distinction in Locke?" pp. 108-23, this volume) and I seem to be in agreement on the centrality of Berkeley's powerful "causal argument" (or arguments) against the primary/secondary quality distinction. My own point of departure, of course, was a question about just how Berkeley's philosophically impeccable argument actually weighed against particular scientific theories of sense perception and judgment. (I used Descartes' theories because Locke, without acknowledgment, relies so heavily upon them in the *Essay*.)

I accept Professor Wilson's gentle reminder (to Alexander) that a distinction between the scientific and the philosophical requires explication. However, her final remarks in

Berkeley's defense seem to me overly generous. Whatever Berkeley himself thought (see n. 12), it is hardly a *virtue* (or as Professor Wilson puts it, "one of the strongest positive features of Berkeley's anti-Lockean metaphysics") that Berkeley "solves" the problem of how matter could possibly produce ideas in the mind by resorting to immaterialism. After all (to persist in the yet unexplicated—though still crucial—distinction), even if Berkeley succeeded in solving the philosophical problem, he did so only at the cost of expurgating all questions about the origins of sensation from the field of scientific debate.

8

Did Berkeley Completely Misunderstand the Basis of the Primary-Secondary Quality Distinction in Locke?

Margaret D. Wilson

I

According to leading seventeenth-century philosophers and scientists, our sensory "ideas" of physical objects are of two importantly different types. Certain sorts of ideas, the "ideas of primary qualities," *resemble* qualities actually existing in the object. While there are some differences about what *exactly* these comprise, size, shape, motion or rest, and number are among the accepted examples. (Locke, notoriously, includes "solidity"; he sometimes mentions position. Gravity, as we will see below, was sometimes included later.) On the other hand, the "ideas of secondary qualities" do not resemble any quality really existing in the object, although they are systematically produced by the interactions of the objects' primary qualities with percipients. Ideas or sensations of colors, odors, tastes, sounds, and temperature (hot and cold) are among the traditional "ideas of secondary qualities."[1]

Berkeley is the best known early critic of this distinction — although, as we shall see, he did have predecessors. In the early twentieth century, the distinction was vigorously attacked by Whitehead, who considered it a prominent manifestation of the "fallacy of misplaced concreteness" — which, he claimed, has "ruined" modern philosophy.[2] More recently, D. J. O'Connor, after critically expounding Locke's doctrine of qualities, dismisses it with the comment:

> Clearly all this is a great muddle. The doctrine of primary and secondary qualities is, in truth, nothing but some scientific truths dangerously elevated into a philosophical doctrine.[3]

But since O'Connor's article was published in 1964, the primary-secondary quality distinction has increasingly been treated with respect, especially by philosophers sympathetic to "scientific realism." In terms of historical criticism, this development has been accompanied by an increasingly sympathetic construal of Locke's philosophy in general, and a tendency to dismiss Berkeley as having had a very poor understanding of Locke's position. The following views, in particular, have been espoused by a number of writers. (1) Locke's distinction should be viewed as principally grounded in the explanatory success of Boylean atomism. (2) Berkeley erroneously and misleadingly construed the distinction as one supposed to rest on ordinary experience of macroscopic objects. More specifically (some have held), Berkeley misinterpreted the "arguments" of the *Essay Concerning Human Understanding*, bk. II, chap. viii, sects. 16-21 — having to do with illusion and the relativity of perception — as Locke's main foundation for the distinction, and therefore falsely supposed that he could refute the distinction by showing that primary-quality perceptions are also subject to relativity considerations. But in fact the issue of perceptual relativity plays no such central role in Locke's thought. (The reasoning of *Essay*, II, viii, 16-21 should be read either as some incidental "bad arguments" for the distinction, or simply as an attempt to bring out the explanatory power of the Boylean conception of body.) (3) Berkeley is responsible, through his stress on relativity considerations, and epistemological issues generally, for a long subsequent history of misinterpreting Locke as relying on such considerations. He is correspondingly responsible for the widespread failure to recognize the truth stated above under (1). (4) When Locke's distinction is correctly reinterpreted as resting on a tacit appeal to the "explanatory success" of contemporary science, it is a much stronger position than traditionally believed. (In fact, at least one prominent philosopher has firmly endorsed Locke's position, with only minor qualifications, relating mainly to scientific progress since Locke's time.)[4]

I fully agree with the view that Locke's distinction was heavily influenced by Boylean science. However, I do not think there is strong reason to suppose that Berkeley seriously "misrepresented" or "misinterpreted" Locke in this connection, is "wholly unfair" to him, read him "carelessly," or produced arguments against Locke that are "wholly [or "simply"] beside the point," as various critics allege.[5] As Barry Stroud has recently noted, this conception of Berkeley, "like the old view of Locke, is a purely fictional chapter in the history of philosophy. . . ."[6] Stroud persuasively demonstrates this claim by a careful examination of the arguments of the *Principles* and the *Dialogues*, in relation to the primary-secondary quality distinction. Stroud stresses throughout that Berkeley is primarily concerned with what he sees as his predecessors' "faulty notion of existence"—specifically, their assumption that something unperceived and unperceiving could exist.[7] It is this assumption that Berkeley sees as their major error, rather than mistakes about the relativity of primary quality perceptions, or the epistemological appearance-reality distinction generally.

In the present essay I will defend a point of view that is similar to Stroud's, but with a somewhat different approach.[8] I will focus on the claims of three commentators—Mandelbaum, Alexander, and Mackie—who hold that Berkeley falsely believed Locke's primary-secondary quality distinction to rest on facts about ordinary perception. After quoting some passages from their writings, I will argue that there is in reality very little basis for attributing this interpretation of Locke to Berkeley. I will suggest, however, that there *is* something of a puzzle about the role of relativity arguments in the history of the primary-secondary quality distinction. (As we will see, the puzzle in question goes back beyond Berkeley; I am unable to resolve it.) I will then show that there is ample evidence that Berkeley was aware that Locke's distinction was supposed to derive major support from arguments from scientific (or corpuscularian) explanation. He in fact deals with such arguments repeatedly, searchingly, and—at least in part—astutely. I will also sketch the variety of considerations by which he tries to meet them.

It is so easy to show that Berkeley was aware of the supposed corpuscularian grounding of the distinction that what really requires explanation is the fact that he has so long been accused of missing it. In conclusion I will point out that two of the three critics indeed seem to acknowledge obliquely that Berkeley is far from simply ignoring the alleged scientific basis of Locke's distinction. But—perhaps out of sympathy for Locke's philosophy?—they do not sufficiently consider the implications of these concessions for their other charges against Berkeley.

While this is strictly an interpretive essay, I would like to mention in passing that I am in some respects quite sympathetic to Berkeley's position on the subject under discussion. That is, I share his view that the primary-secondary quality distinction is an affront to common sense, and I am not convinced that a satisfactory version of the argument from explanation has so far been brought forward to establish it.[9]

II

A key passage from Mandelbaum's influential essay on "Locke's Realism" reads as follows:

> The upshot of our argument . . . is that the basis on which Locke established his theory of the primary qualities was his atomism; it was not his aim to attempt to establish the nature of physical objects by examining the sensible ideas which we had of them. Thus instead of viewing Locke's doctrine of the primary and secondary qualities as a doctrine which rests on an analysis of differences among our ideas, his doctrine is to be understood as a theory of physical entities, and of the manner in which our ideas are caused. To this extent the Berkeleian criticism of Locke's distinction between primary and secondary qualities is wholly beside the point, for it rests on an assumption which Locke did not share—that all distinctions concerning the nature of objects must be based upon, and verified by, distinctions discernible within the immediate contents of consciousness.[10]

Mandelbaum does not explain exactly what he means by "distinctions discernible within the immediate contents of consciousness." However, in a footnote he cites *Essay*, II, viii, 21 as the only passage in Locke where it might seem that the theory of primary and secondary qualities is being supported by such a distinction. (This is the passage in which Locke observed that the corpuscularian theory of warmth in our hands as merely a motion of animal spirits enables us to understand how the same water can feel warm to one hand and cold to another, "Whereas is is impossible that the same Water, if those *Ideas* were really in it, should at the same time be both Hot and Cold."[11] He goes on to indicate that "figure" does not present the same problem, "that never producing the *Idea* of a square by one Hand which has produced the Idea of a Globe by another.") Mandelbaum remarks that the passage is primarily concerned with the causal story of the origin of ideas of secondary qualities, and he suggests that "the contention that we are not deceived by tactile impressions of shape plays no significant part in the discussion."[12]

Rather similarly, Peter Alexander writes in the introduction to "Boyle and Locke on Primary and Secondary Qualities":

> Locke has been seriously misrepresented in various respects ever since Berkeley set critics off on the wrong foot. I wish to discuss just one central view the misunderstanding of which has been particularly gross, namely, the distinction between primary and secondary qualities and,

especially the alleged arguments for this distinction in *Essay* II, viii, 16-21. Robert Boyle is often mentioned in connection with Locke but the extent and importance of his influence on Locke has seldom been realized. [Alexander here cites Mandelbaum as one of two "honourable exceptions."] If the arguments of II, viii were intended, following Berkeley, to *establish* the distinction between primary and secondary qualities then Locke was both foolish and incompetent; a study of Boyle can help us to see that he was neither of these things by making it clear what he was driving at.[13]

And, finally, some excerpts from Chap. I of John Mackie's book, *Problems from Locke:*

But Locke [after well arguing that the corpuscularian science can explain the "illusion" of lukewarm water feeling cold to one hand and hot to the other] throws in, for contrast, the remark that 'figure'—that is, shape—'never produce[s] the idea of a square by one hand [and] of a globe by another.' Though literally correct, this is unfortunate because it has led careless readers from Berkeley onwards to think that Locke is founding the primary/secondary distinction on the claim that secondary qualities are subject to sensory illusion while primary qualities are not. It is then easy for Berkeley to reply that illusions also occur with respect to primary qualities like shape, size, and motion, and hence that there can be no distinction between the two groups of qualities. . . . But of course Locke's argument does not rest on any such claim . . . ; it is rather that the corpuscular theory is confirmed as a scientific hypothesis by its success in explaining various illusions in detail.[14]

The textual support offered for these negative characterizations of Berkeley's understanding of Locke is surely, by anyone's standards, singularly meager. Neither Mandelbaum nor Alexander cites any texts at all, while Mackie refers us (in the paragraph after the one partially quoted) to "especially . . . the First Dialogue." What, then, do they have in mind? Following up Mackie's clue, let us turn first to that Dialogue. One feature of Berkeley's strategy there does afford at least *prima facie* support for the charge against him.

In the first part of the Dialogue, Philonous has argued in a variety of ways (*not* just through notions of relativity or illusion) that sensible colors, sounds, heat and cold, tastes and odors exist "only in the mind." Hylas, reluctantly persuaded of this conclusion, suddenly bethinks himself of the distinction between primary and secondary qualities. "Philosophers," he points out, assert that all of the properties so far covered in the Dialogue "are only so many sensations or ideas existing nowhere but in the mind." The primary qualities, however—"Extension, Figure, Solidity, Gravity,[15] Motion, and Rest"—"they hold exist really in bodies." Hylas concludes his speech as follows: "For my part, I have been a long time sensible there was such an opinion current among philosophers, but was never thoroughly convinced of its truth until now."[16] Philonous then introduces the next phase of the argument for immaterialism in the following terms: "But what if the same arguments which are brought against Secondary Qualities will hold good against [extensions and figures] also?"[17] He then proceeds to argue that perceptions of extension are relative to the condition and situation of the percipient. This discussion includes a passage that does indeed recall the argument of *Essay*, II, viii, 21:

> Phil. Was it not admitted as a good argument [cited in our previous discussion] that neither heat nor cold was in the water, because it seemed warm to one hand and cold to the other?
>
> Hyl. It was.
>
> Phil. Is it not the very same reasoning to conclude, there is no extension or figure in an object, because to one eye it shall seem little, smooth and round, when at the same time it appears to the other great, uneven, and angular?[18]

In response to Hylas' expression of skepticism as to whether this ever happens, Philonous goes on to cite the instance of the microscope.

Now, does this passage, together with Philonous' subsequent development of relativity arguments for motion and solidity, show that Berkeley seriously overestimated the importance of relativity considerations for Locke? This seems to me a rather extravagant supposition, for several reasons. First (and least important), surely there really is a suggestion in *Essay*, II, viii, 21 that relativity considerations show that hot and cold as we perceive them are not really in the water; and *some* contrast is suggested in this respect between hot-and-cold and figure. Second, as Michael Ayers has pointed out, the fact that there is an "association" of Philonous' reasoning with Locke's brief remarks about relativity scarcely shows that Berkeley *sees Locke* as resting the distinction between subjective ideas and real qualities on considerations of relativity or the possibility of illusion.[19] And, finally, the argument of the First Dialogue is clearly not presented in the form of *ad hominem* reasoning at all. That is, the overt strategy is not simply to take a premiss from the opposition—that relativity considerations establish the subjectivity of the "secondary qualities"—and show that anyone who holds *that* can logically be forced into immaterialism. Rather, Berkeley first has Philonous systematically *persuade* Hylas (through relativity and other considerations) that colors, odors, etc., are mere ideas in the mind. Following Ayers, then, I would deny that Berkeley's treatment of relativity arguments in the First Dialogue tends to convict him of a misunderstanding or "careless reading" of Locke.[20]

It might be suggested, however, that the *Principles* actually provide more direct proof than do the *Dialogues* that Berkeley saw Locke and his followers as resting the primary-secondary quality distinction on considerations of perceptual relativity. For we do find in *Principles*, I, sect. 14 the following statement:

> I shall farther add, that, after the same manner as modern philosophers prove certain sensible qualities to have not existence in Matter, or without the mind, the same things may be likewise proved of all other sensible qualities whatsoever. Thus, for instance, it is said that heat and cold are affections only of the mind, and not at all patterns of real beings, existing in the corporeal substances which excite them; for that the same body which appears cold to one hand seems warm to another.[21]

He goes on to claim that the same relativity considerations hold in the cases of extension and motion. It is true, as Ayers points out, that Berkeley immediately goes on (in sect. 15) to observe that this reasoning does not establish the mind-dependence of *either* class of qualities:

> Though it must be confessed this method of arguing does not so much prove that there is no extension or colour in an outward object, as that we do not know by sense which is the true extension or colour of the object.[22]

The passage does, however, provide direct evidence that Berkeley thought that "modern philosophers" drew on relativity arguments to establish the subjectivity of secondary qualities. It appears to imply that he thought they had not noticed that perception of primary qualities, too, could be affected by the position or condition of the percipient. What does this tell us about his reading of Locke?

The first point to observe is that the idea that relativity considerations extend to primary as well as secondary qualities did not originate with Berkeley—nor did the use of this point as a criticism of the view that perceptions of primary qualities possess superior objectivity. The passage quoted above from Berkeley's *Principles* has an extremely close parallel in section G of the article "Zeno of Elea" in Bayle's *Dictionary*, published years before.[23] The likelihood that Berkeley adopted this part of his reasoning from Bayle was apparently first demonstrated by Richard Popkin in 1951, and has frequently been noted in subsequent writings by Popkin and others.[24] Bayle is criticizing "the 'new' philosophers." The following passage is representative:

> . . . all the means of suspending judgment that overthrow the reality of corporeal qualities also overthrow the reality of extension. Since the same bodies are sweet to some men and bitter to others, one is right in inferring that they are neither sweet nor bitter in themselves and absolutely speaking. The "new" philosophers, although they are not skeptics, have so well understood the bases of suspension of judgment with regard to sounds, smells, heat, cold, hardness, softness, heaviness and lightness, tastes, colors, and the like, that they teach that all these qualities are perceptions of our soul and that they do not exist at all in the objects of our senses. Why should we not say the same thing about extension? . . . [N]otice carefully that the same body appears to us to be small or large, according to the place from which it is viewed; and let us have no doubts that a body that seems very small to us appears very large to a fly.[25]

Now, against whom, exactly, does Bayle suppose that such reasoning is effective? In another article Bayle credits Simon Foucher with influencing his views on the indefensibility of the primary-secondary quality distinction.[26] He specifically cites Foucher's *Critique de la Recherche de la Verité*, an attack on Malebranche published in 1675.[27] This would take the criticism of the primary-secondary quality distinction back to fifteen years *before* the publication of Locke's *Essay*. While Foucher does argue that the primary-secondary distinction is indefensible, however, he does not, as far as I can find, focus on the issue of the comparable relativity and variability of primary qualities.[28] It is perhaps logical that he should not, since Malebranche himself makes much of the relativity of perceptions of extension in the *Recherche*![29] Bayle himself notes that such arguments are found in Malebranche and the *Port Royal Logic*, among other sources.[30] It is therefore presently unclear to me just whom Bayle thought he was refuting in the passage quoted, and just what he thought their error was. (Not noticing that perceptions of primary qualities are variable? Not drawing the right conclusion from the observation?)—There certainly seems to be no good reason to suppose he had in mind specifically *Essay*, II, viii, 16-21. The same difficulties then come up at one remove about Berkeley's closely comparable reasoning (and even wording) in *Principles*, sects. 14-15. That is, there may have been "modern" or "new" philosophers who fit the role that Bayle and Berkeley cast them in more closely than

Locke—and Bayle and Berkeley may have had them in mind. Or there may not have been, in which case Berkeley will have taken over from Bayle a piece of reasoning without a proper target. In contrast to this rather murky situation, however, it is possible to show clearly that Berkeley (if not Bayle) fully appreciated the importance of the alleged success of corpuscularian explanations as a basis for the primary-secondary quality distinction. Let us now turn to this task.

III

It is an interesting fact that Mandelbaum, Alexander, and Mackie, in arguing that the explanatory success of corpuscularianism is the main basis for Locke's distinction, particularly cite the ability of this science to explain the production of ideas in us, including the ideas of secondary qualities. But this is, as it happens, a topic with which Berkeley deals repeatedly and emphatically. For instance, at the very beginning of the Second Dialogue, Hylas first admits that he can see no false steps in the reasonings of the previous day. But, he says,

> when these are out of my thoughts, there seems, on the other hand, something so satisfactory, so natural and intelligible, in the modern way of explaining things that, I profess, I know not how to reject it.[31]

The conversation proceeds as follows:

> Phil. I know not what you mean.
>
> Hyl. I mean the way of accounting for our sensations or ideas.
>
> Phil. How is that?
>
> Hyl. It is supposed the soul makes her residence in some part of the brain, from which the nerves take their rise, and are thence extended to all parts of the body; and that outward objects, by the different impressions they make on the organs of sense, communicate certain vibrative motions to the nerves; and these being filled wih spirits propagate them to the brain or seat of the soul, which, according to the various impressions or traces thereby made in the brain is variously affected with ideas.
>
> Phil. And call you this an explication of the manner whereby we are affected with ideas?[32]

In objecting to this reasoning, Philonous first points out that by the previous day's reasoning the brain is just one sensible object among others, and hence itself exists "only in the mind." How could one idea or sensible thing reasonably be supposed to cause all the others? But, he continues, Hylas' position is intrinsically inacceptable, even apart from conclusions previously arrived at.

> Phil. . . . for after all, this way of explaining things, as you called it, could never have satisfied any reasonable man. What connexion is there between a motion in the nerves, and the sensations of sound or colour in the mind? Or how is it possible these should be the effect of that?[33]

As this passage shows conclusively, Berkeley was perfectly aware that the primary-secondary quality distinction was supposed to derive support from the alleged ability of contemporary science to explain perception in terms of materialist mechanism—and hence of primary qualities. His response is straightforward: the purported "explanation" is a sham. In presenting this response he invokes the notion that the production of ideas by states of matter is not "possible." Such an a priori stricture on causal relations would be considered untenable by many philosophers today. It was, however, accepted by Locke, who argued at length that states of matter cannot "naturally" produce "Sence, Perception, and Knowledge."[34] Far from missing Locke's point, Berkeley has come down on a crucial weakness—and problem of consistency—in the Lockean system.[35]

Berkeley raises this issue repeatedly.[36] However, he also deals in other ways with the notion that the contemporary concept of external matter characterized (just) by primary qualities is justified by its "explanatory success." Some of his arguments draw on problematic—even idiosyncratic—views about causal relations. For present purposes there is no need to analyze the relevant passages in detail. I will merely summarize the main considerations he advances.

(1) From the contention that only spirits are active, Berkeley argues that extension, motion, etc.—or unthinking matter characterized by these qualities—cannot be causes of anything. Hence they cannot "explain" the production of any effect.[37]

(2) Even apart from the impossibility of understanding how a motion of matter could produce an idea, or how an "inert" entity could be a cause, contemporary materialism is far from explanatorily adequate. Have the materialists, Berkely demands,

> by all their strained thoughts and extravagant suppositions . . . been able to reach the mechanical production of any one animal or vegetable body? . . . Have they accounted, by physical principles, for the aptitude and contrivance, even of the most inconsiderable parts of the universe?[38]

(3) The explanatory successes that the new science has had can readily be accommodated within the immaterialist philosophy.

They have to do mainly with uncovering regularities and "analogies" in nature. Nothing but confusion results when it is thought that these regularities are leading to the discovery of productive material causes (e.g., "gravitational attraction"). Rather they should be conceived as part of an increasingly comprehensive theory of ideal "signs" to significata. The underlying ground of *this* relation is the causality of the infinite spirit, orderly producer of these ideas or sensible objects that constitute nature.[39]

These contentions range, clearly, from prodigious metaphysics to simple common sense. Taken together, however, they hardly indicate unawareness of the explanatory claims of contemporary mechanism — or of the philosophical significance attributed to these claims.

Two final points should be added, in concluding this discussion of Berkeley. First, the specific considerations against arguments from "explanatory success" for the Boylean concept of matter are offered despite the fact that Berkeley (in the *Principles*, anyway) believes that he can demonstrate the *unintelligibility* of the notion before the issue of its "explanatory power" — which surely is in some sense posterior — is even raised. Second, it would be wrong to suppose (as Mandelbaum sometimes seems to)[40] that Berkeley neglects the prevailing view that qualities of material bodies are supposed to derive from their inner real essences or constitutive corpuscles. He clearly states and disputes this Lockean conception in more than one passage.[41]

IV

In conclusion, I want to acknowledge that both Mandelbaum and Alexander show some recognition that Berkeley's attack on Locke was not wholly a matter of misinterpretation. In the case of Mandelbaum, the recognition is extremely oblique and in several ways puzzling. Mandelbaum points out that Berkeley did not merely overlook the fact that Locke's philosophy was founded on scientific considerations; rather he consciously "sought to free philosophic questions from any direct dependence upon science."[42] From this observation Mandelbaum somehow moves to the conclusion that it is *accordingly* "misleading" to interpret Locke in the light of Berkeley's criticisms. He also seems to think that Berkeley's efforts "to free philosophic questions from any direct dependence upon science" entail his reading the *Essay* "as an epistemological treatise devoid of a scientific substructure."[43] But none of this really follows, unless it be supposed that Berkeley's attempt to free philosophy from dependence on science was somehow a mere blind turning away from the earlier "tradition" without any direct confrontation with its assumptions. Perhaps this inference is tied in with Mandelbaum's undefended claim that Berkeley simply assumes that all distinctions among ideas must be drawn within the contents of ordinary experience of macroscopic objects. In any case, I hope to have shown that Berkeley did understand these "scientific" aspects of Locke's position that Mandelbaum is concerned to stress — and still had reason to regard the position as incoherent.

At the end of his article, Alexander does allow that "perhaps the most difficult objection for Locke to meet," with respect to the primary-secondary quality distinction, "is an argument about causality put by Berkeley. . . ."[44] It appears at first that Alexander means (surprisingly) Berkeley's argument that everything except spirit is "inert" and hence causally inefficacious. But the whole passage gives the impression that "the most difficult objection" that Alexander has in mind is really Berkeley's observation, expounded at some length above, "that no philosopher even pretends to explain 'how matter should operate on a spirit'."

In my opinion, this has to be a crucial point of contention between Berkeley and Locke's present-day apologists, with respect to the primary-secondary quality distinction.[45] Berkeley, I have argued, *rejected* the argument from the explanatory success of mechanistic physics; he did not merely ignore it. And I have also claimed that, insofar as Berkeley was pointing out an inconsistency in the philosophy he opposed, his position is solidly grounded. It is apparently open to the contemporary philosopher, concerned with philosophical truth as well as Locke exegesis to deny that there is, after all, any special problem about causal relations between the mental and the physical, and hence about "explaining" perceptions in physical terms. (In this, I stress again, he would have to disagree with *both* Berkeley and Locke.) Mandelbaum and Mackie do not address this point; they do not seem to see it.[46] Alexander does at least partly see it. But rather than reject the eighteenth-century assumption that there is some special problem about mind-body interaction, he attempts to help Locke out of the difficulty by invoking an unexplained distinction between scientific and philosophical issues:

Locke believes, as does Boyle, that the facts of experience force dualism upon us; the consequent problem is not scientific but philosophical and is therefore not particularly involved in the distinction between primary and secondary qualities.[47]

But surely the whole drift of Berkeley's attack on Locke's distinction is that the "facts of experience" do *not* force dualism upon us—so the philosophical inconsistency that Locke falls into can be avoided. Berkeley thinks that his immaterialism lets us accommodate the facts of experience without *having* a problem—whether "philosophical" or "scientific"—about how matter could possibly produce ideas in the mind. Alexander has not only conceded to Berkeley a relevant, if not powerful, objection to Locke's system.[48] He has unintentionally pointed to one of the strongest positive features of Berkeley's anti-Lockean metaphysics.

Notes

1. See John Locke, *Essay Concerning Human Understanding*, bk. II, chap. viii. Descartes, Galileo, and Boyle are among the other prominent exponents of the distinction.

2. A. N. Whitehead, *Science and the Modern World* (1925; repr. New York: The Free Press, 1967), chap. 3.

3. "Locke," in D. J. O'Connor, ed., *A Critical History of Western Philosophy* (New York: The Free Press, 1964), p. 211.

4. J. L. Mackie, *Problems From Locke* (Oxford: Clarendon Press, 1976), chap. 2. Other sources for the views cited (with less explicit philosophical endorsement of Locke's distinction) are found in the works of Mandelbaum and Alexander, cited below. At the beginning of the paper cited in n. 6, Barry Stroud gives many references to works advancing the "old" interpretation of Locke.

5. All of these comments are from Mackie, Alexander, and Mandelbaum. Some of them occur in the passages I cite from their works at the beginning of pt. II.

6. "Berkeley v. Locke on Primary Qualities," *Philosophy* 55 (April 1980): 150. See also Daniel Garber, "Locke, Berkeley, and Corpuscular Scepticism," this volume, pp. 174-94.

7. Stroud, "Berkeley v. Locke," pp. 150-51 and passim.

8. To the best of my knowledge, my views about the interpretation of Berkeley developed in complete independence from Stroud's. I did not become aware of the similarities between our ideas on this matter until I came across the published version of his paper, after an earlier version of the present article had been submitted for publication. I must acknowledge, however, that I had in my possession all the while a manuscript version of his essay, which constituted part of a much longer paper on Locke and Berkeley that he sent me years ago. Apparently I had never read the section on Berkeley, and had indeed misremembered the paper as being wholly on Locke. (My oversight came to light as a result of recent correspondence with Stroud.)

I have extensively revised pt. I of the present essay to take account of Stroud's prior work. For reasons of structure and exposition, it has proved impractical to remove all overlap from later sections, however. In particular, my treatment of Berkeley on relativity arguments is in several respects close to Stroud's. Stroud also touches briefly on Bayle's precedence to Berkeley, which I discuss in more detail, and on the issue of materialist explanation.

9. I critically discuss Mackie's exposition of the argument in "The Primary-Secondary Quality Distinction: Against Two Recent Defenses," 1979, unpublished.

10. Maurice Mandelbaum, "Locke's Realism," in *Philosophy, Science, and Sense Perception* (Baltimore: Johns Hopkins Press, 1974), pp. 27-28; see also p. 20.

11. John Locke, *An Essay Concerning Human Understanding*, ed. Peter H. Nidditch (Oxford: Clarendon Press, 1960; repr. 1975), p. 139.

12. Mandelbaum, "Locke's Realism," p. 28, n. 52.

13. In I. C. Tipton, ed., *Locke on Human Understanding* (Oxford: Oxford University Press, 1977), p. 62; see also p. 73. (Originally published in *Ratio* 16 [1974].)

14. *Problems From Locke*, pp. 22-23; cf. p. 24.

15. The inclusion of gravity constitutes an important departure from Locke: cf. Margaret D. Wilson, "Superadded Properties: The Limits of Mechanism in Locke," *American Philosophical Quarterly* 14 (April 1979): 148-49. On the other hand, Berkeley does not always include gravity in the list of primary qualities: cf. *A Treatise Concerning the Principles of Human Knowledge*, I, sect. 9. (In A. A. Luce and T. E. Jessop, eds., *The Works of George Berkeley, Bishop of Cloyne*, 9 vols. [London: Thomas Nelson and Sons, 1948-57], vol. II, p. 44. This edition hereafter referred to as *Works*.)

16. *Works*, II, pp. 187-88.

17. Ibid., p. 188.

18. Ibid., p. 189.

19. "Substance, Reality, and the Great Dead Philosophers," *American Philosophical Quarterly* 7 (January 1970): 43. Ayers is disputing a rather different allegation of Berkeleyan misunderstanding—that of Jonathan Bennett—but some of his remarks are relevant to the present context as well.

20. Ayers points out that Berkeley's deployment of relativity arguments in the First Dialogue can well be read as the outcome of "his own quasi-sceptical reflections on the fact that the state, position, etc. of the perceiver help to determine how *any* aspect of the world is perceived." However, as I explain below, there is considerable reason to believe that the "quasi-sceptical reflections" in question were strongly influenced by Bayle.

21. *Works*, II, pp. 46-47. In *Principles*, sect. 14-15, Berkeley specifically mentions relativity considerations as applying to color and taste, as well as hot and cold, among the secondary qualities, and extension, figure, and motion among the primary qualities.

22. Ibid., p. 47. A similar point is made by Bayle in the section of "Zeno" cited in the next note.

23. Pierre Bayle, *Dictionnaire historique et critique*, nov. éd., tome XV (Paris: Desoer, 1820), pp. 44-45; *Historical and Critical Dictionary*, ed. Richard H. Popkin (Indianapolis: Bobbs-Merrill, 1965), pp. 364-66. Subsequent references are to Popkin's edition. The *Dictionary* was originally published in 1697.

24. Richard H. Popkin, "Berkeley and Pyrrhonism," *Review of Metaphysics* 5 (1951-52): 223-46. See also his notes to his edition of Bayle's *Dictionary*, s.v. "Pyrrho" and "Zeno of Elea." See also Richard A. Watson, *The Downfall of Cartesianism, 1673-1712* (The Hague: Martinus Nijhoff, 1966), p. 3: and his *Introduction* to Simon Foucher, *Critique de la Recherche de la Verité* (New York and London: Johnson Reprint Corporation, 1969), p. xxix. I am grateful to Phillip Cummins for calling my attention to Bayle's (and Foucher's) relevance to the present inquiry.

25. *Dictionary*, pp. 364-65.

26. s.v. "Pyrrho," ibid., p. 197.

27. Reprinted 1969: see n. 24. See esp. pp. 76-80 of this work. Foucher's influence on Bayle has been noted by Popkin and Watson in the works cited above. Watson's *Downfall of Cartesianism* contains an especially detailed discussion of Foucher and his relationship

to Malebranche, Bayle, Berkeley, and others. See also Phillip Cummins, "Perceptual Relativity and Ideas in the Mind," *Philosophy and Phenomenological Research* 24 (December 1963): 202-14. Cummins notes Bayle's seemingly erroneous emphasis on the issue of perceptual relativity and provides an interesting analysis of his (and of Foucher's) conception of the issue.

28. Popkin indicates that he does: cf. Popkin, "Skepticism," in Paul Edwards, ed., *The Encyclopedia of Philosophy*, vol. 7 (New York: Macmillan and The Free Press, 1967), p. 454. He does not give an exact reference, however. Watson, in his detailed discussion of Foucher's anti-Malebranche works, does not seem to point to the presence of an "equal variability" argument in Foucher. (I have personally had access to only the first of Foucher's critical works.)

29. *Recherche de la verité*, bk. I, chap. vi, sect. 1, in Nicholas Malebranche, *Oeuvres complètes*, ed. A. Robinet, vol. I (Paris: J. Vrin, 1958), pp. 79ff. However, Malebranche does claim that judgments about bodies' primary qualities involve truths about proportions and relations, while judgments about secondary qualities are more wholly erroneous: cf. Watson, *Downfall*, p. 44.

30. Bayle, *Dictionary*, s.v. "Zeno," nn. 66 and 67, pp. 365-66.

31. *Works*, II, p. 208.

32. Ibid., pp. 208-09.

33. Ibid., p. 210.

34. Cf. Wilson, "Superadded Properties," pp. 144-48; and Stroud, "Berkeley v. Locke," p. 158.

35. Foucher had already observed this inconsistency—and some related ones—in the dualist, realist philosophies of his day, and had dwelt on it emphatically and at length. As noted above, however, his targets were post-Cartesian continental philosophers, especially Malebranche. Foucher's critical arguments and their influence on Berkeley and others have been meticulously detailed by Watson in *Downfall*.

In "Berkeley on the Limits of Mechanistic Explanation" (this volume, pp. 95-107, Nancy L. Maull also stresses Berkeley's use of this line of argument, and mentions its *ad hominem* relevance. Unfortunately, I did not learn of Maull's essay until the present paper had been submitted for publication. While there are a number of points of contact between our approaches, I disagree strongly with Maull's conclusion that we can now see that Berkeley's criticism of contemporary materialist philosophy was "ultimately ineffectual and irrelevant." That is, I do not believe that Berkeley's criticism has been shown to reflect a merely dogmatic distinction between the mental and the physical (as she seems to imply), or that is has been discredited by the subsequent development of psychophysiology.

36. See *Principles*, I, sect. 50 (*Works*, II, p. 62):

. . . you will say there have been a great many things explained by matter and motion: take away these, and you destroy the whole corpuscular philosophy, and undermine those mechanical principles which have been applied with so much success to account for the phenomena. . . . To this I answer, that there is not any one phenomenon explained on that supposition, which may not as well be explained without it. . . . To explain the phenomena, is all one as to shew, why upon such and such occasions we are affected with such and such ideas. But how matter should operate on a spirit, or produce any idea in it, is what no philosopher will pretend to explain.

See also *Philosophical Commentaries*, sect. 476, ed. A. A. Luce (London: Thomas Nelson and Sons, 1944), p. 161.

37. Cf. *Principles*, I, sect. 25, and I, sect. 102, *Works*, II, pp. 51-52, 85.

38. Third Dialogue, ibid., p. 257.

39. *Principles*, I, sects. 58ff. and 103, ibid., pp. 65ff., 86. Compare *Philosophical Commentaries*, sects. 71 and 403, in Luce, ed., pp. 19 and 131. (See also Stroud, "Berkeley v. Locke," pp. 158-59.) As the first of the two passages from the *Commentaries* suggests, Berkeley felt that the mechanists were faced with certain problems in merely understanding *physical* causality, problems that his system avoided. Probably he had in mind, for instance, some of Locke's statements about the incomprehensibility of cohesion on materialist principles: cf. Wilson, "Superadded Properties," p. 149.

40. Cf. Mandelbaum, "Locke's Realism," p. 3.

41. *Principles*, I, sect. 65 and 102, *Works*, II, pp. 69, 85; *Philosophical Commentaries*, sect. 533, in Luce, ed., p. 185. See also Garber's detailed discussion, this volume.

42. "Locke's Realism," p. 3.

43. Ibid.

44. Alexander, "Boyle and Locke," in Tipton, ed., p. 75.

45. At least those discussed in this paper. Jonathan Bennett's defense of the distinction does not focus on the issue of explanatory adequacy, and to this extent avoids completely any problem about body-mind causation: cf. his *Locke, Berkeley, Hume: Central Themes* (Oxford: Oxford University Press, 1971).

46. As becomes clear in a later chapter, Mackie does see a problem about "reducing" phenomenal properties or sensations to states of matter: see *Problems From Locke*, pp. 167ff.

47. "Locke and Boyle," p. 76.

48. Alexander also concedes at the end of his article that he has not "dealt adequately with Berkeley's conclusion from his various arguments that the idea of matter is unintelligible." It seems, then, that Alexander concedes in conclusion that there is *a good deal* that is relevant, if not powerful, in Berkeley's attack on Locke's distinction, and the "idea of matter" that is tied to it.

V Space and Time

9

The Spaces of Berkeley's World

Gary Thrane

I

In a rightly admired[1] passage in the second of the *Three Dialogues Between Hylas and Philonous*, Philonous vividly conjures up various conceptions of the spatial universe.

> How vivid and radiant is the lustre of the fixed stars! How magnificent and rich that negligent profusion, with which they appear to be scattered throughout the whole azure vault! Yet if you take the telescope, it brings into your sight a new host of stars that escape the naked eye. Here they seem contiguous and minute, but to a nearer view immense orbs of light at various distances, far sunk in the abyss of space. Now you must call imagination to your aid. The feeble narrow sense cannot descry innumerable worlds revolving round the central fires; and in those worlds the energy of an all-perfect mind displayed in endless forms. But neither sense nor imagination are big enough to comprehend the boundless extent with all its glittering furniture. Though the labouring mind exert and strain each power to its utmost reach, there still stands out ungrasped a surplusage immeasurable. (*Dialogues*, II)[2]

There is described here the space of ordinary sight, that presented by the telescope, that of imagination, and the space of understanding. "What treatment," Philonous asks, "do those philosophers deserve, who would deprive these noble and delightful scenes of all reality?"

If these passages are any indication, Berkeley recognized the importance of an adequate theory of space. And he does devote a fair portion of his writings to problems connected with space. Yet it can be plausibly argued that, as one commentator puts it, "Berkeley has no positive theory of space at all. . . ."[3] In this paper I will try to give an account of the spaces of Berkeley's world. But before beginning this project, it will be of value to review the reasons for Berkeley's special concerns with the nature of space.

II

One of Berkeley's concerns was theological. The new mechanics was often linked with (what Berkeley regarded as) heretical views concerning the relation of God and space. In the *Principles of Human Knowledge*, he refers to "that dangerous dilemma . . . of thinking either that real space is God, or else that there is something beside God which is eternal, uncreated, infinite, indivisible, immutable. Both which may justly be thought pernicious and absurd notions" (*Principles*, sect. 117). Such views were fairly widespread.[4] Indeed, while Berkeley was in Newport, Samuel Johnson, Berkeley's American correspondent, wrote concerning the passage quoted at the start of this paper, "I don't know how to understand you any otherwise than I understood Sir Isaac, when he uses the like expressions."[5] Johnson goes on to describe his understanding of and agreement with Newton when he describes space as "God's boundless sensorium".[6]

A closely connected reason for Berkeley's worries was the *activity* that Newton seemed to ascribe to space. For Newton, space is active insofar as the dynamical properties of matter are a function of their relation to absolute space. Thus, in Newton's system, absolute space has the features that Berkeley found objectionable in the new physics' description of matter. The attack on matter was only half the battle; absolute and imperceptible space, too, had to be banished.

Everyone is familiar with Berkeley's rejection of matter; few are aware of his rejection of space. From antiquity, however, irreligious materialism has been associated with the doctrine of the void. For the Epicurean, Lucretius, it is not God "in whom we live, and move, and have our being."[7] Rather, it is quite literally the boundless and bottomless pit down which course the mindless atoms.

The new mechanics was inseparably connected with the development of the calculus. Here, again, Berkeley thought error abounded. If the new physics seemed to require the infinitely large void, the new mathematics seemed to require the "infinitesimal," the infinitely small. But Berkeley was quite sure that no one could frame an idea of either an infinitely large or an infinitely small space. In his notebook, he writes, "Our idea we call extension neither way capable of infinity. i.e. neither infinitely small or great" (*Commentaries*, sect. 14).

It must be remembered, too, that the Cartesians made pure extension the essence of matter. Here geometry becomes the science of matter, whereas for Newton geometry is the science of pure space. In either case, geometry (whether as science of void or of plenum) seems incompatible with the metaphysics that Berkeley advocates. It becomes his project, therefore, to show the baselessness of this glorification of geometry.[8]

The idea of space is also a favorite example of an abstract idea. Some philosophers held that the idea of space was common to both the sense of touch and the sense of sight. If this were so, it would count as an important argument for the existence of abstract ideas. The Molyneux problem,[9] which turns on this issue, therefore, looms large for Berkeley.

Finally, the doctrine of immaterialism was resisted by the common-sense experience of *seeing* that there was a space external to oneself. So important a stumbling block did this seem to Berkeley that he devoted his first important work to removing it. The principal doctrine of the *Essay Towards a New Theory of Vision* is that it is not true that sight presents us with any idea of an external, three-dimensional space. In the *Principles* he explains,

> Some perhaps may think the sense of seeing doth furnish them with the idea of pure space; but it is plain from what we have elsewhere shown, that the ideas of space and distance are not obtained by that sense. See the *Essay concerning Vision*. (*Principles*, sect. 116)

In both of his popular works, the *Three Dialogues* and *Alciphron*, Berkeley carefully rehearses the arguments that purport to show that the idea of space does not come from vision. Ordinary folks tend to be quite sure that they just *see* that there is an independently existing external world.

III. The Spaces of Science

In recent times, Berkeley's discussion of Newton's doctrine of absolute space has received a great deal of attention.[10] Indeed, as Jessop concludes, "We must say that he was the only outstanding *modernist* thinker of his period in the British Isles who remained free from the powerful spell of Newton";[11] and A. N. Whitehead remarks, "Quite at the commencement of the [scientific] epoch, he made all the right criticisms, at least in principle."[12] Although Berkeley did not publish his full critique, *De Motu*, until 1721, fifteen years earlier he had posed the problem in the first pages of his notebook.

> N Qu: how to reconcile Newton's 2 sorts of motion with my doctrine. (*Commentaries*, sect. 30)

As is well known, Berkeley rejected the idea of absolute space and motion. As this is well-trodden ground, I shall content myself here with a brief summary of Berkeley's methodological objections to Newton's absolute space. Berkeley objects to absolute space on the grounds that it is (1) imperceptible, (2) unimaginable, (3) incoherent, and (4) useless.

(1)   By Newton's own account, absolute space is imperceptible; absolute space can only be detected (at best) by its dynamical effects. Indeed, in the "Scholium" to the *Principia*, he claims that his main purpose was to discover how to distinguish "true" from "apparent" motion; as he says, "to this end it was that I composed it."[13] That absolute space is imperceptible in part dictates that it is useless. Berkeley concludes,

> No motion can be recognized or measured, unless through sensible things. Since then absolute space in no way affects the senses, it must necessarily be quite useless for the distinguishing of motions. (*De Motu*, sect. 63)

(2)   Furthermore, that absolute space is imperceptible insures that it will be unimaginable.

> But what sort of extension, I ask, is that which cannot be divided nor measured, no part of which can be perceived by sense or pictured by the imagination? For nothing enters the imagination which from the nature of the thing cannot be perceived by sense, since indeed the imagination is nothing else than the faculty which represents sensible things either actually existing or at least possible. (*De Motu*, sect. 53)

There is no difference between absolute and relative space in either sense or imagination.

(3)   There can be no coherent idea of absolute space. In part this is because such a putative idea is subject to all of the logical absurdities that Berkeley attributes to abstract ideas in general. But I would like to call attention to what is, I think, a more interesting cause of Berkeley's objections. In his notebook he writes,

> M In my doctrine all absurditys from infinite space cease. (*Commentaries*, sect. 90)

In fact, Berkeley thinks absolute space is an incoherent response to the inherently unthinkable. We try to think of infinite space, but we inevitably imagine a finite space. In the *Principles*, Berkeley offers the following diagnosis:

> . . . philosophers who have a greater extent of thought, and juster notions of the system of things, discover even the earth itself to be moved. In order therefore to fix their notions, they seem to conceive the corporeal world as finite, and the utmost walls or shell thereof to be the place, whereby they estimate true motions. If we sound our own conceptions, I believe we may find all the absolute motion we can frame an idea of, to be at bottom no other than relative motion thus defined. For as hath been already observed, absolute motion exclusive of all external relation is incomprehensible. . . . . (*Principles*, sect. 114)[14]

The idea of absolute space is incoherent because it involves the attempt to frame an idea of the infinite.

(4)   Finally, the idea of absolute space is quite unnecessary and useless. For we have available an experimentally equivalent and purely sensible reference frame.

> . . . let two globes be conceived to exist and nothing corporeal besides them. . . . a circular motion of the two globes round a common centre cannot be conceived by the imagination. Then let us suppose that the sky of the fixed stars is created; suddenly from the conception of the approach of the globes to different parts of that sky, the motion will be conceived. (*De Motu*, sect. 59)

Thus there is no need for the idea of absolute space.[15]

Thus Berkeley is very hostile to any abstract idea of space. Instead, he insists, there are only sensible spaces. When we imagine, we inescapably imagine a sensory space. Science cannot coherently presuppose, nor has it a need of, nonsensory space. However, there are sensory spaces that are special to science. There is the telescopic and microscopic world.

In the passage from the *Three Dialogues* quoted at the beginning of this paper, Philonous notes that there is not only the naked eye's view of the night sky but also the view through the telescope. The telescope "brings into your sight a new host of stars that escape the naked eye." So, too, does that other important instrument.

> A microscope brings us, as it were, into a new world: It presents us with a new scene of visible objects quite different from what we behold with the naked eye. But herein consists the most remarkable difference, to wit, that whereas the objects perceived by the eye alone have a certain connexion with tangible objects . . . there is not the like connexion between

things tangible and those visible objects that are perceived be help of a fine microscope. (*New Theory of Vision*, sect. 85)

The tangible connection is, of course, also missing in the case of the astronomical telescope. Nevertheless there can be no doubt that the sights revealed by these two instruments are real enough. For they are perceived. Still, there is a problem about how these views are to be related to ordinary visual experience and to the space of touch.

Berkeley is insistent that the microscope does not reveal anything of the substructure of ordinary visible objects. After all, there is nothing in them that does not appear to be there, since *esse* is *percipi*. It is for this reason that Berkeley is forced into holding that the microscope reveals a new visual space. The relation of the ordinary visual world to the microscopic is not one of containment. And the associations with the tangible realm will be very indirect. So, we learn that if we drink water that produces the swarming visions when placed under the microscope, we will become ill.

Such a doctrine is not totally odd. We do quite naturally use the metaphor of the "microscopic world," the microcosm. And, when in imagination we picture microorganisms, we imagine ourselves to be quite small (or them quite large). It is unclear what it is to imagine the microscopic as *in* the ordinary world. When I imagine hundreds of microbes dancing on the head of a pin, I imagine the pinhead to be very large. Just as the visual field is not enlarged by the microscope, so, too, the imagination can conjure up only various scenes, various worlds; the imagination cannot conjure up the microscopic *as microscopic*.

Still, all of this notwithstanding, Berkeley's doctrine here is less impressive than that concerning absolute space. This theory of the microcosm does not do justice to the conviction of most of us that the substructure of ordinary things in part causally accounts for their macroscopic behavior. So I am convinced that it is the microbe *in* me that causes the sickness. And this, even though I cannot imagine (picture) both the microbes and my own body as contained and container. For Berkeley, of course, none of this matters, since God is the cause of all that happens. But he was clearly aware of the last-described objection. He devotes seven complete sections[16] of the *Principles* to his attempt to convince his reader that there is no causally efficacious substructure to sensible objects.

IV. The Spaces of Reason and Imagination

A reading of the *Commentaries* shows that Berkeley was from the first concerned with the relation of his new principle to mathematics. There were two problems, both concerning the mathematical description of space. On the one hand, the newly discovered calculus seemed to require that infinitesimals (or their equivalent) exist. On the other hand, there was the ancient fact that Euclidean geometry required that there be no smallest length. One of the earliest entries in the *Commentaries* is this:

+ Diagonal incommensurable wth ye side Quaere how this can be in my doctrine. (*Commentaries*, sect. 29. Cf. sects. 263, 264.)

In the end Berkeley concluded that it could not be in his doctrine. In a much later entry in the *Commentaries*, we find the following delightful reminder:

X Mem: upon all occasion to use the Utmost Modesty. to Confute the Mathematicians wth the utmost civility & respect. not to stile them Nihilarians etc. (sect. 633)

To see why Berkeley has to "confute the mathematicians," the space that satisfies Euclidean geometry must be considered. I will call this space "mathematical space." Such a space is a continuum. In any given extension there is an (uncountable) infinity of points. Now, this space is a formal space. Its properties are dictated by geometrical principles. We do not observe incommensurable lengths (how could we?). Rather, the Pythagorean theorem requires that, if there be lengths, there be incommensurable lengths.[17] No matter that such a requirement seems "irrational." No formal contradiction results from assuming the existence of such lengths. And, despite such darkling features, geometry was viewed by virtually everyone as the paradigmatic science. A Descartes or a Spinoza believed real space to be described by geometry and dreamed of a general understanding of the world *in more geometrico*. Such a pure understanding was incompatible with Berkeley's empiricism. In his notebook Berkeley writes, "Ridiculous in the Mathematicians to despise sense" (*Commentaries*, sect. 317). Three entries precedent, Berkeley had finally concluded, "Most certainly no finite Extension divisible ad Infinitum" (sect. 314).

Berkeley is driven to such a conclusion because he is convinced that to be is to be perceived. If space exists, all of its existent parts must be perceived. But since we do not perceive an infinite number of points, there cannot be an infinite number of points. But geometry requires that its lines be continuous. For example, to say that the diagonal of a square is incommensurable with the side is to say that there is no "tiny" unit such that a certain integral number of such units will make the diagonal while a certain other integral number of such units will make the side. However small a unit we choose, there is still no fitting an integral number of them into both the side and the diagonal of a square. Geometry rules out minima. Yet Berkeley's metaphysics requires such entities.

Thus Berkeley concludes that mathematical space cannot be sensibly said to exist. What is neither perceivable nor imaginable cannot be. Hence, he begins to write in his notebook,

> X Geometry not conversant about our compleat determin'd ideas of figures, for these are not divisible ad infinitum. (*Commentaries*, sect. 248)

> X The Diagonal is commensurable with the Side. (sect. 264)

> X I say there are no incommensurables, no surds . . . tis impossible 10 points should compose a square . . . the number of points must necessarily be a square number whose side is easily assignable. (sect. 469)

When he comes to the composition of the *Principles*, he urges,

> Every particular finite extension, which may possibly be the object of our thought, is an *idea* existing only in the mind, and consequently each part thereof must be perceived. If therefore I cannot perceive innumerable parts in any finite extension that I consider, it is certain they are not contained in it: but it is evident, that I cannot distinguish innumerable parts in any particular line, surface, or solid, which I either perceive by sense, or figure to myself in my mind: wherefore I conclude they are not contained in it. (sect. 124)

Berkeley chooses his new principle over the standard interpretation[18] of geometry. There are no infinite arrays in thought or perception. Therefore, either to be is not in fact to be perceived or a continuous infinite array of points cannot even exist in thought. Berkeley does not ignore the dilemma. He chooses his principle and forthrightly rejects the fashionable infinitesimals.

It would be a mistake to think that Berkeley rejected all reasoning about infinity. One of his earliest extant works, composed apparently for a philosophical discussion group, is "Of Infinites." In this very brief work, Berkeley cites[19] with approval a passage in Locke's *Essay*, then applies the distinction to the writings of various mathematicians. The passage in Locke's *Essay* continues,

> . . . therefore I think it is not an insignificant subtilty, if I say, that we are carefully to distinguish between the idea of the infinity of space, and the idea of a space infinite. The first is nothing but a supposed endless

progression of the mind, over what repeated ideas of space it pleases; but to have actually in the mind the idea of a space infinite, is to suppose the mind already passed over, and actually to have a view of *all* those repeated ideas of space which an *endless* repitition can never totally represent to it; which carries in it a plain contradiction.[20]

We can imagine that at any point in a progression (any number in a series) there is yet another point (number). But to imagine the whole (infinite) progression is not possible.

Berkeley's thinking about infinite divisibility is roughly similar. We cannot imagine that a finite length consists of an infinite set of points. But we can imagine any particular proportion of a line that we care to imagine. In the *Commentaries*, Berkeley explains how.

> X Suppose an inch represent a mile. $1/1000$ of an inch is nothing, but $1/1000$ of y^e mile represented is something therefore $1/1000$ of an inch tho' nothing is not to be neglected, because it represents something i.e. $1/1000$ of a mile. (sect. 260)

We can imagine any proportion of a line we wish simply by imagining that the line is long enough. It is this reasoning that leads Berkeley to say that to *imagine* a line consisting of infinitesimal points is to imagine a line infinitely long.

> In proportion therefore as the sense is rendered more acute, it perceives a greater number of parts in the object, that is, the object appears greater, and its figure varies. . . . And at length, after various changes of size and shape, when the sense becomes infinitely acute, the body shall seem infinite. (*Principles*, sect. 47)

In practice, then, we can think in terms of the smallest proportion that matters.

Because it is senseless on Berkeley's view to suppose that mathematical space exists, Berkeley concludes that geometry is not pure mathematics if it is really concerned with space. Toward the end of the *Commentaries*, he writes,

> X Qu: whether Geometry may not be properly reckon'd among Mixt Mathematics. Arithmetic and Algebra being the only abstracted pure i.e. entirely Nominal. Geometry being the application of these to points. (sect. 770)

Berkeley apparently settled on this view: insofar as geometry is about the world of things, it must treat of sensibly assignable sizes and is not pure mathematics. It is only partly (roughly) interpretable as about *real* points. In *The Analyst* (1734), Berkeley asks, in the second of the concluding queries,

> Whether the end of geometry be not to measure assignable finite extension? And whether this practical view did not first put men on the study of geometry? (qu. 2)

As for "pure" geometry, it is not about any space. There is no coherent idea of mathematical space. And, if pure geometry is not about any space, then it is purely formal. As Euphranor concludes,

> If I mistake not, all sciences, so far as they are universal and demonstrable by human reason, will be found conversant about signs as their immediate object, though these in the application are referred to things (*Alciphron*, bk. VIII, sect. 13)

Such a view is very different from the standard interpretation of geometry. For geometry, in contrast with arithmetic and other forms of mathematics, is usually conceived of as drawing especially on our power of visualization. It may be hard to understand the nature of the intuitions that support arithmetic; but we *see* (with the inner eye) that the basic propositions of geometry must be so. Thus, for example, Weyl remarks,

> In addition to the physical space one may acknowledge the existence of a *space of intuition* and maintain that its metrical structure of necessity satisfies Euclidean geometry.[21]

Such a Kantian view is still widely held. In Berkeley's day proofs in geometry often required the visualization of transport and congruence.

But it is by no means clear that our spatial visualizations must conform to Euclidean geometry. As Reichenbach notes, "The visualizations of Euclidean geometry should by no means be taken for granted. . . ."[22] Mental images tend to be vague and indeterminate. And it seems more likely that we picture in accordance with geometrical principles rather than draw our geometrical principles from the way we must picture. (In Reichenbach's language, there is a "logical" rather than a "visual compulsion."[23]) Although it is sometimes claimed that we cannot visualize non-Euclidean geometries, this, too, is suspect.

Berkeley does not find in imagined (visualized) space anything that could serve as the support or even interpretation of Euclidean geometry. Imagined space is derived from our visual experiences.

[1]X[1] A man born Blind would not imagine Space as we do. we give it always some dilute or dark color. in short we imagine it as visible

or intromitted by the Eye wch he would not do. (*Commentaries*, sect. 454)

Visualized space is subject to all of the features of the space of vision. We cannot visualize a line as consisting of an infinite number of points any more than we can see such a line. Further, the visualization of an object is only partial and incomplete. This is a feature of visual space, too. In his notebook Berkeley notes,

> ^{1}X^3 Qu: if there be not two kinds of visible extension. one perceiv'd by a confus'd view, the other by a distinct successive direction of the optique axis to each point. (sect. 400)

Neither the visual field nor the objects of visualization have the transcendental clarity that is sometimes claimed for them.

Furthermore, visualized objects must be visualized from a point of view. What would it be like to visualize, say, a cube, but not from a point of view? Various problems of deformation of figure under transport will therefore occur (see next section). Indeed, the example of the man born blind and this last reflection make it clear that it is not unthinkable that there be no visual space. Even the sighted person can ask himself if there is a visual space *behind* his head. Visual space (as well as space in visualization) just is distinct from the abstract space required by Euclidean geometry.

I conclude that there is justice in Berkeley's claim that the truth of Euclidean geometry is neither insured nor illustrated by our visualizations. But it is hard to follow Berkeley all the way. As G. J. Warnock writes,

> It seems clear that Berkeley is really committed to wreaking more havoc in geometry than he recognized. . . . At best some parts of geometry could be regarded as roughly true; but much of it would have to be rejected as false, much as dubious, and much as nonsense.[24]

Still, it is not clear yet exactly what status to accord "pure" geometry. As uninterpreted, formal system, geometry is nonsense. And it is not clear that physical space can interpret geometry. Is physical space continuous? What operational definition can be given to the notion of incommensurability in real, practical measurement?[25] These questions are still not definitively answered.

Before moving on to Berkeley's doctrine concerning sensory space, it may be useful to consider his theory of the *minimum sensible*. As has been seen, Berkeley holds that sensible objects can have only a finite number of parts. If so, there must be minimal parts. Also, he apparently reasons that (infinitesimal) mathematical points cannot ever add up to real space.

^{2}X^1 No stated ideas of length without a minimum. (*Commentaries*, sect. 88)

Again, Berkeley would have to reject the dimensionless, mathematical point as self-contradictory. Or he may well have thought of the obvious fact that our eyes are not perfectly acute. Perhaps he thought of the stars in the night sky or reasoned along the lines Hume does when he concludes that there must be *minima*.[26] The *minimum sensibile* also does for sensory space what Newton's absolute space is to do for physical space. The *minimum* provides an intrinsic metric for sensory space.[27]

Although there are a number of arguments in support of *minima sensibilia*, they are also subject to sundry objections. The doctrine of *minima* is a favorite of commentators; it is not hard to devise difficulties. Many of these puzzles are from geometry and are forestalled by Berkeley's claim that geometry does not apply to the sensible realm. In other cases it is not so clear that the doctrine escapes.

One interesting objection that does not involve geometry is Armstrong's. He urges that "surfaces look continuous, and if they look continuous, then, on Berkeley's view, what is immediately perceived *is* continuous and so not made up of minima."[28] Berkeley considers this problem in his notebook[29] and in the *Essay Towards a New Theory of Vision* he writes,

> The visive faculty . . . may be found to labour of two defects. . . . It can take in at one view but a certain number of *minima visibilia*, beyond which it cannot extend its prospect. *Secondly*, our sight is defective in that its view is not only narrow, but also for the most part confused . . . and the more we fix our sight on any one object, by so much the darker and more indistinct shall the rest appear (sect. 83)

Although our powers of attention are undoubtedly limited, this does not seem to be an adequate account. But Berkeley is not alone in having difficulties here. Those who are inclined to subscribe to the so-called "Constancy Hypothesis" have a similar problem. The photosensitive surface of the eye, the retina, consists of discrete nerve endings. Thus, one nineteenth-century theorist concludes, "The utmost I can really see is a panorama painted in mosaic."[30] And leaving aside the constancy hypothesis, if experiences are understood in the strictest materialist way as brain states, still how can such discrete states exhibit "the continuous character of an expanse of red"? The problem of continuous experiential contents resulting from a finite number of discrete states remains unresolved.[31]

V. The Spaces of Sense

Berkeley tells us (*Principles*, sect. 116), that the reason he composed his *New Theory of Vision* was to combat the "vulgar" belief that we see external space. Berkeley was well aware of the very natural belief that we just *see* that there is a world of external and independently existing objects. Convincing his readers of the immaterialism of sight was an important first step in his general program. To establish the immaterialism of sight, it sufficed to establish that we do not see "into" external space. Accordingly, the immaterialism of sight is established by arguments designed to show that we get from sight no idea of external space (or "outness," as Berkeley quaintly calls it).

The nature and validity of these arguments have been much discussed in the literature, and as I have discussed these at length elsewhere,[32] I will not do so here. Instead, I will here concentrate on the spatial character of the visual field according to Berkeley. As has been seen, Berkeley claims that there is no relation between the objects of vision and Euclidean geometry. He is quite aware that this is bound to seem very peculiar.

> Some things there are which at first sight incline one to think geometry conversant about visible extension. . . . It would, without doubt, seem odd to a mathematician to go about to convince him the diagrams he saw upon paper were not the figures, or even the likeness of the figures, which make the subject of the demonstrations. . . . It being by them assigned as one reason of the extraordinary clearness and evidence of geometry that in this science the reasonings are free from those inconveniences which attend the use of arbitrary signs, the very ideas themselves being copied out and exposed to view upon paper. (*New Theory of Vision*, sect. 150)

Nonetheless, Berkeley goes on to insist in the same section that "visible extension and figures are not the object of geometry."

There are a number of reasons for holding a view initially so counterintuitive. First, the visual field is only clear and distinct at its "center." Figures taking up any considerable part of the visual field must be scanned if their parts are each to be seen clearly.[33] Visible figures, then, lack the precision to be treated by geometry. Another important reason for thinking that the visual field is unsuitable for treatment by geometry is that there are no "rigid rods" in the visual field. Objects are foreshortened and deformed by perspective. There is no guaranteed congruence of visual objects after transport; indeed, the usual case is that change of position means change of shape.

> . . . a visible inch is itself no constant determinate magnitude and cannot therefore serve to mark out and determine the magnitude of any other thing. (*New Theory of Vision*, sect. 61[34])

Thus, Berkeley concludes,

> All that is properly perceived by the visive faculty amounts to no more than colours, with their variations and different proportions of light and shade: But the perpetual mutability and fleetingness of those immediate objects of sight render them incapable of being managed after the manner of geometrical figures . . . (sect. 156)

The visual field, then, is a two-dimensional manifold filled with ephemeral and constantly deforming color expanses. But, those expanses, as Berkeley makes quite clear, are neither planes nor solids: ". . . plains are no more the immediate object of sight than solids" (*New Theory of Vision*, sect. 158). The reason for this is that we can get no idea of a third dimension from sight on Berkeley's theory; and yet "some idea of distance is necessary to form the idea of a geometrical plain, as will appear to whoever shall reflect a little on it" (sect. 155).

Visual space is very odd. In the usual sense it is not space at all. It is two-dimensional, but it has no determinate "shape" in a third dimension.[35] Its relation to the space of touch is purely associative. Visual space is naturally isotropic; it has no natural orientation. There is no intrinsic "up" or "down" in the visual field; the visual field is "free-floating" and is not oriented with respect to tactile space.[36]

Still the visual field is a kind of space; it has describable topological features. But the very abstract geometry that describes such a space will not be Euclidean geometry. Ernst Mach, carrying on in the Berkeleyan tradition, concludes, "Visual space resembles the space of metageometry rather than that of Euclid."[37] Such a "space" is not space in the ordinary sense.

Because the space of sight is so odd, there is only one plausible source remaining as the origin of the idea of (three-dimensional) space: touch. In his notebook Berkeley writes,

> X· Geometry seems to have for its object tangible extension, figures & motion & not visible. (*Commentaries*, sect. 101)

The *New Theory of Vision* takes for granted that, through the sense of touch, we are presented with externally existing, three-dimensional objects. In the *Principles*, Berkeley makes clear that tangible objects, too, are mind-dependent. But can space be a tactile idea? As George Stack argues, "Obviously not, since space is, by its very nature, intangible."[38] Berkeley himself seems to draw this very conclusion:

> And perhaps, if we inquire narrowly, we shall find we cannot even frame an idea of *pure Space exclusive of all body*. This I must confess seems impossible, as being a most abstract idea. When I excite a motion in some part of my body, if it be free or without resistance, I say there is *Space*. But if I find a resistance, then I say there is *Body*: and in proportion as the resistance to motion is lesser or greater, I say the space is more or less *pure*. So that when I speak of pure or empty space, it is not to be supposed that the word *space* stands for an idea distinct from, or conceivable without, body and motion. When, therefore, supposing all the world to be annihilated besides my own body, I say there still remains *pure Space*; thereby nothing else is meant but only that I conceive it possible for the limbs of my body to be moved on all sides without the least resistance: but if that too were annihilated then there could be no motion, and consequently no space. (*Principles*, sect. 116)[39]

It appears then that, from an epistemological point of view, motion is not to be defined in terms of space. Rather, what are first given in experience are kinesthetic sensations and the sensations of localization that tell a man that his hand, say, is moving relative to his torso.[40] It is the perception of motion, then, that is primitive. This view is to be found early in his notebook.

> M Space not imaginable by any idea receiv'd from sight, not imaginable, without body moving not even then necessarily existing (I speak of infinite Space) for w^t the body has past may be conceived annihilated. (*Commentaries*, sect. 135)

As will soon be seen, Berkeley still holds this view of "pure" space in the much later *De Motu*.

There is no escaping the obvious consequence of Berkeley's new principle: every perceived extension must be *filled*. There is no feeling what is not there. Since to be is to be perceived, there can be no such thing (idea) as empty space. Analogously, there is no seeing empty space, either. All seen spaces are visibly filled. We cannot see what is not there. In another way we see here why the visual field is bidimensional for Berkeley. Every line of sight terminates at a surface. Solids, therefore, cannot be seen.

Berkeley often used the *Gedankenexperiment* of being blind from birth (*à la* Molyneux's question) to clarify his thinking about the relation of touch and sight. It is, indeed, vision that most leads us to think we perceive *empty* space spread out around us. But a man born blind would likely give Berkeley's hypothetical account of (pure) empty space. In any case, there is no escaping the fact that Berkeley holds this view. In *De Motu*, he again emphasizes this account.

> We are sometimes deceived by the fact that when we imagine the removal of all other bodies, yet we suppose our own body to remain. On this supposition we imagine the movement of our limbs fully free on every side; but motion without space cannot be conceived. None the less if we consider the matter again we shall find, 1st, relative space conceived defined by the parts of our body; 2nd, a fully free power of moving our limbs obstructed by no obstacle; and besides these two things nothing. It is false to believe that some third thing really exists, *viz.* immense space which confers on us the free power of moving our body; for this purpose the absence of other bodies is sufficient. And we must admit that this absence or privation of bodies is nothing positive. (*De Motu*, sect. 55)

Thus, Berkeley refuses to admit the concept of "container" space. Instead, pure space is to be understood as an "absence or privation" and "nothing positive." Quite clearly, then, we have not yet gotten a positive idea of real space. From this last passage it is clear that real space is "relative space conceived defined by the parts of our body." But nowhere does Berkeley explain in any detail what he means by this. We are forced to eke out an account.

There are, in fact, a number of ways in which spatial relations can be thought of as presented in experience. First, a human being knows where the parts of his body are. We "sense" where our hands and feet are; we need not look at our feet as we dance. The contortions of the body, the way it is "shaped" in space, is itself something felt, something given in experience. My knowledge of how my body is "arranged" in space is a presentation of a three-dimensional array.

Second, there are sensations felt throughout the body. These sensations, from headache to foot cramp, also constitute a three-dimensional presentation. The case of the amputee shows that it is possible to feel pain as being "out there." In a way, there is nothing especially mysterious about vision in this regard. Just as a question can be raised about how I come to position my visual sensations *out there*, so, too, we may wonder how we come to localize our tactile sensations as occurring here and there in the body. In the end it is equally odd that I localize my visual experience of the chair *over there* as that I localize my foot cramp in that region of space that (as it happens) is occupied by my foot. Still, we know that those born blind make such localizations; but if we consider a purely visual intelligence, as does Berkeley (*New Theory of Vision*, sects. 153ff.), it seems unlikely that he will be able to "place" his visual sensations. Hence the priority of touch.

Yet another presentation connected with the idea of space is our sense of balance. For we also "feel" our body's total orientation. In Berkeley's discussion of retinal inversion, it is important that the field of touch is oriented (is not isotropic), whereas the visual field has no natural, unlearned orientation (*Theory of Vision . . . Vindicated*, sect. 146). The prejudice against the antipodes shows how deep is the intuition that we sense the *downward direction of space*.[41]

Finally, and most important, are the surface sensations. These are the touchings of "external" things. Now, touch, unlike vision and the other senses, is proprioceptive: when we feel objects, we also feel the part of our body that is in contact. Moreover, these touchings must be oriented in various ways. That is, when we hold, say, a ball in our hand, we feel tactile sensations all along the surface of the hand. And these sensations are themselves oriented in a space. (The great Helmholtz, often seen as being in the Berkeleyan tradition, apparently thought the idea of the third dimension could be derived from the sensations of the hand grasping an object.[42]

Berkeley's only real three-dimensional space is on and under the skin. But it is not clear that the space of tactile sensation is really Euclidean. Ernst Mach, who took this whole project very seriously, refers to the "great anomalies of the skin's spatial sense as against metrical space."[43] He notes that,

> The distance between two points of a compass at which contact in two adjacent places can just be distinguished is 50–60 times smaller on the tip of the tongue than in the middle of the back. The parts of the skin show large gradations of spatial sensitivity.[44]

Indeed, Mach concludes, "To the skin's space there corresponds a two-dimensional, finite unbounded (closed) Riemann space."[45] Berkeley did not foresee such difficulties. Yet he was surely aware of problems concerning the *minimum tangibile*. The spaces of Berkeley's world are constricted and "odd."

At the start of this paper I cited Philonous's brilliant description of the universe as a "boundless extent with all its glittering furniture." But Berkeley would lead us from the infinite universe to the closed world of our sensations. *In reality*, space is confined beneath the integument. In *Siris*, Berkeley refers to real, external space as "that phantom of the mechanic and geometrical philosophers" (*Siris*, sect. 271). And he urges that real spaces are "in truth but hypotheses, nor can they be the objects of real science" (sect. 293). Finally, he concludes,

> And though the moderns teach that space is real and infinitely extended, yet, if we consider that it is no intellectual notion, nor yet perceived by any of our senses, we shall perhaps be inclined to think . . . that this is also . . . spurious reasoning, and a kind of waking dream. (sect. 318)

External space thus goes the way of matter.

Many have noted that Berkeley's arguments seem to turn on supposing the existence of what he tries to deny. His arguments concerning the nature of the visual field seem to be a function of knowledge concerning the physiology of the eye. And it can be argued that Berkeley's reasonings concerning space presuppose the existence of the very space he seems at pains to deny.[46] As one philosopher concerned with surface irritations notes, "even as we try to recapture the data, in all their innocence of interpretation, we find ourselves depending upon sidelong glances into natural science."[47]

Still, it can be argued that Berkeley's arguments are best viewed as *reductio ad absurdum* arguments. They are meant to show the mere *formality* of science and mathematics. But true understanding of the world occurs "when we enter the province of the *philosophia prima*, we discover another order of beings, mind and its acts, permanent being . . . " (*Siris*, sect. 293). But, here, too, there are difficulties aplenty. Samuel Johnson, Berkeley's American critic, objects,

> You allow spirits to have a real existence external to one another. Methinks, if so, there must be distance between them and space wherein they exist, or else they must all exist in one individual spot or point, and as it were coincide with another. I can't see how external space and duration are any more abstract ideas than spirits. (*Works*, II, p. 276)

Just as one can wonder how the unextended mind can "contain" extended ideas, so too one may wonder "where" minds exist. It is here that Berkeley is likely to seem the most foreign to the modern critic. For Berkeley would surely reply that it is not in space but "in Him we live, and move, and have our being."

Notes

1. Samuel Johnson, Berkeley's American correspondent, wrote to Berkeley during his sojourn in Newport, R.I., referring to the passage quoted as "that most beautiful and charming description" (Letter of Feb. 5, 1729/30; see *Works*, II, p. 287).

2. All references to the works of Berkeley are to A. A. Luce and T. E. Jessop, eds., *The Works of George Berkeley, Bishop of Cloyne*, 9 vols. (London: Thomas Nelson and Sons, 1948-57); hereafter *Works*. The quotation from the *Dialogues* is in *Works*, vol. II, pp. 210-11.

3. George J. Stack, "Berkeley's New Theory of Vision," *The Personalist* 51, 1 (1970): 133.

4. Berkeley certainly had specific philosophers in mind. In the *Philosophical Commentaries*, he notes that "Locke, More, Raphson, *et al.* seem to make God extended" (sect. 298). For more, see "The Divinization of Space" in Alexander Koyré's *From the Closed World to the Infinite Universe* (New York: Harper Torchbooks, 1958), pp. 190ff.

5. Johnson, Letter of Feb. 5, 1729/30. In his reply, Berkeley mentions Raphson as well as Newton and remarks, "As to Space. I have no notion of any but that which is relative" (see *Works*, II, p. 292).

6. Johnson wrote, "External space and duration therefore I take to be those properties or attributes in God, to which our ideas, which we signify by those names, are correspondent, and of which they are the faint shadows. This I take to be Sir Isaac Newton's meaning when he says, *Scol. General. Deus — durat semper et adest ubique et existendo semper et ubique, durationem et spacium, aeternitatem et infinitatem constituit"* (*Works*, II, p. 292, n. 5).

7. The remark of St. Paul's was certainly Berkeley's favorite scriptural citation. See *Principles*, sect. 149, and *Dialogues* (*Works*, II, p. 214). The quotation was often construed by the followers of Newton as supporting his doctrine. See Koyré, *From the Closed World*, pp. 227 and 270. For the connection with ancient atheism, see *Siris*, sect. 271.

8. In *Commentaries*, sect. 425, Berkeley notes, "Aristotle as good a Man as Euclid but He was allow'd to have been mistaken."

9. Molyneux's problem was this: Would a man born blind, his sight restored, be able to distinguish a sphere from a cube? See *New Theory of Vision*, sect. 132.

10. See, for example, Karl Popper, "A Note on Berkeley as a Precursor of Mach and Einstein," in *Conjectures and Refutations* (New York: Harper Torchbooks, 1968); G. J. Whitrow, "Berkeley's Critique of the Newtonian Analysis of Motion", *Hermathena* 82 (November 1953); 90-112; John Myhill, "Berkeley's *De Motu* — An Anticipation of Mach," in *George Berkeley* (Berkeley: University of California Press, 1957); W. A. Suchting, "Berkeley's Criticism of Newton on Space and Motion," *Isis* 58 (1967): 186-97. Finally, one should note the excellent discussions in Koyré's work (cited in n. 4) and in Max Jammer, *Concepts of Space* (New York: Harper Torchbooks, 1960).

11. T. E. Jessop, "Berkeley and the Contemporary Physics," *Revue Internationale de Philosophie* 7, 23-24 (1953): 89.

12. *Science and the Modern World* (New York: Mentor Books, 1958), p. 67.

13. Isaac Newton, *Mathematical Principles of Natural Philosophy* (Berkeley: University of California Press, 1934), p. 545.

14. Absolute space is sometimes called "container space." See Adolf Grünbaum, *Philosophical Problems of Space and Time* (New York: Alfred A. Knopf, 1963), p. 4.

15. Berkeley's argument here may be styled a *kinematic* one; Berkeley does not contest that there would be a tension in a rope joining the two globes. Still, as many have noticed, Berkeley's view here is very close to the *dynamical* critique of Ernst Mach. As Mach remarks of Newton's bucket experiment, "No one is competent to say how the experiment would turn out if the sides of the vessel . . . [were] several leagues thick." (*The Science of Mechanics* [Lasalle, Ill.: The Open Court Publishing Company, 1960], p. 284) So, too, no one can say whether there would be a tension in the rope.

16. *Principles*, sects. 60-66. See also *Siris*, sect. 283.

17. Thus Berkeley concludes, ". . . the Pythagoric theorem [is] false" (*Commentaries*, sect. 500).

18. In the first two editions of the *New Theory of Vision*, Berkeley describes his thinking about geometry as "most anxious" and describes his conclusions as "far out of the common road of geometry . . . in an age, wherein that science hath received such mighty improvements by new methods. . . ." See *New Theory of Vision*, sect. 159.

19. *Works*, IV, p. 235.

20. John Locke, *An Essay Concerning Human Understanding* (New York: Dover Publications, 1959), p. 281 (vol. I, bk. II, chap. XVII, sect. 7).

21. Hermann Weyl, *Philosophy of Mathematics and Natural Science* (Princeton: Princeton University Press, 1949), p. 135.

22. Hans Reichenbach, *The Philosophy of Space and Time* (New York: Dover Publications Inc., 1957), p. 38.

23. Ibid., pp. 37-43.

24. *Berkeley* (Baltimore: Penguin Books, 1953), p. 209.

25. See, for example, Carl Hempel's discussion of the diagonal of the square and operational definitions in "Empiricist Criteria of Cognitive Significance." *Aspects of Scientific Explanation* (New York: The Free Press, 1965), pp. 110-11.

26. David Hume, *A Treatise of Human Nature* (Oxford: The Clarendon Press, 1960), p. 27. Hume writes, "Put a spot of ink upon paper, fix your eye upon that spot, and retire to such a distance, that at last you lose sight of it; 'tis plain, that the moment before it vanish'd the image or impression was perfectly indivisible."

27. Cf. Grünbaum, *Space and Time*, p. 6.

28. D. M. Armstrong, *Berkeley's Theory of Vision* (Parkville, Victoria: Melbourne University Press, 1960), p. 44.

29. Cf. *Commentaries*, sect. 321.

30. The remark is from W. K. Clifford. Cited by Nicholas Pastore in *Selective History of Theories of Visual Perception* (New York: Oxford University Press, 1971), p. 181.

31. The problem of the continuous expanse of red is discussed by Thomas Natsoulas in his "Subjective, Experiential Element in Perception," *Images, Perception and Knowledge* (Boston: D. Reidel Publishing Company, 1974), pp. 241-49.

32. "Berkeley's Proper Object of Vision," *Journal of the History of Ideas* XXXVIII, 2 (April-June 1977): 243-60.

33. See *New Theory of Vision*, sect. 83.

34. Cf. *Dialogues*, in *Works*, II, p. 189; and *Commentaries*, sect. 514-16.

35. See Gary Thrane, "The Proper Object of Vision," *Studies in the History and Philosophy of Science* 6, 1 (1975): 3-41.

36. Cf. Michael Morgan, *Molyneux's Question* (Cambridge: The University Press, 1977), p. 62.

37. *Knowledge and Error* (Boston: D. Reidel Publishing Company, 1976), p. 251.

38. "Berkeley's New Theory of Vision," *The Personalist* 51, 1 (1970): 132.

39. Cf. *Commentaries*, sect. 496.

40. This interpretation is vigorously denied by John Wild in his *George Berkeley* (Cambridge, Mass.: Harvard University Press, 1936), p. 104. There Wild urges that "this 'kinesthetic' theory . . . is . . . a passing phase in the development of his thought." But Wild's view of Berkeley as a proto-Kant seems to me not to be supported by the text.

41. Cf. Mach, *Knowledge and Error*, pp. 261-62.

42. Cf. Pastore, *Selective History*, p. 164.

43. *Knowledge and Error*, p. 252.

44. Loc. cit.

45. Loc. cit.

46. Cf. Colin Turbayne, "Berkeley and Russell on Space," *Dialectica* 8, 3 (1954): 210-27.

47. W. V. O. Quine, *Word and Object* (Cambridge, Mass.: The M.I.T. Press, 1960), p. 2.

10

On Being "Embrangled" By Time

E. J. Furlong

I. The Berkeley–Johnson Correspondence

During the period 1729-1730, four quite long letters passed between George Berkeley and his American friend Samuel Johnson (*Works*, II, pp. 271-94).[1] The first letter from Johnson ranged widely over difficulties that Johnson and a group of friends had found in Berkeley's immaterialism. Berkeley replied at length to this letter. In his second letter, Johnson declares (ibid., p. 285) that he is "content to give up the cause of matter . . . " and he adds that "of all the particulars I troubled you with before, there remain only these that I have any difficulty about, *viz.* archetypes, space and duration, and the *esse* of spirits." Of these topics, the one to which he gives most space is the "*esse* of spirits." " . . . I know Descartes held the soul always thinks, but I thought Mr. Locke had sufficiently confuted this notion . . . " (ibid., p. 288).

> There is certainly something passive in our souls, we are purely passive in the reception of our ideas; and reasoning and willing are actions of something that reasons and wills, and therefore must be only modalities of that something. (p. 289)

> And therefore when I suppose the existence of a spirit while it does not actually think, it does not appear to me that I do it by supposing an abstract idea of existence, and another of absolute time. The existence of John asleep by me, without so much as a dream is not an abstract idea, nor is the time passing the while an abstract idea. . . . And I think it as easy to conceive of him as continuing to exist without thinking as without seeing. (p. 289)

148

Has a child no soul till it actually perceives? And is there not such a thing as sleeping without dreaming, or being in a *deliquium* without a thought? If there be, and yet at the same time the *esse* of a spirit be nothing else but its actual thinking, the soul must be dead during those intervals; and if ceasing or intermitting to think be the ceasing to be, or death of the soul, it is many times and easily put to death. According to this tenet it seems to me the soul may sleep on to the resurrection, or rather may wake up in the resurrection state, the next moment after death. Nay I don't see upon what we can build any natural argument for the soul's immortality. . . . (p. 289)

In his reply to Johnson (letter IV), Berkeley explains that, because of the arrival of a ship on which he hopes to travel, he has to write "in a hurry." However, he does deal with the points that Johnson has raised (in *Works*, II, pp. 292-93).

1. I have no objection against calling the ideas in the mind of God archetypes of ours . . .

2. As to Space. I have no notion of any but that which is relative . . .

By the τὸ νῦν I suppose to be implied that all things, past and to come are actually present to the mind of God, and that there is in Him no change, variation, or succession. A succession of ideas I take to *constitute* Time [Berkeley, like Descartes and Locke, meant by ideas here what we broadly mean by experiences, e.g., sounds, sights, etc], and not to be only the sensible measure thereof, as Mr. Locke and others think. But in these matters every man is to think for himself and speak as he finds. One of my earliest inquiries was about Time, which led me into several paradoxes that I did not think fit or necessary to publish; particularly the notion that the Resurrection follows the next moment to death. We are confounded and perplexed about time. (1) Supposing a succession in God. (2) Conceiving that we have an *abstract idea* of Time. (3) Supposing that the time in one mind is to be measured by the succession of ideas in another. (4) Not considering the true use and end of words, which as often terminate in the will as in the understanding, being employed rather to excite, influence, and direct action, than to produce clear and distinct ideas. (Ibid.)

All four of these latter positions were ones that Berkeley clearly considered to be mistaken, e.g., (1) and (2).

II. The *Philosophical Commentaries*

The reference to "my earliest inquiries" is importantly confirmed by the fact that the first sixteen entries in the *Philosophical Commen-*

taries all concern time. Most have, in fact, the plus sign (+), which broadly means "do not publish," or "this is a mistake." (Cf. entry 375: "+ Mathematicians have some of them good parts, the more is the pity. Had they not been Mathematicians they had been good for nothing, they were such fools they knew not how to employ their parts"; and entry 422: "+ No word to be used without an idea.")[2]

The third, fourth, ninth, and thirteenth entries do not have the plus sign, however. Let us take these entries in order. Entry 3: "G.T Whether succession of ideas in the divine intellect." This is a question which, as we see from Berkeley's second letter to Johnson, he answered in the negative. Entry 4: "T Time train of ideas succeeding each other." This was the paradoxical position that Berkeley mentions in the same letter ("A succession of ideas . . . "). Entry 9: "The same τὸ νῦν not common to all intelligences." This may be taken with letter IV, "By the τὸ νῦν . . . " Entry 13: "Time a sensation, therefore onely in the mind." This has the same import as entry 4. In Luce's valuable note on entry 4, he summarizes the treatment of time in the *Commentaries* and uses his findings as evidence that Berkeley probably "wrote an essay on time as part of his first study of immaterialism."[3]

III. The *Principles*

So far I have been concerned with Berkeleian writings on time that Berkeley did not publish. Let us now consider what Berkeley did publish on time in his *Principles* twenty years before the correspondence with Johnson. Here sects. 97 and 98 are especially relevant. I quote from the first edition as being the one that Berkeley and Johnson would have used: T. E. Jessop, ed. (London and Hull: A. Brown and Sons, Limited, 1937); or *Works*, II, using footnote variants. These sections give us what we might call a pragmatic view. The passage I have in mind is as follows:

> Time, place and motion, taken in particular, or concrete, are what everybody knows; but having passed thro' the hands of a metaphysician, they become too abstract and fine to be apprehended by men of ordinary sense. Bid your servant meet you at such a *time*, in such a *place*, and he shall never stay to deliberate on the meaning of those words: in conceiving that particular time and place, or the motion by which he is to get thither, he finds not the least difficulty. But if *time* be taken, exclusive of all those particular actions and ideas that diversifie the day, meerly for the continuation of existence, or duration in abstract, then it will perhaps gravel even a philosopher to comprehend it.

At sect. 98, Berkeley gives us a view of time that he rejects, and follows it with one that he accepts:

> For my own part, whenever I attempt to frame a simple idea of *time*, abstracted from the succession of ideas in my mind, which flows uniformly, and is participated by all beings, I am lost and embrangled in inextricable difficulties. I have no notion of it at all, only I hear others say, it is infinitely divisible, and speak of it in such a manner, as leads me to harbour odd thoughts of my existence: since that doctrine lays one under an absolute necessity, of thinking, either that he passes away innumerable ages without a thought, or else that he is annihilated every moment of his life: both which seem equally absurd.

Now for the view that he accepts:

> Time therefore being nothing, abstracted from the succession of ideas in our minds, it follows, that the duration of any finite spirit must be estimated, by the number of ideas or actions succeeding each other, in that same spirit or mind. Hence it is a plain consequence that, the soul always thinks: and in truth whoever shall go about to divide in his thoughts, or abstract the *existence* of a spirit from its *cogitation* will, I believe, find it no easy task.

We note the categorical affirmations, (1) "Time therefore being nothing, abstracted from the succession of ideas in our minds, it follows that the duration of any finite spirit must be estimated, by the number of ideas or actions succeeding each other, in that same spirit or mind," and (2) "Hence it is a plain consequence that the soul always thinks: . . . " These were two of the positions that Berkeley had reiterated in the correspondence with Johnson.

IV. Two Major Problems in Berkeley's Theory

I think there are two major problems in Berkeley's curious views on time, as stated in his second letter to Johnson and in his *Principles*. The first concerns the nature of time, the second the paradox of private times. I shall grapple with them shortly.

Before I do so, however, I may mention the results of an enquiry into the *Oxford English Dictionary* concerning the verb "embrangle." The dictionary notes, as meanings of the verb, to "entangle, confuse, perplex." The few references given include Samuel Butler, Berkeley, and Lord Morley.

I thought I might effect a minor lexicographical novelty by calling, in what follows, an attempt to "disembrangle" Berkeley's paradoxical views on time. When I turned again to the *O.E.D.*, however, I found that the word did exist and there are in fact two, and only two, recorded occurrences of the word "disembrangle." As it happens, both occurrences are in letters mainly concerning Bermuda written by Berkeley to his lifelong friend Thomas Prior.[4]

V. What Is Time? Berkeley's Answer

Let us now attempt to disembrangle Berkeley's puzzlements about time. There are, as stated above, at least two main problems to consider: first, what is time? and, in particular, why did Berkeley say that time is *constituted* by the succession of ideas in our minds? There were several considerations at work in his mind here. He did not want to say, with Locke and others, that time is an abstract idea. He held, as we know, that abstract ideas are a main cause of scepticism, irreligion, and other defects in contemporary thought. Yet Berkeley felt that time must be something. So he gave us the curious view just noted that time is constituted by the succession of ideas in our minds.

The word "constituted" may ring a bell for a reader of the *Principles*, pt. I. I quote the latter part of the first section of this work.

> And as several of these [smells, tastes, colors, etc.] are observ'd to accompany each other, they come to be marked by one name, and so to be reputed as one thing. Thus, for examples, a certain colour, taste, smell, figure and consistence having been observ'd to go together, are accounted one distinct thing, signified by the name *apple*. Other collections of ideas constitute a stone, a tree, a book, and the like sensible things. . . .

The sentence that I have just quoted is a hard saying, though there are modern philosophers who have said something similar. Common sense, however, which Berkeley generally wishes to have on his side (he had written in his notebooks, "I side in all things with the Mob" [entry 405]), would find it hard to believe that an apple is made up of a color, a taste, a smell, etc. Even W. B. Yeats, who remarked that Berkeley had "given us back the world that sounds and shines," would probably have found it difficult to believe that the world around us *consists* of sounds and shines.

Returning to time, we are told, as I have quoted, that it is also *constituted*—in this case, constituted by the succession of our experiences or ideas. I think that Berkeley's unplausible statement about time here might be accounted for as follows:

He did not want to assert that there is no such thing as time. After all, we speak of time passing, of arriving in time, of saving time, losing time, etc. We are aware in our experience of succession, of duration.

But, as we have noted, he did not wish to admit an abstract idea of time.

His difficulties, which led him to be "lost and embrangled," might have been removed if he had noticed a difference between the following two propositions:

(1)   There is no such *thing* as time.
(2)   There is *no* such thing as time.

Berkeley could have assented to proposition (1), but what he needed to see, if he were to escape his perplexities, was that an assent to proposition (1) need not imply an assent to proposition (2). In other words, we can accept that there are many temporal aspects of our experience, without supposing that the word "time" names a thing.

I think some support for the distinction I have just been making can be derived from Lewis Carroll's *Alice in Wonderland*. (Carroll, as we know, was no mean philosopher.)

> Alice sighed wearily. "I think you might do something better with the time," she said, "than waste it asking riddles with no answers."
>
> "If you knew Time as well as I do," said the Hatter, "you wouldn't talk about wasting *it*. It's a *him*."
>
> "I don't know what you mean," said Alice.
>
> "Of course you don't!" the Hatter said, tossing his head contemptuously. "I dare say you never even spoke to Time!"
>
> "Perhaps not," Alice cautiously replied: "but I know I have to beat time when I learn music."
>
> "Ah! that accounts for it," said the Hatter. "He won't stand beating."

It is interesting that Lewis Carroll should have chosen time as a subject with which to drive home the fact that not every word names a thing. It is also remarkable that Berkeley should have supposed that he must find some object for which the word "time" stands, in view of *Commentaries*, entry 422: "+ No word to be used without an idea."[5] [We note the +.]

VI. Private Times

I come now to the second problem, which has to do with private times. Here I must quote another entry from Berkeley's notebooks (entry 713):

The Concrete of the Will and understanding I must call Mind not person, lest offence be given.

Dr. Luce, in his note on this entry, remarks that "Berkeley uses it [the term *person*] freely in the early part of [his notebooks], but he decides to avoid it [in what he will publish] owing to its use in the Trinitarian and Christological *formulae*."[6]

However, I doubt whether theological orthodoxy was the whole story about Berkeley's rejection of the word "person." He was almost certainly influenced, in his decision to treat human beings as minds rather than minds and bodies, by the tradition going back through Descartes (What am I?) to Plato, whose writings Berkeley much admired, though he did indeed believe that a mind was united with a body—a body as understood in his sense, i.e., a certain collection of ideas. He writes (*Works*, II, p. 241) of being "chained to a body."

It is tempting to think that if Berkeley had allowed himself to use the word "person," he would have avoided his difficulties about private times. But in fact, as is clear from *Commentaries*, entry 713, he was using the word "person" as equivalent to "mind."

Must we then conclude that we cannot help Berkeley about private times? No, I think there is a way out. We recall that Berkeley's was essentially a religious philosophy: 'in Him we live and move and have our being'. Why should He not therefore keep each one of us in being between the moment of going to sleep and the moment of waking up, so that the latter would not follow immediately after the former? Likewise for the moment of death and the resurrection.

It might be objected to this that, if God is to do these things, there will be a succession of ideas in Him. Berkeley had denied that there was such a succession of ideas in God. Perhaps the way to meet this difficulty is to recall that God is not in time—nor in space. "A thousand ages in Thy sight are like an evening gone," wrote Isaac Watts, echoing Psalm 90. This line of a popular hymn, taken literally, traverses Berkeley's philosophy. In his view, a thousand ages are no time for God—not even an evening gone. And here we may also refer to a well-known passage in the *Principles*: "yet we may not hence conclude that they [chairs, tables, etc.] have no existence except only while they are perceiv'd by us, since there may be some other spirit that perceives them though we do not" (sect. 48). Again, we need not worry about an implied succession of ideas in God's mind, because He is not in space.

Notes

1. References to the works of Berkeley are to A. A. Luce and T. E. Jessop, eds., *The Works of George Berkeley, Bishop of Cloyne*, 9 vols. (London: Thomas Nelson and Sons, 1948-57), except where noted.

2. Cf. Luce, Introduction, in Luce, ed., *Berkeley's Philosophical Commentaries* (London: Thomas Nelson and Sons, 1944). See also my "Some Puzzles in Berkeley's Writings," *Hermathena* CXX (1976).

3. Luce, Introduction to *Commentaries*, p. 319.

4. Berkeley has been credited with adding about 90 words to the English language: Roland Hall in *Berkeley Newsletter* (ed. D. Berman and E. J. Furlong) 3 (Dublin, 1978): 4-8.

5. It is, perhaps, curious that we are, on the whole, more concerned about time than about space. Two dictionaries of quotations showed about 150 entries for time, but only six to seven concerning space.

6. Luce, Introduction to *Commentaries*, p. 445.

VI Aether and Corpuscles

11

The "Philosopher by Fire" in Berkeley's *Alciphron*

I. C. Tipton

I

There is a passage in Berkeley's *Alciphron* (bk. VI, sects. 13-14) in which Lysicles, one of the "minute" philosophers, claims that the human soul is subject to death in the ordinary course of nature. This, he says, has been revealed by "a modern free-thinker, a man of science," whose views he proceeds to outline. We are not surprised when Crito, speaking for Berkeley, fails to be impressed. We know it to be Berkeley's view that *"the soul of man is naturally immortal."*[1]

The passage in *Alciphron* has not been much discussed, but Hone and Rossi, and, later, Jessop, do comment on it,[2] and they agree in seeing it as raising two questions. We shall look at these questions in a moment. First, though, we should see what the views are that Lysicles attributes to his "free-thinker."

The first point that emerges is that the scientist is decidedly an experimentalist. He has revealed the "whole secret" of the nature of the soul, but he has done this "not by a tiresome introversion of his faculties, not by amusing himself in a labyrinth of notions, or stupidly thinking for whole days and nights together, but by looking into things, and observing the analogy of nature." The crucial analogy here is between animals (including men) on the one hand and plants on the other: animals being "moving vegetables" and vegetables, "fixed animals." The "great man" holds that "men and vegetables are really of the same species" and that, for example, "blossoms and flowers answer to the most indecent and concealed parts in the human body." *Life*, in plants and animals alike, is "a certain motion

159

and circulation of juices through proper tubes or vessels," while the *soul* in both is "that specific form or principle from whence proceed the distinct qualities or properties of things." Because "vegetables are a more simple and less perfect compound, and consequently more easily analysed than animals," we begin with them. And we find that "the soul of any plant . . . is neither more nor less than its essential oil," this being made up of "a gross unctuous substance, and a fine subtle principle or volatile salt imprisoned therein." The "resolution of this essential oil into its principles" amounts to the death of the soul of the plant; and at this stage, Lysicles says, "that volatile essence of the soul, that ethereal aura, that spark of entity . . . returns and mixes with the solar light, the universal soul of the world, and only source of life, whether vegetable, animal, or intellectual." We must note that reference to intellectual life here. For Lysicles goes on to stress that the soul of man is subject to a similar dissolution, the intellect being destined for "reunion with the sun."

As I said, the commentators see this passage as raising two questions. In the first place, we want to know who Lysicles's "great man" was. And here I am inclined to accept, somewhat hesitantly, that Jessop is right in thinking that he was the chemist, physician, and botanist Herman Boerhaave, professor at Leyden, whose important textbook on chemistry had been published in an unauthorized edition in 1724, with an English translation appearing three years later. It must be said at once that if Boerhaave is intended, Lysicles misrepresents him in one important respect. But I have looked closely at what Boerhaave says and I find that, apart from that element of misrepresentation, there is a fairly good fit. We might note here his insistence that "the truths of chemistry are none of 'em deduced *à priori*, from any abstract contemplations of the mind; but collected *à posteriori*, from innumerable experiments"; his claim that "the proper genuine characteristic . . . of an animal, is to be free, and at large," while "all plants are connected . . . to the body which furnishes 'em food," this together with his observation that they are to be distinguished "on this only account"; and his resolve to start his investigation of bodies with "a subject, which, of all others, is at once the most simple, easiest resolvable, or whose parts are separable by the smallest force," this being "one taken from the vegetable kingdom".[3] The apparent misrepresentation of Boerhaave is too serious to be ignored, and I shall say something about it in my second section, but the parallels are impressive, most particularly perhaps the fact that where Lysicles's "free-thinker" experiments with the plant rosemary, Boerhaave's first process is one in which he extracts "the native or presiding spirit" from that very plant.

We can turn now to the second problem that has been raised in connection with the passage in *Alciphron*. For the commentators have been struck by the fact that the views Lysicles attributes to his "great man" have much in common with the "fire-theory" that Berkeley was himself to put forward just twelve years later in *Siris*. Hone and Rossi suggest that in *Alciphron* "this 'philosopher by fire' is readily discarded as a dreamer of no importance," and they contrast Berkeley's attitude here with that in *Siris* where he himself talks of "the elementary fire or light, which serves as an animal spirit to enliven and actuate the whole mass, and all the members of this visible world" (sect. 291). Hone and Rossi are concerned to illustrate Berkeley's supposed lack of concern for consistency in his writings, and they will not allow that *Siris* reveals a simple change of mind, that judgment being ruled out in their view by the fact that "he republished the *Alciphron* as it stood eight years after *Siris*." This seems unduly harsh to me. But Jessop detects at least a change of mind. The question for him becomes: "Why did [Berkeley] dismiss the theory in 1732, and embrace it not long afterwards?" It is worth noting that this question is given extra bite for Jessop because it is quite clear that one of the most prominent positive influences on *Siris* was none other than Herman Boerhaave, the very man Jessop identifies with the philosopher by fire in *Alciphron*. In *Alciphron* Boerhaave's views are, apparently, summarily dismissed. But in *Siris* he has become a respected authority.[4]

That, then, sets out what has been taken to be the most interesting question raised by the passage in *Alciphron*. And by way of response it seems to me worthwhile to stress that the question itself reflects a misunderstanding of the passage; the point being that there is no evidence of any change of mind, and that what Berkeley attacks here is quite different from what he accepts in *Siris*. For the point at issue in *Alciphron* is not whether there are important analogies between plant and animal structures, a view Berkeley accepts in *Siris*;[5] nor is it whether "pure fire" is, in the words of *Siris*, that which imparts "different degrees of life, heat, and motion to the various animals, vegetables, and other natural productions" (sect. 190). The one issue in *Alciphron* concerns the human soul, its nature and its destiny, and on *that* issue Berkeley never wavered, at least not if "soul" is equated, as it is in the *Principles*, for example, with "mind." Admittedly, complications arise if the word is taken in some other sense. In a note Jessop tells us that, in the passage in *Alciphron*, "'soul' has its old sense of 'anima', that which makes animate things animate,"[6] but this is surely misleading.[7] In *Siris* Berkeley allows that souls in this sense are corporeal, and if Lysicles had gone no further than offering a chemist's account of "that which makes animate things animate" there is no evidence that Berkeley would have quarreled with him. Certainly in *Alciphron*, III, 14, he looks with some degree of favor on a Stoic distinction between a mortal soul "containing the brutal part of our nature" on the one hand, and mind on the other, where the latter is described as "a *particle of God*." And it seems clear that if Berkeley, or Berkeley's Crito, quarrels with Lysicles, it is because the account is supposed to touch intellect or mind. The issue is whether chemistry has anything to teach us about *that*. And if this is the issue, then *Alciphron* and *Siris* give precisely the same—negative—answer.

So far as *Siris* is concerned, Berkeley's position is well known and, I think, fairly well understood. After commending tar-water as at least a candidate panacea, Berkeley indulges in some, to our minds quaint, scientific speculation in order to account for the efficacy of the remedy. In an open letter published in the same year as *Siris*, he tells us that even when he began experimenting with tar-water he "had of a long time entertained an opinion . . . *that fire may be regarded as the animal spirit of this visible world*," adding that "it seemed to me that the attracting and secreting of this fire in the various pores, tubes, and ducts of vegetables, did impart their specific virtues to each kind; that this same light or fire was the immediate instrumental or physical cause of sense and motion, and consequently of life and health to animals."[8] The thinking here is, of course, reminiscent of the philosopher by fire in *Alciphron*, and in *Siris* Berkeley appeals to Boerhaave and other moderns, as well as to the ancients, in developing the notion. But we need not dwell in this area. The important point is that it is one of the main aims of *Siris* to distinguish between this sort of scientific speculation about the corporeal world on the one hand, and the realm appropriate to metaphysics, or what he here calls the *philosophia prima*, on the other. *Siris* is in many ways a strange work, but we have here a clear link between it and the earliest works. Once more a clear distinction is drawn between the corporeal world and the mental; once more minds are said to be the only true causes; and once more minds are said to lie outside the scope of the experimental sciences.

Now when we turn our attention back to *Alciphron*, we find that, far from there being any inconsistency, the only point Crito makes in answer to Lysicles is one we should expect the author of *Siris* to make: that the human soul is not a subject for the natural scientist. "But what relation," he asks, "hath the soul of man to chemic art?" He goes on: "The same reason that bids me trust a skilful artist in his art inclines me to suspect him out of his art." The reply is disappointingly brief,[9] and it does not tell us whether Berkeley was sympathetic or unsympathetic to the general line that the philosopher by fire takes on plants, animals, or humans, except so far as that claim about mind is concerned, and there he is definitely hostile. But, Crito's refusal to trust an artist "out of his art" clearly carries no implication that he would not respect the philosopher by fire up to that point where he exceeds his competence. In a footnote following Crito's response, Jessop observes that "Berkeley was sharply aware of the limitations of each and all natural science." To substantiate this he gives references to the *Principles* and *De Motu,*[10] and he could have referred to *Siris* as well. Certainly I take Jessop's point here to be quite crucial to understanding the philosopher by fire passage. Indeed it is because I take it to be crucial that I think we must go against what Jessop says in his main discussion. We should accept, against him, that the passage we are examining involves *only* "a refusal to resolve the soul 'chemically' into fire," rather than a rejection of the fire theory as a whole. And this means that we should conclude, against Hone and Rossi, and Jessop too, that there is no inconsistency between this passage and *Siris*. Instead we find only the simple assertion of a basic tenet that Berkeley adhered to throughout his life.[11]

II

The view that the passage involves more than I have suggested may well owe something to a feeling that, as an immaterialist, Berkeley certainly should have been opposed to even those aspects of Lysicles's story that could be presented as perfectly proper scientific theorizing about "this visible world." And while, at one level, any argument based on this feeling could be countered simply by insisting that in *Siris* he embraces such theorizing enthusiastically, as involving notions he "had of a long time entertained," and therefore seems not to have seen things this way, I intend to return to this point in my third section. There is an important issue here. In this section, however, I want to look at a minor issue that arises only if we suppose Lysicles's "great man" was indeed Boerhaave.

The problem that arises in this connection is that if Jessop is right and the philosopher by fire is intended to be Boerhaave, it does seem clear that Lysicles misrepresents him in one very important respect. Indeed the misrepresentation could hardly be more dramatic, for the truth seems to be that Boerhaave himself always stopped short of claiming to reveal the nature of the human mind. For example, in the authorized edition of *Elementa Chemiae*, published in the same year as *Alciphron*, we find him stressing that when he refers to animals he means "the bodies of animals, and the parts thereof: the other principle, *viz.* the mind, being no way the subject of chemical enquiries."[12] This, of course, coincides exactly with Berkeley's own position. So it would seem that in *Alciphron* Berkeley gets Boerhaave wrong. Having rejected certain hypotheses that spring to mind, I suggest that we can best account for this misrepresentation by considering, first, a general characteristic of Berkeley's approach to freethinkers and freethinking in *Alciphron*, and secondly, Boerhaave's reputation.

For the first point we can take our text from Berkeley himself in his Advertisement, where he warns us that "the author hath not confined himself to write against books alone." What he presents us with in *Alciphron* is essentially a conversation, and he warns that: "A gentleman [such as Alciphron or Lysicles] in private conversation may be supposed to speak plainer than others write, to improve on their hints, and draw conclusions from their principles." It would seem, then, that if an author is represented in *Alciphron*, he might appear franker, more outrageous, than he would in his own works. And, quite generally, this can lead to an impression of unfairness. Many commentators have complained at Berkeley's unfairness to Shaftesbury in particular, and this is not the only case.[13] The trouble is that the misrepresentation of Boerhaave is particularly gross. And my own hunch is that if Berkeley allows Lysicles to present his scientist as a "free-thinker," he must have thought or suspected that this is what he was.

The speculation here is not entirely without foundation, for I find that though G. A. Lindeboom in his biography lays stress on Boerhaave's piety[14] — and Lindeboom has assured me in a letter that Boerhaave's view on the mind-body relationship was "more or less Cartesian" — there is evidence that this was not always recognized, just as it was not always recognized that he was, in Hone and Rossi's words, "the enemy of Spinoza, Epicurus, Hobbes."[15] It is significant that in his *History of Materialism*, F. A. Lange notes that, while Boerhaave was not an avowed materialist, "his whole influence cannot but have favoured the spread of materialistic views among his pupils," but it is even more interesting that Lange refers to his "unconcealed adhesion to the philosophy of Spinoza," adding that "Spinozism was to the theologians the same thing as Atheism."[16] I must stress that if Lindeboom is correct, Boerhaave's reputation for Spinozism was based on extremely shaky foundations.[17] But it remains the case that the rumor was spread as early as 1693, and that it gained sufficient ground to persuade him to abandon his hopes of a ministry in the church. If Berkeley knew of Boerhaave's reputation for Spinozism, and if he took that reputation seriously, this would go a long way toward explaining the philosopher by fire passage. In *Alciphron*, VII, 26 Spinoza is referred to as "the great leader of our modern infidels," and one of the views attributed to him is that "men are mere machines impelled by fatal necessity."

There is an interesting footnote to this, for even if Lysicles, and arguably Berkeley too, is unfair to Boerhaave, we do know that one of Boerhaave's pupils was to become a very prominent materialist. This pupil was La Mettrie, who attended Boerhaave's lectures in 1733 and who later wrote *Traité de l'Ame*, *L'Homme Machine*, and, indeed, *L'Homme Plante*. La Mettrie's claim in *Man a Machine* that "only the physicians have a right to speak" on the subject of the soul, and his insistence that we "take in our hands the staff of experience, paying no heed to the accounts of all the idle theories of philosophers,"[18] alien though this might have been to the teaching of Boerhaave, is surely strikingly reminiscent of Lysicles's attitude when he introduces the philosopher by fire. And while a teacher must not be unfairly blamed for the excesses of a pupil, we should note that elsewhere, La Mettrie did go so far as to try to tar Boerhaave himself with the materialist brush. Though La Mettrie recognizes that Boerhaave "divise l'homme en corps & en ame," he claims that "il ne donne jamais à l'ame les épithetes de spirituelle & d'immortelle," adding that "il explique par le seul méchanisme toutes les facultés de l'ame raisonnable." La Mettrie concludes that "il m'est évident qu'il n'a connu dans l'homme qu'une ame sensitive plus parfaite que celle des animaux."[19] Lindeboom asserts roundly that "La Mettrie wronged his former teacher when he presented Boerhaave's psychology as mechanistic, and even dared to assert that he never spoke of an immortal soul."[20] And it is not my intention to argue with this. It is at least interesting, however, that if Lysicles, a fictional character, wrongs Boerhaave by drawing him into his own materialism, so, not much later, does one of Boerhaave's own pupils.

III

There is just one more question I want to raise in this paper. I want to ask how it was that Berkeley, the idealist, could at any stage have come to accept that "fire may be regarded as the animal spirit of this visible world." No doubt this question becomes pressing only if our concern is with *Siris*, but it is desirable to raise it here if only to correct an impression that may have been given by what was said earlier. For it is one thing to say, as I think we should say, that Berkeley's criticism of the philosopher by fire involves no more than an insistence that a natural science can tell us nothing about mind, but it is quite another to claim that the *sort* of theorizing that Berkeley countenances concerning the corporeal world in *Siris* is compatible with immaterialism. My own view is that it is compatible. But there is, surely, a genuine question here.

Certainly some commentators have thought that there is. Thus John Wild, for example, refers to "Berkeley's abandonment of the *esse percipi* thesis in his discussion of inorganic nature and that fiery energy which is its activating principle."[21] Wild associates this fiery energy with "matter," and concludes that in *Siris* "matter has an independent existence of its own, and can act." Few commentators have gone this far, but I suspect that most have been somewhat embarrassed by what Berkeley says concerning the "invisible fire," light, or aether. There has not even been agreement on what Berkeley took its nature to be. For Wild it is material. For J. O. Wisdom it is "incorporeal."[22] While for Hone and Rossi it is both a "natural" and an "intellectual" element, which they describe as "the real medium between spirit and idea."[23] If there is one thing we can say with confidence here it is that Wisdom is wrong, as sect. 220 of *Siris* makes clear.

Now it must be said at once that *some* of the qualms that might be felt about Berkeley's espousal of the fire theory can be quickly dispeled, given that distinction, so important for Berkeley, between strict philosophical *truth* and what scientists and others can be allowed to *say*. For example, we need not be too worried when he refers to aether as a "mighty agent" (sect. 152), given that he goes on to stress that "mechanical causes . . . are by no means active in a strict and proper signification" (sect. 155). In the *Principles,* he had insisted that in this area "we ought to *think with the learned, and speak with the vulgar*" (sect. 51). And in *Siris* the view is similar: "In compliance with established language and the use of the world, we must employ the popular current phrase." Again, there is sufficient in the later sections of *Siris* to make it abundantly clear that Berkeley did not see himself as having abandoned the basic tenets of his earlier idealism. If we have serious qualms, this will be, surely, because Berkeley makes it quite clear that the aether is not something we can *perceive*. Thus Wild stresses that it is an "unseen principle" (*Siris*, sect. 176) and "the object of no sense" (sect. 175),[24] and R. J. Brook, too, is struck by "the clear suggestion in the *Siris* that the 'aether' . . . is 'insensible'." "In what sense," Brook says, "can this 'aether' (or its constituent particles) be called 'ideas'?"[25] Basically, the problem concerns how Berkeley is prepared to cut the world up. We want to know how he can allow for an "invisible" component if, as in the *Principles* (sect. 99), "objects of sense are nothing but . . . sensations combined, blended, or . . . concreted together." Brook raises a related question, however, when he notes that the particles of aether are "not causally required by the 'Creator,' but rather a 'sign' for the 'creature'." Brook asks how it is that "if the particles are 'insensible'" they can "be considered 'signs' if by this term we mean an 'idea' separable from and suggestive of another 'idea'."

The issue here is important, indeed more important than Wild suggests when he concentrates on the question of whether Berkeley, in his later life, discarded the *esse percipi* thesis. As Brook makes clear, it relates to the question of Berkeley's attitude to the insensible atoms of the contemporary corpuscularians, and, given that "the relation between Berkeley's thought and 'corpuscularianism' is not as simple as may appear at first glance,"[26] Berkeley scholars ought to treat that issue as one of pressing concern.[27] Clearly, an adequate treatment of the wider issue would involve paying close attention to Berkeley's various references to corpuscles, in the earlier works and the later, and, indeed, to the notions of the corpuscularians themselves. But here my aim must be more modest. On the question of the particles in *Siris*, I want to agree with Brook that we do not find "a straightforward contradiction with the earlier work," but, against him, I want to deny that there is "an unresolved dilemma." Brook thinks there is a dilemma because he is impressed by Berkeley's instrumentalist treatment of certain of the notions used in natural science, and then supposes that when faced with talk of insensible particles Berkeley ought to have been *either* totally dismissive *or* an instrumentalist. Against this background, Brook is naturally puzzled when he finds that "contra Warnock there is . . . no evidence that Berkeley did, or would treat the ultimate particles of the 'aether' as a 'mathematical hypothesis', as he would so treat 'gravitational force'."[28] Brook's dilemma disappears, however, once we appreciate that his options are not the only ones open to Berkeley, and that even the earlier work suggests that there is scope for Berkeley to be a realist about insensible things.

The clue here lies in Berkeley's interest in the very minute, an interest wholly natural in the age of the development of the microscope, and an interest well documented in the *Principles* (sects. 60-66) where he dwells at length on "that curious organization of plants, and the admirable mechanism in the parts of animals," which he describes as "the clockwork of Nature . . . hid as it were behind the scenes." And, of course, the issue in the relevant sections is at no stage whether "all that variety of internal parts" really exists, but rather what its *purpose* is, given that for Berkeley it can play no genuinely causal role. The answer to *that* question is that even in considering "the inward parts of bodies" we are still in the area of "marks or signs for our information," and this is precisely what Berkeley says about the aether in *Siris*. If *Siris* raises problems not raised by the discussion in the *Principles*, it must be because in the *Principles* we never leave the realm of "inefficacious perceptions," or ideas, or the sensible, this because the mechanisms he has in mind are *discernible*, if only with the aid of microscopes. But even here he allows, significantly, that a "great part" of the clockwork "is so wonderfully fine and subtle, as scarce to be discerned by the best microscope." What we find in *Siris* is enthusiastic speculation about the subtlest part of the clockwork, or what "no eye could ever hitherto discern, and no sense perceive" (sect. 159). But there is no suggestion that we have left the realm of what could, ultimately, be sensed, could we but "pry" deeply enough.[29] It seems fairly clear that the aether is, *in that sense*, perceivable.

What I am suggesting, of course, is that, for Berkeley in *Siris*, there is nothing corporeal that is "insensible," except in the sense that, because it is "inconceivably small" (sect. 261), it lies, and may always lie, beyond the range of our most powerful microscopes. (One would expect Berkeley to hold that if no human will ever perceive the aether, other spirits can or could.) And this means that his acceptance of very minute particles in *Siris* provides no support for the view that he could or would have accommodated atoms or corpuscles such as those postulated by Boyle and Locke, given, that is, that Brook is right in supposing that the unobservability of the latter is "not rooted in some empirical limitation of our powers of perceptual discrimination," and that the atoms are "theoretical" entities in the *strong* sense of that term whereby such entities must be "in principle unobservable."[30] There is, however, a complication here, and it arises because it is by no means as clear as Brook thinks that the atoms were consistently thought of as theoretical entities in this strong sense, even by their supporters. There is, for example, Locke's well-known observation that "had we senses acute enough" we should "discern the minute particles of bodies," an observation linked with thoughts concerning angelic perception, and the powers of one who could "so fit his eye to all sorts of objects as to see . . . the figure and motion of the minute particles in the blood and other juices of animals as distinctly as he does, at other times, the shape and motion of the animals themselves."[31] The burden of *this* passage is that our inability to discern the innermost structure of things is indeed the consequence of empirical limitations on *our* powers of perceptual discrimination, so that *we* can only theorize where others can perhaps perceive, and the thinking here is, surely, reminiscent of Berkeley's attitude in *Siris* as I have interpreted it. As I said earlier, an adequate treatment of Berkeley's attitude to corpuscularianism would involve a careful study of the relevant passages in the various works. We can already see, however, that the background is not quite as Brook supposes. Indeed, if Berkeley is less outrightly dismissive of talk of corpuscles than we might have expected, even in the *Principles*, we might expect that one strand in his thought will be that, if talk of real essences and atomic structure goes along with what Gerd Buchdahl has described as "a theory of the two-layered universe: the 'ideal' and the 'non-ideal',"[32] it will fall foul of the *esse percipi* thesis, but that if the atoms are taken as theoretical entities only in a weak sense, it will not. There will be nothing here to embarrass Berkeley. For if his opponents do treat the corpuscles as "material," they will be condemned on Berkeley's principles: while if they treat them as "ideal," Berkeley's immaterialism will stand.[33]

A word more is necessary on Berkeley's attitude to the fire theory. In the first place, we should note that if the reading given above is correct, there will be certain consequences. In particular, the aetherial particles, if they are insensible because minute, will, in

Berkeley's terms, be "ideal," and this will, agreeably to Berkeley's intentions, allow for their passivity as well as their reality, thus putting them firmly in the realm of the corporeal, but as things that must *require* mind, and that could not constitute it. And we can see too that Berkeley would reject certain of the interpretations of his position that we met earlier, notably that he makes aether either "matter" or "the real medium between spirit and idea." More generally, we can say that the fire theory, thus conceived, turns out to be fully compatible with Berkeley's idealism. And this is not really surprising. It is perhaps worth noting that while the degree of speculation in *Siris* about what we cannot perceive may be new, a cautious readinesss to allow for its possible (though "ideal") existence is not.[34]

In conclusion, however, I should point out that the reading offered in this paper receives very strong support from the section in the *Principles* where Berkeley makes that claim, quoted at the outset, that "the soul of man is naturally immortal." This section has a number of interesting features. In the first place, we find that, as in *Alciphron*, when Berkeley looks for a rival to his view, the view he immediately thinks of is that of those "who hold the soul of man to be only a thin vital flame, or system of animal spirits." This was the view he attributed to the "great man" in *Alciphron*, and which he seems to have thought Boerhaave held. The second feature concerns Berkeley's response. For we find that in the *Principles*, as in *Alciphron*, his instinct is not to pour scorn on the notion of a "system of animal spirits," but simply to insist that the soul must be distinct from any "thin vital flame." And the third feature brings us to Berkeley's reason for insisting on this. For he tells us that "bodies *of what frame or texture soever*, are barely passive ideas in the mind" [my emphasis]. We may perhaps feel embarrassed when Berkeley speculates at length in the later work about bodies of the subtlest texture, if only because the science is outmoded. But on the strength of this passage in the *Principles*, we should expect him to treat the aether as ideal.

Notes

1. *Principles*, sect. 141, in A. A. Luce and T. E. Jessop, eds., *The Works of George Berkeley, Bishop of Cloyne*, 9 vols. (London: Thomas Nelson and Sons, 1948-57); hereafter, *Works*. In the Preface to the *Dialogues*, Berkeley claims that "the sublime notion of a God, and the comfortable expectation of immortality, do naturally arise from a close and methodical application of thought." He goes on to refer to the different conclusion

that may result from "that loose, rambling way, not altogether improperly termed *free-thinking*, by certain libertines in thought, who can no more endure the restraints of *logic*, than those of *religion*, or *government*."

2. J. M. Hone and M. M. Rossi comment on the passage in their *Bishop Berkeley* (London: Faber & Faber, 1931), pp. 218-19 and a long footnote on pp. 228-29. T. E. Jessop's discussion is in *Works*, V, pp. 10-12.

3. The quotations in this paragraph are taken from *A New Method of Chemistry*, which was edited by P. Shaw and E. Chambers and published in London in 1727. This was based on *Institutiones et Experimenta Chemiae*, which had appeared, without Boerhaave's consent, in 1724. Boerhaave detested the "spurious" edition, which was taken from student notes, but in his *Herman Boerhaave* (London: Methuen, 1968) G. A. Lindeboom expresses what seems to be the accepted view when he says that its blemishes "appeared much greater to him than they did to others," and that it "was not so bad as he often made it appear to be" (pp. 179 and 181).

4. In *Works*, V, pp. 233-35, Jessop has collected a number of passages from *Elementa Chemiae* to illustrate Berkeley's debt to Boerhaave. The authorized edition of Boerhaave's textbook was published in the same year as *Alciphron*. We might note here that a comparison of *Siris*, sects. 42-43, with Lysicle's account in *Alciphron* makes the identification of his "great man" with Boerhaave almost irresistible.

5. Sects. 29ff.

6. *Works*, III, p. 244.

7. One recurring theme in *Alciphron* is whether mind and "that which makes animate things animate" are different in kind. In IV, 4, Alciphron accepts the existence of animal spirits (inferred from "animal functions and motions") *and* of a reasonable soul, though he insists that the latter "may be no more than a thin fine texture of subtle parts or spirits residing in the brain." And this is the notion accepted by Lysicles in the passage we are examining. Later, in VII, 16, Alciphron bases a case for denying free will on the identification of soul or mind with "animal spirit in the brain or root of the nerves." Berkeley's Euphranor replies that Alciphron is just assuming that the soul is corporeal. In all these passages the basic issue is whether a discussion of mind can be subsumed under a discussion of *anima*.

8. *Works*, V, p. 176.

9. The main ground for disappointment is that Crito assumes, but makes no attempt to *show*, that the soul is not a subject for "chemic art." We know that Berkeley has arguments he could offer, based on his immaterialism. But in this passage Lysicles capitulates, or withdraws from discussion, far too quickly. "My notions sit easy. I shall not engage in pedantic disputes about them."

10. The passage from *De Motu* (sect. 42) is particularly relevant. Here Berkeley tells us that "a knowledge of incorporeal and inextended things" cannot be arrived at by the natural philosopher, who "should concern himself entirely with experiments, laws of motions, mechanical principles, and reasonings thence deduced." Berkeley continues that "if he shall advance views on other matters, let him refer them for acceptance to some superior science." In *Alciphron*, Lysicles's "great man" is presented as having overstepped this limit. And that is the *only* criticism Crito offers.

11. It seems strange that the only passage Hone and Rossi quote from *Siris* to prove inconsistency with *Alciphron* is one in which Berkeley's *main* point is not that fire is the animal spirit of the world, but that "a divine Agent" governs the fire. As Berkeley goes on to say (still in sect. 291), reflection leads us *from* fire "naturally and necessarily to an incorporeal spirit or agent." If in *Alciphron* Berkeley opposes someone whose reflections lead *no further than* fire, this hardly suggests inconsistency.

12. The quotation is taken from the translation by Peter Shaw of the authorized edition of Boerhaave's textbook. The translation was published in London in 1741 as the second edition of *A New Method of Chemistry*, and the quotation comes from Vol. I, Part 2, p. 148. Of course Berkeley could not have read the authorized edition before writing the passage in *Alciphron*, so it is worth noting that even in the 1727 edition we find Boerhaave remarking that in treating of animals he considers "the body, not the soul."

13. See for example Hone and Rossi, *Bishop Berkeley*, pp. 174-76; G. Dawes Hicks, *Berkeley* (London: Ernest Benn, 1932), pp. 189-91; B. Dobrée, "Berkeley as a Man of Letters," *Hermathena* 81 (1953): 64-65; and Jessop's comments in *Works*, III, pp. 10-12. It is interesting that while Jessop admits that "Berkeley *did* misrepresent Shaftesbury," he also says that "in attacking him, Berkeley was . . . attacking what he took to be his contemporary influence." Dobrée makes a similar point about Berkeley on Mandeville: "if . . . [Berkeley] may be defended as describing the kind of person a follower of Mandeville might become, he traduces Mandeville himself." If we took seriously F. A. Lange's observation on the likely influence of Boerhaave (quoted on p. 165), we might argue that Berkeley's unfairness to Boerhaave fits into a pattern.

14. Lindeboom, *Herman Boerhaave*, pp. 261-63.

15. Hone and Rossi, *Bishop Berkeley*, p. 229.

16. F. A. Lange, *The History of Materialism*, 3rd ed. (3 vols. in 1), (London: Kegan Paul, 1925), vol. ii, p. 55.

17. Lindeboom, *Herman Boerhaave*, pp. 45-47 and 264-65.

18. J. Offray de La Mettrie, *Man a Machine*, tr. G. M. Bussey (Chicago: Open Court Publishing Co., 1912), p. 89.

19. Offray de La Mettrie, "Abrégé des Systêmes," *Œuvres Philosophiques de Mr. de La Mettrie* (Berlin, 1774), vol. i, pp. 212-13.

20. Lindeboom, *Herman Boerhaave*, p. 266 (cf. p. 238).

21. John Wild, "Berkeley's Theories of Perception: A Phenomenological Critique," *Revue Internationale de Philosophie* VII (1953): 147.

22. J. O. Wisdom, *The Unconscious Origin of Berkeley's Philosophy* (London: The Hogarth Press, 1953), p. 73.

23. Hone and Rossi, *Bishop Berkeley*, p. 215.

24. Wild, "Berkeley's Theories," p. 147. No great harm is done if we take the quotations here to reflect Berkeley's own view, but this may be the place to observe that great care should be taken when quoting from *Siris*, where Berkeley is often reporting views that are not necessarily his own. Thus it is Hippocrates who is said to make fire "the object of no sense," and in Hippocrates the notion goes along with the view that it is "something immortal which understands all things" (*Siris*, sect. 174). In sect. 176, Theophrastus is being reported.

25. R. J. Brook, *Berkeley's Philosophy of Science* (The Hague: Martinus Nijhoff, 1973). The relevant discussion is on pp. 99-101.

26. Ibid., p. 16.

27. The importance of the topic lies in the fact that Locke scholars are putting increasing stress on Locke's interest in the distinction between the phenomenal qualities of things (those we see and feel them as having) and the corpuscular structure of the same objects. At the same time, they are playing down the importance of his representationalism, some going so far as to deny that he was a representationalist at all. Against this background, and if Locke is still to be seen as one of Berkeley's main targets, the question of Berkeley's attitude to corpuscularianism becomes crucial.

28. For Berkeley to say that they were a "mathematical hypothesis" would be to say that they are not to be regarded "as anything really existing in nature" (*Siris*, sect. 234). Indeed the point can be put rather more strongly. The claim that gravitational force is a

mathematical hypothesis goes along, in Berkeley, with the notion that it is impossible that it should exist in nature. For G. J. Warnock's examination of Berkeley's attitude to corpuscularianism, see his *Berkeley* (London: Penguin Books, 1953), pp. 207-15.

29. The talk of microscopic "prying" is in sect. 283 where Berkeley describes "the fine mechanism of nature" as "endless or inexhaustible," thus suggesting, surely, that there are things to be observed that we will never discern.

30. Brook, *Berkeley's Philosophy*, pp. 94-95.

31. John Locke, *An Essay Concerning Human Understanding*, bk. II, chap. xxiii, sects. 11-13.

32. Gerd Buchdahl, *Metaphysics and the Philosophy of Science* (Cambridge, Mass.: The M.I.T. Press, 1969), p. 296. There is much of value in chap. V of Buchdahl's book: "Berkeley: New Conceptions of Scientific Law and Explanation," though he does not touch on Berkeley's aether, and is not, to my mind, wholly convincing on Berkeley's attitude to corpuscularianism.

33. Of any number of qualifications that might be made here, I shall mention just two. First, it will not follow from anything I have said that we should expect the Berkeley of the *Principles* to think that scientific theorizing in terms of minute but "ideal" particles is likely to be a useful exercise. And, secondly, it will not follow that the corpuscles he might be able to accept would have the characteristics the atomists attributed to theirs. In particular, the notion that they lack all secondary qualities would seem to go along with the conception of them that Berkeley must repudiate. On a more positive note, the suggestion that Berkeley can think in terms of presenting his opponents with the sort of choice indicated is supported by one of the first of the sections in the *Principles* usually cited by those who want to draw attention to his hostility to corpuscles. Here, in sect. 50, he meets the challenge that the effect of his views is to "destroy the whole corpuscular philosophy," first by attacking "matter," and then by insisting that "they who attempt to account for things, do it not by corporeal substance [or matter], but by figure, motion, and other qualities, which are in truth no more than mere ideas, and therefore cannot be the cause [i.e., the true cause] of any thing."

34. For example, in sect. 78 of the *Principles*, he stresses that *all* qualities are mind-dependent, and that "this is true not only of the ideas we are acquainted with at present, but likewise of all possible ideas whatsoever." The point is made in the rather special context of what a *totally new* sense might reveal, but it clearly applies equally well to what *acuter* senses might show. The distinction is important, however, for I think that Berkeley can allow detailed speculation about things too small for us to see, where he cannot allow it about what a totally new sense might acquaint us with.

12

Locke, Berkeley, and Corpuscular Scepticism

Daniel Garber

It is no news to be told that much of Berkeley's thought derives from his acquaintance with Locke's *Essay Concerning Human Understanding*. Berkeley's debt to Locke, both negative and positive, both as a source of positions to criticize and as an inspiration for positions taken, has been studied at great length. It is thus particularly strange that Berkeley's commentators have given so little attention to one of the central concerns of Locke's writings. What I have in mind is the particular brand of scepticism with respect to our knowledge of external objects that infects the *Essay*. Unlike the sceptical problems that figure most prominently in the Berkeley commentaries, Locke's own worries do not derive in any *direct* way from problems connected with the representative theory of perception and the veil of perception difficulties it raises for establishing the existence or real nature of external objects. Locke himself is not particularly worried about how we can know what things are like on the other side of our ideas, as the veil-of-perception sceptic is. In the very few places where Locke even opens the door to such worries, he quickly (*too* quickly, perhaps) closes it again. What concerns Locke is something quite different. If the gross bodies of our everyday experience are

Versions of this paper were read at the 1979 Conference of the International Berkeley Society, the University of Missouri at St. Louis, Illinois State University, and the University of Cincinnati. I would like to thank audiences there, as well as Ian Tipton, Phillip Cummins, Roger Ariew, and Burnham Terrell for helpful discussions. I would also like to express my gratitude to the gracious ladies of the Colonial Dames of Rhode Island and Providence Plantations for allowing me to reside at Whitehall, Berkeley's American home, while this paper was being written.

really made up of parts too small for us to sense, as the corpuscular-ians tell us, Locke asks, then how could we ever discover the hidden nature and real constitution of things? How, with our weak senses, could we ever discover the hidden properties that bodies really have, as opposed to the way they appear to us? Most Berkeley scholars have concentrated their attention on veil-of-perception scepticism and have neglected even to look for Berkeley's response to Locke's corpuscular scepticism, as I shall call it. In the few places where Locke's corpuscular scepticism is even recognized, Berkeley's commentators have tended to assimilate it to the veil-of-perception scepticism by identifying the world of corpuscles with the world on the other side of the veil.[1] In this paper I shall argue that these readings will not do. I shall show that Berkeley did not simply iden-tify the corpuscular substructure of a body with the unperceivable thing-in-itself, and that he did distinguish Locke's corpuscular scepticism from the sceptical problems raised by the representative theory of perception.

I

Before entering into Berkeley's response to Locke, it will be help-ful to outline one aspect of Locke's ambitious program. Locke's announced goal in the *Essay* is an examination of the "Original, Certainty, and Extent of humane Knowledge" (*Essay*, 1, 1, 2).[2] What I have called the corpuscular scepticism arises in the context of the limits that Locke places on our knowledge of body.

The importance of the corpuscular theory to Locke's philo-sophy is something that recent students of his thought have em-phasized.[3] As Locke understood that theory, it holds that the gross bodies of our everyday experience are made up of a multitude of smaller bodies, corpuscles. The claim is that *all* the observed proper-ties of bodies, their color, temperature, the effects they have on one another, can be explained in terms of their primary qualities, i.e., the solidity, size, shape, position, and motion of the particular corpuscles that make up the body in question.[4] As Locke puts it:

> Beside these before mentioned *primary Qualities* in Bodies, *viz.* Bulk, Figure, Extension, Number, and Motion of their solid Parts [i.e., cor-puscles]; all the rest, whereby we take notice of Bodies, and distinguish them one from another, are nothing else, but several Powers in them, depending on those primary Qualities; whereby they are fitted, either by immediately operating on our Bodies to produce several different *Ideas* in us; or else, by operating on other Bodies, so to change their primary

Qualities, as to render them capable of producing *Ideas* in us different from what before they did. (*Essay*, 2, 8, 26. See 2, 8 passim; 2, 21, 75; 2, 23, 8; 2, 23, 11-13.)

Locke stops short of claiming that we *know* the truth of the corpuscular theory in the strict philosophical sense of that word. But he clearly endorsed the corpuscular theory as the best account of the makeup and properties of bodies that he knew of, and the one that "the Weakness of humane Understanding" would be unlikely to better (*Essay*, 4, 3, 16).

This corpuscularian picture shaped Locke's conception of a body. Locke took very seriously the distinction between the corpuscular substructure and the other qualities of bodies, like color, sound, smell, and taste, which are "only Powers to act differently upon other things" (*Essay*, 2, 8, 23). Thus Locke refers to the corpuscular substructure as "the internal Constitution, and true Nature of things," (2, 23, 32), and goes so far as to argue that the corpuscular substructure represents the only qualities that bodies *really* have:

> The particular *Bulk, Number, Figure, and Motion of the parts of Fire or Snow are really in them*, whether any ones Senses perceive them or no: and therefore they may be called *real Qualities*, because they really exist in these Bodies. But *Light, Heat, Whiteness,* or *Coldness, are no more really in them, than Sickness or Pain is in* Manna. (*Essay*, 2, 8, 17)

Or, even more clearly:

> There is nothing like our *Ideas*, existing in the Bodies themselves. They are, in the Bodies, we denominate from them, only a Power to produce those sensations in us: and what is Sweet, Blue, or Warm in *Idea*, is but the certain Bulk, Figure, and Motion of the insensible Parts in the Bodies themselves, which we call so. (2, 8, 15)

The corpuscular substructure of a body is also identified by Locke with its *essence* in the proper sense of the word:

> *Essence* may be taken for the very being of anything, whereby it is, what it is. And thus the real internal, but generally in Substances unknown Constitution of Things, whereon their discoverable Qualities depend, may be called their *Essence*. This is the proper original signification of the Word. . . . (3, 3, 15)

This notion of essence is usually called the *real essence* of a body by Locke in order to distinguish it from the *nominal essence*, which is just the collection of manifest properties that make up the abstract idea in accordance with which we divide bodies into species and genera (see *Essay*, 3, 3 and 3, 6 passim).

This view of body has a profound effect on Locke's epistemology and sets a significant limit on our knowledge of body. Locke seems to have no doubt that the insensible parts of bodies that corpuscularians deal with are *in principle* observable:[5]

> Had we Senses acute enough to discern the minute particles of Bodies, and the real Constitution on which their sensible Qualities depend, I doubt not but they would produce quite different *Ideas* in us; and that which is now the yellow Colour of Gold, would then disappear and instead of it we should see an admirable Texture of parts, of a certain Size and Figure. (*Essay*, 2, 23, 11)

Had we sufficiently powerful microscopes or the microscopical eyes that God could have given us and might have given angels (*Essay*, 2, 23, 11-22), then we would be able to actually *see* the real essences of bodies, the corpuscular substructure that is responsible for the properties that we observe in bodies. But, of course, we don't have such acute senses, or even microscopes powerful enough to penetrate to the level of the supposed corpuscles and discover the *real* properties that bodies have. Consequently, we have no knowledge of the "internal Constitution and true Nature of things, being destitute of the Faculties to attain it" (2, 23, 32; see 3, 6, 9.).[6] Put quite bluntly, Locke says that:

> There is not so contemptible a Plant or Animal, that does not confound the most enlarged Understanding. (*Essay*, 3, 6, 9)

This pessimism with regard to our ability to know the real properties that bodies have, their true natures, can be thought of as a kind of scepticism, and is what I earlier characterized as corpuscular scepticism.[7] It should be emphasized how different this corpuscular scepticism is from the sceptical worries deriving from the representative theory of perception, what I called veil-of-perception scepticism earlier. For the veil-of-perception sceptic there is something in the world, a mind-independent physical thing, which is represented in our ideas, but which is by its very nature inaccessible to our senses. While we *may* have reason to believe that it exists, we are *in principle* unable to discover its properties through experience, since all we *can* ever acquire through those senses are the *ideas* that it is supposed to cause in us. The problem that the corpuscular sceptic calls attention to is very different. For the corpuscular sceptic, his physical theory tells him that the sensible properties of objects are grounded in the parts of objects that are too small for *us* to sense. Here the difficulty is not one of *in principle* inaccessibility. What makes the world of corpuscles, and thus the *real* properties that bodies have, inaccessible to us is only the weakness of our senses. If we had more acute senses or powerful enough microscopes, the restrictions would be lifted, and the corpuscular sceptic would be a sceptic no more.

While Locke's pessimism may look sceptical to us, it is interesting to note that Locke did not take it in that way. Locke, in fact, saw the enterprise of setting limits on human knowledge as an important step in the *cure* of scepticism:

> . . . When we have well survey'd the *Powers* of our own Minds, and made some Estimate what we may expect from them, we shall not be inclined either to sit still, and not set our Thoughts to work at all, in Despair of knowing any thing; nor on the other side, question every thing, and disclaim all Knowledge, because some Things are not to be understood. (*Essay*, 1, 1, 6)

Locke's theme, repeated over and over again, is that "the Candle, that is set up in us, shines bright enough for all our Purposes. The Discoveries we can make with this ought to satisfy us" (*Essay*, 1, 1, 5). While we may be doomed forever to ignorance with regard to the true, hidden nature of things, our faculties are sufficient to "draw Advantages of Ease and Health, and thereby increase our stock of Conveniences for this Life" (4, 12, 10).

II

While Locke did not find his conclusions sceptical, Berkeley most certainly did. Unfortunately, though, Berkeley is often not as precise as one would like about pinpointing the kind of scepticism that concerns him. But the language he uses shows that Berkeley was well aware of the problems that the corpuscular sceptic was concerned to emphasize. For example, the entire opening section of the third of the *Three Dialogues Between Hylas and Philonous* seems to be devoted to a discussion of corpuscular scepticism. Hylas presents his position as follows:

> You may know that fire appears hot, and water fluid: but this is no more than knowing what sensations are produced in your own mind, upon the application of fire and water to your organs of sense. Their internal constitution, their true and real nature, you are utterly in the dark as to *that*. (*Works*, II, p. 227)

The reference to the "internal constitution," the identification of that with the "true and real nature," and the reference to the distinction that Locke makes between the real properties and mere powers of a body are all strikingly reminiscent of Locke. Locke's position and language are also alluded to in the opening sections of the Introduction of *Treatise Concerning the Principles of Human Knowledge*, where Berkeley is setting out his whole project. There Berkeley talks of a kind of "forlorn scepticism" that looks very much like Locke's position:

> But no sooner do we depart from sense and instinct to follow the light of a superior principle, to reason, meditate, and reflect on the nature of things, but a thousand scruples spring up in our minds, concerning those things which before we seemed fully to comprehend. . . . The cause of this is thought to be the obscurity of things, or the natural weakness and imperfection of our understandings. It is said that the faculties we have are few, and those designed by Nature for the support and comfort of life, and not to penetrate into the inward essence and constitution of things. (Introduction, *Principles*, sects. 1-2)

The discussion of the "obscurity of things," "the natural weakness and imperfection of our understandings," and our inability "to penetrate into the inward essence and constitution of things" all recall Locke's discussions of the corpuscular substructure. Later in the *Principles*, Berkeley characterizes his opponent in a way that leaves even less doubt that he was aware of the peculiarities of Locke's corpuscular scepticism, using Locke's own terminology and a virtual paraphrase of the *Essay*:

> . . . I shall say somewhat of natural philosophy. On this subject it is, that the *sceptics* triumph: all that stock of arguments they use to depreciate our faculties, and make mankind appear ignorant and low, are drawn principally from this head, to wit, that we are under an invincible blindness as to the *true* and *real* nature of things . . . We are miserably bantered, they say, by our senses, and amused only with the outside shew of things. The real essence, the internal qualities, and constitution of every [sic] the meanest object, is hid from our view; something there is in every drop of water, every grain of sand, which it is beyond the power of human understanding to fathom or comprehend. (*Principles*, sect. 101; cf. *Essay*, 3, 6, 9)

The "something there is in every drop of water" which is "beyond the power of human understanding" is nothing but the corpuscular substructure, the "real essence, the internal qualities, and constitution." It is hard to see how Berkeley could have referred to Locke's corpuscular scepticism any more clearly than he did.

These passages show that Berkeley was aware of Locke's corpuscular scepticism. Unfortunately, though, all these passages are perfectly consistent with the possibility that Berkeley simply identified the hidden nature of the corpuscularian with the unperceivable thing-in-itself, and thus saw no difference between the corpuscular scepticism that worried Locke and the veil-of-perception scepticism that is Berkeley's more visible target. If we are to make the case that Berkeley did distinguish the two theories and the two scepticisms, further evidence must be presented. This is the project of the following sections.

III

There are some considerations that might lead one to think that Berkeley simply identified the scientific world of corpuscles with the inaccessible world on the far side of the veil of perception in his early writings, and thought that both could be rejected with a single argument.[8] If we think of corpuscles as the materialist does, as mind-independent hunks of corporeal substance, there is no doubt that it is on the other side of the veil that the corpuscular substructure belongs. Berkeley also makes a number of apparently anti-corpuscularian remarks in which he treats corpuscles in a way very reminiscent of the way in which he treats mind-independent material bodies. Berkeley, for example, does recognize that ideas are made up of smaller parts. The ideas of sense are resolvable into their *minima, minima visibilia* in the case of sight and *minima tangibilia* in the case of touch (see *Essay Towards a New Theory of Vision*, sect. 54). Each such idea may be thought of as composed of a certain finite number of these *minima* arranged in a certain pattern. But Berkeley seems to have the corpuscular theory in mind when he insists that these *minima* be *sensible*. Though we can divide a visible idea into its visible corpuscles, so to speak, Berkeley insists that "that wch is visible cannot be made up of invisible things" (*Philosophical Commentaries*, sect. 438; see sects. 249, 439, 464).[9] This looks very much like Berkeley's rejection of mind-independent physical objects, invisible things thought to stand behind our sensible ideas of things. Some of Berkeley's remarks on microscopes are similarly anticorpuscular, and resemble his treatment of mind-independent bodies. For example, shortly after Philonous exhorts Hylas to trust his senses, Hylas asks, naturally enough:

. . . why should we use a microscope the better to discover the true nature of the body, if it were discoverable to the naked eye? (*Dialogues*, in *Works*, II, p. 245)

Philonous replies:

Strictly speaking, Hylas, we do not see the same object that we feel; neither is the same object perceived by the microscope which was by the naked eye. (ibid.; see *Commentaries*, sects. 236, 249; *New Theory of Vision*, sect. 85)

This, of course, is reminiscent of Berkeley's remarks to the effect that no new sense could ever inform us of the existence of mind-independent bodies, since all a new sense could give us is new ideas (see *Principles*, sects. 77-78).

But it would be a mistake to read these passages uncritically. They are tied closely to a certain conception of the contents of Berkeley's world of ideas that he sometimes emphasizes and at other times does not. Sometimes Berkeley is at pains to emphasize that each separate idea of sensation is a separate sensible thing, strictly speaking. Thus in the *New Theory of Vision*, Berkeley emphasizes that "the tangible and the visible magnitude do in truth belong to two distinct objects" (sect. 55). In the *Dialogues*, he goes even further, suggesting that the visible object that he discusses in the *New Theory of Vision* is, in truth, a *series* of visible objects, so that when we are normally said to be moving closer to a single object, what is really happening is that we perceive "a continued series of visible objects succeeding each other" (*Works*, II, p. 201). These individual ideas of sensation, conceived of as sensible things, are what might be called *idea-things*. It is with idea-things in mind that Berkeley makes some of the statements quoted earlier. Since "there is nothing in [an idea] but what is perceived" (*Principles*, sect. 25), idea-things can contain no insensible parts. And since each idea may be thought of as a separate sensible thing, the microscope will not give us a more detailed view of an individual idea-thing. All it can give us is a *new* idea-thing.

Elsewhere, though, Berkeley takes a different view of the contents of his immaterialist world, one that offers more room for insensible corpuscles. Often Berkeley means by a sensible thing some regular and recurrent collection of ideas of sensation.[10] For example, Berkeley says in the opening section of the *Principles*:

Thus, for example, a certain colour, taste, smell, figure and consistence having been observed to go together, are accounted one distinct thing, signified by the name *apple*; other collections of ideas constitute a stone, a tree, a book, and the like sensible things. (sect. 1; see *Dialogues*, in *Works*, II, p. 249)

Later in the *Principles*, Berkeley seems to indicate that such *idea-cluster things*, as I shall call them, are what correspond in this world to the physical objects in Locke's:

> But, say you, it sounds very harsh to say we eat and drink ideas, and are clothed with ideas. I acknowledge it does so, the word *idea* not being used in common discourse to signify several combinations of sensible qualities which are called *things*. . . . But this doth not concern the truth of the proposition. . . . The hardness or softness, the colour, taste, warmth, figure and such like qualities, which combined together constitute the several sorts of victuals and apparel, have been shown to exist only in the mind that perceives them; and this is all that is meant by calling them *ideas*. . . . (*Principles*, sect. 38)

With the idea-cluster things, much of the complexity and obscurity of Locke's physical objects makes its way back into Berkeley's world. Unlike idea-things and like Locke's objects, idea-cluster things can have properties that are not immediately evident. Because of an imperfect knowledge of the regularities in accordance with which God produces sensory ideas in us, we may fail to know all of the ideas that are connected together in the order of things and hence belong together in a given idea-cluster thing. With the complexity of idea-cluster things comes the possibility of an immaterialist corpuscularianism, a possibility that I think Berkeley embraces.

The most convincing evidence that Berkeley admitted that there is a proper sense in which bodies can be said to be made up of corpuscles is found in the *Principles*, in sects. 60-66. There Berkeley takes up an objection to his claim that God is the true efficient cause of all our ideas of sensation. Why, if God is the immediate source of all of our sensible ideas, do objects have to have the complex inner structures that they do? Why do clocks have to have wheels, and animals, hearts?

Berkeley's answer is very interesting. Never once in the course of his lengthy response does he suggest that the objects in question do not really have internal parts. Berkeley takes it for granted that they do and attempts to explain why God may have made things in the way in which he did. Berkeley reminds us that the laws of nature are, properly, the regularities that God imposed on the phenomena, "the set rules, or established methods, wherein the mind we depend on excites in us the ideas of sense" (*Principles*, sect. 30). It is, of course, for our benefit that God set up these regularities, which give us "a sort of foresight, which enables us to regulate our actions for the benefit of life" (sect. 31). Now, God could certainly produce any effect he liked directly, without the need of any hidden mechanism. He could move the dial of a clock without wheels, or the body of a cat without internal organs. But, Berkeley argues, the hidden mechanisms are necessary if the effects we observe are to have a mechanical explanation, if they are to be subsumable under the laws of nature, the "rules of mechanism, by Him for wise ends established and maintained in the Creation" (sect. 62). As Berkeley argues:

> . . . it must be observed, that though the fabrication of all those parts or organs be not absolutely necessary to the producing any effect, yet it is necessary to the producing of things in a constant and regular way, according to the Laws of Nature . . . A particular size, figure, motion, and disposition of parts are necessary, though not absolutely to the producing any effect, yet to the producing it according to the standing mechanical Laws of Nature. (sect. 62)

Two things should be noted about this argument. First of all, Berkeley does *not* say that God set things up in such a way that we can always *actually discover* the mechanism behind the manifest properties of things. Berkeley seems to think that if *anything* in the world is to be intelligible to us, then God must have framed some simple sets of laws of nature under which *all* phenomena (miracles excepted, of course) can be subsumed. The *universality* of the laws then entails that there must be a mechanism behind (most) manifest phenomena. But nothing Berkeley says commits him to the claim that all the mechanisms can actually be discovered by us.[11] Secondly, there is no suggestion that the mechanisms that Berkeley is talking about are any less real than tables or chairs. The mechanisms that must exist are *not* presented as fictional, instrumental things, terms in a mathematical theory of nature that have no significance outside of that theory, a status he explicitly gives forces and attractions (*De Motu*, sects. 17-18). Berkeley does not say that such mechanisms are *posited* in order that we might think of the laws of nature *as if* they were universal; the mechanisms must exist, there must be wheels behind the clock face and a heart in the cat's chest because the laws *are* universal.

But what are these hidden mechanisms whose existence this argument is intended to justify? Berkeley quite explicitly includes mechanisms like the internal organization of plants and animals and the wheels and springs that make up the internal mechanisms in clocks (see *Principles*, sect. 60). But it seems clear that Berkeley meant to include the hidden corpuscular substructure of things as well. For one, the argument that is meant to render the existence of internal mechanisms compatible with his immaterialism works as well for corpuscles as it does for the wheels of a watch. It would seem as difficult to explain magnetic and chemical phenomena, and phenomena clearly relating to heat and fire on mechanical principles without corpuscles, as it would be to explain the movement of a watch dial on mechanical principles without wheels and springs. Furthermore, while Berkeley does not explicitly use the *word* "corpuscle" in these passages, his language is virtually identical with the language that Locke uses when talking about corpuscles. Like Locke, he talks of the "size, figure, motion, and disposition of *parts*" (*Principles*, sect. 62 [emphasis added]; cf., e.g., *Essay*, 2, 8, 14). Recalling Locke's discussion of microscopes and microscopical eyes, Berkeley talks of mechanisms "so wonderfully fine and subtle as scarce to be discerned by the best microscope" (*Principles*, sect. 60; cf. *Essay*, 2, 23, 11-13). Almost paraphrasing Locke's description of corpuscles, Berkeley talks of the hidden mechanisms "which seem like so many instruments in the hand of Nature that, being hid as it were behind the scenes, have a secret operation in producing those appearances which are seen on the theatre of the world, being themselves discernible only to the curious eye of the philosopher" (*Principles*, sect. 64; cf. *Essay*, 4, 3, 25). And finally, Berkeley makes use of the most characteristic metaphor of the corpuscularians when he compares the mechanisms of nature to the workings of a clock.[12] In stating the objection to which he is to reply, Berkeley says:

> By this doctrine [i.e., immaterialism], though an artist hath made the spring and wheels, and every movement of a watch . . . yet he must think all this done to no purpose, and that it is an intelligence which directs the index, and points to the hour of the day. . . . The like may be said of all the clockwork of Nature, great part whereof is so wonderfully fine and subtle as scarce to be discerned by the best microscope. (*Principles*, sect. 60; cf. *Essay*, 3, 6, 9; 3, 6, 39; 4, 3, 25)

Berkeley thus seems quite prepared to accord corpuscles the same real existence that he gives to the inner mechanism of the watch, the parts of a tree, and the organs of an animal.

But how can Berkeley recognize the existence of insensible corpuscles if external objects are to be clusters of *ideas*? While Berkeley never addresses this question directly, it is not difficult to reconstruct one way that corpuscles could be accommodated within his system. Berkeley certainly felt that he had to give some account of the real existence of external objects when no one is sensing them. Berkeley seems to have settled on the position that sensible things, when not being perceived by finite minds, exist as ideas in God's mind, ideas that He would produce in us if we were in appropriate circumstances.[13] Thus, the mechanism of the watch, hidden in the watch case, exists as a cluster of ideas in God's mind, some of which he would produce in us if we were to open the watch case and inspect its innards. This same account can be extended to accommodate corpuscles as well. As I pointed out earlier, Locke and his contemporaries did not think that corpuscles are *in principle* unobservable. They seemed to believe that if we had appropriate sense organs, or appropriately strong microscopes, we could actually see the corpuscular substructure of bodies. There is reason to believe that Berkeley shared that view. When he is not emphasizing the fact that each idea is, in a sense, a separate thing, Berkeley sounds very much like Locke when he speaks about microscopes and the possibility that we could have been given more acute sense organs. As quoted earlier, he refers to the "clockwork of Nature" as being so fine as "scarce to be discerned by the best microscope" (*Principles*, sect. 60). In the *Dialogues*, Berkeley (in the person of Philonous) talks of microscopes as "that which best sets forth the real nature of the thing, or what is in it self" (*Works*, II, p. 185).[14] In that passage he also takes it to be "not only possible but manifest, that there actually are animals whose eyes are by Nature framed to perceive those things which by reason of their minuteness escape our sight" (ibid.). Given that it is not in principle impossible to observe the corpuscles, one can give an account of their real existence that is exactly parallel to Berkeley's account of the real existence of the hidden wheels of the watch. The insensible corpuscles may be said to exist as ideas in God's mind, which we would have if we were in appropriate circumstances. Of course, the specification of appropriate circumstances involves more than just opening the watch case; it involves positing appropriately strong microscopes or appropriately penetrating sense organs. But this makes no difference with regard to the question of their real existence.[15]

With the existence of corpuscles comes the possibility of a Berkeleyan corpuscular science, a corpuscularian science of idea-cluster things. The materialist corpuscularian tries to find the hidden structures of insensible parts that are invariably correlated with and productive of the more easily observed properties of bodies. So, for example, the corpuscularian would try to find that configuration of corpuscles that all gold has in common and that is responsible for its color, weight, malleability, and so on. Berkeley's immaterialist version of the corpuscularian program will be very similar. Like the materialist, the immaterialist corpuscularian will try to find the underlying corpuscular structure invariably correlated with the manifest properties of bodies, and from which those manifest properties can be derived (or at least predicted). But for the immaterialist, the claim that a given body has such-and-such a corpuscularian substructure will be cashed out in terms of the existence of certain ideas in God's mind and the possibility (under appropriate circumstances) of our having those ideas. So the immaterialist corpuscularian deals, properly speaking, with the correlations among ideas, the ideas that constitute the corpuscular substructure of a given body, and the *other* ideas that make up the idea cluster that Berkeley identifies with that body. Thus Berkeley says:

> . . . they [the corpuscularians] who attempt to account for things do it, not by corporeal substance, but by figure, motion, and other qualities, which are in truth no more than mere ideas . . . (*Principles*, sect. 50; see *Commentaries*, sect. 403)[16]

Since, Berkeley argues, ideas cannot be efficient causes, such structures cannot be the real *productive* causes of the manifest properties of bodies:

> . . . One idea of object of thought cannot produce, or make any alteration in another . . . Whence it plainly follows that extension, figure and motion cannot be the cause of our sensations. To say therefore, that these are the effects of powers resulting from the configuration, number, motion, and size of corpuscles, must certainly be false. (*Principles*, sect. 25; cf. sects. 50, 102)

Thus, in rejecting the materialists' mind-independent corpuscles, Berkeley finds that he must reject the claim that the corpuscular substructure is the *real cause* of the sensible properties we observe in things. But this does not eliminate the basic program of the corpuscularians. Even in Berkeley's immaterialist and noncausal corpuscularianism, there will be good reasons for wanting to find the corpuscular substructure of a body. Knowledge of the corpuscular substructure will still be of use in predicting the unknown properties that a body has, in the sense that *if* we knew that structure (i.e., what ideas we would have if our senses were sufficiently acute), then we could use our knowledge of that (and the laws of nature) to derive others of that body's properties:

> By this means [i.e., by means of the laws of nature] abundance of information is conveyed unto us, concerning what we are to expect from such and such actions, and what methods are proper to be taken, for the exciting such and such ideas: which in effect is all I conceive to be distinctly meant, when it is said that by discerning the figure, texture, and mechanism of the inward parts of bodies . . . we may attain to know the several uses and properties depending thereon, or the nature of the thing. (*Principles*, sect. 65)

In short, an immaterialist corpuscularian science would be like any other Berkeleyan science: it would deal not with efficient causes but with the relations of concurrence and succession that hold among ideas.[17]

If my case is right, then it is not strictly speaking correct to say that Berkeley identified the world of corpuscles with the world on the dark side of the veil of perception. Conceived properly, that is, conceived *immaterialistically*, there is room for corpuscles on our side of the veil. What puts the materialist's corpuscles on the wrong side of the veil is not their *corpuscularity*, but their *materiality*. The corpuscularian is wrong not in thinking that corpuscles really exist, but in thinking that they exist independent of minds and cause the sensory ideas that we have. In this respect, the corpuscular theory is entirely different from the representative theory of perception, with its objects in *principle* unperceivable. While the corpuscular theory has its core of truth, there is *no way* in which Berkeley can accept mind-independent material things. But if Berkeley could distinguish between the representative theory (which he rejected) and the corpuscular theory (which he could accept, in his own way), then there is reason to believe that he may have distinguished between the sceptical worries that these two theories generated. In the following section, I shall argue that Berkeley did distinguish the two scepticisms by showing that he offers different arguments against each of them.

IV

Berkeley is convinced that the root of *all* scepticism is the belief in mind-independent material substance. Berkeley repeats over

and over again that "the doctrine of matter or corporeal substance . . . [is] the main pillar and support of scepticism" (*Principles*, sect. 92), that "the arguments urged by *sceptics* in all ages,
depend on the supposition of external objects" (sect. 87). His
claim is that:

> So long as we attribute a real existence to unthinking things, distinct
> from their being perceived, it is not only impossible for us to know with
> evidence the nature of any real unthinking being, but even that it exists.
> (*Principles*, sect. 88; see *Dialogues*, in *Works*, II, p. 229)

The clear implication is that when we eliminate mind-independent
external objects, our scepticism will be cured.

It is obvious how the denial of mind-independent material objects
cuts against the veil-of-perception sceptic. In denying that there even
exists a hidden nature of the sort that the veil-of-perception sceptic
aspires to know, Berkeley sets those sceptical worries to rest. But it
is more difficult to see how the denial of mind-independent material
bodies affects the corpuscular sceptic. If the corpuscularian were
willing to accept Berkeley's immaterialist version of his program,
then he could accept this argument without *necessarily* giving up
his scepticism, it would seem. As long as Berkeley recognizes *some*
sense in which corpuscles can exist in the world of ideas, the corpuscularian could try to press the sceptical worries that seem to follow
out of the fact that we lack senses appropriate to penetrate to the
corpuscular substructure. Clearly, some additional argument is
needed if Berkeley is to hold that the rejection of mind-independent
material substance leads to the collapse of the corpuscular scepticism.

This, I think, gives us a possible way of determining whether or
not Berkeley distinguished between the two scepticisms. If Berkeley
saw no difference between the corpuscular sceptic and the veil-of-
perception sceptic, then we should expect no special argument,
directed specifically at the corpuscular sceptic, designed to connect
the denial of material substance with the refutation of that particular variety of scepticism. If Berkeley did not distinguish the two
sorts of scepticism, then it is plausible that he would have thought
the denial of material substance *by itself* sufficient to silence both
opponents in one fell swoop. But if, on the other hand, he saw the
corpuscular sceptic as making claims different from those made by
the veil-of-perception sceptic, then we should expect to find such
additional argument in the texts. When we examine the texts carefully, it turns out that there *is* such an argument, one that has
generally been overlooked by the commentators. In the *Principles*,

we find an argument which, though grounded in the denial of material substance, provides just the additional argument that Berkeley needs to address the corpuscular sceptic.

This argument is given in sects. 101-02 of the *Principles*. There Berkeley characterizes the kind of scepticism that he means to attack in terms that strongly suggest the corpuscularian. He talks of this kind of scepticism being derived from "*natural* philosophy," according to which "the real essence, the internal qualities, and constitution of every [sic] the meanest object, is hid from our view." The argument against this variety of scepticism then proceeds as follows:

> One great inducement to our pronouncing our selves ignorant of the nature of things, is the current opinion that every thing includes within it self the cause of its properties: or that there is in each object an inward essence, which is the source whence its discernible qualities flow, and whereon they depend. Some have pretended to account for appearances by occult qualities, but of late they are mostly resolved into mechanical causes, to wit, the figure, motion, weight, and such like qualities of insensible particles: whereas in truth, there is no other agent or efficient cause than *spirit*, it being evident that motion, as well as all other *ideas*, is perfectly inert. See *Sect.* 25. Hence to endeavor to explain the production of colours or sounds by figure, motion, magnitude and the like must needs be labour in vain. (*Principles*, sect. 102)

This argument might strike us as curious. Why does Berkeley emphasize the fact that spirit is the only efficient cause? How is the inertness of ideas supposed to count against the corpuscular sceptic? But despite the initial strangeness of the passage, Berkeley is clearly addressing Locke's position here. As I pointed out earlier, Locke grounds his identification of the nature, essence, and real qualities of a body with the corpuscular substructure on the claim that the color, taste, temperature, and so on that a body has are causal consequences of the corpuscular substructure, and thus are "only Powers to act differently upon other things" (*Essay*, 2, 8, 23). Since the secondary qualities are only powers, grounded in the corpuscular substructure, Locke concludes that the corpuscular substructure must be that which constitutes the "true Nature of things" (2, 23, 32). Thus, in being ignorant of the corpuscular substructure, we are ignorant of the nature of things. Berkeley's strategy in this argument is to defuse the corpuscular sceptic's position by eliminating one of his essential premises, the claim that the sensible qualities that a body exhibits are, properly speaking, *caused* by the corpuscular substructure. In the argument quoted, as in *Principles*, sect. 25, which Berkeley cites and which I quoted earlier, Berkeley argues that since "motion, as well as all other *ideas* is perfectly inert," the corpuscular substructure, itself just a collection of ideas, cannot be the efficient cause of anything at all. The implication is obvious: this removes the principal motivation for considering the corpuscular substructure to constitute the real nature of body. Since the corpuscular substructure is not the productive cause of the manifest properties of bodies, it has no claim to represent the real nature of bodies.[18] And since the corpuscular substructure does not constitute the real nature of body, ignorance of the corpuscular substructure does not constitute ignorance of the real nature of material things. Once we have understood that there are no mind-independent bodies and that the corpuscular substructure is just a collection of inert ideas, on a par with all other such collections, Berkeley thinks, there will no longer be any reason for "pronouncing our selves ignorant of the nature of things."

Berkeley's answer to the corpuscular sceptic, as I have interpreted it, may look like a mere linguistic move. One might object that Berkeley's answer does not cure our ignorance but only relabels it. In the end, Berkeley's argument seems not to touch the hard core of corpuscular scepticism: whether the corpuscular substructure constitutes the true nature of things or just concurrent ideas, it remains unknown and for all practical purposes unknowable. But this is not entirely fair to Berkeley. Berkeley's argument transforms the ignorance of the corpuscular substructure from a matter of great importance, ignorance of the true nature of things as they really are, to ignorance of a much more benign sort. If ignorance of the corpuscular substructure is mere ignorance of the interconnection of ideas, then it is no more serious than ignorance of the chemical properties of lead or the geography of the dark side of the moon. To claim that we are ignorant of the "*true* and *real* nature of things" is indeed to "make mankind appear ignorant and low," and to claim that "we are miserably bantered . . . by our senses, and amused only by the outward show of things," as Berkeley characterizes the corpuscular sceptic's position in *Principles*, sect. 101. But to claim that there are empirical facts about the interconnection of ideas in what we take to be the material world that we do not know is only to remind us of our finite intellects, to remind us that we are not God.

Berkeley's argument against the corpuscular sceptic, like the more direct argument against veil-of-perception scepticism, depends essentially on the rejection of mind-independent material substance. It is because nothing exists independently of mind that bodies must be just clusters of ideas, and it is because of this that corpuscles cannot be efficient causes. But it should be evident how different the strategies Berkeley uses against the two scepticisms are from one another. The veil-of-perception sceptic is refuted by showing that the hidden nature of whose ignorance he complains does not exist. In Berkeley's new world of minds and ideas, the veil-of-perception sceptic's questions cannot even be raised. But the corpuscular sceptic is treated in an entirely different way. The hidden nature of the corpuscularian, the corpuscular substructure, is not eliminated by Berkeley. In finding a place in Berkeley's world as a collection of ideas, however, it loses its causal efficacy and, with it, its special claim to represent a body the way it really is in itself. The corpuscular sceptic is thus refuted not by elimination but by reinterpretation. Once we realize that there are no mind-independent bodies and that the corpuscular substructure is just a collection of ideas, part of a larger cluster of ideas, we will realize that ignorance of it is not the serious matter that the corpuscular sceptic makes of it. The radical difference between these two immaterialist strategies that Berkeley uses—refutation by elimination, directed against the veil-of-perception sceptic, and refutation by reinterpretation, directed against the corpuscular sceptic—strongly suggest that Berkeley did distinguish between the two scepticisms.

If my readings are correct, then Berkeley seems to have understood his Locke much better than commentators have usually given him credit for. His many discussions of the "clockwork of Nature" (*Principles*, sect. 60) show that he could separate the world of corpuscles from the world of mind-independent external objects. And though he deplored the sceptical dangers inherent in both theories, he seems to have understood the difference between the two varieties of scepticism. The different strategies he used to refute the two scepticisms testify to the fact that Berkeley recognized that, while all scepticism may have its root in the belief in mind-independent material substance, significantly different plants can spring from the same root.

Notes

1. For example, George Pitcher, in his recent *Berkeley* (London: Routledge and Kegan Paul, 1977), is typical in not mentioning Locke's corpuscularianism and Berkeley's response to it at all. His chap. VII, on Berkeley's response to Locke's concept of matter, deals

entirely with mind-independence and veil-of-perception problems. R. J. Brook, on the other hand, slurs the corpuscular theory together with the representative theory in his *Berkeley's Philosophy of Science* (The Hague: Martinus Nijhoff, 1973), pp. 94-95. I. C. Tipton seems to make a similar mistake by identifying the scientific world of corpuscles with the world on the dark side of the veil of perception in *Berkeley: The Philosophy of Immaterialism* (London: Methuen, 1974), pp. 28ff. and 31ff. Prof. Tipton has assured me that, even if he may once have held such a view, he does no longer.

2. References to Locke and Berkeley will be given in the text. Locke references are taken from John Locke, *An Essay Concerning Human Understanding*, ed. P. H. Nidditch (Oxford: Clarendon Press, 1975). References to this work consist of the book, chapter, and section, given in that order. References to Berkeley are to A. A. Luce and T. E. Jessop, eds., *The Works of George Berkeley, Bishop of Cloyne*, 9 vols. (London: Thomas Nelson and Sons, 1948-57). References to the text cite the work by section number, except for references to the unsectioned *Dialogues*, references to which are given by the page number in vol. II of the *Works*.

3. The most influential source for this is Maurice Mandelbaum, *Philosophy, Science, and Sense Perception* (Baltimore: The Johns Hopkins University Press, 1964), chap. I. Mandelbaum's thesis, that Locke must be read in the context of the corpuscular theory, has been accepted by virtually all recent writers on Locke.

4. There is an ambiguity in Locke's use of the term "primary quality" that should be noted. Sometimes Locke thinks of the primary qualities as being solidity, size, shape, etc. Elsewhere, though, he identifies the primary qualities with the corpuscular substructure, i.e., the solidity, size, shape, etc., of the *corpuscles*. Berkeley reads Locke exclusively in the former way. See, e.g., *Principles*, sects. 9-15. Consequently, none of Berkeley's discussion of the distinction between primary and secondary qualities touches on issues directly related to the corpuscular theory, as such discussions often do in Locke.

5. See L. Laudan, "The Clock Metaphor and Probabilism," *Annals of Science* 22 (1966): 73-104, esp. pp. 101-03 where Laudan gives examples of some of Locke's contemporaries who thought that microscopy would eventually progress to the point where we could actually *see* the corpuscular substructure.

6. There are some places, however, where Locke suggests that through experiment we can make probable conjectures about the corpuscular substructure. See, e.g., *Essay*, 4, 6, 13; 4, 12, 10; 4, 16, 12. These passages are emphasized by L. Laudan in "The Nature and Sources of Locke's Views on Hypotheses," *Journal of the History of Ideas* 28 (1967): 211-23, repr. with an interesting postscript as essay X in I. C. Tipton, ed., *Locke on Human Understanding* (Oxford: Oxford University Press, 1977). On the other hand, J. W. Yolton reads Locke in a more Baconian way, and de-emphasizes the importance of framing hypotheses about corpuscular substructures for Locke. See his *Locke and the Compass of Human Understanding* (Cambridge: Cambridge University Press, 1970), esp. chaps. 2 and 3.

7. What I have called the corpuscular scepticism is only one of the limits that Locke places on our knowledge of body. For a *complete* understanding of body, Locke sometimes argues that we need to know more than just the corpuscular substructure, though knowledge of that is certainly necessary. For a complete understanding of body, Locke sometimes thinks that we would need to know how it is that the corpuscles cohere (*Essay*, 2, 23, 23-28) and that we would need an *a priori* knowledge of the connection between any given configuration of corpuscles and the ideas that it causes in us (4, 3, 12-14; 4, 6, 14). It is the lack of *all* of this that seems to make a science of body impossible (4, 12, 9-10). See Yolton, *Locke and the Compass of Human Understanding*, pp. 79ff., and M. Wilson, "Superadded Properties: The Limits of Mechanism in Locke," *American Philosophical Quarterly* 16 (1979): 143-50.

8. In this paper I shall not deal with Berkeley's corpuscularianism in the later *Siris*, since to do so would necessitate dealing with the questions of continuity and change in Berkeley's writings. For an account of Berkeley's treatment of the corpuscular theory in *Siris*, see G. Moked, "A Note on Berkeley's Corpuscularian Theories in *Siris*," *Studies in History and Philosophy of Science* 2 (1971): 257-71.

9. It is interesting to note that, in the *Commentaries*, Berkeley did consider adopting a position according to which sensible colors are composed of ideas that we are incapable of distinguishing. See *Commentaries*, sects. 151, 153, 664. All these passages are marked by the obelus (+), which, according to Luce, indicates those positions that Berkeley rejected by the time he composed the *New Theory of Vision* and the *Principles*.

10. While Berkeley is usually clear that objects are composed of ideas of sensation, some of the arguments he uses suggest that ideas of imagination are included as well. See *Principles*, sect. 23, and *Dialogues*, in *Works*, II, pp. 200ff. The particular regularities that cause us to bind single ideas into complex sensible things are complex, and constitute the divine sensible language that Berkeley often talks about. A detailed discussion of this topic, though, is beyond the scope of this paper.

11. It is because he misses this point that Brook is led to difficulties in his interpretation of Berkeley's attitude toward corpuscles. See Brook, *Berkeley's Philosophy of Science*, pp. 100-01.

12. See, e.g., Laudan, "The Clock Metaphor and Probabilism," loc. cit.

13. Berkeley's position on this question is more complex than usually thought, and what I have presented is only a simplification. For a discussion of the ins and outs of Berkeley's thinking on the existence of unperceived objects, see Pitcher, *Berkeley*, chap. X.

14. The supposed contradiction between this passage and the one quoted earlier from the *Dialogues* (*Works*, II, p. 245) is discussed in B. Silver, "The Conflicting Microscopic Worlds of Berkeley's *Three Dialogues*," *Journal of the History of Ideas* 37 (1976): 343-49. Because Silver misses the distinction between idea-things and idea-cluster things, I think that he neglects an obvious way of resolving the apparent contradiction.

15. While usually ignored by commentators, the question of the existence of corpuscles in Berkeley has received varied treatments in the literature. Brook, seemingly troubled that Berkeley's God would have fashioned signs insensible to us, thinks that, in his early writings, Berkeley denied that corpuscles exist. See Brook, *Berkeley's Philosophy of Science*, pp. 93, 100-01. For a similar position see Moked, "Berkeley's Corpuscularian Theories in *Siris*," pp. 258, 267-68. Though G. J. Warnock (*Berkeley* [London: Penguin Books, 1953], pp. 212-13) considers the possibility that corpuscles might exist as ideas in God's mind, he rejects this view in favor of an instrumentalist interpretation of corpuscles. Gerd Buchdahl, in *Metaphysics and the Philosophy of Science* (Cambridge, Mass.: M.I.T. Press, 1969) sees a serious conflict in Berkeley between wanting to deny corpuscles and wanting to admit a version of corpuscularian science. See pp. 292ff. and 308ff. Buchdahl's position comes closest to my own, though I do not see quite as much inner conflict in Berkeley's position as Buchdahl does.

16. Brook, *Berkeley's Philosophy of Science*, p. 93, uses this passage to argue that Berkeley denied the existence of corpuscles. Needless to say, I think that he radically misconstrues the meaning of Berkeley's words here.

17. For an account of Berkeley's conception of what science, properly understood, is, see Buchdahl, *Metaphysics*, chap. V, and K. R. Popper, "A Note on Berkeley as a Precursor of Mach and Einstein," *British Journal for the Philosophy of Science* 4 (1953). It is tempting to object here that Berkeley's immaterialistic corpuscularianism would have to be very different from Locke's or Boyle's, since, unlike classical corpuscularians, Berkeley cannot say that his corpuscles lack color. Cf., e.g., *Principles*, sect. 10, with *Essay*, 2, 8, 15, 17, 19.

VII Idealism and Universals

13

Berkeley's Idealism Revisited

Edwin B. Allaire

In a 1963 issue of *Theoria*, there appeared an essay, "Berkeley's Idealism," which has attracted considerable attention. Some have used it; others have abused it. The former have taken it as a starting point for explorations of Berkeley's treatements or nontreatments of solipsism, individuation, and so on. The latter have attacked it for advancing the so-called inherence interpretation of Berkeley.

Upon recently becoming aware of just how much attention has been given to that 1963 essay, I decided to reread it. (I use 'reread' because, having once had a bit more than a passing interest in Berkeley, I suspect I read it when it appeared; though if I did, I doubt that I gave it much critical thought.) Having reread that essay with, I believe, as much thought as it deserves, I find myself puzzled as to why it has received so much attention.

That '63 essay is plainly not an interpretation of Berkeley, notwithstanding that it contains some passages from the *Principles* and *Three Dialogues*. Midway through the essay, its author writes:

> I am, of course, not claiming that Berkeley himself unfolded idealism as described above; nor am I claiming that he was aware that it could be so unfolded. The *Principles* is clearly not developed in strict conformity with that pattern [i.e., what has come to be called the inherence interpretation].

The author of that '63 essay plainly acknowledges (a) that he does not know and is indifferent to finding out whether or not he is talking about Berkeley the author and (b) that he is not talking, at least not strictly, about Berkeley the text. Of course, the just-

197

quoted sentences begin a paragraph that is immediately preceded by a paragraph that begins with the sentence 'Berkeley's steps to idealism are firm and definite' and that goes on to state the so-called inherence interpretation. That is confusing, to say the least. Who *is* the Berkeley of the firm and definite, inherence-interpretation steps to idealism? Whoever he is, he is plainly not Berkeley the text (and not likely to be Berkeley the author); and yet some have spilled much ink to make the small but always visible point that the inherence-interpretation Berkeley is not Berkeley the text. That puzzles me.

That '63 essay is not only confusing, it is confused. Here is how it opens:

> Berkeley's idealism may be expressed as follows. (1) There are only two kinds of existents, minds and sensible objects. (2) . . . The *esse* of sensible objects is *percipi*. Though many philosophers accept (1), few accept (2). Whereas the former seems commonsensical, the latter does not. That chairs, tables, mountains and so on must be perceived seems beyond understanding, let alone conviction. Yet Berkeley was convinced of it. Why?

In light of that opening, I am in the dark concerning how anyone could have entered into the essay. The claim that many philosophers accept (1) is outlandish, and it was so in 1963. Further, the claim that (1) seems commonsensical is grotesque. Finally, there is no real mystery concerning why Berkeley the text is convinced that a sensible object cannot exist apart from a mind. Even an untutored reader of the *Principles* can see straightway that Berkeley's commitment to idealism is rooted in the claims that sensible objects are composed of ideas and that ideas cannot exist independently of minds, or, perhaps differently, of being perceived by minds.

The author of the '63 essay, having fabricated a mystery, solves it brilliantly: he creates a fictitious Berkeley, diagnoses that Berkeley's mistake, and then confusingly suggests that the fictitious Berkeley is or could be or might as well be the real Berkeley.

That '63 essay is so plainly confusing and confused (and, incidentally, confused in ways too numerous to detail) that I am genuinely puzzled by the considerable attention it has received; and a good deal of that attention is informed by great seriousness. I can but speculate concerning a solution to my puzzle.

The fictitious Berkeley of that '63 essay has, I believe, at least two useful uses. (I shall henceforth use 'Berkeley*' to refer to this fictitious Berkeley and 'Berkeley' to refer to Berkeley the text.)

First, a familiarity with Berkeley* forces one to pursue a central issue concerning Berkeley: what account, if any, of the connection between a mind and a simple sensed item (say a color or colored shape) underlies or supports his claim that the latter cannot exist apart from or independently of the former (or, perhaps differently, of being perceived by the former?) Second, Berkeley* enables contemporary philosophers to engage idealism rather more seriously than Berkeley does.

That '63 essay has received so much attention because, I suspect, those who have addressed it have sensed at least one of the useful uses of Berkeley*; but no one has yet to get clear concerning how to make good use of him. Like the author of the '63 essay, they have allowed themselves to be distracted by the idle issues of whether or not Berkeley* and Berkeley are identical and, of not, whether or not they are closely related.

Let me now introduce Berkeley* and, in the course of doing so, point to the likely inspiration for him. The following passage from the *Principles*[1] expresses Berkeley's idealism:

> . . . houses, mountains, rivers, in a word all sensible objects have not any subsistence without a mind, that their being is to be perceived or known; that consequently so long as they are not actually perceived by me, or do not exist in my mind, they must either have no existence at all, or else subsist in the mind of some eternal spirit. (sects. 4 and 6).

That passage is encapsulated in the '63 essay as follows: a sensible object cannot exist independently of a mind, the author allowing 'perceived by the mind' to be replaced by 'in the mind'.

The inspiration for Berkeley* is this remark by Philonous (*Dialogues*, in *Works*, II, pp. 235-36):

> I own the word *idea*, not being commonly used for *thing*, sounds something out of way. My reason for using it was, because a necessary relation to the mind is understood to be implied by that term; and it is now commonly used by philosophers, to denote the immediate objects of the understanding.

That passage inspires the creation of a Berkeley who argues for idealism without making use of the word *idea*. Here is Berkeley*— or, more precisely, Berkeley*'s argument for idealism.

1. Minds are the only substances.
2. Sensible objects are composed of qualities.
3. Qualities must inhere in a substance.

∴ 4. Sensible objects cannot exist without, independently of minds.

This fictitious philosopher is entitled to be called Berkeley* because Berkeley would assent to the premises used by Berkeley*. Of course, Berkeley would not support them in the same way as Berkeley*; nor would Berkeley arrange them in the same order as Berkeley*. Still, the author of the '63 essay remains in touch with the text.

Berkeley* has at least one great virtue: he provides us with a simple and immediately discernible view concerning the relation between a mind and an item that it senses; and, further, the view supports the claim that sensed items cannot exist independently of minds. Sonewhat differently, Berkeley*'s embrace of idealism is understandable and interesting in light of the tradition's commitment to the Aristotelian inherence dictum and, I should add, our own sympathies for similar dicta.

A familiarity with Berkeley* compels us, as earlier remarked, to ask this question about Berkeley: what is his view concerning the relation or connection between a mind and a sensed item (or, if one prefers, between a sensing item and a sensed item) such that the latter cannot exist independently of the former? That question is compelling; only a dull, indifferent reader of Berkeley could fail to ask it.

The author of that '63 essay allowed himself to be tempted to suggest that Berkeley himself advanced the inherence view concerning the relation between a mind and an item that it senses; and the temptation is perhaps difficult to resist. On the one hand, the early sections of the *Principles* seem to express it at least implicitly, and, on the other hand, if Berkeley does hold that view, then we are able to understand his insistence on the dependency claim; and our need to understand that is particularly urgent for the reason that his embrace of idealism is not essential to his rejection of representative realism.

Regrettably, in sect. 49, Berkeley explicitly rejects the inherence account of sensing, if I may so put it. (In that '63 essay, one gets a muddled discussion of sect. 49, the muddle being due to the author's failure to be clear about whether he is trying to reconcile sect. 49 with the early sections of Berkeley or trying to reconcile Berkeley* with a revised version of sect. 49.) Berkeley's rejection of the inherence account of sensing is rooted in his recognition of a seemingly abysmal consequence of such an account, the consequence being that a mind, when sensing red, *is* red. Berkeley expresses himself this way: "Those [sensible] qualities are in the mind only as they are perceived by it; that is, not by way of *mode* or *attribute*, but only by way of *idea*." That Berkeley rejects the inherence account is plain, unarguable; but he offers us nothing in its stead. The words 'qualities are in the mind as they are perceived by it' do not even hint at an account of sensing, an account of how sensed (or perceived) items are related either to the mind or to a sensing of them. Further, the words 'qualities are in the mind by way of idea' point, if anywhere, to an account that Berkeley explicitly rejects in sect. 8. It is an account that partakes of a distinction like Descartes' distinction between formal and objective reality. For Berkeley, a sensed item is neither an item that represents nor an item that is represented. Whatever sensing is for Berkeley, it is not a mediated relation. The compelling question remains: what is Berkeley's account of sensing, what is his account of the relation between a mind and an item sensed? And this question is not answered, I should add, by pointing out that Berkeley uses 'idea' as a category word for sensed items. Even Berkeley himself came to realize that the use of that word leaves open the question concerning the nature of sensing; though he also, it seems, came to realize that the use of that word tempts one to attribute to him the inherence account, which he explicitly rejects.

Now, I have no doubt that there are some plausible readings of sect. 49 that will render it compatible with imputing an inherence account of sensing to Berkeley. For example, if one draws a distinction between perceiving a sensible object and sensing a quality or collection of them, then one can suggest that sect. 49 bespeaks Berkeley's failure to pay attention to that distinction; for perceiving, but not sensing, is a mediated relation for Bekeley. Or one could read sect. 49 as an instance of Berkeley's failure to explore the difference between sensing something and recognizing or identifying the something. Such efforts are not worth the effort, though. Why insist that Berkeley is Berkeley*, just because the latter has what the former could use? Why not allow Berkeley* to exhibit that which one wants from Berkeley; namely, an account of sensing that will give at least plausible support to the dependence claim regarding sensible objects.

Two recent critics of the inherence interpretation have, I think, sensed the usefulness of Berkeley* for coming to terms with Berkeley; but neither critic puts the fiction to good use. Nathan Oaklander ("The Inherence Interpretation of Berkeley: A Critique," *The Modern Schoolman* LIV [1977]: 261-69) argues that, for Berkeley, a mind and a sensed item stand in what Oaklander calls the intentionality relation. He does so largely as a result of confronting Berkeley with Berkeley*. Oaklander's argument rests primarily on his reading of sect. 49; he is convinced that Berkeley rejects the inherence account of sensing. Oaklander naturally attempts to construct an alternative account, one which will accommodate sect. 49. My lament concerning Oaklander's essay is certainly not that he tries to offer an alternative to the inherence account; nor that he fails to elaborate and clarify the intentionality account. My lament is that he does not appreciate and clarify the intentionality account. My lament is that he does not appreciate that his confronting Berkeley with Berkeley* requires him to explain how Berkeley's alleged account of sensing supports the dependence claim. The best that one can attribute to Oaklander is the conviction that Berkeley's claim that ideas cannot exist apart from the mind wears its support on its words and thus that his, Oaklander's, task is merely to show that Berkeley does not hold that sensing is inhering. Well, both Berkeley and Berkeley* deserve a better fate than that.

Robert Muehlmann ("Berkeley's Ontology and the Epistemology of Idealism," *Canadian Journal of Philosophy* VIII [1978] : 89-111) devotes much energy and detail to showing that Berkeley is not Berkeley*. He also tries to show that the mere entertaining of the view that Berkeley holds that sensing is inhering is implausible, for, according to Muehlmann, Berkeley has a Humean rather than a substantialist account of mind. That seems a bit far to go in order to persuade one that Berkeley* is different from Berkeley. But that is not at all distressing in comparison with Muehlmann's failure to face the compelling question concerning Berkeley's basis for the dependence claim. That is a bit inaccurate. Rather than failing to face the compelling question, Muehlmann tries to laugh it off. He seems to allow Berkeley to arrive at idealism on the wings of the word *idea*; and he rather stridently claims that that is the appropriate mode of travel, since Berkeley has no ontological view, implicit or explicit, regarding the sensing relation. Muehlmann tries heroically to make a virtue of Berkeley's omission. That would be a virtue, however, only if Berkeley were offering us a *reductio* of representative realism; but Berkeley is plainly not doing that. Berkeley's failure to yield an answer to the compelling question concerning the relation between either a mind and a sensed item or a sensing and an item sensed ought to disturb, not amuse us. Of course, Muehlmann may be right that Berkeley disappoints us at the crucial point; but Muelhmann fails to appreciate that Berkeley* does not disappoint us and that Berkeley deserves our disdain in so far as he does. At any rate, Muehlmann devotes many pages to showing that Berkeley is little like Berkeley* and urging us to believe that the less like him the better; but all that devotion serves only to present us with a displeasingly shallow Berkeley. Better, I think, to believe mistakenly that Berkeley is Berkeley*; the latter at least makes an interesting mistake.

Another critic of the inherence interpretation, George Pappas ("Ideas, Minds, and Berkeley," *American Philosophical Quarterly* 17, 3 [July 1980]: 181-94), seems to sense but not master the fact that Berkeley* enables us to engage somewhat seriously (Berkeley's) idealism. Toward the end of a long, careful, and sympathetic discussion of the inherence interpretation, Pappas writes:

> It is tempting to interpret *esse est percipi* as the thesis that no idea can exist unperceived. Indeed, I think this is a common interpretation. But, though this is surely *part* of what Berkeley intends, it is not all. For on this interpetation, *esse est percipi* is an *obvious* necessary truth, one that no one, including Berkeley, would have regarded as a daring and original claim. Any philosopher of the period, that is, would have granted that the *esse* of *ideas*, phenomenal entities of some sort, is *percipi*, provided 'percipi' is understood broadly enough. What is *not* obvious, and not obviously necessarily true, is the claim that no *sensible quality* can exist unperceived. It is in establishing the latter that Berkeley can maintain that sensible qualities just *are* sensible ideas. And it is the thesis that the *esse* of sensible qualities is *percipi* that Berkeley argues for.
>
> It is a merit of the IA [Inherence Interpretation] that it contains an argument for this last-mentioned thesis. (p. 193)

That passage is, I believe, confused, though rather fascinatingly so. Pappas is right to remark that the claim that ideas cannot exist unperceived or without the mind would have been neither daring nor original to Berkeley's contemporaries. Furthermore, they would not have been thrown off balance by Berkeley's claim that sensible objects are composed of ideas and thus cannot exist unperceived; but they would have been deeply upset by the so-called likeness principle that Berkeley puts forth in sect. 8; for it is that principle that undercuts representative realism. The principle is thus an essential part of Berkeley's argument for idealism.

Consider this passage from sect. 1:

> Thus, for example, a certain colour, taste, smell, figure and consistency having been observed to go together, are accounted one thing, signified by the name *apple*.

That claim, when conjoined with (a) the likeness principles, (b) the claim that sensible qualities are ideas, and (c) the claim that ideas cannot exist without the mind, is what yields idealism. In the light of Berkeley's argument for idealism, it is perhaps better to cast idealism in this way: 'house', 'mountain', and all words that signify the so-called furniture of the world have only one signification; namely, ideas of sense.

That point is important for it reveals a significant difference between Berkeley* and Berkeley. The former does not need the likeness principle in order to reach idealism, for the simple sensible items are not deemd ideas. There is thus no possibility of thinking that they might be representative items. Further, Berkeley* can use the claim that sensible objects are composed of qualities in a straightforward way, for sensible objects will naturally be construed as the furniture of the world.

Imagine, now, that Berkeley argued for idealism this way:

1.   Ideas cannot exist apart from the mind.
2.   Sensible objects are composed of ideas.

∴ 3.   Sensible objects cannot exist apart from the mind.

Berkeley's contemporaries would surely have been amused by that argument; but they would not have been amused by the addition of the likeness principle. Were they to assent to that principle, they would have been forced to abandon such distinctions as that between formal and objective reality and that between nominal and real essence.

Once we see what Berkeley's argument for idealism is, we realize, of course, that his idealism is secured independently of his attack on material substance. Moreover, we understand why Berkeley* must argue from the nonexistence of matter to idealism. Curiously enough, Berkeley's argument for idealism is not incompatible with the admission that material substance exists.

Pappas' failure to appreciate Berkeley's argument for idealism distracts him, I believe, from the compelling question concerning the dependence claim. Somewhat differently, though his remark that *esse est percipi* would have been taken as an *obvious* necessary truth is true, the remark does not point to the account of sensing that supports the necessity of that claim.

Berkeley need not be, I submit, Berkeley* in order for the former's contemporaries to perceive him as a threat. Pappas' preference for Berkeley* or, more accurately, for Berkeley*'s exclusive use of 'quality' as the category term for sensible items is rooted, then, in Pappas' own inability to take seriously that sensed items are ideas. Somewhat differently, he can take seriously that red is a quality but not that red is an idea. Pappas thus wonders whether or not one can get the dependence claim without having to rely on the inherence account of sensing and on the Aristotelian dictum. If that were possible, idealism would gain our attention in a way even more serious than when we encounter it in Berkeley*. Unfortunately, Pappas no sooner intimates his profound wonder than he becomes again intimate with the text. He concludes his paper by expressing the hope that one can find in sects. 22 and 23, an argument for the dependence claim, which argument will allow one to dispense with the word *idea*, using instead the word *quality*, but which argument will not make use of the Aristotelian dictum. Pappas' hope is to see Berkeley as claiming that sensed items are qualities, that sensing is not inhering, and that sensed items nevertheless cannot exist apart from minds.

I, for one, doubt that such a Berkeley can be found in the text. My doubt does not rest on a reading of sects. 22 and 23, though a close reading of them should dash Pappas' hopes. My doubt rests instead on this consideration. If Berkeley is to have a basis for his dependence claim, then he will have to have an ontology. (Needless to say, I take a dim view of arguments to the effect that Berkeley's idealism is epistemologically rooted. Such arguments serve only to disguise that Berkeley has no basis for *esse est percipi*; those arguments are most generously construed as trying to show how Berkeley stumbled into idealism.) The dependence claim will have to be to the effect that one basic kind of entity cannot exist apart from another basic kind. I am persuaded that all such dependence claims come down to the Aristotelian dictum or to a variant of it. (Needless to say, the dependence claims I have in mind are of the ontological, not the causal, kind.) I do not mean to say that Aristotle's dictum and its variants are unproblematic; I am quite persuaded that they need a thorough examination. I mean only to say that I know of no dependence claim concerning basic kinds of entity that does not have it that the entities of those kinds stand in the inherence relation or a variant of it.

As I have indicated in several earlier comments, I believe both that Berkeley* is not Berkeley and that the latter disappoints us at just the point that the former pleases us. Berkeley* has an account of sensing that structurally supports the dependence claim; Berkeley does not. Accordingly, I believe that most who have used or defended that '63 essay are as misguided as those who have abused it. No worthwhile purpose is served by trying to show that Berkeley and Berkeley* are or may as well be identical twins.

Even though Berkeley disappoints us by failing to speak to a critical issue, he pleases us in many other ways. His attack on representative realism, his consequent phenomenalism, and, most important, his criticisms of the traditional ontological account of that which is expressed by subject-predicate statements are immensely pleasing: they mark Berkeley's depth. Besides, Berkeley* is a fiction and, further, depends for his existence on Berkeley.

Note

1. References to Berkeley are to A. A. Luce and T. E. Jessop, eds., *The Works of George Berkeley, Bishop of Cloyne*, 9 vols. (London: Thomas Nelson and Sons, 1948-57); hereafter, *Works*.

14

Berkeley and Others on the Problem of Universals

Joseph Margolis

The famous problem of universals is too complex to be captured by a single formulation. But the impulse of the empiricists—in rather different ways focused on the notion of natural kinds or *sorts* (to use a term that Locke and Berkeley appear to share)—may reasonably be taken to be the locus for the most promising and most sensible (and even the most appropriately earthly) speculations on the issue. Whatever else may be true about classification, universals, essences, properties in common, predicates uniformly used, the recognition of natural kinds represents the beginning of responsible reflection on the nature of universals. It is Berkeley's distinction to have focused this finding in a powerful and peculiarly modern way.

In order to make this claim both fresh and telling, however, we cannot avoid presenting a reasonably comprehensive picture of contemporary analytic speculation about the problem of universals. We shall, in effect, place Berkeley in the contemporary scene as if he were a current participant—which, doubtless, would have pleased him. The principal thread of the argument, then, will trace a certain persistent conceptual difficulty confronting nominalistic solutions to the problem of universals. The intended theme is not to be taken as disqualifying nominalism, but rather as enabling us to see that—and why—nominalism and realism need not be construed as incompatible. Thus developed, our account will enable us to assess the full relevance of Berkeley's contribution, in the sense in which: (i) Berkeley has as clear an understanding of the conceptual difficulty currently debated as any contemporary philosopher; and (ii) he provides a clue regarding its resolution that is essential to any successful account. These remarks may perhaps serve as an *apologia* for an otherwise rather indirect approach to Berkeley's theory. In any event, it is to read with the ancients and to think with one's contemporaries, or, again, to preserve the most effective arguments within the historical tradition.

In our own time, Anthony Quinton has characterized natural classes, informally, as those "[in which] people who are introduced to a few of the members can go on to pick out others without hesitation or idiosyncrasy. . . ."[1] D. M. Armstrong, who has undoubtedly offered the most recent and most fully ramified theory of universals within the Anglo-American tradition, construes Quinton's thesis about the naturalness of classes in terms "of degrees of resemblance of universals." He then criticizes Quinton for not having admitted, or recognized, "that these aboriginal classifications are not sacrosanct." As Armstrong claims, "the original classifications may be shown to rest upon relatively trivial resemblances which are replaced, when the scientific enterprise gets under way, by quite different and much more significant classifications. In general, what Quinton omits to note is that the original classifications can be subjected to criticism."[2]

In an important sense, what Armstrong says is true; but in an equally important sense, his remark is profoundly beside the point, effectively undermines his appreciation of the problem of universals, and inevitably confirms the stubborn good sense of the empiricists, who refuse to be deflected from the critical issue. For what Armstrong fails to credit sufficiently, in Quinton's view—and what the empiricists never tire of puzzling over—is the simple fact that (as Quinton puts it) "I cannot be introduced to the entire extension of a predicate."[3] That is, it really makes no difference to the admission of universals as such, that universals corresponding to certain superficially appealing resemblances *should*, with the development of the sciences, *be replaced by other universals*. On Quinton's thesis—and, ultimately, on Armstrong's thesis, in spite of his apparent demurrer—the replacing universals (conditionally admitted to be such) must either be as "natural" as those they replace or else must (somehow) be suitably linked (both psychologically and conceptually) to those that are. Otherwise, we should never be able to resolve satisfactorily Quinton's version of the empiricists' puzzle: how can I go on applying predicates to the things of the world, which were never included among the paradigms of its original use, if I do not rely on the natural affinities among things?

There is a second peculiarity in Armstrong's paraphrase of Quinton's query. Quinton addresses himself deliberately to the problem of extending the use of a predicate with regard to particulars; so, too, do the empiricists. Armstrong takes the solution of this problem to be entailed in effect in resolving the problem of resemblances *among universals*. But this is an unsupported claim. If it were the same issue, then the formulation would be redundant—and even unwise, given the trouble with talk about universals. But it is clear that Armstrong believes that the solution to the problem of resemblance among particulars is both formally distinct from, and entirely dependent upon, the solution to the problem of resemblance among universals; he says explicitly: "we cannot gain a full view of the resemblance of particulars until we understand the resemblance of universals"; for "a particular *a* resembles a particular *b* if and only if:

> There exists a property, P, such that *a* has P, and that there exists a property, Q, such that *b* has Q, and either P = Q *or* P resembles Q.[4]

We shall see, later, that this somewhat familiar shift in emphasis bears rather instructively on the empiricists' characteristic maneuver— in particular, on Berkeley's. In fact, an effective survey of the entire issue of universals is much facilitated by providing a contemporary context in which to review the theories of the empiricists.

Even the naive reminders of the problem of universals just sketched generate a remarkable number of queries. The empiricists—say, from Hobbes to Hume—were obliged to face the issue in a particularly touching and exposed way because, in one fair sense at least, they were all committed to nominalism. Hobbes, for example, asserts: "[T]here being nothing in the world universal but names; for the things named are every one of them individual and singular."[5] In the *Elements of Philosophy*, he is more explicit: "This word universal is never the name of any thing existent in nature, nor of any idea or phantasm formed in the mind, but always the name of some word or name."[6] Similarly, Locke insists that "All things that exist are only particulars."[7] He adds that universals, including species and genera, remain, though they "have their foundation in the similitude of things," "the workmanship of the understanding"; "*general* and *universal* belong not to the real existence of things; but are the inventions and creatures of the understanding, made by it for its own use, and concern only signs, whether words or ideas."[8] There is an uneasy softening here, away from Hobbes' uncompromising nominalism and rather in the direction of

Descartes' conceptualism: the juggling between "words" and "ideas" confirms this.[9] Berkeley is as explicit as Hobbes and Locke: "It is a universally received maxim that *every thing which exists is particular.*"[10] And Hume construes his own contribution to the theory of universals as essentially Berkeleyan in nature: assuming "*all our ideas are copy'd from our impressions,*"[11] "Abstract ideas are . . . in themselves individual, however they may become general in their representation. The image in the mind is only that of a particular object, tho' the application of it in our reasoning be the same, as if it were universal";[12] general ideas are "nothing but particular ones, annexed to a certain term, which gives them a more extensive signification, and makes them recall upon occasion other individuals, which are similar to them."[13] Here, too, the inkling of a concession going beyond Hobbes may be remarked; also, going beyond Berkeley, insofar as Hume's theory of resemblance is distinctively his own.

Now, we must be careful in speaking of nominalism. Quinton takes it to be a "nominalistic alternative" to platonism to hold that "the things to which a general predicative term applies are related by similarity."[14] On that score, both Hobbes and Locke may pass for nominalists. But R. I. Aaron identifies (at least) the principal forms of nominalism with what amounts to the Hobbesian thesis, that the members of a class share only a name in common, or that classifying is a purely verbal process involving no appeal to non-verbal resemblances.[15] These alternatives, essentially for Quinton's reason, are either absurd or false. There is then—in a strong sense of nominalism—no nominalistic solution of how to go on beyond some initially specified extension of a predicate. Technically, Aaron is not explicit enough, of course. The reason is an important one, but only because contemporary nominalists are, contingently, reluctant or unwilling to recognize two quite distinct senses of *class*: one, that of the modern notion of an extensionally defined set; the other, that of a natural class, or sort, or similarly specified aggregate, in which the members are identified *only in virtue* of their being instances of some determinate kind. In the first sense, no appeal to universals is required (unless it is already invoked in individuating the things that *are to form* the class, or set, in question; therefore, there never arises any need to attend to Quinton's worry: we never go beyond the defined membership of the set as first introduced, there are no further discoveries to be made. But in the second, membership in the class in question is itself defined in terms of instantiating attributes—hence, membership is defined intensionally.

Aaron overlooks the difference, understandably enough. Whether, in so saying, one is committed to universals depends entirely on what one means by "universals." But, in any case, the distinction about classes lies at the very foundation of such extensionalist (and nominalist) programs as are recommended by W. V. Quine and Nelson Goodman.[16]

Armstrong's definition of nominalism is particularly apt, both because it accords with the view of the empiricists *and* because it betrays the essential weakness of extreme nominalism (Hobbes's doctrine) with respect to the problem of universals. On Armstrong's view, "nominalism is defined as the doctrine that everything there is is a particular and nothing but a particular."[17] On one reading, nominalism is simply irrelevant to the problem of universals, since, as the empiricists make abundantly clear, its admission does not preclude speculation about the valid and nonvacuous use of general terms. On another, favored by both Armstrong and Aaron, nominalism is invalid because something like Quinton's query must be answered: even if only particulars exist, they must be structured in such a way that the use of general predicates may be vindicated. If this is equivalent to realism, so be it: universals may then be said to exist *in some sense*. But in the sense in which the denial of platonism, or "transcendent realism"—the doctrine that universals exist *ante rem,* independent of, or separated from, particulars[18]—is compatible with the thesis that existent particulars may resemble one another, Quinton's conception of nominalism will be seen to be closer to the empiricists' than is Armstrong's. We must always bear in mind that either the admission of universals is doctrinally neutral, in the sense in which it is a casual way of conceding that the *real* resemblances among particulars must be accounted for in some ontological way; or it entails the claim that some particular theory or other about the existence of certain abstract entities (universals) somehow accounts for our recognition of the resemblances among particulars. In the sense in which extreme nominalism is hopelessly inadequate, *all* viable theories of particulars are realist theories, committed (we may say) to universals. But that is scarcely enough to commit anyone to such quarrelsome and substantive doctrines as that universals exist *ante rem, in re,* or *post rem.* It is quite conceivable that a kind of nominalistic realism (like Quinton's) may be defended at the same time one rejects the claim that universals *exist* (as in any of the traditionally disputed senses). There is good reason to think that, speaking of universals, the empiricists favored the benign and neutral sense of the term, not the ontologically bolder sense in which entities of a certain peculiar sort could be said to exist. In any case, no empiricist (except perhaps Hobbes) was disposed to dismiss the problem of universals as inessential to human knowledge—such as it is. In that respect, seventeenth- and eighteenth-century nominalism was, in a double sense, more realistic than contemporary nominalism. It never sought to deny—in fact, it actually overstated—the deeply intentional character of science.

There is, however, an important sense in which the empiricists resisted the more robust forms of ontological realism. Certainly, they were all disinclined to admit that the generality of predicates invariably corresponded to the objectivity of properties, without regard to the initiating activity of human intelligence and of contingent human interests. In this sense, their view was intended at least to combat the apriorism of the rationalists. They were not typically concerned to deny universals but to domesticate them, so to say, to yoke them to the specific investigative efforts of the human mind. For that reason—as Locke, Berkeley, and Hume, in various ways, attest—the empiricists were not always disposed to deny that the human mind *could* actually descry resemblances among particulars themselves. In that sense, it is not at all certain, even in Locke, that a mere conceptualism is intended: as long as the resemblances posited result from, and are not merely (passively) discovered by the human scanning of actual particulars, Locke does not invariably insist that particulars are subsumed under a universal merely in the sense that they are subsumed under a common concept supplied by the human mind. This, perhaps, is the point of the otherwise curious remark that universals are "the workmanship of the understanding," though they also "have their foundation in the similitude of things." That thesis is both helpful and profound, for the least reflection shows that if nominalism is inadequate (in the restricted sense that Hobbes so often seems to favor), then so also must be a comparably restricted conceptualism. Quinton's question is addressed to both. The empiricists, then, in their different ways, were opposed to apriorism and the cognate doctrine of the accessibility of independently real essences. They found it necessary, therefore, to reject realism, for that is what they apparently meant by that doctrine. But *if* realism, in the more contemporary sense, signifies that there are natural affinities on which the success of our generalizing depends (universals in the benign sense), then the empiricists were surely realists, because, as with Locke, they realized that they could not rest with Hobbes's doctrine.

Anachronistically, they realized that they would not have been able to answer Quinton's question.

In effect, then, in rejecting apriorism, the empiricists opposed utterly the idea that universals exist *ante rem* or *in re*, that is, independent of the activity of the investigative mind. In this sense, they also implicitly rejected the idea that universals are immutable, uncreated, indestructible, and the like, or, at any rate, that, if there were any such entities, we could have access to them relative to our cognitions. The insistence on the activity of the human mind makes it pretty clear that the notion of universals employed by the so-called conceptualist (if we may call the relevant abstractive regularities such) is radically different, in the ontological sense, from the apriorist's notion. It may well be (we shall return to the issue) that such abstractive regularities ought not to be called universals at all—even if they are taken in some sense to exist—simply because they appear to be created, to be historically and culturally contingent, in spite of their abstractness. Let us, then, mark the apriorist's notion of universal, "universal$_a$"—classically formulated in platonism. There arises, then, a conceptual difficulty confronting the *in re* theorist: for, if he concedes that universals$_a$ are neither created nor destroyed, he apparently must deny that natural species, for instance, have evolved or exist contingently; and he must explain the nondestruction of universals despite the destruction of all their instances. (But that is not our present concern.) The empiricists hold to a notion—call it "universal$_e$"—that either (a) is a casual, ontologically indifferent label for the minimal realism that Quinton's observation marks (that is, that we use general terms effectively beyond some paradigm extension), or (b) itself marks an abstractive regularity that depends essentially on the inventive and originative activities of the human mind. It is, of course, in connection with alternative speculations about (b) that Berkeley's intended solution gains its particular force. But, for the moment, we may notice that the (a) sense does not entail any version of the usual doctrine of universals at all; and the (b) sense (which may well be shared with rationalists—for instance, with Descartes, as in the *Principles of Philosophy*)[19] is utterly unlike the apriorist's sense (including that of the platonizing Descartes) in requiring attention to the contingently creative activity of the human mind. This is a more careful way of putting the distinction than to speak of creat*ed* and perish*able* universals, because the latter way of speaking (apart from its oddity, given the traditional view) entails admitting in some ontologically robust sense the existence of universals as such.

The point of this insistence is that, in context, one might almost say that neither realism nor nominalism is directly concerned with the problem of universals. Nominalism insists only that only particulars are real; and realism may be understood to hold that, since particulars must be supposed to have properties, it is impossible to specify an actual particular without invoking considerations which (somehow) universals$_a$ and universals$_e$ are independently intended to explain. In that sense, realism is an amplification of nominalism, not its opponent: nominalism simply opposes platonism, and realism simply offers a less elliptical account of the very particulars that the nominalist insists on. This comes rather close, in fact, to Armstrong's thesis, except that Armstrong believes (contrary to the very efforts of the empiricists) that "the Nominalist errs in trying to reduce universals to particulars,"[20] and except that Armstrong is premature about the nature or existence of universals. It is quite fair to say that the empiricists were inclined to view particulars—particular ideas or impressions—as somehow discriminable *prior* to considering resemblances among them or their being instances of common kinds. This has partly to do with their peculiar theories about physical objects as "collections of ideas" and partly to do with their avoidance of apriorism. But the fact remains that they admitted "sorts" or natural kinds and construed particulars as spontaneously, recognizably similar to other particulars; they tended to express themselves in terms of elementary ideas, but their admission was intended to apply to physical objects and organisms as well as to their properties and relations. Hence, there is a fair sense in which empiricist particulars may be construed as propertied particulars— or, as one might also say, individuals (that is, instances or cases of recognizable kinds). The point is that, for all its apparently radical new beginning, empiricism is not entirely at variance with classical views about the nature and intelligibility of complex individual entities. On the contrary, as we shall see, it actually recovers such views in a way that is distinctly modern.[21]

No doubt, this summary is a distortion, for there can be no question that nominalists, both classical and contemporary, *have been* concerned to solve the problem of universals. Perhaps, then, with some justice, we may conclude that the nominalist/realist controversy has been focused *both* on the theory of the nature of particulars *and* on the theory of the role of universals in human knowledge. It then becomes pertinent to emphasize that these are scarcely the same issue and ought not to be conflated.

Characteristically, the empiricists fared poorly on the first and promisingly on the second.

There is another by-benefit that illuminates the empiricists' endeavor. The problem of universals has sometimes been thought, notably by David Pears,[22] to lead to circular solutions. For example, Pears explicitly holds that "realism is necessarily a circular explanation of naming."[23] Similarly, he holds that the statement "'Universals exist' has a deceptive logic . . . it cannot be understood as a verifiable statement of fact."[24] And he adds that "any comprehensive explanation of naming [that is, the naming of attributes] is necessarily circular."[25] Pears was effectively criticized on this score by Alan Donagan, who, taking one of Bertrand Russell's accounts of universals, instructively admits: "The form of realism which Pears chose to attack is not precisely Russell's. Russell's premise was not that we are able to call things red, but that some propositions containing the primitive predicate ' . . . is red' are true; and his argument did not purport to explain such truths, but only to exhibit a necessary condition of their existence."[26] Donagan claims that Russell's thesis *is* informative. "Russell argued," he says, "that a necessary condition of the truth of propositions of the form 'x is red' is that the universal *red* be real: this 'shifts to another level,' i.e., shifts from the level of words like ' . . . is red' to the level of real beings, and so looks informative."[27] Armstrong construes the maneuver as "formally correct," but find it too good to be true. "There seems to be no honest toil in it!"[28] Now, the resolution of this confusing quarrel about realism is essential to an adequate understanding of the empiricists' enterprise regarding universals—and it will lead us conveniently to a strong view regarding the problem of universals. The reason, of course, is simply that Russell's claim (and Donagan's defense) gains its force from its implied appreciation of the problem of how "to go on" in making attributions, or using general predicates, *beyond* any initial (paradigm) set "named." This is what Pears apparently failed to grasp.

Pears' objection obtains *if* what is wanted is an account of an *independent* access to universals, in virtue of which the naming of attributes can be "*verified*" or confirmed. This is the sense in which he holds that the statement "Universals exist" cannot be verified as a matter of fact. His reason is a perfectly simple and compelling one: "Universals are specifiable only by reference to words."[29] He also says, in the same context, that "universals, like facts and propositions, are . . . shadows [cast by words and sentences as if they were separately identifiable] ."[30] But this is not quite the same claim. The difference is crucial. Pears' objection is that there is, and can be, no cognitively independent way of confirming the validity of "naming" attributes *by* access to universals. In this, he is surely right. But to deny independent access is *not* to deny that there are empirical ways of confirming the validity of favoring one attributive characterization over another, for example, general arguments regarding the success of the physical sciences.[31] This explains both why the infinite regress of the Third Man argument is fatally incapable of accounting "for our ability to ascribe general predicative terms to things by reference to our *awareness* [italics added] of some antecedent relation between the thing to be classified and an intermediary, predication-guiding object"[32] and, also, why it is easily obviated. It is obviated because the cognitive issue does not depend on a *cognitive* awareness of, or confirmation of, the relation to universals; it is fatal because that putative relationship cannot be discerned in any way at all. Russell's argument (which recalls that of the empiricists again) involves an inference to the (best) ontological explanation of our generalizing capacity, *not*, as Pears seems to suppose, a drift toward platonism.

The empirical move regarding *choice* among posited attributions presupposes, of course, an answer to the problem of universals; it certainly cannot supply it. Intuitively, Donagan *replaces* Pears' question with another that is more manageable and also more pertinent. What Donagan shows, *à la* Russell, is that universals must be real (one supposes, in the neutral sense supplied) if statements using the predicate " . . . is red" are true. The *sense* in which universals must be real is *not* supplied by Donagan—except to rule out a reliance on platonism. Armstrong acknowledges the force of Donagan's objection—though he misconstrues it as a matter merely of distinguishing between the mention and the use of such predicates as "red," whereas Donagan explicitly shifts from words to "real beings." So even the (a) sense of universals is a realist sense, since it acknowledges that attributions may be true. Armstrong is dissatisfied, because *he* wishes to make clear—in the spirit of the empiricists themselves—that it does not follow that "just because the predicate 'red' applies to an open class of particulars, therefore there must be a property, redness. There must be an explanation why the predicate is applicable to an indefinite class of particulars which played no part in our learning the meaning of the word 'red.' Furthermore, this explanation must in the end appeal to the *properties* (or relations) of these particulars. But none of this shows that there is a property, *redness.*"[33] Armstrong is dead right here, though, as we have already seen, he invokes universals just at this point. We simply cannot (he stresses) infer corresponding (and determinate) universals for each and every applicable predicate.

Here, then, Armstrong oscillates between Donagan's and Pears' questions. With Donagan, he admits that the epistemic circularity of any effort to explain naming does not affect the thesis of the reality of universals. But, rather in Pears' direction, he longs for an explanation of the empirical grounds for *attributing* properties to particulars. He points out that "there may be none, one or many universals in virtue of which the predicate applies."[34] But this simply undermines the presumption of a one-one correspondence between predicates and properties; it does not touch at all Russell's (and Donagan's) argument that a necessary condition for the truth of propositions of the form "x is red" is that the universal red be real. For, if the predicate "red" (as is supposed in the argument) designates a simple quality, then the argument goes through—and, in effect, Armstrong accepts it. But if it does not designate a simple quality, then, it is true, alternative possibilities arise regarding the matching of particular predicates and properties.[35] Nevertheless, the general strategy of realism in science shows how to *choose* between alternative matchings. In that sense, Armstrong's demurrer is irrelevant to the question as to why realism regarding universals must be defended; and, in conceding Donagan's distinction, he has effectively confirmed the force of the realist position—provided we do not draw any conclusions, from that alone, as to the particular sense in which universals are said to be real. But that returns us to Quinton's version of the empiricists' puzzle: "I cannot be introduced to the entire extension of a predicate."

The issue is certainly open to misunderstanding. Appeal to universals, in either the (a) or (b) senses given, is an attempt to *explain* in general the condition of valid *predication*. It is *not* an attempt to explain in general the *meaning* of predicates; it appeals rather to some ontological condition. The (a) sense takes the resemblance between particulars to be actual (in some sense); and the (b) sense holds (in some sense) that universals exist (apart from the resemblance of particulars), account for such resemblance, *and*, therefore, account for the success of predication.[36] The (b) sense is closely linked to essentialism; the (a) sense is not, but is linked with natural kinds—in the sense of spontaneously favored resemblances. Universals obtain (in either the neutral or the robust sense) whether or not we have predicates to pick them out; that is the

respect in which even a nominalist may be said to be a realist. And
that, precisely, is the direction in which the empiricists were drawn.
If we combine the lesson of these various distinctions, we may say
that the problem of universals concerns *the ontological conditions of
cognition*, that it does not concern at all *the epistemic, semantic, or
methodological conditions of cognition.* This is the point of admitting
the force of Pears's charge of circularity, the force of Donagan's charge
of the irrelevance of Pears's argument; the force of Armstrong's division between predicates and universals; the force of Quinton's appeal
to natural classes; and the force of the attempted solutions of the
empiricists themselves.

We may now justifiably claim that Berkeley's solution is a peculiarly strategic one, both for his own time and for ours. But in reviewing it, we must keep in mind that its bearing on the analysis of
particulars must be distinguished (and assessed independently) from
its bearing on the ontological conditions of cognition. The Berkeleyan
(and, in general, the empiricist) theory of particulars as "collections
of ideas" may well be indefensible and may even affect the consistency of empiricist solutions of the cognition issue;[37] but that need
not detain us if we ourselves avoid their theories about particulars.
Now, Berkeley's strategy involves sorting two different kinds of "abstract ideas," neither of which he admits as possible, but one of which
presupposes that the other obtains. It is very difficult to disengage
this argument from Berkeley's attack on the kind of "abstraction"
that involves assuming that one can "distinguish the existence of
sensible objects from their being perceived, so as to conceive them
existing unperceived."[38] But, of course, it is quite pointless to attempt to salvage Berkeley's contribution to the problem of universals
if we may not fairly disregard or neutralize this complication.

Consider the following well-known passage:

> . . . when we attempt to abstract extension and motion from all other
> qualities [likewise, time], and consider them by themselves, we presently
> lose sight of them, and run into great extravagancies. All which depend on
> a two-fold abstraction: first, it is supposed that extension, for example,
> may be abstracted from all other sensible qualities; and secondly, that the
> entity of extension may be abstracted from its being perceived. But . . .
> where the extension is, there is the colour too, to wit, in his mind. . . .
> [Similarly] to frame an abstract idea of happiness, prescinded from all
> particular pleasure, or of goodness, from every thing that is good, this is
> what few can pretend to.[39]

Berkeley, then, recognizes at least three kinds of abstraction that
he opposes: (1) the alleged abstraction of ideas from the condition of

their being perceived—which we may disregard; (ii) the alleged abstraction of certain ideas, as of extension from color, which are always co-present though distinct from one another—and which, on Berkeley's view, cannot "really exist each of them apart by itself, and separated from all others";[40] (iii) the alleged abstraction of ideas of what is common to particular qualities or particular things without "considering" as well those particular qualities or things—which, on Berkeley's view, results in the nonsense (attributed to Locke) of, say, the abstract idea of "some colour" that is "neither white, nor black, nor any particular colour," or the abstract idea of man, which includes "stature, but then . . . neither tall stature nor low stature, nor yet middle stature."[41] Berkeley's interesting thesis is that the impossibility—at once psychological and conceptual—of forming an idea of certain sensible qualities without forming at the same time an idea of certain other sensible qualities (which ideas nevertheless remain intelligibly distinct) depends on what it means to form a determinate idea of some particular quality or thing. On Berkeley's nominalist view, then, the onus regarding abstract ideas rests with the abstractionists. But it is not merely that abstract ideas involve inconsistencies—which there is reason to believe that Locke specifically wished to avoid[42]—but also (and more tellingly) that *whatever* may be said in favor of general ideas and abstraction must be keyed to the fact that our experience is the experience of particular things. Abstraction (ii) prepares the way for supposing that abstraction (iii) need not be linked to our experience of particular things.[43] Berkeley's point, then, is not to deny generalization or the valid use of general terms (however much he may have been tempted to), but rather to preclude the admission of such entities as separable universals, general properties, and abstract ideas. On the contrary, he expressly concedes the resemblance among particular things and particular qualities *just at the point* of rejecting abstract ideas. So he typically begins: "For example, the mind having observed that Peter, James, and John, resemble each other, in certain common agreements of shape and other qualities, leaves out of the complex or compound idea it has of Peter, James, and any other particular man, that which is peculiar to each, retaining only what is common to all. . . . "[44] What we may say, then, is that, as a nominalist—in our sense, not in the sense in which he condemns Locke—Berkeley is committed to realism, in the minimal, ontologically neutral sense supplied above. But in spite of the fact that he criticizes Locke, Berkeley really agrees with him to the extent at least of rejecting universals independent of our conceptions, *and* to the extent of rejecting the thesis that valid general ideas are merely the product of our conceptions.[45] Berkeley is quite explicit.

He first cites Locke's view: "'Since all things that exist are only particulars, how come we by general terms?' *His [Locke's] answer is*, 'words become general by being made the signs of general ideas.'" And then he proceeds to say: "And here it is to be noted that I do not deny absolutely there are general ideas, but only that there are any *abstract general ideas*."[46] What he objects to, in Locke, are "abstract general ideas"; *he does not object to general ideas*. But this is just the (a) sense of universals noted above, in which their admission is no more than a casual way of admitting genuine resemblance among particulars.

Even this much of Berkeley's theory is surprisingly potent—viewed in the context of current speculations about universals. For, *if* one is a nominalist (in restricting what exists to what is particular) and *if* one is also a realist (in admitting that predications extending beyond some original paradigm specimens may be valid), then *it becomes quite impossible to appeal to universals* in either of at least two ways: (1) in any *ante rem* sense—against platonism; and (2) in any sense in which the resemblance between particulars is itself to be explained by reference to the resemblance between universals. There is a sense in which most contemporary nominalistically inclined philosophers are realists as well. Certainly, of those already mentioned, Armstrong, Pears, and Quinton are nominalistic realists. Armstrong himself cites favorably both Quine's "innate quality space" and Wilfrid Sellars' "manifest image."[47] Possibly, Goodman would be the only relatively clear exception, though this is not entirely certain either.[48] On Berkeley's argument, however, Armstrong himself violates the second constraint; for he explicitly holds (as we have seen) that "we cannot gain a full view of the resemblance of particulars until we understand the resemblance of universals." On Berkeley's view, either the appeal to universals trivially restates what is admitted regarding particulars (that they resemble one another), or the appeal constitutes an illicit reference to abstract ideas. We cannot *explain* the resemblance of particulars by reference to the independent resemblance of universals, because the generality supported by the first cannot be strengthened in any conceivable way by appeal to anything separable from particulars; also, since the resemblance between particulars is, in some sense, cognitively accessible to begin with, an appeal to the putative resemblance of universals must also be cognitively intended. If it is, then Pears's circle cannot be escaped; and if it is not, then it appears that our understanding of the *resemblance* of universals (if we admit the notion) must itself depend, *cognitively*, on the resemblance of particulars. It would take us too far afield to consider Armstrong's thesis about "second-order" relations between "first-order" universals. His point is that causality and nomo-logicality "constitute a powerful argument for Realism about uni-versals."[49] But the argument is marred both because, contrary to his view, and given the actual practice of the sciences, it is not clear that causality entails either "constant conjunction" or "nomic necessita-tion,"[50] and because the regularities that, in terms of a general scien-tific realism, favor supporting either causal or nomological hypotheses strengthen universals only in the (a) sense, the ontologically neutral sense, not the (b) sense.

The force of Berkeley's distinction is supported as well by recalling Nicholas Wolterstorff's thesis that "predicables are just kinds, of a certain sort. They are certain kinds of cases." Being such, they are universals.[51] Wolterstorff wishes to countenance the kind, the Dodo, as well as the Unicorn. Certainly, he is right in holding (implicitly, here) that the criteria for the identity of cases of a kind cannot be the same for the identity of the predictable or kind of which they are the cases. (And he is also right in holding that kinds are not "instance-kinds," since what may be an instance of a kind may be an instance of plural kinds, and since the same things that are instances of one kind may be instances of *another* kind.) But *if* we countenance predicables as universals, then we inevitably face the problem of their *application*, which is to say, of our *cognitive* use of them. And then, it becomes quite clear that, for uninstantiated kinds (the Unicorn, for instance), it is quite impossible to know how to begin or to go on —in Quinton's sense—without it being the case that the use of such a predicable presupposes the prior applicability of other kinds. But that is just to say that the explanation of resemblance among uni-versals (speaking contrary to Berkeley's constraint) would itself, on Berkeleyan terms, have to be explained in terms of the resemblance of particulars. Put another way, Armstrong's attempted explana-tion of the resemblance of particulars utterly fails; and Wolterstorff's characterization of universals as predicables is not an explanation of such resemblance, but rather a misleading version of the original realist thesis itself. In fact, Wolterstorff's position is inadequate for Berkeley's purpose, because, on Berkeley's view (rightly), what is predicable of a thing need not correspond to a property that it has. For example, it *is* predicable of a book that it have a certain color, without predicating that it have this *determinate* color or that. On Wolterstorff's view, then, "having color" designates a "kind" or uni-versal; but, on Berkeley's view, it does not, since mere determinables are abstract ideas.[52] Here, then, is a fresh way of viewing Berkeley's seemingly muddled attack on abstract ideas. Abstract ideas are what we may call mere *predicables*, not universals—or Berkeleyan "general ideas." General ideas are universals in the (a) sense given, that is, ideas ranging (in some sense) over particular ideas that resemble one another. They are, of course, predicables also. Alternatively put, general ideas form a subset of predicables, namely, just those conformable with Berkeley's nominalistic constraint.

We are now in a position to appreciate the full power of Berkeley's solution to the problem of universals, whatever its vagueness and incompleteness may be. We have, for one thing, constrained the theory of universals nominalistically. And, for another, we have provided the sense in which universals identify an ontological—rather than semantic, epistemic, or methodological—condition of cognition. Berkeley shows the sense in which the resemblance of particulars is cognitively prior, or equivalent, to the defense of universals; also, the sense in which abstraction (iii)—which amounts to the admission of determinables—violates the principle of the determinateness of the properties of particulars and cannot, therefore, satisfactorily capture the concept of a universal; also, for similar reasons, the sense in which universals, if admitted, cannot be mere predicables. We may incidentally notice that the distinction between predicables and universals facilitates an answer to the vexed question of the production and destruction of universals. For predicables (culturally generated features, for instance) can surely be contingently generated and lost; and, minimally, universals correspond to what is true of anything—relative to what is predicable—consistent with the nominalistic constraint of determinateness. For that, we are indebted to Berkeley. So contingency holds of predicables, and the applicablility of predicables is a necessary condition for the detection of a universal. In other words, apriorism aside, the question of the ungenerated nature of universals cannot meaningfully arise.

But we are indebted to Berkely for more as well. Consider the following well-known illustration of his theory of general ideas:

. . . suppose a geometrician is demonstrating the method, of cutting a line in two equal parts. He draws, for instance, a black line of an inch in length, this which in itself is a particular line is nevertheless with regard to its signification general, since as it is there used, it represents all particular lines whatsoever; for that what is demonstrated of it, is demonstrated of all lines or, in other words, of a line in general. And as that particular line becomes general, by being made a sign, so the name *line* which taken absolutely is particular, by being a sign is made general. And as the former owes its generality, not to its being the sign of an abstract or general line, but of all particular right lines that may possibly exist, so the latter must be thought to derive its generality from the same cause, namely, the various particular lines which it indifferently denotes.[53]

Particular words and things "become" general only in a functional sense: they "represent" things "in general" by functioning as the sign of them. But, of course, they may do so in either of two ways—answering to the two distinct senses of "class" already introduced. Only in the sense in which membership in a class depends on recognition of things being of a similar kind or sort (in that they resemble one another) could Berkeley's thesis have any genuine force at all. But he himself recognizes this, for he admits that particulars are perceived to resemble one another.

In this extremely important regard, Berkeley's solution of the problem of universals is a genuine and direct improvement of Locke's solution. Locke's is inconsistent with the nominalistic constraint that he and Berkeley share. Hence, Locke introduces general ideas as *distinct* (therefore, on Humean grounds, also separable) from particular ideas of particulars. For Locke, words become the signs *of (particular) general ideas*—hence, general terms. Berkeley, grasping Locke's inconsistency (which he, perhaps not altogether fairly, puts in terms of a contradiction regarding determinate properties—color, for instance, that is neither this nor that nor any particular color), treats general ideas themselves in terms of selecting a particular idea to represent other particular ideas that it determinately resembles. With that important adjustment, Berkeley and Locke then converge again; for *both* are committed to the notion of natural kinds, or "sorts," and both are committed to the notion that these depend (in Locke's terms) on "the workmanship of the understanding" while at the same time they "have their foundation in the similitude of things."

The *only* way to understand this thesis defensibly—also, the only way to solve the problem of universals—entails (A) that we must be biologically disposed, disposed in a species-specific way, to favor at least certain determinate perceptual discriminations, and that these form the "foundation" of the determinate resemblances that we actually mark among particular things; (B) that this biological disposition is not itself a fixed template that determines "true" universals, but is rather our incompletely plastic nature, on which an enormous variety of alternative schemes of predicables may, by our "workmanship," be erected; and (C) that universals are (or are, at least, initially) those subsets of predicables that, because of our biological disposition, may, when once introduced by the use of predicates, be used (in Quinton's terms) "without hesitation or idiosyncracy," in ranging beyond initial paradigm instances to "the entire extension of a predicate." These conditions, then, clarify the profound sense in which the explanation of universals is an ontological, not an epistemic, matter—though it concerns the ontological constraints on which cognition itself depends. Berkeley, in effect, provides an original, forceful, and peculiarly modern way of understanding this. He himself acknowledges (despite earlier doubts): "It is I know a point, much insisted on, that all knowledge and demonstration are about universal notions, to which I fully agree." But he goes on, in the same passage:

> [B]ut then it doth not appear to me that those notions are formed by *abstraction* in the manner premised; *universality*, so far as I can comprehend not consisting in the absolute, positive nature or conception of any thing, but in the relation it bears to the particulars signified or represented by it: by virtue whereof it is that things, names, or notions, being in their own nature *particular*, are rendered *universal*.[54]

Berkeley realizes that he cannot defend this view without adhering to a doctrine of "sorts" or natural kinds. He is also aware that the required theory must depart from *both* the usual *ante rem* or *in re* realism *and* the usual mere conceptualism. Apparently, he never succeeded in refining the theory of sorts required. But he is quite explicit, at least in the *first draft* of the *Principles*, about what must be rejected. "These sorts," he says, "are not determin'd & set out by Nature. . . . Nor yet are they limited by any precise, abstract ideas settled in the mind . . . nor do they in truth, seem to me to have any precise bounds or limits at all."[55] Here, Berkeley opposes "most philosophers" and the "author of the *Essay*" (the latter, perhaps not entirely accurately); but he also affirms the remarkable plasticity with which diverse schemes of sorts can be linguistically introduced. The solution is a doctrine that as yet has no name. It must combine the biological component (which predisposes us, in dealing with nature, to favor certain discriminations *as* similar) and the linguistic (by which, within the tolerance of the biological, we invent alternative conceptual schemes that we may cognitively apply "to the entire extension of a predicate"). The theory required may not unfairly be called a theory of imagination, rather in the Kantian sense.[56] But it requires a fresh start. The fact remains that Berkeley provides us with one of the most acute anticipations of the nature and details of an adequate theory of universals. And in doing so, he shows us a very forceful sense in which, though universals cannot be the mere set of the particular cases or instances that instantiate them, the concept of a universal may be understood in terms of predicables constrained by a nominalistic reading of the determinate resemblances among particulars. In that sense, predicables—and the universals that are taken to be a subset of them—are heuristically introduced to correspond to our *actual* ability to apply a predicate "to [its] entire extension."[57] There need, then, be no separable universals; and the question of their existence, apart from the actual resemblances among particulars, is either obviated or trivialized.

Notes

1. Anthony Quinton, "Properties and Classes," in *Proceedings of the Aristotelian Society* XLVIII (1957): 33-58; see also his *The Nature of Things* (London: Routledge and Kegan Paul, 1973), chap. 9.

2. D. M. Armstrong, *Universals and Scientific Realism*, vol. II: *A Theory of Universals* (Cambridge: Cambridge University Press, 1978), pp. 49-50.

3. Quinton, *Nature of Things*, p. 261.

4. Armstrong, *A Theory of Universals*, p. 96.

5. Thomas Hobbes, *Leviathan*, ed. Michael Oakeshott (Oxford: Basil Blackwell, n.d.), bk. 1, chap. iv.

6. *Elements of Philosophy* (London: Molesworth, 1939), bk. I, chap. ii, sect. 9.

7. John Locke, *An Essay Concerning the Human Understanding*, ed. A. C. Fraser (Oxford: Clarendon, 1894), bk. III, chap. iii, sect. 6; hereafter referred to as *Essay*.

8. Ibid., III, iii, 13, 11.

9. Cf. R. I. Aaron, *The Theory of Universals* (Oxford: Clarendon, 1952), p. 19.

10. George Berkeley, *Three Dialogues Between Hylas and Philonous*, in A. A. Luce and T. E. Jessop, eds., *The Works of George Berkeley, Bishop of Cloyne*, 9 vols. (London: Thomas Nelson and Sons, 1948-57), vol. II, p. 192; hereafter referred to as *Works*. The quotation is from the first *Dialogue*.

11. David Hume, *A Treatise on Human Nature*, ed. L. A. Selby-Bigge (Oxford: Clarendon, 1888), p. 72.

12. Ibid., p. 20.

13. Ibid., p. 17.

14. *Nature of Things*, p. 259.

15. *Theory of Universals*, p. 226.

16. W. V. Quine, *Words and Objects* (Cambrdige: MIT Press, 1960); Nelson Goodman, *The Structure of Appearance*, 2nd ed. (Indianapolis: Bobbs-Merrill, 1966). Cf. Joseph Margolis, "The Problem of Similarity: Realism and Nominalism," *The Monist* (LXI (1978): 384-400. I have discussed the issue also in an unpublished paper, "Attribution and Intensional Problems of Classes."

17. *A Theory of Universals*, p. 3; cf. p. 8, n. 1.

18. Ibid., p. 176.

19. Cf. Aaron, *Theory of Universals*, p. 19.

20. Armstrong, *A Theory of Universals*, pp. 3, 8 n. 1.

21. This is both to sympathize with, and to oppose, Marjorie Grene's sharp opposition between empiricist particulars and Aristotelian individuals. Empiricist assumptions about the origination of our concepts appear to be inadequate; similarly, their reductive tendencies regarding the analysis of complex entities are correspondingly inadequate. But their nominalistic realism remains ontologically decisive, precisely because it is so grudgingly and irresistibly won. Cf. Marjorie Grene, "Individuals and Their Kinds: Aristotelian Foundations

of Biology," in S. F. Spicker, ed., *Organism, Medicine, and Metaphysics* (Dordrecht: D. Reidel, 1978).

22. D. F. Pears, "Universals," *Philosophical Quarterly* I (1951); repr. in Michael Loux, ed., *Universals and Particulars* (Garden City: Doubleday Anchor Books, 1970). Page references are to the Loux volume.

23. Ibid., p. 37.

24. Ibid., p. 35.

25. Ibid., p. 37.

26. "Universals and Metaphysical Realism," *The Monist* XLVII (1963); repr. in Loux, ed., *Universals and Particulars*, p. 150. Page references are to the Loux volume.

27. Ibid., p. 151.

28. *A Theory of Universals*, p. 7.

29. "Universals," p. 39.

30. Ibid.

31. This is characteristically formulated in terms of scientific realism (as opposed to idealism); for instance, by Hilary Putnam, *Meaning and the Moral Sciences* (London: Routledge and Kegan Paul, 1978), and Richard Boyd, "A Causal Theory of Evidence," *Nous* VII (1973): 1-12. But the "realistic" success of science is actually *empirically* neutral as between realist and idealist interpretations of science—which is not our present concern. Cf. Joseph Margolis, "Cognitive Issues in the Realist-Idealist Dispute," *Midwest Studies in Philosophy* V (1980): 373-90.

32. Quinton, *Nature of Things*, p. 259.

33. Armstrong, *A Theory of Universals*, p. 8.

34. Ibid., p. 9.

35. Cf. Ibid., pp. 32-33; also Bertrand Russell, *My Philosophical Development* (London: Allen and Unwin, 1959), pp. 165-66 (cited by Armstrong).

36. Cf. Armstrong, *A Theory of Universals,* pp. 10-14.

37. Cf. Monroe C. Beardsley, "Berkeley on 'Abstract Ideas'," *Mind* LII (1943); repr. in C. B. Martin and D. M. Armstrong, eds., *Locke and Berkeley* (Garden City: Doubleday Anchor Books, 1968).

38. *Treatise Concerning the Principles of Human Knowledge*, sect. 4, in *Works*, II; hereafter referred to as *Principles*.

39. *Principles*, sects. 99-100.

40. Ibid., sect. 7. Berkeley's argument is certainly open to challenge and departs from Hume's; cf. Beardsley, loc, cit.

41. *Principles*, sects. 8-9.

42. Cf. Aaron, *Theory of Universals*, p. 31; *Essay*, III, iii, 19.

43. Cf. A. A. Luce, *Berkeley's Immaterialism* (London: Thomas Nelson and Sons, 1945), chap. 2.

44. *Principles*, sect. 9.

45. Cf. the interesting passage of Berkeley's draft efforts, cited by Aaron, *Theory of Universals*, pp. 53-54.

46. *Principles*, Introduction, sects. 11-12. Cf., also, J. L. Mackie, *Problems from Locke* (Oxford: Clarendon, 1976), chap. 4.

47. *A Theory of Universals*, p. 50.

48. Cf. Margolis, "The Problem of Similarity: Realism and Nominalism."

49. *A Theory of Universals*, p. 151.

50. I have explored these issues in "Puzzles About the Causal Explanation of Human Actions," presented at the Center for the Philosophy of Science, University of Pittsburgh, fall 1978; forthcoming in Larry Lauden and Adolf Grünbaum, eds., *Topics in Explanation in the Biological and Behavioral Sciences* (Berkeley: University of California Press).

51. "On the Nature of Universals," in Loux, ed., *Universals and Particulars*, p. 185; cf. also his *On Universals* (Chicago: University of Chicago Press, 1970).

52. Cf. Armstrong, *A Theory of Universals*, pp. 130-31; see also Phillip D. Cummins, "Berkeley's Likeness Principles," *Journal of the History of Philosophy* IV (1966); repr., with minor corrections, in Martin and Armstrong, *Locke and Berkeley*.

53. *Principles*, Introduction, sect. 12.

54. Ibid., sect. 15.

55. "First Draft of the Introduction to the Principles," *Works*, II, p. 128.

56. Cf. P. F. Strawson, "Imagination and Perception," in Lawrence Foster and J. W. Swanson, *Experience & Theory* (Amherst: The University of Massachusetts Press, 1970).

57. On this use of the term "heuristic," see Joseph Margolis, *Knowledge and Existence* (New York: Oxford University Press, 1971).

VIII The "Doctrine of Signs" and "The Language of Nature"

15

Berkeley's Doctrine of Signs

William McGowan

In Rhode Island some 250 years ago, George Berkeley, exempt from public haunt, penned this sentence for the seventh dialogue of his *Alciphron*:

> I am inclined to think the doctrine of signs a point of great importance and general extent, which, if duly considered, would cast no small light upon things, and afford a just and genuine solution of many difficulties.[1]

This sentence echoed a passage on the doctrine of signs in the final chapter of John Locke's *Essay concerning Human Understanding* (1690):

> The Consideration then of *Ideas* and *Words*, as the great Instruments of Knowledge, makes no despicable part of their Contemplation, who would take a view of humane Knowledge in the whole Extent of it. And, perhaps, if they were distinctly weighed, and duly considered, they would afford us another sort of Logick and Critick, than what we have been hitherto acquainted with.[2]

Locke had divided knowledge into the speculative, the practical, and the instrumental, dubbing the last division "σημειωτική, or the Doctrine of Signs."[3] Locke's two rubrics for signs, '*ideas*' and '*words*', were supposed to denote the two great instruments of knowledge.

Berkeley agreed with Locke that ideas and words have both a semiotic and an epistemic status. But some of the Lockean metaphors for ideas and for words tend to insinuate false or self-defeating support for that contention. By revising these metaphors, Berkeley rendered them more suitable as support for the claim of a combined

231

semiotic and epistemic status for ideas and for words. By way of introduction to Berkeley's contribution, I propose to sketch with a few rough strokes the background of this advancement of the doctrine of signs.

I start with ideas. (Whereas Locke meant by 'idea' "whatsoever is the Object of the Understanding when a Man thinks,"[4] I shall follow Berkeley in restricting the term to Locke's "ideas of sensation.") To reach the relevant metaphors for ideas, we need to examine Locke's various models for the human understanding in its *passive* phase. The understanding generally he took to be active, and perhaps implicit in Locke's thought is (what I shall call) the Builder[5] as just one of his comprehensive models. Such a model would be congruent with Locke's opposition to intellectual sloth, an opposition which in turn prompted his denial of the doctrine of innate knowledge, the last theoretical resort of the rigidly self-righteous. In rendering the Builder initially passive in the reception of his simple ideas, which are his materials, Locke was led to the explicit use of additional models to spell out this passive phase of the understanding. But these additional models were not meant to stand alone so as to usurp the active understanding.

Locke's core model for the passive understanding is that of the celebrated *Tabula rasa*, or blank tablet.[6] This model complements the mechanical Clockwork[7] that he used as his chief model for the physical world, for the *Tabula rasa* allowed Locke to think of a simple idea in the understanding *as if* it were mechanically produced by a physical object, just as what appears on the face of a clock is the mechanical effect of hidden Clockwork. The impression mechanically produced on the *Tabula rasa* can be construed as a self-portrait of the signet-ring or printer's type. This construal gives the impression semiotic status both as an *index*, by virtue of its being a causal effect of the die, and as an *icon*, by virtue of its being a copy, however defective. (In Locke's theory of perception, the ideas of secondary qualities are defective as icons in that they do not resemble, as the ideas of the primary qualities do, the powers that produce them.) The impression could be granted semiotic status also by construing it as a character, or letter of the alphabet, used as a purely arbitrary *symbol*.[8] But, whereas an act of the author produces the character, it is the impact of the die that produces its self-portrait. For the purpose of opposing innatism, Locke found it useful to dwell on the indexical and iconic properties of the impression, treating it as a self-portrait of the die. Its symbolic properties as a character were not as useful to him. (Locke does consider it as a character when focusing on the principles of which the simple ideas are ingredients.) What Locke especially wanted was not the author's intent but the impact of the die, without which the *Tabula rasa* remains blank. It should be noted, however, that resemblance and physical causality offer only the respective *grounds* for the iconic and the indexical modes of signification, not the signification itself. In *any* of its modes, signification is a triadic relation that includes not just the sign and the thing signified, but also at least a potential sign user as a third term. And, whatever else could be said to be the sign user, the *Tabula rasa* cannot. A piece of paper cannot use or interpret the impression written on it as an icon or index, much less as a symbol. Granted, the paper in Locke's mechanical model is the analogue of the understanding in his perceptual theory, but only of the understanding as passive. His analogy cannot illustrate the *understanding* putting its own ideas to semiotic use. The analogy, of course, might illustrate an omniscient epistemologist using as signs the ideas in the understanding of someone *else*. But this could hardly be what Locke had in mind when he declared that ideas are semiotic instruments of our knowledge. And if one *were* to make the analogy between the *Tabula rasa* and the understanding a basis for the contention that the understanding acquires knowledge by using its own ideas as signs, then the stronger the analogy, the weaker the argument. So it would be self-defeating to use the metaphor of the idea as an imprint to support that contention.

There is little temptation at this point to develop such an argument, however, if only because of the weakness of the analogy. The *Tabula rasa* is a physical object, and the impression is a mechanical alteration. The understanding is not a physical object, and an idea is not a mechanical alteration. We can, however, produce a stronger analogy by shifting the model from mechanics to optics. In seventeenth-century physics, mechanical models were being used successfully to explain nonmechanical effects produced with optical instruments, and so it was open to Locke to develop his core model for the passive understanding so as to incorporate it in an optical instrument. One of these devices is the *Speculum*, or mirror.[9] This extended analogy makes an idea in the understanding the analogue of the virtual image in the *Speculum*, just as the mirror image in turn is the analogue of the impression on the *Tabula rasa*. Another optical model that Locke used for the passive understanding is the *Camera obscura*, or dark room.[10] With this model the analogue of the idea becomes the inverted real image. Using the *Camera obscura*, Locke could extend his analogy even further by appealing to the great discovery made by

Kepler in physiological optics at the beginning of the seventeenth century. What Kepler had discovered is that light behaves in the mammalian eye just as it does in the *Camera obscura*, except that the effect produced is not merely optical but also a temporary neurophysiological alteration of the sense organ.[11] Locke, then, could move easily in his string of analogies from the *Camera obscura* to the *Oculus*, or eye,[12] to find his most comprehensive model for the passive understanding. With this traditional physiological model, as newly "understood" in the "light" of Kepler, the analogue of the idea becomes the inverted retinal image. Of course, the *Oculus* does not use the retinal image as a sign any more than the *Tabula rasa* uses the impression as a sign. But there is a complication now. The retinal image is not just the *analogue* of any (simple) idea, but it is also a normal physiological *condition* of perceiving any (complex) visual idea. Notwithstanding, not even the perceiver who possesses the *Oculus* as an organ of vision uses the retinal image as a sign. The user of a retinal image as a sign, if there ever is such a user, can only be an outside observer, such as René Descartes or Christoph Scheiner, who experimented with the eyes of oxen. Just because the experimenter takes the retinal image as a self-portrait of an object situated before the *Oculus* does not mean that the ox uses that physiological effect as a semiotic instrument in its knowledge. God did not give the ox its two *Oculi*—yes, there are usually *two* retinal images—so that Descartes or Scheiner could see pictures in them (though they could), much less so that the ox could see pictures in them (for it could not). Seeing is not a matter of using one's own retinal images as signs, and so the analogy between the *Oculus* and the understanding cannot illustrate ideas as semiotic instruments of our knowledge.

If an analogy cannot illustrate a point, then it is wrong to use it as evidence to support the point. Consider what the argument from the analogy between the passive understanding and the *Oculus* would be. *First premise*: The idea (in the perceptual theory) is like the retinal image (in the physiological model) in several respects (such as the passivity of its receptor and the need for "openings" in the receptor). *Second premise* (regarding only the model): The retinal image is used as a sign (*not* by its receptor, the *Oculus*, or even by the possessor of the *Oculus*, but) by the likes of Scheiner and Descartes. *Conclusion* (regarding only the theory): The idea is used as a sign by its receptor, the understanding. When the argument is stated so baldly it is easy to see that the second premise does nothing whatsoever to support the conclusion.

We need not ascribe this argument from Locke's analogy to Locke himself in order to consider the possibility that it has been an influential argument in winning converts to his dualistic theory of perception, indeed possibly more influential than any of Locke's own actual arguments. In Locke's epistemological dualism, as traditionally understood, ideas are only representations or copies, however inadequate, of what we would know. The defectiveness of the argument lies not in a failure to show that ideas can be pictures, images, representations, self-portraits, or the like of original corporeal qualities—the analogy could provide at least some support for *that* view—but in its failure to show the possibility of the *understanding* using its *own* ideas as signs in this or any other way. Indeed, to the extent that the analogy *were* to support the contention that ideas only represent corporeal qualities, it would equally support the contention that it is *not* the understanding that so interprets them. The analogy *taken by itself* offers no aid to the epistemological dualist. But if the argument under consideration is so defective, then how could it ever have gained a foothold, as I suggest it has? It strikes me, as I think it did Socrates at his trial, that the most influential and at the same time the most pernicious arguments are sometimes unstated ones working surreptitiously, because they are unexamined, through imagination and passion. Mists of confusion arise to obscure their defectiveness, and in the argument at hand I believe that there have been two sorts of confusion. One is the confusion of three things within the physiological model: the *Oculus* itself, the possessor of the *Oculus*, and the experimenter using the retinal image in the *Oculus* as a sign. The other is the confusion of the image in the physiological model with the idea in the perceptual theory, a confusion that Locke himself fostered by using his theoretical term 'idea' to designate the optical and physiological images in his models. When one confuses the model with the theory, the argument takes on an air of conclusiveness inappropriate to this type of argument from analogy, and the question is begged.

Part of Berkeley's advancement of the doctrine of signs was through a reconstruing of the Lockean metaphor of the idea as imprinted character or image. By transforming the metaphor, Berkeley, unlike Locke, was able to use it in support of the claim that our ideas are semiotic instruments of our knowledge. This seemed to necessitate, however, abandoning the dualistic claim that ideas are (sometimes defective) self-portraits of corporeal qualities without the mind.

In transforming the metaphor, Berkeley dropped the *Tabula rasa* as a model for the understanding after first appropriating its impressions. Berkeley did not want these impressions as self-portraits produced by the impact of independently existing bodies. Instead he treated them merely as symbolic characters produced by the act of an *Auctor*, or author. This shift allowed Berkeley to replace Locke's occult Clockwork with the *Scriptura*, or written characters, as a new model for the physical world, a model that Colin Murray Turbayne has drawn to our attention.[13] The understanding perceptually affected by the *Scriptura* becomes the *Lector*, or reader. With the *Lector*, Berkeley could reinterpret what the Fellow of the Royal Society does in his scientific work. Locke, having come upon the medieval system of science—like Old St. Paul's Cathedral—in ruins, had set himself the task of clearing the rubbish for the Builders like Christopher Wren to erect a new structure. But the building blocks that Locke allowed the Builder were only surrogates—and sometimes misleading ones at that—for the real features of nature. Berkeley, believing that the scientist confronts the book of nature more immediately, transformed Locke's construction worker, who deals in bloodless "images," into an interpreter of cordial "words." In making this transformation, Berkeley hoped to draw the mind toward the *Auctor* "in whom we live, and move, and have our being."[14] Locke, too, had recognized features common to the arbitrary signification of words and the natural signification of ideas, as evidenced by his allowance that neither sort of signification requires resemblance between the sign and what it signifies. But Berkeley, after all, held that we see the color white because of a direct act of (divine) volition, whereas Locke held that the immediate cause probably had to do with something like corpuscles. For Locke, although the signification of words depends on volition, at least the natural signification of ideas does not. The differences between the conventional and the natural went deep. I think that Locke could look on with some approval as his colleagues in the Royal Society dreamt the Baconian dream of forsaking the artifice of the court for the golden world of the Forest of Arden. But to Berkeley this was the impossible dream, and so he was so bold as to declare that the general principles of signification governing the world of human contrivance are the very ones governing the natural world as well. All the world's a stage.

When Berkely assigned linguistic, arbitrary signification to natural signs, he was not thereby barring them from epistemic use, nor was he necessarily confusing truth with meaning. The infallibility or unreliability of a sign *of* something, of course, is something other than the rightness or wrongness of a sign *for* something. But Berkeley should not be disallowed the possibility of books in the running brooks and sermons in stones on the supposition that the same sign cannot be both correct *and* fallible.[15] That the supposition is mistaken should be obvious when one considers *artificial* signs. Thomas Hobbes gave as an example of an artificial sign a bush hung up by the door to signify that wine is sold there.[16] This signification of the bush was correct seventeenth-century usage. But its reliability can also be brought into question, for we could wonder whether someone had neglected to take down the bush or even whether someone intended to mislead the traveler. Consider now *natural* signs. *If* natural signs can be thought to have linguistic signification, then one can make *that* the basis for putting them to epistemic use. When Berkeley made the *Lector* an analogue of the understanding, he was indeed granting linguistic meaning to natural signs, but this in itself is not evidence that he confused truth with meaning.

The *Scriptura* model is rich enough to provide several different sorts of linguistic rules, which the *Lector* might make the basis for his epistemic use of natural signs. Among the semantic rules there are not just those of reference, in either the object language or the metalanguage, but also semantic rules of translation, such as those governing the transliteration of characters from one alphabet into another, or the translation of written words from one language into another, or the translation of written into spoken words within the same language. Turbayne has succeeded in showing, I believe, that, although Berkeley's theory of vision relies heavily on the last kind of translation rule, his more general theory of knowledge appeals more to syntactical rules of combination. In considering the Fellow of the Royal Society in the narrowness of his scientific approach, which finds him reducing the various combinations of ideas to rule, Berkeley characterized him as the Grammarian of nature. Ideally, however, the *Lector* has the enlarged vision that permits him to approach the *Scriptura* with the full hermeneutic apparatus of the true literary Critic.

How is the literary work to be interpreted?[17] It is a mirror held up to nature. Art imitates life. The literary work is a representation of the world. So goes the *mimetic* theory of interpretation. No, the work of art is self-contained. It is not to be judged by external standards, such as how well it copies nature, but it is a universe in its own right, governed by its own laws. The work is to be understood in terms of the formal relations among its parts. This is the *objective* theory of interpretation. No, a poem or book does have a function, which is to move its reader in some specific way—by "recreating and exalting the mind," by edifying, by purging, by entertaining, or whatever. It is the effect produced on the audience or reader that counts. Here we have the *pragmatic* theory of interpretation. Finally, the real function of the work of literary art is to express the writer's feelings and intentions—indeed, the very being of the author. What is important in the words is what they reveal of the artist. Any work of art is a veil, but one which is also an epiphany, a manifestation of its creator. This is the *expressive* theory of interpretation.

The basic insights embodied in these four theories of interpretation can be reconciled within a semiotic approach to the work of art.[18] As a sign, or system of signs, the work has some sort of semantic relation to *the world*, which the mimetic theory emphasizes. But the formal relations among the various parts of *the work itself* require the syntactical anaylsis demanded by objective theorists, such as the New Critics of the early *Kenyon Review*. The pragmatic dimension of sign usage brings in the triadic nature of the sign relation. The pragmatic theory of criticism, by considering the work's "perlocutionary" force, as J. L. Austin called it,[19] measures the success of the work in terms of whether it is capable of producing in *the audience* certain results, such as a purging of pity and terror. But the work also has "illocutionary" force, and the expressive theory, by asking what the artist was doing in the making of the work, considers what it discloses of *its author*.

Berkeley's *Scriptura* model allows physical nature to be interpreted in similar ways. The mimetic theory tells us that nature itself is a mirror. A mirror of what? It imitates the language with which we are already familiar. Its semantic referent is the English language. The golden world of nature reflects a product of human contrivance. But nature is also a self-contained—or nearly self-contained—system. The objective theory tells us that one of the jobs of the physical scientist is to try to reduce the connections between phenomena to syntactical rule. There are limits to formalization, however, and the pragmatic theory tells us that the rules are meant to have utility. Armed with counterfactual conditionals derived from our systematization of nature, we can steer the most likely courses for avoiding harm and gaining benefit. If we were to perform such-and-such an operation, then we would likely be confronted with such-and-such a phenomenal result. When we interpret the discourse of nature in this way, it can offer nourishment, comfort, and delight. But Berkeley also believed, in line with the expressive theory, that the *Scriptura* of nature manifests the goodness and power and wisdom of its Creator. Berkeley's ideas of sense veil reality, but not as Lockean ideas that screen the would-be knower from an abstract matter. Berkeley's ideas themselves are an immediate physical reality, and the reality they seem to conceal, which is spiritual, they partially reveal.

Let me now turn from this veil of ideas to a matching veil of words, thereby passing from the philosophy of perception to the philosophy of language.

Locke had used the metaphor of a mist of words to express both his worry about the natural *imperfection* of language and his worry about the willful *abuse* of language. In complaining about the imperfection of language Locke wrote that words

> interpose themselves so much between our Understandings, and the Truth, which it would contemplate and apprehend, that like the *Medium* through which visible Objects pass, their Obscurity and Disorder does not seldom cast a mist before our Eyes, and impose upon our Understandings.[20]

The paradoxical nature of a verbal attack on words was at least dimly recognized by Locke himself when he admitted that "so hard is it, to shew the various meaning and imperfection of Words, when we have nothing else but Words to do it by."[21] In complaining about the abuse of language, Locke asked:

> Whether it would not be well . . . that the Use of Words were made plain and direct; and that Language, which was given us for the improvement of Knowledge, and bond of Society, should not be employ'd to darken Truth, and unsettle Peoples Rights; to raise Mists and render unintelligible both Morality and Religion?[22]

Now, Locke held that "all the artificial and figurative application of Words Eloquence hath invented . . . are certainly, in all Discourses that pretend to inform or instruct, wholly to be avoided."[23] Because Locke's advocacy of plain speaking included this ban on figurative language, it brings to notice the paradox of a metaphorical assault on metaphor. And, as we have already seen, the verbal "mist" is but *one* example of Locke's use of metaphor in his theorizing about the understanding.

The complaints about verbal mists, however, were scarcely original with Locke. Throughout the seventeenth century, English spokesmen for both science and religion used the mist and related metaphors to plead the cause of "naked" truth.[24] In part they were advocating discourses stripped "bare" not just of obscure or affected speech but of all figurative language whatsoever. During the Restoration period, reformers of pulpit oratory blamed fancy language for the incivility of the recent civil strife. One reason for opposing figurative speech—the reason that Thomas Hobbes gave for banning metaphor from the speech of the counselor—was the supposition that its tendency to stir up the passions makes it useful only to deceive.[25] Also suspect, however, was the similitude grounding a figure. The authority of

Aristotle's *Rhetoric* could be invoked for using a good metaphor to get hold of a new idea easily, and Francis Bacon allowed that similitude could appropriately be used in the infancy of learning in order to make formerly unfamiliar notions capable of being conceived.[26] But what facilitates familiarization with knowledge may obstruct its advancement. Figures may be justified for pedagogical but not investigative purposes. The sixteenth-century magician, through his belief in divine "signatures" as a form of the world secretly bound to it by affinity, could hail the walnut as a cure for headaches because of its resemblance to the brain.[27] Once the seventeenth century had renounced such occult similitudes, resemblance seemed to smack of illusion. Locke could praise the faculty of "judgment," which discriminates or distinguishes between ideas, only at the expense of the faculty of "wit," which pleases the "fancy" by putting together ideas "wherein can be found any resemblance or congruity."[28] When Locke's age assigned metaphor, simile, and allegory to the imagination or fancy, it was officially barring the conceits of John Donne, Henry Vaughan, Thomas Herbert, and the other metaphysical poets from the scientific language of reason. The doctrine of signatures had been ousted by the doctrine of signs. Signs were supposed to be only a neutral and transparent means of ordering things in terms of their identities and differences. Once words were distinguished from things, discourse could stop pretending to be anything more than what it said. By the "naked" truth was meant, then, not just plain speech, in which *language* is stripped, even of figures, but our *ideas* stripped of the artifice and alleged cheat of words themselves.

What words were thought to veil was a *mental* discourse. Yet no one was really willing to rest content living the life of just his own mental discourse, even assuming that to be possible. ("In respect that it is solitary, I like it very well; but in respect that it is private, it is a very vile life.") What was envisioned was an ideal language, which, according to Thomas Sprat, historian for the Royal Society, would deliver so many things in an equal number of words.[29] Bishop Sprat believed that the natural languages had once approximated this primitive purity and shortness. Perhaps it could be recaptured. The Royal Society assigned to another of its Fellows, John Wilkins, the task of constructing an artificial language of real rather than nominal characters.[30] Bishop Wilkins's program had already been proposed by Francis Bacon,[31] that great master of figurative language who had damned words as the most troublesome of all the idols that beset men's minds.[32] The Royal Society welcomed Bacon's declaration that words are but the images of things, and that the learned are too enamored with words.[33] The view was not confined to the Fellows of the Royal Society. Alexander Ross, for instance, had already written in the "Epistle Dedicatorie" to his *Medicus Medicatus* (1645), "Expect not here from me Rhetorical flourishes: I study matter, not words: *Good wine needs no bush*."

So pervasive a metaphor as that of the mist or veil of words had no difficulty spilling over into the eighteenth century and into the thought of Berkeley. Indeed, this particular metaphor seemed to determine his very aim. In the *Philosophical Commentaries*, we find (in entry 567) his praise of Locke for having seen through the "mist" as far as he had, and (in entry 642) his proclamation that "the chief thing I do or pretend to do is onely to remove the mist or veil of Words." Entry 717 declared that Locke should have begun, at least in his thinking, with the third book of the *Essay*, which dealt with words; and that is where Berkeley began his own *Principles of Human Knowledge*. The verbal mist or veil, along with related metaphors, crop up innumerable times in the Introduction to the *Principles*, especially in the Manuscript Introduction. What we are in danger of overlooking, however, is that Berkeley was pouring new wine into an old bottle. Berkeley's radical transformation of the veil of words merits a separate detailed study. (Anyone undertaking this task will find Bertil Belfrage's forthcoming diplomatic edition of the Manuscript Introduction indispensable.) The significance of this transformation lies in its departure from the seventeenth-century dogma of the solitary, private thinker in his golden world.

Without this important departure Berkeley could not have reached his new understanding of the nature of generality in scientific law. The mind, wrote Berkeley in the seventh dialogue of *Alciphron*, is designed "not for the bare intuition of ideas, but for action and operation about them, and pursuing her own happiness therein." For this purpose the mind needs general rules, which

> are not to be obtained by the mere consideration of the original ideas, or particular things, but by means of marks and signs, which being so far forth universal, become the immediate instruments and materials of science.[34]

This was no American afterthought. Berkeley had already reached this view in Ireland years earlier while reworking the Manuscript Introduction to the *Principles*. Berkeley had indeed used the conceit of the Solitary Man in the first stratum of his manuscript, but his revisions show him recognizing legitimate scientific uses of words and other symbols that go beyond the mere recording or communicating of ideas. Berkeley struck out the Solitary Man, leaving only his shadow to guarantee that among the scientist's ideas there are none framed by abstraction. Elsewhere in the Manuscript Introduction, he introduced the notion of the algebraic variable used in calculations when its assigned value is not actually in mind. Lurking in this notion was the conceit of the Reckoner or Gamester, who operates at the card table with counters. Berkeley made this conceit explicit in the seventh dialogue of *Alciphron*,[35] but it was already in embryo form in "*De Ludo Algebraico*," one of the papers that Berkeley had gathered up in 1707 for his first publication, the *Arithmetica* and *Miscellanea Mathematica*. There Berkeley had shown how algebra could be treated as a game in which its symbols are manipulated without regard for their application.

What, then, was the new meaning carried in the metaphor of the mist or veil of words? Locke had used the metaphor to warn his reader of the self-deceit which arises from the natural imperfection of words and their willful abuse in affected and figurative language for cognitive purposes. Berkeley, on the other hand, found the source of self-deceit in misconstruing the use of words. Where Locke had worried about *words*, Berkeley worried about the *doctrine* of words.[36] It is a false doctrine that when a word is kept to a single definition it must always stand for the same idea;[37] that the idea it is appointed to stand for must be suggested to the mind each time the word is used;[38] that the chief or sole end of language is the communication of ideas;[39] and that figurative speech in cognitive discourse is an abuse of language.[40] Because he was directing the Introduction to his *Principles* against the doctrine of abstract ideas, it was beside his purpose to consider figurative language there. But his refusal to fault our natural faculties opened the way for his fully explicit acknowledgment in the seventh dialogue of *Alciphron* that models, metaphors, analogies, and the like are essential to science. It is through figures that we move from the known to the unknown, from the familiar to the unfamiliar, from the more immediate to the more important, from the more actual to the more real.[41] Berkeley ordered and presented his own philosophical vision on a hierarchal scale that starts with the objects of vision, moves thence to the objects of the other senses by way of the imagination, and then ascends from sensory ideas to the objects of reason. The physical world is the mind's road to God. Nor is there any abuse as such in using figurative language, which is inevitable. There is abuse, however, in misconstruing it. For instance, when we use physical models to speak of the spiritual, we should not suppose that the actions of the spirit, of which we can have only "notions,"[42] are like the motions of billiard balls.[43] Another instance, examined earlier in this paper, is the assignment of semiotic status to ideas on the basis of a misuse of Locke's physical models for the passive understanding. The very riskiness of metaphor, however, might be taken as an indication of the power that metaphor has in doing good.

If the English mist of words is a gross concealment and even a misrepresentation of reality by the words themselves, then the Irish mist is more subtle and fine. Though as a false doctrine of words the verbal veil does indeed misrepresent reality, as the properly construed words themselves—especially in their figurative use—it discloses the reality it first seems to conceal. In any good book, however, the disclosure will not be complete or final. Berkeley's lifelong opposition to the deists shows that his devotion to the Enlightenment ideals of a clarification and enlargement of our vision was never intended as a belittlement of the genuinely mysterious. Berkeley was an enemy only of crippling or "uncouth" paradox. In the words of Heraclitus, "The lord whose oracle is in Delphi neither speaks out nor conceals, but gives a sign."[44]

In the background of Berkeley's advancement of the doctrine of signs was his revision of the Lockean metaphor of the idea as an imprinted character and the Lockean metaphor of the word as a veil or mist. Without these revisions our understanding of the understanding is threatened by fruitless paradox. With these revisions the metaphors can offer support for the claim that ideas and words are semiotic instruments of the understanding. But if it be true that a good wine needs no bush, 'tis true that a good performance needs no epilogue. And so what I have said here is meant only as prologue to Berkeley's own words, which I hope will disclose the doctrine of signs as you like it.

Notes

1. *Alciphron: or, The Minute Philosopher. In Seven Dialogues. Containing An Apology for the Christian Religion, against those who are called Free-Thinkers* (1732), dial. VII, sect. 13. All Berkeley quotations are taken from A. A. Luce and T. E. Jessop, eds., *The Works of George Berkeley, Bishop of Cloyne*, 9 vols. (London: Thomas Nelson and Sons, 1948-57); hereafter referred to as *Works*.

2. Bk. IV, chap, xxi, sect. 4. All Locke quotations are taken from John Locke, *An Essay concerning Human Understanding*, ed. Peter H. Nidditch (Oxford: Oxford University Press, 1975); hereafter referred to as *Essay*.

3. *Essay*, IV, xxi, 4.

4. *Essay*, I, i, 8.

5. The implicit model of the Builder is suggested early in the *Essay* in "The Epistle to the Reader" in the figures of the "master-builders" and the "under-labourer," which figures might be said to reinforce the hunter who "hawks" at his "quarry" and to offer a contrast to the beggar with his "alms-basket." See also I, iv, 25.

6. The comparison of the mind to a blank tablet was made as early as Aristotle, *De Anima*, II, 12; III, 4. For the Stoic use of the comparison, see *Stoicorum Veterum Fragmenta*, ed. Hans von Arnim (Leipzig, 1903-24), II, 53-56; 59; 63. The comparison is rejected in Plotinus, *Enneads*, IV, vi, 1-3. In Locke's day, the *"abrasa tabula"* was used in Nathanael Culverwel, *An Elegant and Learned Discourse of the Light of Nature* (1652) and in Benjamin Whichcote, *Works*, II, 4. The *"rasa tabula"* makes its appearance in Draft A of Locke's *Essay*, sect 2, fol. 58; and in Draft B, sect. 17. In the published *Essay* (in II, ii, 2), Locke compares the mind to "white paper, void of all characters." (The figure is already implicit in I, ii, 1; 22; 25; and II, i, 2.) In *Nouveaux Essais sur l'entendement humain* (1765 posthumous), Leibniz objected to Locke's comparison of the mind to *"une Table rase."* Published nearly half a century after Leibniz's death, the *New Essays* (according to Wilhelm Windelband) had a great influence on Kant's *Inaugural Dissertation* (1770).

7. Descartes compared the human body to a mechanical clock in *L'Homme*, a part of *Le Monde ou Traité de la Lumière* (1662 posthumous, completed 1633) and in Part V of *Discours de la Méthode* (1637). Thomas Hobbes compared the animal body to the mechanism of a watch in *Leviathan* (1651), Introduction. Locke used "the inward contrivance of that famous Clock at *Strasburg*" as a model for any body in the *Essay*, III, vi, 9. The use of the Cartesian model of a machine to provide a world view is discussed in Colin Murray Turbayne, *The Myth of Metaphor* (New Haven: Yale University Press, 1962). The present paper owes much to Prof. Turbayne's notion of model and metaphor.

8. The terminology 'index', 'icon', and 'symbol' is taken from the classification of signs provided by Charles Sanders Peirce.

9. The *Speculum* appears as a model for the mind at least as early as Plato, *Timaeus* 71. Each link in the Neoplatonists' Great Chain of Being was a microcosm "reflecting" the One. The mirror was a favorite Renaissance analogue for both painting and the painter's mind, and—by extension—the poet and his work. Francis Bacon used the (smooth) mirror as a metaphor for the *ideal* mind in *The Advancement of Learning* (1605), I, i, 3; also in the Plan of the Work of *The Great Instauration*, prefixed to its second part, the *Novum Organum* (1620). (Ideally, the understanding is a *Speculum non coloratum*, whereas in actuality it is a *Speculum inaequale*.) The *Speculum* found its way into Draft B of Locke's *Essay*, sect. 21, in a passage reproduced in the published *Essay*, II, i, 25, thus:

> These *simple Ideas*, when offered to the mind, *the Understanding can* no more refuse to have, nor alter, when they are imprinted, nor blot them out, and make new ones in it self, than a mirror can refuse, alter, or obliterate the Images or *Ideas*, which, the Objects set before it, do therein produce.

Note how Locke uses the term 'ideas' as an alternate way of denoting mirror images when he is setting up his model.

10. Although perhaps the earliest mention of the *camera obscura* in England, though not referred to by that name, was in Bacon's *De Augmentis Scientiarum* (1623), Bacon did not use it there as a model for the understanding. Culverwel, despite his claim that the natural law is written in our hearts, required the senses as "windows" of the understanding in *The Light of Nature* (1652), and Locke was already employing the *Camera obscura* as a model for the mind as early as his fourth essay on the law of nature (after 1660). The "dark room" appears in Draft B of the *Essay*, sect. 31; and "a little hole" of that draft becomes "some little opening[s]" in the published *Essay*, II, xi, 17. (Note that the plural 'openings'

becomes singular in the fourth and fifth editions.) This is related to "the yet empty Cabinet" in I, ii. 15.

11. As early as the tenth/eleventh century, Alhazen had used the *Camera obscura* in optical anatomy, but Kepler was the first to publish an account of how it can be used consistently as a model allowing for an *inverted* "image" projected onto the *retina* of an eye. See his *Ad Vitellionem paralipomena* (1604) and *Dioptrica* (1611). Some of Kepler's Renaissance predecessors (such as Leonardo da Vinci and Giambattista della Porta) had also tried to use the *Camera obscura* as an ocular model, but they mistook the *lens* for the receptor and demanded an *erect* image.

12. If, as Aristotle said, thinking is analogous to perceiving, then, just as the eye is the organ of vision, so the understanding is the organ of thought. Bacon wrote of the "eye" of the understanding in the Preface to *The Great Instauration*, as did Culverwel in *The Light of Nature*, IX. This analogy, a commonplace in the seventeenth century, was introduced by Locke into the second paragraph of the "Epistle to the Reader" and reappeared (in a passage similar to that in Draft B, sect. 1) in the second sentence of the opening paragraph of the "Introduction" to the *Essay*, I, i, 1.

13. C. M. Turbayne, *The Myth of Metaphor*, contrasts Berkeley's "language" model with the Cartesians' "machine" model. The Berkeleyan model is spelled out (if the pun may be permitted) as an "alphabet" model in Turbayne, "Berkeley's Metaphysical Grammar," in his edition of *Berkeley: Principles of Human Knowledge, Text and Critical Essays* (Indianapolis: Bobbs-Merrill, 1970), pp. 3-36.

14. Acts 17:18.

15. This is in opposition to J. L. Austin, "Truth," *Proceedings of the Aristotelian Society*, Supplementary Volume XXIV (1950); repr. in J. L. Austin, *Philosophical Papers* (Oxford: Oxford University Press, 1961), pp. 85-101.

16. *Elements of Philosophy* (1656, Latin edition 1655), pt. I, chap. ii, sect. 2.

17. The following classification of theories of interpretation is from M. H. Abrams, *The Mirror and the Lamp: Romantic Theory and the Critical Tradition* (New York: Oxford University Press, 1958; first published Oxford, 1953).

18. The notion of the three dimensions of sign usage is taken from Charles Morris, *Foundation of the Theory of Signs. International Encyclopedia of Unified Science*, vol. 1, no. 2 (Chicago: University of Chicago Press, 1938).

19. For the terms 'perlocutionary' and 'illocutionary' see Austin, *How to Do Things with Words* (New York: Oxford University Press, 1965; first published 1962).

20. *Essay*, III, ix, 21.

21. Ibid., III, vi, 19.

22. Ibid., III, x, 13.

23. Ibid., III, x, 34.

24. For this story see, for example, George Williamson, *The Senecan Amble: A Study in Prose Form from Bacon to Collier* (Chicago: University of Chicago Press, 1951). Some seventeenth-century titles, prior to Locke's *Essay* (1690), in the assault on language and metaphor: Francis Bacon, *The Advancement of Learning* (1605); Alexander Ross, *Medicus Medicatus* (1645); Alexander Ross, *The Philosophicall Touch-stone* (1645); Thomas Hobbes, *Leviathan* (1651); Meric Casaubon, *A Treatise of Enthusiasme* (1655); Samuel Parker, *A Free and Impartial Censure of Platonick Philosophie* (1666); Thomas Sprat, *History of the Royal Society*, with Abraham Cowley's "Prefatory Ode," (1667); John Wilkins, *An Essay towards a Real Character, and a Philosophical Language* (1668); and John Eachard, *Grounds and Occasion of the Contempt of the Clergy* (1670). Locke wrote the first drafts of the *Essay* in 1671.

25. *Leviathan*, pt. II, chap. 25.

26. *The Advancement of Learning*, bk. II, chap. xvii, sect. 10.

27. On the magical mode of thought, see Michel Foucault, *The Order of Things* (New York: Pantheon Books, 1971).

28. *Essay*, II, xi, 2.

29. *History of the Royal Society* (1667).

30. *An Essay towards a Real Character, and a Philosophical Language* (1668).

31. See, for instance, *The Advancement of Learning*, II, xvi, 1.

32. Aphorism LIX in *The New Organon*.

33. See, for instance, Abraham Cowley's Prefatory Ode to Sprat's *History of the Royal Society*.

34. Sect. 11.

35. Sect. 5.

36. Compare the passage from Berkeley with the parallel passage from Locke quoted on p. 231.

37. *Principles*, Introduction, sect. 18.

38. Ibid., sect. 19.

39. Ibid., sect. 20.

40. *Three Dialogues Between Hylas and Philonous* (1713), Third *Dialogue*, in *Works*, II, p. 250.

41. Sect. 13.

42. A technical term added in 1734 to the second edition of the *Principles*.

43. *Principles*, sect. 144.

44. G. S. Kirk and J. E. Raven, *The Presocratic Philosophers* (Cambridge: Cambridge University Press, 1960), p. 211.

16

Dynamical Implications of Berkeley's Doctrine of Heterogeneity: A Note on the Language Model of Nature

Lawrence A. Mirarchi

Berkeley's analysis of the Newtonian concept of force continues to pose a problem for contemporary commentators. On the one hand, Berkeley insists that there are no physical forces in nature: "*Force, gravity, attraction,* and terms of this sort are useful for reasonings and reckonings about motion and bodies in motion, but not for understanding the simple nature of motion itself or for indicating so many distinct qualities."[1] On the other hand, he accepts Newtonian dynamics with its distinction between force-free and accelerated motion and even appears to invoke the presence of a force as a criterion of absolute motion: "For to denominate a body 'moved' it is requisite, first, that it change its distance or situation with regard to some other body; and secondly, that the force or action occasioning that change be applied to it" (*Principles,* sect. 115).[2] According to Richard Brook in his book *Berkeley's Philosophy of Science,* ". . . there is a central ambiguity concerning how Berkeley understands Newton's first two laws of motion. At times he suggests that they are empirical generalizations of a rather straightforward sort; . . . at other times he suggests that the legitimate use of 'forces' in mechanics is comparable to using a mathematical fiction, like the 'lines and angles' of geometers."[3] The prevailing critical attitudes seem to fall into two categories: Popper, Whitrow, and Myhill[4] pay tribute to the contemporary empiricist character of Berkeley's philosophy of science, viewing Berkeley as a precursor of Mach and Einstein but not addressing the specific problems of interpretation surrounding his concept of force. Others, such as Brook, Silver, and Ritchie,[5] view Berkeley as

247

being at odds with himself, or inconsistent with Newton's laws, or generally "weak in dynamics." The latter commentators have together brought to light some crucial issues in the interpretation of Berkeley's philosophy of science. How can Berkeley deny the existence of forces and yet accept their validity in Newtonian dynamics? In what sense can Berkeley accept Newton's laws as empirical generalizations, relating force and acceleration while regarding "force" as a mathematical fiction? Is Berkeley refuted by Newton's crucial experiments with the rotating globes and the whirling bucket designed to demonstrate the empirical connection of force with absolute motion? In a recent paper, I gave one approach toward resolving these problems through metaphorical extension of haptic force experiences to inanimate objects.[6] I now wish to approach the same issues by way of Berkeley's unique and as yet not fully appreciated approach to contemporary logical empiricism. This approach is embodied in a semiotic interpretation of nature, that is, that nature is a collection of heterogeneous signs constituting a language. It is not my purpose here to develop a language model of Newtonian mechanics, or even to defend Berkeley's doctrines. I wish instead to undertake the more modest project of showing how Berkeley's doctrine of heterogeneity and his language model of nature, insofar as he himself articulated them, serve to clarify his views on the concept of force along with the associated concepts of absolute space and absolute motion.

Berkeley's doctrine of the heterogeneity of objects of sight and touch is developed at great length in the *Essay Towards a New Theory of Vision* and in *The Theory of Vision . . . Vindicated and Explained.*[7] The doctrine is introduced in the *New Theory of Vision*: "The extensions, figures and motions perceived by sight are specifically distinct from the ideas of touch, called by the same names; nor is there any such thing as one idea, or kind of idea, common to both senses" (sect. 127). On this claim, the coordination of the visual roundness of a baseball with its tactual counterpart is not a priori. Though the visual and tactual baseballs are "called by the same names," they are distinct objects that are reputed to be one thing through their repeated association in experience. In the context of Berkeley's phenomenalism, this means that no third object or "common sensible" can be invoked to account for our experienced coordination of the visual and tactual baseball. The tactual baseball and the visual baseball are related in experience so that each becomes a sign for the other. If the experienced coordination of the heterogeneous qualities of sight and touch is not due to an independently existing common sensible, it follows that the coordinating principle must be either another idea or a transcendent immaterial cause. But ideas are passive: "[A]ll our ideas, sensations, or the things which we perceive, by whatsoever names they be distinguished, are visibly inactive—there is nothing of power or agency included in them. So that one idea or object of thought cannot produce or make any alteration in another" (*Principles*, sect. 25). It follows that objects of sight and touch, which can exist only as ideas in a perceiver, are rendered active and are ordered and coordinated not by any material principle but by the mind of a perceiver.

There are two levels at which this coordination and ordering occur. The first is at the level of a transcendent Spirit or Mind, which is the first cause of ideas and their relations: "The ideas of sense . . . are not excited at random . . . but in a regular train or series, the admirable connection whereof sufficiently testifies the wisdom and benevolence of its Author" (*Principles*, sect. 30). At this level the claim is relevant to science only to the extent that the scientist presupposes an objective order of nature, which is given in experience and which provides the basis for testing the truth of scientific claims. Transcendent Spirit apart, belief in an objective order of nature is a starting point for all scientific investigation and poses no issues peculiar to Berkeley's system. The second level is that of the individual perceiver or community of perceivers, the scientists, who select from among the infinite number of possible objective relations given in experience those particular groupings that suit the needs of the investigators. Turbayne[8] has explained how in Berkeley's sense we are all both readers and *authors* of natural relations. This process of selection and grouping is a part of the *creative* function of the scientist as exercised in formulating laws or sorting the appropriate variables to relate in experimentation. The association of force and motion represents a selection, from an infinite number of possibilities, which is deemed significant. On a more primitive level, the idea of a moving automobile and the associated potential experience of force are selected from a myriad of sensations given in experience not because that grouping is unique or absolute but because there could be disastrous consequences to ignoring it while crossing a street. But the coordination of heterogeneous elements in symbolic relations that imbue them with meaning is an essential characteristic of language.

Berkeley introduces his language model of nature in the *New Theory of Vision*: "Upon the whole I think we may fairly conclude that the proper objects of vision constitute a universal language of the Author of nature, . . . and the manner wherein they signify and mark unto us the objects which are at a distance is the same with that of languages and signs of human appointment which do not suggest the things signified by any likeness or identity of nature, but only by a habitual connection that experience has made us to observe between them" (sect. 147). The fact that this passage is a conclusion following Berkeley's extensive discussion of the heterogeneity of objects of sight and touch serves to underline the importance of heterogeneity for the language model. As discussed in articles by Turbayne,[9] the association between written and spoken words of a language is purely one of "human appointment"; the one cannot be inferred from the other for they are arbitrarily associated. These sets of written and spoken words comprising two heterogeneous classes Berkeley calls *artificial language*.[10] One can draw the analogy between written and spoken words on the one hand and visual and tactual ideas on the other. Berkeley does so in the *Principles*: " . . . [v]isible ideas are the language whereby the governing spirit on whom we depend informs us what tangible ideas he is about to imprint upon us in case we excite this or that motion in our own bodies" (sect. 44). The identification of visual ideas with a language leaves no doubt of Berkeley's intention. Especially significant is the association of tangible ideas with (1) an "imprinting," as of words on paper; (2) motion, as in the relation between tangible force and visible acceleration; and (3) "our own bodies," without which tangible ideas would not exist. This suggests that the haptic sensation of force is not in the moving object but must be construed as a haptic experience within ourselves. In the *Principles*, Berkeley then extends his language model to include not only ideas of sight and touch but all natural phenomena. The set of natural phenomena, viewed as the signs of a language, Berkeley refers to as *natural language*. Heterogeneity and the language model imply that when a physicist seeks relations among phenomenal objects, those relations are never necessary but must be viewed semiotically, as relations of signs to things signified. Moreover, only signs (ideas) and minds (perceivers) exist. Therefore, since physics is confined to the domain of ideas, any sign in the artificial language of the theoretical physicist must be a sign of something—either of a phenomenal sign or idea in natural language or of a written sign or grouping of signs in artificial language. These points will now be brought to bear in clarifying some of Berkeley's views on three related Newtonian concepts, those of absolute space, absolute motion, and force.

1. *Absolute space*. Berkeley maintained that space and motion are inherently relational. Thus, in describing a body in motion a reference frame must be chosen. The choice of reference frame is a matter of

convenience, but the same body may be at rest or in motion depend-ing on the reference frame chosen. Although Newton believed that there is no way to establish that a given reference frame is absolute, he maintained that all motion could ultimately be referred to an abso-lute space with respect to which a body is absolutely at rest or abso-lutely in motion: "Absolute space, in its own nature, without rela-tion to anything external, remains always similar and immovable."[11] Newton's definition implies that there is something called 'space' that is without relation to anything apart from itself. But for Berkeley our conception of space is a construct drawn from our experienced coordination of two distinct and heterogeneous spaces, visual space and tactual space. This inherently relational character of space is revealed in Berkeley's claim that visual space has no depth until the objects of sight are augmented with tactual experience: "So that in strict truth the ideas of sight, when we apprehend by them distance and things placed at a distance, do not suggest or mark out to us things actually existing at a distance, but only admonish us what ideas of touch will be imprinted in our minds at such and such dis-tances of time, and in consequence of such and such actions" (Prin-ciples, sect. 44). In keeping with the argument against common sen-sibles used to establish his immaterialist claim, Berkeley is committed in a similar way to the claim that there is no single entity, or com-mon sensible, called 'space' that accounts for the perceived associ-ation of visual and tactual spaces. Newton's absolute space would therefore, at best, be a composite of two heterogeneous parts with each part requiring an external relation to define it relative to the other. Moreover, the whole, as a composite of heterogeneous parts, could not be absolute in Newton's sense because its dichotomous parts cannot be analytically connected with one another. Thus with-out a specification of how the visual and tactual parts are experien-tially related to construct the whole, there would be no space, abso-lute, or otherwise.

Although heterogeneity is a sufficient condition for denying the possibility of absolute space, Berkeley's language model makes his case with more immediacy. The passage from Principles, sect. 44 quoted in the previous paragraph suggests that visual space is a lan-guage wherein the dimension of depth is signified for those who have learned the meaning of its visual symbols by their association with tactual experience. If we draw an analogy between visual and tactual space and the written and spoken words of a language, it is clear that to claim the existence of an absolute space apart from the visual and tactual signs that define it would be akin to claiming the existence of the word "cat" apart from the written sign CAT and the spoken word kat, which are signs of one another. Referring to heterogeneous objects of sense, Berkeley says: "And as several of these are observed to accompany each other, they come to be marked by one name, and so to be reputed as one thing" (*Principles*, sect. 1). Thus the visual and tactual signs of space are mistakenly reputed to be a single entity, which Newton would refer to as his absolute space. But the language model forces an even more fundamental ground for denying the existence of an absolute space. In terms of the language model, the universe is a collection of signs and minds. So absolute space must be either a sign or a mind. The latter possibility was in fact entertained by Newton when he referred to space as the "sensorium of God." Spiritual entities have no place in physics, so absolute space would have to be a sign; that is, absolute space is a word in some language. Since a word has meaning only in terms of what it signifies, if absolute space is "without relation to anything external," then absolute space is not a sign of any language for it fails to signify. Claiming the existence of a sign that does not signify is like claiming the existence of a word that has no meaning and therefore is not a part of any language. In either case, a self-contradiction is unavoidable.

2. *Absolute motion.* According to Newton, "Absolute motion is the translation of a body from one absolute place to another; and relative motion, the translation from one relative place into another."[12] But we have seen that, in Berkeley's phenomenological framework, space is purely relational and absolute space is a self-contradictory concept. It follows that absolute motion cannot be meaningfully defined in terms of absolute places. This leaves the question of whether there is some phenomenal criterion that could distinguish absolute from relative motion. Newton denies that there is any phenomenal criterion that can distinguish absolute from relative motion when that motion is uniform. However, he believed that in the case of accelerated motion the presence of an impressed force establishes that the motion is absolute: "The causes by which true and relative motions are distinguished, one from the other, are the forces impressed upon bodies to generate motion."[13] As proof for his identification of force with motion, Newton offered two examples: the whirling bucket, which has received extensive discussion in the literature,[14] and the two globes connected by a string:

> For instance, if two globes, kept at a distance from one another by means of a cord that connects them, were revolved about their common center of gravity, we might, from the tension of the cord, discover the endeavor of the globes to recede from the axis of their motion, and from

thence we might compute the quantity of their circular motions and then if any equal forces should be impressed at once on the alternate faces of the globes to augment or diminish their circular motions, from the increase or decrease of the tension of the cord, we might infer the increment or decrement of their motions; . . . and thus we might find both the quantity and the determination of this circular motion, even in an immense vacuum, where there is nothing external or sensible with which the globes could be compared.[15]

Berkeley insists that the motion of the globes is purely relative:

> Then let two globes be conceived to exist and nothing corporeal besides them. Let forces then be conceived to be applied in some way; . . . a circular motion of the two globes around a common centre cannot be conceived by the imagination. Then let us suppose that the sky of fixed stars is created; suddenly . . . the motion will be conceived. That is to say that since motion is relative in its own nature, it could not be conceived before the correlated bodies were given. (*De Motu*, scct. 58)

The fact that the absolute motion of the globes "could not be conceived" is significant in view of the language model: If the universe is a collection of signs, then that which could not be conceived cannot be a sign and therefore does not exist. Although Berkeley would grant the association of force and motion, heterogeneity precludes any necessary connection between the two. The existence of a force does not necessitate the motion of the globes, though it may stand as a sign for that motion. But a sign belonging to either natural or artificial language must be a sign of something, that is, of another sign in either the natural or the artificial language. Thus the tension in the string, if it exists, cannot signify that which cannot be conceived. At best, the tension in the string can only signify the potential occurrence of relative motion upon introduction of a suitable reference frame, such as the fixed stars. Ernst Mach also rejects the physical validity of the concept of absolute motion. In comparing the Copernican and Ptolemaic models of the solar system, he says:[16]

> Both views are, indeed, equally *correct*; only the latter is more simple and more *practical*. The universe is not *twice* given, with an earth at rest and an earth in motion; but only *once*, with its relative motions alone determinable. . . . We may interpret the one case that is given us in different ways. . . . The principles of mechanics can, indeed, be so conceived, that even for relative rotations centrifugal forces arise.

Implicit in these passages by Berkeley and Mach is also a recognition of the *reconstitutive* feature of a language: that signs of a language can be reconstituted in different ways to form different messages.[17] For Berkeley, the scientist as reader of natural language studies its "syntax" as dictated by its objective order. The scientist as author chooses the particular grouping of signs that are deemed appropriate in formulating laws. The particular grouping of force and motion is alluded to by Berkeley in the *Principles*: "Now I ask anyone whether, *in his sense* of motion as he walks along the streets, the stones he passes over may be said to move, because they change distance with his feet?" (sect. 113[my emphasis]). Relativity makes nature indifferent as to whether I move or the cobblestones move, for the translational motion of my body along the ground could be viewed as a rotation of the earth beneath my feet. Since I am aware of force, as a manifestation of my own volition or agency as I walk, however, then, in *my sense* of motion, I am in motion. But it does not follow that my motion is absolute, it only follows that I have *defined* motion in this way through an *anthropocentric* choice of phenomenal sign groupings.[16]

But, aside from one's own sense of volition or agency, what is the phenomenal counterpart of force as applied to inanimate objects? Here Berkeley cuts deeper, for he not only denies the necessity of associating force and motion, he denies that there are forces, e.g., the tension in the string, if by 'force' is meant anything more than the observed motions. The balance of my discussion will therefore be devoted to Berkeley's concept of force.

3. *Force*. Through his introduction of the concepts of force and mass, Newton was able successfully to coordinate visual and tactual elements in a science of dynamics. Newton defines force as ". . . an action exerted upon a body, in order to change its state, either of rest or of uniform motion in a right line."[19] Implicit in this definition are the first law, that "Every body continues in a state of rest, or of uniform motion in a right line, unless it is compelled to change that state by the forces impressed upon it,"[20] and the second law, that "The change of motion is proportional to the motive force impressed."[21] These distinctions, between force-free and accelerated motion, pose a problem in the context of Berkeley's phenomenalism. An "action exerted" suggests an efficient cause having a change of motion as effect, but, in accordance with his claim that ideas are passive, Berkeley denies the existence of efficient causes in inanimate objects except in the sense of a first cause or Spirit. Berkely supports his claim on phenomenal grounds: "While we support heavy bodies we feel in ourselves effort, fatigue, and discomfort. We perceive also in heavy bodies falling an accelerated motion towards the center of the earth; and

that is all the senses tell us" (*De Motu*, sect. 4). Apart from first causes and occult qualities, which are ruled out of scientific discourse, how is one to construe the term 'force' as applied to the inanimate bodies of mechanics? The following alternatives arise:

i. Force is an essential attribute of matter. In his introduction to the second edition of Newton's *Principia*, Roger Cotes argues that "in short, either gravity must have a place among qualities of all bodies or extension, mobility, and impenetrability must not."[22] But gravity is not a quality of objects in the same sense as are extension, mobility, and impenetrability. As effect, gravity is a complex idea so it cannot *be* a primary quality. Gravity, as an unobservable entity apart from its observable effects, cannot be a primary *quality*. Moreover, the set of primary qualities is heterogeneous and forms a 'basis set' for the construction of complex ideas from groupings of its heterogeneous and independent elements. By the same token, one primary quality cannot be expressed in terms of the others nor can one primary quality interact with another in any way. Thus gravity as a primary quality cannot be the cause of its observable effects, that is, of the alterations occurring in other primary qualities. Therefore, for Berkeley, gravity as an unobservable entity cannot exist nor could it have any explanatory power: ". . . [T]his also is accounted for by attraction; but, in this as in the other instances, I do not perceive that anything is signified besides the effect itself; for as to the manner or action whereby it is produced, or the cause which produces it, these are not so much as aimed at" (*Principles*, sect. 103). The claim that a nonobservable entity, known only by its effects, should take its place among the observable primary qualities only begs the question of its nature in a materialistic scheme and relegates it to nonexistence in Berkeley's phenomenalistic scheme. Terms like 'gravity' and 'force' must therefore be construed in other ways.

ii. A second way to construe the term 'force' is in the instrumental sense of what Berkeley calls a "mathematical hypothesis": ". . . [T]he physicist makes use of certain abstract and general terms, imagining in bodies force, action, attraction, solicitation, etc. which are of *first utility for theories and formulations, as also for computations about motion,* even if in the truth of things, and in bodies actually existing, they would be looked for in vain . . ." (*De Motu*, sect. 39 [my emphasis]). Although Berkeley asserts that 'forces' and 'attractions' are looked for in vain, their existence or nonexistence is irrelevant to their instrumental function. Perhaps because of its similarity to contemporary logical empiricism, Berkeley's instrumentalism has received considerable discussion by commentators such as Popper and Myhill.[23] Berkeley's views on force are only partially accounted for in instrumental terms, however, for he refers to their "first utility for theories and formulations," which suggests that they serve as aids to discovery or to formulating concepts and theories. In this sense, terms like 'force' would need to have some reference to experience, for it is only through the reconstitution of elements of experience that new theories are developed. In this connection I discern a third sense of the term 'force' as denoting a haptic experience arising from tactual ideas.

iii. Force is a haptic experience of action exerted or resistance felt, of the sort encountered in lifting a weight or coming to a stop in a moving vehicle. Viewed purely as a mathematical hypothesis, Newton's second law would amount to a stipulative definition, and the relation $F = ma$ would be analytic.[24] But a law of nature must make an empirical claim, so the term 'force' or the symbol 'F' on one side of the equality must have an empirical referent that differs from the acceleration symbolized by 'a' on the other side. The only empirical referent that Berkeley recognizes is the haptic sensation of force that a sentient being experiences under conditions of exertion or of changing motion. But such forces belong to sentient beings alone and cannot be attributed to inanimate bodies: "All that which we know to which we have given the name *body* contains nothing in itself which would be the principle of motion as its efficient cause" (*De Motu*, sect. 22). Given Berkeley's claim, how can the equation $F = ma$ be applicable to mechanical systems and lay claim to being a law of nature, that is, an empirical claim, when the term 'force' and the symbol 'F' cannot refer to any quality of the body to which the equation is applied? The key to resolving the ambiguity lies in making Berkeley's distinction between the requisites for *discovery* of empirical laws as opposed to the *role* played by those laws in a logicomathematical deductive system. Discovery involves a search among the objects of experience for syntactical relations of natural signs given to us in natural language. The relations of signs are then translated into relations of artificial signs, which, in conjunction with the logicomathematical system, constitute the artificial language of the theoretical physicist. Once the translation has been made, the theoretical physicist no longer deals with phenomena but with artificial signs, manipulated according to the rules of the logicomathematical system.

The relation of force and motion in Newton's laws of dynamics may be viewed as summarizing a wide variety of experiences, some of which are catalogued by Turbayne in *The Myth of Metaphor*:[25]

"We are aware that we can make and do things, push and pull them, act and react to them; we are aware of ourselves as agents, causes, forces, or minds; . . . there, it seems, lies the origin of all our notions of cause." Specifically, the relation between force and acceleration is experiential; we experience force in lifting a weight, walking along a road, or coming to a stop in a moving car. The relation between a haptic experience of force and a visual acceleration is an association of heterogeneous signs. The idea of acceleration now stands as a sign for a potential haptic experience. Thus I anticipate the experience of force if I see that I am standing under a falling object or coming to a stop in a car. The visual signs do not contain the forces, they merely signify the forces contained within ourselves. We now translate our experience into the signs of artificial language by introducing the signs 'F' for force, 'a' for acceleration, and 'm' for a numerical factor that quantifies the relation $F = ma$. But *heterogeneity stops the process here*. The symbol 'F' stands for a haptic experience of force that has been related to a visual acceleration. The relation, being one of mere association between heterogeneous qualities, is of no further use as it stands, Berkeley says:

> . . . it is, I think, an axiom universally received that quantities of the same kind may be added together and make one entire sum. Mathematicians add lines together; *but they do not add a line to a solid*, . . . A blue and a red line I can conceive added together into one sum and making one continuous line; but, to make, in my thoughts, one continued line of a visible and tangible line added together is, I find, a task far more difficult, and even insurmountable. (*New Theory of Vision*, sect. 131 [my emphasis])

Berkeley's comments give rise to the question of how it is possible for variables representing tactual and visual qualities, e.g., 'F' and 'a', to become related in a mathematically functional way. So long as the symbol 'F' refers to a tactual concept, the relation $F = ma$ cannot be further unplaited. The solution is to replace the haptic force by another associated visual concept. This is accomplished by expressing the force as a function of a visual position. For example, if the force is due to a stretched metal spring, it is assumed to be proportional to the displacement x of the spring from its equilibrium configuration. If the function $F = -kx$ is introduced, where k is a numerical factor and x is the displacement, a new empirical relation, $-kx = ma$, is established. Acceleration and position are visual signs of natural language amenable to being translated into the geometric language of Newton's mathematics. Or, in effect, acceleration as the second time derivative of the displacement is analytically related to it, thereby allowing the equation to be further developed or 'solved' according to the rules of logic and mathematics. Having served their purpose as aids to discovery, the haptic force and the heterogeneous relation between force and acceleration are dropped from further consideration. Instead, a new relation among the visual elements of position and acceleration, which are analytically related, forms the basis for derivation of consequences. The natural signs of force and acceleration have now been completely translated into the artificial signs of the mathematical system.

But once the symbolic relations have been established in artificial language, all or some of the experiential antecedents to the established law may become irrelevant, for the justification and utility of the established axioms lie in their predictive power, that is, the extent to which they allow deductions of true observational consequences. Thus the relation $F = ma$ is empirical insofar as the symbol 'F' stands for a haptic force; it is a mathematical hypothesis insofar as the symbol 'F' becomes a nonreferring sign of the logicomathematical deductive system, that is, insofar as the symbol 'F' is intended to refer to a characteristic of inanimate objects. The error made in using force as a criterion of absolute motion lies in confusing the term 'force' as a symbol of the haptic sign for motion that occurs in natural language with the term 'force' as a written sign in the artificial language. The written sign in artificial language, when applied to inanimate bodies, has no phenomenal referent in the natural language but retains meaning by standing for a grouping of signs in artificial language, e.g., $F = ma$. Heterogeneity precludes any necessary connection between haptic force and acceleration, whereas the written relation $F = ma$ has all the 'force' of a definition. In terms of "computations about motion," the connection between the symbols is necessary. In terms of the existence of a phenomenal counterpart to the symbol 'F' other than the perceived motions themselves, the written symbol 'F' makes no claim. It is not possible therefore to use an unobservable force to demonstrate that an observed motion is absolute.

In sum, I have shown how Berkeley's concepts of space, motion, and force are illuminated when understood in the context of his doctrine of heterogeneity and language: yes, Berkeley can deny the existence of forces and accept their validity in Newtonian mechanics, he can maintain that Newton's laws are mathematical hypotheses that have a basis in experience, and he is not refuted by Newton's examples of the rotating globes and the whirling bucket—on the contrary, Berkeley refutes Newton. The strikingly contemporary flavor of Berkeley's views is impressive, for they are characterized by physical

relativism, a verificationist criterion of meaning, a deductive nomological model of scientific explanation, and an instrumentalist view
of the role of theoretical entities. But this coincidence with contemporary thought should not obscure the fact that these tenets arise
from the uniquely Berkeleyan framework of heterogeneity and the
language model.

Notes

1. Berkeley, *De Motu*, in A. A. Luce and T. E. Jessop, eds., *The Works of George Berkeley, Bishop of Cloyne*. 9 vols. (London: Thomas Nelson and Sons, 1948-57).

2. In C. M. Turbayne, *Berkeley: Principles of Human Knowledge, Text and Critical Essays* (Indianapolis: Bobbs-Merrill, 1963). The Berkeley work is hereafter referred to as *Principles*.

3. Richard J. Brook, *Berkeley's Philosophy of Science* (The Hague: Martinus Nijhoff, 1973), p. 142.

4. Karl R. Popper, "A Note on Berkeley as Precursor of Mach and Einstein," *British Journal for the Philosophy of Science* 4 (May 1953-Feb. 1954): 26-36 (also in Turbayne, *Berkeley: Principles of Human Knowledge* [1970 ed.]); G. J. Whitrow, "Berkeley's Philosophy of Motion," *British Journal for the Philosophy of Science* 4 (May 1953-Feb. 1954): 37-45; and John Myhill, "Berkeley's De Motu—An Anticipation of Mach," in *George Berkeley*, University of California Publications in Philosophy (Berkeley, 1957), vol. 29.

5. Brook, *Berkeley's Philosophy of Science*, pp. 104-45; Bruce Silver, "Berkeley and the Principle of Inertia," *Journal of the History of Ideas* 34 (1973): 599-608; and A. D. Ritchie, *George Berkeley: A Reappraisal*, ed. G. E. Davie (Manchester: Manchester University Press, 1967).

6. "Force and Absolute Motion in Berkeley's Philosophy of Physics," *Journal of the History of Ideas* 38 (1977): 705-18.

7. Both essays are in C. M. Turbayne, ed., *Works on Vision* (Indianapolis: Bobbs-Merrill, 1963).

8. See C. M. Turbayne, "Berkeley's Metaphysical Grammar," in *Berkeley: Principles*. On p. 21, Turbayne says: "The language of nature is conceived on the model of the written Greek that Plato read, in which there were no gaps, no periods, and no lower case letters. There were, therefore, no words in the text until Plato 'read them into' it." Of course, nei-
ther I nor Turbayne claim that God speaks Greek! Nor would I deny that there are ways in which nature fails to be a language. But, in philosophy as in science, one may use the time honored practice of constructing a model suitable to the task at hand, preserving those features that are useful and discarding those that are not. There are a number of ways in which gases fail to be ideal, yet much of thermodynamics is an attempt to bring data into congruence with equations based on the ideal gas model.

9. In the Introduction to his edition of the *Principles* and in his introduction to the *Works on Vision*.

10. Berkeley's use of the terms 'natural language' and 'artificial language' should not be confused with the use of these terms in computer science. Berkeley's artificial language is the natural language of computer science. Berkeley's natural language has no counterpart in computer science, for it refers to natural phenomena as language.

11. *Mathematical Principles of Natural Philosophy*, tr. Motte, rev. Cajori (1934; repr. Berkeley: University of California Press, 1971), vol. I, p. 6. Hereafter referred to as *Principia*.

12. Ibid., p. 7.

13. Ibid., p. 10.

14. For a discussion of the whirling bucket, see Ernest Nagel, *The Structure of Science* (New York: Harcourt, Brace and World, 1961), chap. 8. For discussions of Berkeley and the whirling bucket, see also Myhill, "Berkeley's De Motu," and Brook, *Berkeley's Philosophy of Science*, chap. 3.

15. *Principia*, I, p. 12.

16. *The Science of Mechanics*, tr. T. J. McCormack (La Salle, Ill.: Open Court Publishing Co., 1907), p. 284. Mach also discusses absolute motion and the whirling bucket (pp. 279-84).

17. Gordon G. Gallup, Jr., in an article "Self-Awareness in Primates," *American Scientist* 67, 4 (1979), refers to three characteristics of language use that also "appear to be part and parcel of the complex motor and intellectual skills underlying tool use and fabrication." They are *syntax, reconstitution*, and *displacement*. Syntax is a "basic grammar," which "governs the way in which elements can be combined to achieve a particular goal." Of reconstitution, he says: "Just as the elements contained in a message can be reconstituted to form new messages, the fabrication of tools also requires reconstituting aspects of the environment as a means to an end" (p. 417).

18. This point is discussed in more detail in my paper "Force and Absolute Motion," cited in n. 6.

19. *Principia*, I, p. 2.

20. Ibid., p. 13.

21. Ibid.

22. Ibid., p. xxvi.

23. Popper, "A Note on Berkeley," and Myhill, "Berkeley's De Motu," are cited in n. 4.

24. Although Newton's own mathematical treatment of dynamics is primarily geometrical, I will refer throughout to the more familiar and concise algebraic formulations. My arguments are not affected by this choice.

25. Colin M. Turbayne, *The Myth of Metaphor*, rev. ed. (Columbia, S.C.: University of South Carolina Press, 1971), p. 48.

17

Berkeley's Argument from Design

Michael Hooker

While he was in Newport, Berkeley spent a good part of his time in composing *Alciphron*, a work that is as sadly neglected by philosophers today as Berkeley was by King and Parliament during his stay in Newport. Although *Alciphron* is foremost an apologia for the Christian faith, it is also rich in discussion of philosophical issues related to theistic doctrine. My aim here is to focus on Berkeley's discussion of the existence of God in Dialogue IV, which bears the title "The Truth of Theism." In my view, the arguments presented there are at first more intersting and more challenging to the critic than the theistic argument of the *Principles*. Ultimately, I will contend, the *Alciphron* arguments are very much akin to that found in the *Principles*.

I

One of the features of the work that makes *Alciphron* especially refreshing is the extent to which its doctrines are developed free of the context of the immaterialist arguments of the *Principles*. In this regard, Berkeley's argument for the existence of God in the Fourth Dialogue appears to follow suit. The argument is by analogy, and its development follows a lengthy course as the author, speaking through Euphranor, re-educates the freethinker Alciphron.

The first stage of Berkeley's argument from design looks like a version of the classical argument by analogy. The speaker is Euphranor.

From motions, therefore, you infer a mover or cause; and from reasonable motions (or such as appear calculated for a reasonable end) a rational cause, soul or spirit? . . . The soul of man actuates but a small body, an insignificant particle, in respect of the great masses of nature, the elements, and heavenly bodies and system of the world. And the wisdom that appears in those motions which are the effect of Human reason is incomparably less than that which discovers itself in the structure and use of organized natural bodies, animal or vegetable. A man with his hand can make no machine so admirable as the hand itself; nor can any of those motions by which we trace out human reason approach the skill and contrivance of those wonderful motions of the heart, and brain, and other vital parts, which do not depend on the will of man . . . Doth it not follow, then that from natural motions, independent of man's will, may be inferred both power and wisdom incomparably greater than that of the human soul? (*Alciphron*, bk. IV, sect. 4)[1]

From this beginning Euphranor goes on to point out that from the unity of design, fit, and purpose of nature we may infer a single organizing intellect as its cause. Just as we infer a rational soul behind the actions of a human body, so we infer an infinitely wise and powerful director behind the orchestra of nature.

Alciphron demurs in the face of this conclusion and expresses doubt that the strength of Euphranor's inference to God can match the conviction that attaches to Euphranor's belief in the existence of other persons. To combat this challenge, Euphranor exacts the concession that we do not strictly see other people, that is, the thinking being behind the flesh, but rather we see the outward or visible signs and tokens from which we infer the existence of a thinking soul that is more properly the person we are interested in. Euphranor drives home the point by noting that

. . . in the self-same manner, it seems to me that, though I cannot with eyes of flesh behold the invisible God, yet I do in the strictest sense behold and perceive by all my senses such signs and tokens, such effects and operations, as suggest, indicate, and demonstrate an invisible God, as certainly, and with the same evidence, at least, as any other signs perceived by sense do suggest to me the existence of your soul, spirit, or thinking principle . . . (sect. 5)

The argument here presented is a kind of double analogy, though its structure does not immediately reveal it as such. The first analogy, which is not fully developed by Berkeley, is an analogical argument for the existence of other minds. From Alciphron's behavior I infer the existence of his rational mind. The basis for inference is my acquaintance with my own mind and the relation between it and my behavior. The second analogy is a second-order comparison. By analogy with our proof of the existence of Alciphron's soul from its outward signs, we also can establish the existence of a rational world soul behind its outward signs, that is, behind nature and its manifold workings.

God's existence, then, is proved by an argument analogous to the analogical argument for other minds. The argument for God's existence is parasitic on the argument for other minds, not because God's existence presupposes the existence of other minds, but rather because the persuasive force of the theistic argument derives its strength from its similarity to the analogical argument for other minds. Without the latter analogy to predispose the reader, or interlocutor in Alciphron's case, the analogical argument to God's existence would not carry what persuasive force it does.

At this juncture Alciphron, though wavering, is still unwilling to join the ranks of the devout, and his reluctance finds expression in a last line of defense. He announces to Euphranor that reflection has enabled him to recognize that the real proof of another's rational soul lies not in his actions, but in his speech. According to Alciphron, "It is my hearing you talk that, in strict and philosophical truth, is to me the best argument for your being" (sect. 6). It is, says Alciphron, "the arbitrary use of sensible signs, which have no necessary connection with the things signified" that convince him of an unseen intelligence (sect. 7). Such signs, Alciphron tells Euphranor,

> . . . suggest and exhibit to my mind an endless variety of things, differing in nature, time, and place; thereby informing me, entertaining me, and directing me how to act, not only with regard to things near and present, but also with regard to things distant and future. No matter whether these signs are pronounced or written; whether they enter by the eye or the ear: they have the same use, and are equally proofs of an intelligent, thinking, designing cause. (sect. 7)

Euphranor follows these remarks by taking Alciphron through a long discussion in which he presents the theory of the divine visual language, which had been expounded in the *Essay towards a New Theory of Vision* and summarized in the *Principles*, sects. 43ff. The discussion concludes with Euphranor's summary:

> Upon the whole, it seems the proper objects of sight are light and colours, with their several shades and degrees; all which, being infinitely diversified and combined, form a language wonderfully adapted to suggest and exhibit to us the distances, figures, situations, dimensions, and various

qualities of tangible objects: not by similitude, nor yet by inference of necessary connection, but by the arbitrary imposition of Providence, just as words suggest the things signified by them. (sect. 10)

Euphranor, picking up Alciphron's earlier characterization of language as the arbitrary use of signs that have no necessary connection to the things signified, reminds him that nature has been shown to be just such a language, through which God, the author of nature, constantly speaks to us. The Dialogue ends finally with a characterization of the theophanic God as "a provident Governor, actually and intimately present, and attentive to all our interests and motions . . . throughout the whole course of our lives, informing, admonishing, and directing incessantly, in a most evident and sensible manner" (sect. 14).

II

Such is the argument of *Alciphron*, IV. What are we to make of it? Clearly Berkeley intends the most weight to be borne by the notion of God as the author of the language of nature. To the extent that the classical form of the argument from design is relied on by Berkeley, it is used only to smooth the way for our acceptance of the final argument from the language of nature. Unfortunately, it is not so easy to discern the exact structure of that argument. On first inspection it appears to be only a special case of the argument from design. According to that interpretation, our senses inform us just as the spoken language of another informs us, so the data of our senses can be viewed as a kind of language. Since tokens of spoken language each have intelligent speakers behind them, so too must the language of our senses have an intelligent "speaker" behind it.

Viewed in this way, the argument, as a special case of the standard design argument, should be assessed by standards appropriate to such arguments. We begin by reminding ourselves that arguments by analogy, and in particular arguments from design, are not amenable to assessment in a straightforward way. There is no knock-down refutation of the argument from design, such as the devastating refutation of *a priori* arguments that Hume gives us in pt. IX of the *Dialogues*. Analogical arguments are to be assessed by rules of thumb, and in the *Dialogues* Hume offers a number of such rules.

In pt. II, Hume counsels against analogical arguments from unique effects to their causes. When we encounter a watch in the woods, it would be acceptable to argue that it has a maker, because the found watch is not unique. It is like other watches that we know to have makers. The origin of watches has been witnessed, but the origin of worlds has not. Also in pt. II, Hume tells us that the degree of confidence appropriate to the conclusion of an analogical argument is proportional to the degree of similarity between the things being examined. Even though worlds are unique, Hume says, it would be safer to argue to the existence of a world-maker if worlds were more like watches than they are.

In the case of Berkeley's argument, both rules of assessment apply: the world of sense is a unique effect, and it is questionable whether that world is really very much like a language. We have witnessed the intelligent intention behind the production of language, but we have no experience of the origin of other sense data. We could partially overcome the barrier created by the uniqueness of the world of sense if we could really establish that sense data are like a language, but it is not clear that Berkeley has presented a strong case for that analogy.[2] Another of Hume's rules of analogy tells us that it is unsafe to reason from the similarity of parts to the similarity of wholes. That rule applies here when Berkeley would have us reason from the fact that one sense datum signals another to the view that a collection of such signals constitutes a language. On the basis of Hume's three rules, I conclude that the analogy is weak in important respects, and for that reason the argument is less than wholly persuasive.

Obviously, more needs to be said before the argument can be rejected finally on the grounds that the analogy put forward is a weak one. However, there is a possibly more powerful and certainly more tantalizing argument that is suggested by the passages under discussion. Berkeley takes pains to note that our sense data are like language in a deeper respect than just their informing character. The deeper similarity is in the connection between symbol and thing symbolized. The connection, Berkeley points out, is a contingent one both in the case of the word-world connection and in the case of sense data and the things about which they inform us. Berkeley does not tell us why the contingency of the connection is important, but clearly he thinks it is. While we may dispute that a dark cloud informs us of approaching rain in any respect that would point to an intelligent intention that we be so informed, Berkeley thinks we should be convinced of an intelligence behind the connection, given that it is contingent and not necessary. We must ask why Berkeley thinks so. We should begin to search for an answer by drawing an important distinction. There are two very different kinds of correlations to be dealt with. Burnham Terrell refers to them as the epistemological and ontological dimensions of the sign relation.[3] The epistemological dimension of the sign relation refers to one idea of sense being a sign for or signifying an-other, e.g., in the way that the sight of fire signals the feeling of warmth that will follow from approaching it. Here, of course, we are referring just to sense data, sight and feeling. In the case of the onto-logical dimension, we refer to the relation between sense data and the objects in the world that they signify. According to Terrell, it is the fact of signification within the world of sense that grounds the significance *of* the world of sense as a sign of God.[4] That is, because ideas of sense are signs of one another, epistemologically speaking, the world of sense is a sign of God, ontologically speaking.

We have then two kinds of contingent correlations to consider: first, the relationship in which some sense data are contingent signs of others, and, second, the relationship in which sense data are signs of the world. Viewed from the first perspective, an argument to the effect that God preserves the connection between contingent ideas of sense is not straightforwardly an analogical argument from design. What is needed is an explanation of why contingently connected sense data show the remarkably regular co-occurrence that they do. With-out the assurance of some ordering force behind the world of sense data, we should not expect the feeling of warmth to accompany the sight of fire. But it does, with remarkable regularity, so there must be an ordering force. By this mode of arguing, then, God is posited as the best explanation of the uniformity of experience.

So viewed, however, the argument of *Alciphron* is neither an argu-ment from design, nor is it an argument so very unlike the theistic argument of the *Principles*. In that work, God is postulated as the preserver of the world of experience when I am inattentive to it or of that portion of the world to which I am inattentive at a given time. An assessment of the *Alciphron* argument interpreted as a best ex-planation argument will turn on the degree to which one accords weight to the Principle of Sufficient Reason in the present case, that is, to the view that there must be an explanation of the order and unity of sense experience. The value of Berkeley's explanation, for those persuaded that there is something that demands explanation, will have to be assessed against competing explanations. The Lockean realist affords for Berkeley an obvious competitor explanation. Berkeley's own strategy, of course, is to defeat causal realism by at-tacking directly its presuppositions, and thus to leave the field free for God as the only reasonable explanation of our sense experience. Berkeley's degree of success or failure has been widely and repeatedly assessed, so I will refrain here from adding to the assessment.

Let us turn to an examination of the relationship between sense data and the world about which they inform us. In respect to this examination, it is important to remember that what is a problem for Berkeley in *Alciphron* would not have arisen in the *Principles*, where there is no such eternal world. And in spite of the fact that ideas of sense are defended in *Alciphron* as the immediate objects of experience, Berkeley is at pains to keep his apologia free from reliance on his ill-received immaterialist metaphysics. He tells us then that the senses inform us regarding the world of which they are signs and to which they are only contingently connected. Possibly it is in the fact of this connection that Berkeley finds an argument for God's existence.

To see where the argument may lie, it would be useful to look at a contemporary theistic argument, advanced by Richard Taylor. In his book *Metaphysics*, Taylor offers what he calls an argument from design with a peculiarly rational twist.[5] It rests upon the fact that we rely upon our sensory faculties to give us information about the world.

Taylor begins by setting the stage for an analogy with the following story. Suppose that an archaeologist unearths a stone with a strange pattern of markings. The markings *can* be taken to be the result of natural diastrophic forces, but suppose further that they are recognized to be similar to the markings of ancient language and that the markings are taken to spell out the message HERE KIMON FELL LEADING A BAND OF ATHENIANS AGAINST THE FORCES OF XERXES. Now, it is possible that natural forces could have produced markings that spell out that message; but if we suppose on the basis of the message that there was actually a person named Kimon who died in battle at some previous time, then we must assume that the markings on the rock were put there for the purpose of providing that information.

In a similar manner, Taylor says, whereas it is possible for our sensory organs to be the result of the purely natural forces of evolution with no purposeful design behind them, we in fact treat them more like the rock interpreted as bearing a message. Speaking of our sensory faculties, Taylor says:

> The important point, and one that is rarely considered, is that we do not simply *marvel* at these structures, and wonder how they came to be that way. We do not simply view them as amazing and striking things and speculate upon their origins. We, in fact, whether justifiably or not, *rely* on them for the discovery of things that we suppose to be true and which we suppose to exist quite independently of those organs themselves.[6]

Such reliance upon our faculties, Taylor claims, must presuppose that they were designed for the purposes for which we use them. In his words:

> We saw that it would be irrational for anyone to say *both* that the marks he found on the stone had a natural, nonpurposeful origin and *also* that they reveal some truth with respect to something other than themselves . . . One cannot rationally believe both of these things. So also, it is now suggested, it would be irrational for one to say *both* that his sensory and cognitive faculties had a natural, nonpurposeful origin and *also* that they reveal some truth with respect to something other than themselves . . .[7]

Taylor's argument is difficult to assess. We might be inclined to object that our cognitive and sensory faculties are part of the system of nature and that they have evolved within that system to give us the information they do because our possession of such information has survival value. Further, we do not just blindly trust that our faculties give us information about a world apart from them, but rather we have good inductive evidence that they do; our reliance upon them is constantly rewarded. We might be inclined to so object, and Taylor attempts to forestall such objections by boldly claiming that they beg the question.[8] The problem, he says, is that we can never rely upon our faculties without using them to test their own reliability.

On the face of it, Taylor seems to be appealing to a principle to the effect that, whenever we assume that something is informative or performs some function, we must assume also that it was designed for that purpose. Such a principle is obviously false. In responding to our aforementioned objections by branding them as question-begging, however, Taylor reveals, I think, the true nature of his argument. The real issue concerns whether our cognitive and sensory faculties give us information about the world, and Taylor disallows our checking their reliability through further use of them. The problem has a familiar ring. It is the great barrier objection to causal realism that Berkeley thought showed Locke's position as one that ultimately entails skepticism. Taylor can be interpreted then as raising the objection that any use of our sensory faculties to test our sensory faculties will only tell us about their internal consistency, not about their reliability as guides to an external world beyond themselves. On this interpretation, Taylor is assuming a causal realist's view of the world and holding that, if we assume that skepticism is false, then we must have some guarantee of the reliability of our sensory faculties. That guarantee lies in God's intentional design of our faculties for the purpose of informing us.

My aim in introducing this discussion of Taylor was to shed light on Berkeley, so let us return again to *Alciphron*. The point should be obvious. In *Alciphron*, though he refers obliquely to the immaterialist doctrine of his developed philosophy, Berkeley is speaking to the philosophically unsophisticated. His audience will hold a common sense view of our senses as giving us information about a world that is really out there and represented to us by the data of our senses. However, and this is the important point, there is no guarantee, in virtue of a necessary connection, that our senses do accurately inform us. But because we think we are informed we must suppose that something exists as the guarantor of the reliability of our cognitive and sensory faculties. Hence we conclude that God exists. The analogy to language is just this: In the case of language, there is a contingent or conventional connection between words and the things they signify; in the case of the language of nature, there is similarly a contingent connection between our experiences and the wordly things they signify. In the case of spoken language, it is the speaker's intention that ensures the reference relationship, and in the case of the language of nature, it is the theophanic diety, always speaking to us through our senses, who ensures the reference of our sense experience.

In the present argument, as well as in the argument offered by Taylor, the starting point is with an assumption and a problem that the assumption creates. The assumption is that our sense experience is informative of a world beyond itself, and the problem is to ensure the truth of that assumption. In both cases, God provides the needed guarantee. The weakness in both arguments is in the acceptability of the generating assumption. A skeptic would disallow it. What is really required is a transcendental route to a defense of the assumption of knowledge, and neither Taylor nor Berkeley has found such a route.

In summary, then, on our fullest and best interpretation of *Alciphron*'s theistic argument from the divine natural language, there are two possible arguments. In the one, God is posited as the best explanation of the order, regularity, and predictability of the world of sense experience. In the other, God is posited as the guarantor of a connection between our sense experiences and the world about which they inform us. In both interpretations, the function assigned to God and the argument by which we get to his existence is akin to that found in the *Principles*. In that work as well as here, God is introduced to avoid skepticism or to explain why we are not faced with skepticism. The story told about the nature of the world may differ in *Alciphron* and the *Principles*, but the skeptical problem at root is the same in each.

I should not close without a concluding postscript to address one likely objection to my interpretation of Berkeley's argument in *Alciphron*. In a thorough and impressive study of *Alciphron*, Paul Olscamp has presented an interpretation of Dialogue IV that is at variance with my own.[9] Olscamp sees Berkeley as offering a two-part argument concerning God. The first part, which is in the *Principles*, is an argument to the necessity of God's existence, and the second part, which is in *Alciphron*, is an argument that has the probable conclusion that God is benevolent, provident, wise, and good. In an admittedly too brief reply to Olscamp, I would say only that the ostensible purpose of *Alciphron*, IV, as established in the dramatic stage setting at the beginning of the dialogue, is to prove God's existence rather than his nature. Certainly his nature is referred to throughout as following from considerations adduced in favor of his existence, so it is at least part of Berkeley's purpose to address the question of God's nature in *Alciphron*. Further, toward the end of the dialogue, Euphranor's attention is turned exclusively to treating God's nature. I think it is clear, however, that the prior intent is to establish the truth of theism and only later to establish God's attributes.[10] So far as I can tell, the truth of theism is argued in the manner that I have characterized.

Notes

1. Quotations from Berkeley, *Alciphron*, are from A. A. Luce and T. E. Jessop, eds., *The Works of George Berkeley, Bishop of Cloyne*, 9 vols. (London: Thomas Nelson and Sons, 1948-57), Vol. III, pp. 141-73.

2. Colin M. Turbayne has argued fairly persuasively that Berkeley has succeeded in establishing a strong analogy. See "Berkeley's Metaphysical Grammar" in his edition, *Berkeley: Principles of Human Knowledge, Text and Critical Essays* (Indianapolis: Bobbs-Merrill, 1970), and *The Myth of Metaphor* (Columbia, S.C.: University of South Carolina Press, 1971), pp. 208-17.

3. "Dean Berkeley's ABC's," read at the International Berkeley Society meeting, Washington, D.C., December 1978. Terrell credits Robert Armstrong with first characterizing the distinction in this way.

4. Ibid.

5. New York: Prentice-Hall, 1974, pp. 114-19.

6. Ibid., p. 117.

7. Ibid., p. 118.

8. Ibid., p. 119.

9. *The Moral Philosophy of George Berkeley* (The Hague: Martinus Nijhoff, 1970).

10. A philosophically sound examination of the issue of God's attributes interestingly, is precluded by Alciphron's announced intention (sect. 2) to avoid discussion of the problem of evil. Such a discussion would be required, since the proof of God's goodness is taken to lie, for example, in his warning us through appropriate sensory evidence of potential harm. The problem is that God is responsible for producing not only the warning, but the harm as well.

IX Mind

18

Is Berkeley's a Cartesian Mind?

Willis Doney

Classical British empiricism has been viewed as a progressive under-mining or step-by-step razing of Descartes's metaphysic of substance. In Descartes, we find a trichotomy of uncreated substance—substance in the strict sense or God—on the one hand and created substances (in a sense and as it were) on the other, the two varieties of which are mind or finite spirits—a second part of the trichotomy—and matter or bodies, the third.[1] From one long-range, all-encompassing per-spective, Berkeley, pursuing Locke's probing questions regarding the idea of corporeal substance in general, rejects outright this part of Descartes's trichotomy and retains without serious question or res-ervation the remaining parts of the Cartesian metaphysic of sub-stance, namely, finite minds or spirits and God.[2] Berkeley's is the Cartesian edifice without one major wing; or, to vary the metaphor, Berkeley is an amputated Descartes, matter having been lopped off. To complete the picture from this rather one-sided point of view, Hume does for mental substance what Berkeley accomplishes with the corporeal. God aside, nothing of the Cartesian trichotomy is left. The metaphysic of substance itself is thus demolished; and thereafter, as with Bertrand Russell, the very word "substance" is suspect.[3]

In reaction in part to this account of Berkeley's rôle in the devel-opment of modern thought, there has been a tendency in the recent literature to stress differences between Berkeley's conception of self or mind and Descartes's. Berkeley's finite spirit is not just, as on the foregoing view, the Cartesian *res cogitans* sans actual or possible

273

body, and, according to certain observers of the tortuous "way of ideas,"[4] the ideas in that spirit differ from Descartes's *modi cogitandi* to the extent that they appear to correspond in name only. With due respect for Berkeley's originality and with all deference to his colossal stature in modern philosophy, I want to affirm here that there is more than a little truth in the view of Berkeley as a truncated Descartes—as a castrated Cartesian without matter. No doubt there are a number of differences, but there are on the other side counterbalancing and weighty likenesses between Descartes's and Berkeley's conceptions of the self and the substance in which its various activities and ideas are supposed to reside. I shall not give a list of similarities. Instead, I want to call attention to a similarity that seems to me to have been neglected, and I shall do this by concentrating on one term of the likeness relation rather than the other, on Berkeley rather than Descartes. Even so, the story is somewhat long, and I shall give only a bit of it.

A common feature I have in mind is their warning about harmful effects of abstraction. For Descartes as for Berkeley, abstraction in a certain sense or of a certain kind is an evil and a cause for concern to the right-minded philosopher. Conjoined with this theme about abstraction is, I believe, a shared confusion and inconsistency in their notions of possibility and impossibility. My limited objective is to point out this confusion in Berkeley's *Principles* as it surfaces in views expressed there about conceivability and the possibility of separate existence. I want to call attention to an inconsistency between what Berkeley says or implies in the diatribe against abstract ideas in the Introduction to the *Principles*, sect. 10 in particular, and what he says or implies in the body of the *Principles*, notably in sects. 4-5 and 10, when he attempts to put his anti-abstractionist view to work in order to impugn the matter of the Philosophers and the bodies of Locke and the Cartesians. I aim to show that Berkeley is committed to two propositions both of which cannot be true. To anticipate: he is committed in the Introduction to the proposition that there is a way of telling whether putatively two parts, qualities, or states X and Y that are invariably perceived together (or as one) can, or cannot, exist apart that is other than the way in which we tell whether X and Y can, or cannot, be conceived apart; whereas, in the arguments against material substance in the body of the *Principles*, he is committed to the proposition that there is no way of telling whether or not it is possible for X and Y to exist apart that is other than the way in which we ascertain that X and Y can or cannot be conceived apart.

I

In sect. 10 of the Introduction, Berkeley makes a general claim about the limits of conception or conceivability, and the way in which he is prepared to support this claim commits him to the first of the two propositions that I have distinguished. In sect. 10, he tells us that, in one sense of the term "abstraction," we are able to abstract, but he maintains that in two other senses—in the "proper acceptations of the term"—we cannot:

> I own my self able to abstract in one sense, as when I consider some particular parts or qualities separated from others, with which though they are united in some object, yet, it is possible they may really exist without them. But I deny that I can abstract one from another, or conceive separately, those qualities which it is impossible should exist so separated; or that I can frame a general notion by abstracting from particulars in the manner aforesaid. Which two last are the proper acceptations of *abstraction*.

Part of the claim about conceivability to which I want to call attention is contained in Berkeley's statement in this passage about the first of the two kinds of abstraction, which he says are abstraction in the proper acceptations of the term and which he maintains are impossible, i.e., in his statement, "I deny that I can abstract one from another, or conceive separately, those qualities which it is impossible should exist so separated . . . ." The generality of Berkeley's contention in this sentence can be made explicit if we rephrase it, "In no instance can I abstract one from another, or conceive separately, qualities which it is impossible should exist so separated" or "Any conceivable separation of qualities entails the possibility of a real separation." This part of the claim can be restated using quantifiers without (I trust) altering its import: $(x)(y)(x$ cannot be conceived separately, or apart from, y if it is not possible that x can exist separately, or apart from, $y)$. The other part of the claim is contained in the sentence immediately preceding: "I own my self able to abstract in one sense, as when I consider some particular parts of qualities separated from others, with which though they are united in some object, yet, it is possible they may really exist without them." The statement here is also a general statement about conceivability, which can be rephrased in a manner suggested in the Draft Introduction (*Works*, II, p. 125): "Any separation of parts or qualities that is possible *in re* is also possible *in intellectu*." Reformulating this part of the claim in the same way as the part of the claim in the following sentence, we get: (x)(y)(x can be conceived separately, or apart from, y, if it is possible that x can exist separately, or apart from, y). Putting the two parts together, we have the claim: (x)(y)(x can be conceived separately, or apart from, y if, and only if, it is possible for x to exist separately, or apart from, y).

Exception to this paraphrase of the claim in sect. 10 can be taken for a variety of reasons. (a) There is a well-known ambiguity in "conceiving apart," for one thing. Does it mean thinking of X without thinking of Y? or does it mean thinking of X that is not Y? My paraphrase leaves this and related questions unattended to. (b) It might be argued that Berkeley's claim here is specifically about "particular parts or qualities . . . united in some object" and is not intended to be, as the paraphrase suggests, about the possibility of separation in general or of no matter what. Something relevant to this point will be said at the beginning of the next part of the paper. Finally: (c) The modalities in Berkeley's claim are not made perspicuous in this gloss. Should, for instance, the claim be prefaced, "Necessarily . . . ?" Interesting as these questions are (and difficult as they are to answer), I believe my restatement of the claim will do for my present purpose, viz. to show how, in making this claim, Berkeley commits himself to the first of the two propositions distinguished earlier about a way or ways in which the possibility or impossibility of separate existence can be determined.

In addition to this first-order claim, there is also in sect. 10 a second-order claim about a procedure or procedures for establishing the first-order claim. In the preceding sections of the Introduction (7-9), Berkeley describes various feats of conception that he thinks would have to be performed if the doctrine of abstract ideas were correct. The view of the opposition set forth and explained in this way, sect. 10 begins, "Whether others have this wonderful faculty of *abstracting their ideas*, they best can tell: for my self I find . . . ." What Berkeley goes on to tell us that he finds in his own case, and implies that someone else can find in his own case, is *inter alia* that the feats of conception required by his adversaries to attain their alleged abstract ideas cannot be performed. About their putative abstract idea of man, he says, "I cannot by any effort of thought conceive the abstract idea above described"; and, with regard to the proposed separation of qualities in an object, he says, "It is equally impossible for me to form the abstract idea of motion distinct from the body moving . . . ." Although the thought-experiments suggested to him by his opponents' accounts of abstraction and abstract ideas yield negative results, i.e., his "effort of thought" in each case is unsuccessful, he also reports attempted separations in which he succeeds. "I can," he says, "imagine . . . the upper parts of a man joined to the body of a horse . . . [or] the hand, the eye, the nose, each by it self abstracted or separated from the rest of the body." Not content simply to register successes and failures in particular cases, he proceeds to make his general claim about the limits of conception.

As the description of particular cases is followed immediately by the general statement, the view expressed here seems clearly to be that the former provide evidence for the latter and that the latter can be supported or confirmed by the former. If I am right, the view expressed is (in other words) that, by performing such thought-experiments as are indicated, each of us can be assured that Berkeley's claim about the limits of conception is true. Farther on in sect. 13, after quoting Locke on the general idea of a triangle, he suggests an alternative way in which his generalization can be supported:

> All I desire is, that the reader would fully and certainly inform himself whether he has such an idea or no. And this, methinks, can be no hard task for any one to perform. What more easy than for any one to look a little into his own thoughts, and there try whether he has, or can attain to have, an idea that shall correspond with the description that is here given of the general idea of a triangle, which is, *neither oblique, nor rectangle, equilateral, nor scalenon, but all and none of these at once?*

Here the test proposed—"to look a little into his own thoughts . . ."—seems to involve a kind of internal observation of the contents of one's mind in order to discover the presence or absence there of the supposed abstract ideas described by Locke and others, i.e., of ideas that would be there if their supposed feats of abstraction had been accomplished, though the expression "whether he has, or *can attain to have* . . ." (my italics) appears to encompass the previously described "effort of thought" as well. The second-order claim that I find then in sect. 7-10 and 13 can now be stated briefly in the following way: the first-order claim about the bounds of conception can be supported by internal observations or thought-experiments of the kinds suggested in these passages.

From this second-order claim, it can be shown to follow that there must be some way of determining the possibility of real separations that is other than the tests he proposes involving internal observations or thought-experiments. For, according to Berkeley, these tests yield conclusions about the possibility of *mental* separations; and, on the supposition that it is the same tests that establish the possibility of real separations, it makes no sense to hold that the performance of these tests supports the claim that the possibilities of mental separations and of real separations are co-extensive. It might be argued that, because the tests are the same, that claim is true and indeed necessarily true. But that is not the way in which Berkeley argues in the Introduction, sects. 7-10 and 13. His second-order claim there is that the results of performing these tests provide evidence for his first-order claim, and his second-order claim makes sense only if there is some way of ascertaining the possibility of real separations that is other than by means of these tests, i.e., the tests that establish the possibility of mental separations. If this is right, it follows that Berkeley is committed to the proposition that there is some way of telling whether or not separate existence is possible that is other than the procedure by which we determine whether separate existence is conceivable.

Two comments are appropriate to anticipate and perhaps forestall (though not indeed answer) objections to what I have concluded so far, namely, that Berkeley is committed to the first proposition, distinguished earlier, that there is a way of telling whether putatively two parts, qualities, or states X and Y that are invariably perceived together or as one can, or cannot, exist apart that is other than the way in which we tell whether X and Y can, or cannot, be conceived apart. First, I have not maintained that Berkeley *asserted*, or indeed that he would have been prepared to assert, the proposition to which I contend he is committed. In the next part of my paper, I give reasons for thinking that, on the contrary, he would not have been prepared to assert that proposition. My argument here is that he would have to accept the proposition if the line of reasoning in the passages cited in the Introduction is to make sense, i.e., on pain of incoherence. Second, at the beginning of sect. 7, Berkeley makes a (very puzzling) statement about what "is agreed on all hands." It might be supposed on the basis of this statement that his reasoning in the following sections is supposed to rest on an assumption that there is general agreement about what is and is not objectively possible and hence he does not commit himself to the proposition that there is some way of determining the possibility or impossibility of separate existence and a fortiori he does not commit himself to the proposition that there is a way of determining the possibility or impossibility of separate existence that is other than the internal observations or thought-experiments that he thinks can be used to find out whether separate existence is or is not conceivable. Both Berkeley and his opponents, he suggests in sect. 7, agree about what is and is not objectively possible — they differ only with regard to what is or is not conceivable. To this objection, it can be pointed out that, since general agreement is in a sense a "way" of determining possibility and impossibility, my point is made. But, more importantly, it should be noted that Berkeley cannot consistently base his reasoning on the proposition that there is general agreement about objective possibilities and impossibilities. For he is firmly committed to the view that it is *not* agreed on all hands that primary and secondary qualities can "never really exist . . . apart . . . ." That is why the statement about what is agreed on all hands in sect. 7 is both surprising and puzzling.

2

In sects. 4-5 and 10 in the body of the *Principles* (among other places), Berkeley argues from the impossibility of conceiving X apart from Y to the impossibility of X existing apart from Y. In both arguments, he claims that impossibility of conception is an incontrovertible proof of impossibility of existence, and he implies thereby that there is no way of determining the possibility or impossibility of separate existence other than by the tests for conceivability.

Berkeley's procedure in sects. 4-5 is to claim at first in sect. 4 that it is a "manifest contradiction" or "plainly repugnant" that sensible objects should exist apart from sensations or perceptions of them. It may be, as some have thought, that he takes this ostensible repugnancy or contradiction to be something that is simply and unarguably self-evident. But, as I read sect. 4 in conjunction with sect. 5, he takes the position that, although it is indeed self-evident and as clear as anything can be that sensible objects cannot exist apart from perceptions of them, still an argument can be given proving that such a separation is impossible. Moreover, the stand that he takes is that this argument is absolutely conclusive. In sect. 5, referring to the pernicious doctrine of abstract ideas, he maintains, "It is impossible for me to conceive in my thoughts any sensible thing or object distinct from the sensation or perception of it." If we put sects. 4 and 5 together and take this claim to be the suppressed premise of an argument suggested in sect. 4, we can construe that argument in the following way: since it is impossible to conceive a sensible object apart from the sensation of it and since what cannot be conceived apart cannot exist apart, it follows like the night the day that a sensible object cannot exist apart from the sensation of it. The inference I wish to attribute to Berkeley in these sections is from inconceivability to impossibility; and, since he implies here that the impossibility of "dividing in my thoughts" what is sensed from the sensing of it is an absolutely knock-down, demonstrative proof of the impossibility of what is sensed existing apart from the sensing of it, it can also be argued that he implies that there is no way in which the possibility or impossibility of separate existence can be established other than the tests for conceivability or (as it turns out) inconceivability. If there were some other way, it would seem that we might discover in that way that it is possible for a sensible object to exist apart from the sensation of it; and it would then have seemed to Berkeley that, if he wished to give an incontrovertible proof, he would have to show that the other way could not yield a result different from the conclusion reached by the tests for conceivability. But he is prepared to rest his case on the outcome of these tests and thereby implies that there is no other test to be taken account of.

In sect. 10, arguing against the distinction of primary and secondary qualities, Berkeley again makes the move from inconceivability to impossibility:

> I see evidently that it is not in my power to frame an idea of a body extended and moved, but I must withal give it some colour or other sensible quality . . . In short, extension, figure, and motion, abstracted from all other qualities, are inconceivable. Where therefore the other sensible qualities are, there must these be also. . . .

He implies here, too, that there is no criterion of the possibility and impossibility of separate existence other than conceivability or inconceivability. If there were, then, though something having, say, shape without any sensible quality might admittedly be inconceivable, it would not follow necessarily that it is impossible. By the other test it might for all one knows turn out to be possible; and the argument here would not be, as Berkeley clearly thinks it is, a demonstative refutation of the Philosophers' bifurcation of primary and secondary qualities. If I am right in my reading of sect. 10, Berkeley clearly implies here too that there is no way of determining whether X can, or cannot, exist separately from Y that is other than the procedure for determining whether X can, or cannot, be conceived apart from Y. If I am also right in my reading of sects. 7-10 and 13 of the Introduction, we can impute to Berkeley two propositions that are contradictory, viz. that there is a way of determining possibility and impossibility of separate existence that is other than the procedures for determining the possibility or impossibility of conception; and that there is no way of determining possibility and impossibility of separate existence that is other than the tests of possibility or impossibility of conception.

3

I shall now quote some passages from Descartes paralleling views that I have attributed to Berkeley. The first is from the Replies to the Second Set of Objections appended to the *Meditations*, which contains Descartes's denial that sense can be attached to notions of possibility and impossibility that are not based on our conceptions and ideas: "All contradictoriness or impossibility is only in our conception wrongly conjoining ideas that are mutually opposed; it cannot be attributed to any thing outside the intellect since, by the very fact that something is outside the intellect, it is clear that it is not contradictory but it is possible" (AT, VII, p. 152; HR, II, p. 46[5]). On the other side of the Cartesian coin, we find that there is, for Descartes, some other (higher) standard of possibility and impossibility that differs from, and is acknowledged to be other than, the human capacity or incapacity of conception. A number of passages about God's creation of the eternal truths can be cited to this end; for instance, from the Sixth Replies, Sixthly, "It is because he [God] willed the three angles of a triangle to be necessarily equal to two right angles that this is true and *cannot be otherwise* . . ." (my emphasis, AT, VII, p. 432; HR, II, p. 248). A double standard of possibility and impossibility one side of which we humans cannot admittedly apply is tacitly acknowledged farther on in the Sixth Replies, Eighthly, when Descartes observes that "there is no need to ask in what way God could bring it about from all eternity that it not be true that twice four is eight, etc., for I admit that that cannot be understood by us" (AT, VII, p. 436; HR, II, p. 251). In the next sentence, he adds, "It would have been easy for Him so to establish that we human beings could not understand that these very things could be otherwise than they are. . . ."

I also want to quote some passages in which we are warned of the dangers of abstraction. In *Rules*, XIV, Descartes admonishes:

> If it is a problem regarding number, we are to imagine some substance (*subjectum*) measurable in many units. Though it is permissible for the intellect to confine its attention for the time to this multiplicity, we must yet be on our guard not on that account to conclude afterward something in which the thing numbered is supposed to have been excluded from our conception, as is done by those who ascribe mysterious and empty absurdities to numbers, which they certainly would not believe in so strongly if they did not conceive number to be distinct from things numbered. (AT, X, pp. 445-46; HR, I, pp. 59-60).

The danger of abstraction in geometry is also noted in Rule XIV:

> In [Geometry] almost everyone goes wrong in conceiving three species of quantity: line, surface, and solid (*corpus*). For . . . line and surface are not conceived as really distinct from solid or from one another; and, if in fact they are considered simply as abstracted by the intellect, they are no more diverse species of quantity than animal and living in man are diverse species of substance. (AT, X, pp. 448-49; HR, I, p. 62)

Another passage, from a later published work, is in the Letter to Clerselier in the French translation of the *Meditations*:

> There is a great difference between distinguishing and abstracting, for in distinguishing a substance from its accidents we must consider the one and the other, which greatly helps in knowing the substance; if, instead, we separate the substance from its accidents merely by abstraction, that is, if we consider it all alone without thinking of them, this prevents us from knowing it so well. . . . (AT, IX, p. 216; HR, II, p. 134)[6]

Notes

1. The threefold division is perhaps most perspicuous in *Principles of Philosophy*, pt. I, sects. li-liv (AT, VIII, pp. 24-26; HR, I, pp. 239-41). ("AT" stands for the edition of Charles Adam and Paul Tannery, *Oeuvres de Descartes* [Paris: Léopold Cerf, 1897-1913]; "HR" refers to the English translation by Elizabeth S. Haldane and G. R. T. Ross, *The Philosophical Works of Descartes* [Cambridge: Cambridge University Press, 1931].)

2. Citations of Berkeley's *Treatise Concerning the Principles of Human Knowledge* — hereafter referred to as *Principles* — are from A. A. Luce and T. E. Jessop, eds., *The Works of George Berkeley, Bishop of Cloyne*, 9 vols. (London: Thomas Nelson and Sons, 1948-57), vol. II. This edition is hereafter called *Works*. References to the *Principles* are by section numbers.

3. See, for instance, Bertrand Russell, *A History of Western Philosophy* (New York: Simon and Schuster, 1945), pp. 571, 609, 662, 832. Even Thomas Reid, who is careful to note differences in Berkeley's use of the term "idea," tells part of this story in *Essays on the Intellectual Powers of Man*, Essay II, especially at the beginning of chap. XII, in *The Works of Thomas Reid* (Edinburgh: Maclachlan and Stewart, 1872), I, p. 293.

4. A forthright statement of a "realist" interpretation of Berkeley is made by A. A. Luce in "Berkeley's Existence in the Mind," *Mind* L, 199 (July 1941): 258-67.

5. "AT" and "HR" are defined in n. 1.

6. It should be added that *abstrahere* for Descartes does not always or indeed usually carry a pejorative connotation. See the references under "Abstraction" in Étienne Gilson, *Index Scholastico-Cartésian* (Paris: Alcan, 1912), p. 1. It should also be noted that Berkeley sanctions abstraction in two senses or of two sorts, one in the passage quoted from the Introduction, sect. 10, and the other in the Introduction, sect. 16 (2nd ed.), where he says: "And here it must be acknowledged that a man may consider a figure merely as triangular, without attending to the particular qualities of the angles, or relations of the sides. So far he may abstract. . . ." This passage is added in the second edition, and it can be argued that it shows a change in Berkeley's view. I am not of the opinion that it does.

19

Hylas' Parity Argument

Phillip Cummins

This paper explores some aspects of a well-worn topic—Berkeley on spirit. It is concerned with that familiar episode in the third of the *Three Dialogues* when Hylas propounds and Philonous parries a series of objections to what may be called Berkeley's official account of mind. Three arguments are stated by Hylas. The final two were inserted at the third (1734) printing of the *Dialogues*.[1] Of these additional criticisms, the first differs from the original only in being more general in scope and thorough in formulation. Appropriately, Philonous' response to the original limited version, which explicitly concerns only God, is rich enough to answer in advance the more sweeping version. The reply given to the latter actually adds but little to the original reply. For these reasons, the first and second of Hylas' three arguments are best treated as a single objection. Since it turns on the allegation that it is impossible to conceive of a spirit, be it divine or human, it will be styled the *inconceivability argument*. The final argument, the second of the 1734 additions, will be called the *substance argument*. Besides it and the inconceivability argument, Philonous answers a third objection, one which is not explicitly given in the *Dialogues* but is akin to and suggested by those that are. This implicit argument will be termed the *nescience argument*.[2] For convenience we shall consider Hylas its author.

The three objections have a common pattern. All charge Philonous with failure to observe parity of reasoning. In each case, the criticism is that Philonous' negative position on matter is founded on arguments that apply with equal force to mind, but that his position on mind reverses rather than parallels his position on matter. Matter he denies; mind he affirms. Yet his reasons for denying the former tell equally well against the latter. In each objection a specific line of reasoning is said to have been used by Philonous against material substance, but not used, though equally applicable, against mental substance. Hylas' conclusion is that there is parity between matter and mind; either both must be retained or, using Berkeleyan principles, both must be rejected. At bottom, then, the parity arguments charge Philonous and his creator with nothing less than deeply rooted inconsistency.

Let us formulate the three parity arguments, beginning with the *inconceivability argument*. As with the others, it is constructed in response to a double contrast that is one of the central elements in Berkeley's philosophy. Not only are ideas categorically different from material substances, they are also categorically different from spirits.[3] It is no surprise, then, that Hylas begins his presentation of the inconceivability argument with a series of questions designed to elicit from Philonous the admission that God, particularly, and spirits, generally, have nothing in common with ideas. Not only is God not an idea, but, more importantly, "No idea therefore can be like unto, or represent the nature of God" (*Works*, II, p. 231). Later this is broadened to:

> . . . You acknowledge you have, properly speaking, no idea of your own soul. You even affirm that spirits are beings altogether different from ideas. Consequently that no idea can be like a spirit. We have therefore no idea of any spirit. (p. 232).

This conclusion becomes the basis for the inconceivability argument. Hylas continues:

> You admit nevertheless that there is spiritual substance, although you have no idea of it; while you deny there can be such a thing as material substance, because you have no notion or idea of it. Is this fair dealing? To act consistently, you must either admit matter or reject spirit. (p. 232)

Why does inability to have an idea of some putative being provide grounds for denying the existence of that thing? In discussing the case of God, Hylas suggests an answer. He says, "Since therefore you have no idea of the mind of God, how can you conceive it possible, that things should exist in his mind?" (p. 231) If one equates conceivability with possibility, what cannot in principle be conceived, that is, what is inconceivable, is impossible. Thus, if to conceive of something is to have an idea of it, neither matter nor mind is possible.

Neither is conceivable, since neither can be represented by an idea. Alternatively, if it is granted one can conceive of God or any other spirit without an idea of it, why not also conceive matter without using ideas? So goes the dilemma.

The *substance argument* alleges that Berkeley asserted the unintelligibility of the category of substance, concluded that "material substance" is a meaningless or incoherent phrase, yet affirmed, no, celebrated, the existence of mental substance. As Hylas puts it,

> Notwithstanding all you have said, to me it seems that according to your own way of thinking, and in consequence of your own principles, it should follow that you are only a system of floating ideas, without any substance to support them. Words are not to be used without a meaning. And as there is no more meaning in spiritual substance than in material substance, the one is to be exploded as well as the other. (p. 233)

On what basis does Hylas charge Philonous with holding, inconsistently, that "material substance" is meaningless, but "mental substance" is meaningful? Presumably Hylas is alluding to principles invoked in the First Dialogue to discredit his defence of material substance. There he conceded that he had no proper positive conception of substance, but claimed a relative notion on which to base a definition of material substance. Substance is substratum, he held, that which stands under its qualities (*Works*, II, pp. 197-99).[4] This account proved indefensible, since it generated an infinite regress of supports. Hylas, however, may be recalling the Second Dialogue, in which Philonous confronted him with arguments designed to show that the phrase 'material substance' is either meaningless or contradictory (pp. 216-26). In the Third Dialogue, Hylas seeks revenge. Mind is in the same fix as matter, since mental substance is no less meaningless than material substance. Hylas implies that Philonous inferred that material substance is meaningless or contradictory because substance, as such, is meaningless or contradictory. If this is so, Philonous must grant that mental substance is equally unintelligible. Once again parity of reasoning is demanded. If 'substance' is meaningless, then both material and spiritual substance are indefensible; if, on the other hand, substance can be given sense, both mind and matter should be granted.

In the process of answering this and the preceding argument, Berkeley insisted that minds are known. He discussed in some, though insufficient, detail how different kinds of spirits are known. It is helpful, I think, to consider his arguments on these topics as a full reply to the claim that minds cannot be known. This thesis is one of the conclusions of the *nescience argument*, which consists of the following seven premises, all of them allegedly drawn from Berkeley's presentation of immaterialism.

1. If some being is known, it is either directly known or inferred from some other being or beings that are directly known.

2. Something is directly known if and only if it is an object of immediate experience.

3. Something, X, can be inferred from some other being, Y, which is directly known, if and only if X has previously been directly known to be connected or conjoined to Y or is similar to something, Z, which is directly known to be connected or conjoined to Y.

4. No material substance is an idea.

5. No spiritual substance is an idea.

6. Only ideas are objects of immediate experience.

7. Something can be similar to an idea if and only if it is itself an idea.

Neither matter nor spirit are ideas. Hence neither can be like ideas. Consequently, neither can be immediately experienced nor inferred from what is. In short, neither matter nor spirit can be either directly or indirectly known. Both are in principle unknowable on immaterialist principles. Berkeley was thus inconsistent in proclaiming knowledge of spirit and ignorance of matter. Parity of reasoning is required.

The three parity arguments constitute a sustained attack on spiritual substance. Some scholars think that Philonous repulsed it, but many more seem to find Hylas' criticisms convincing. Of these, some, such as Thomas Reid, maintain that one must secure mind and matter by repudiating Berkeley's epistemology.[5] Others hold that Berkeley failed to realize that his radical epistemology required a new metaphysics, not just the more refined half of Descartes' dualism. They endorse the epistemology. Allaire, among others, has taken this line.[6] Still others—Turbayne, their leader—see Berkeley as adroit, consistent, and cunning.[7] The official account of mind, they say, is mere tactical sham, analogous to the account given of touch in the *Essay Towards a New Theory of Vision*. Needless to say, Berkeley's critics, whatever their differences, find Philonous' response to the parity arguments inadequate. Let us next assess that opinion, beginning with the attempt to answer the inconceivability argument.

The heart of Berkeley's response to both the inconceivability and the nescience arguments is his contention that each spirit, by a reflex act, has itself and its activities as immediate objects of experience. This contention flatly contradicts the sixth premise of the nescience argument. More importantly, it provides the starting point for both an account of how spirits of various kinds can be conceptualized and an account of our knowledge of the existence of spirits, human and divine. Before considering them, let us examine the evidence that Berkeley avowed direct self-knowledge on the part of minds. Consider these passages. First:

> I own I have properly no idea, either of God or any other spirit; for these being active, cannot be represented by things perfectly inert, as our ideas are. I do nevertheless know, that I who am a spirit or thinking substance, exist as certainly, as I know my ideas exist. Farther, I know what I mean by the terms *I* and *myself*; and I know this immediately, or intuitively, though I do not perceive it as I perceive a triangle, a colour, or a sound. (*Works*, II, p. 231)

Again:

> My own mind and my own ideas I have an immediate knowledge of; and by the help of these, do immediately apprehend the possibility of the existence of other spirits and ideas. (p. 232)

Further along, Philonous says,

> Whereas the being of my self, that is, my own soul, mind or thinking principle, I evidently know by reflexion. (p. 233)

Finally, responding to the substance argument, he says,

> How often I must I repeat, that I know or am conscious of my own being; and that I my self am not my ideas, but somewhat else, a thinking active principle that perceives, knows, wills, and operates about ideas. (p. 233)

Through his spokesman Berkeley makes it evident that in his view each conscious mind has immediate knowledge of itself and so knows both that it is and what it is. Though direct, this knowledge is said to be reflexive, presumably because Berkeley shared Locke's view that a knower's knowing of itself and its knowing involves a redirection of attention.[8] Reflexive awareness of a cognitive activity need not involve an idea as its object, even though the object of that activity is an idea. Hence, besides immediate experience of ideas, there is held to be immediate experience of mind and mental activities. Let us next consider the significance of this position in Berkeley's refutation of the inconceivability argument.

Hylas maintained that Philonous argued against the existence of matter on the grounds, first, that since one cannot have an idea of matter, it cannot be conceived and, second, that since it cannot be conceived, matter is impossible. He proceeded to draw the obvious consequences of Berkeley's view that one cannot have an idea of spirit. The argument presupposes that Berkeley held two crucial principles: (1) What is not an idea cannot be conceived; and (2) what cannot be conceived is impossible. In response, Berkeley denied both principles. To reinforce that denial, he sketched an account of how spirits are conceived and offered a more accurate characterization of his grounds for denying the existence of matter.

His account of how one can think about spirits begins, as we have seen, with the claim that each spirit has direct experience of itself and its activities. Hence, each center of consciousness can apprehend what it, *qua* center of consciousness, is. Philonous proceeds to argue that one can think of or conceive other minds, even though 'idea', strictly used, cannot be applied to a mind, and an idea, correctly understood, cannot represent one either. If a representative entity or model is in any way involved when one mind conceptualizes other minds, that entity is the conceptualizing mind itself. Consider this statement:

> However, taking the word *idea* in a large sense, my soul may be said to furnish me with an idea, that is, an image, or likeness of God, though indeed extremely inadequate. For all the notion I have of God, is obtained by reflecting on my own soul heightening its powers, and removing its imperfections. I have therefore, though not an inactive idea, yet in my self some sort of an active thinking image of the Deity. (*Works*, II, pp. 231-32)

Other spirits can be conceived in much the same way. If, for that, a paradigm or model of what a mind is is needed, one's own mind can serve. It is directly known. And, unlike a sensed object, it can always be apprehended. A reflexive act of awareness does the trick. Hence nothing corresponding to pictorial ideas of imagination is required. It must be conceded that Berkeley never spelled out an account of thinking about thinking or thinking about minds, but it is not difficult to fit what he did say in his published works to the sketch just presented.

Conceiving (thinking) of an object is an activity of mind. It is either adequate or inadequate. The conditions for adequate conception may be met in one of two ways. First, an item may be directly apprehended. Once apprehended, it may be thought. In the light of Philonous' statements in response to the parity arguments, it would seem that for Berkeley ideas of sense, various activities of mind, and even the conscious mind itself can be thought on the basis of direct apprehension. Second, what is not so apprehended may nevertheless be adequately conceived by being conceived as the same or similar in kind or character to one or more items that are directly known. For example, one may think of an as yet unperceived, but perceivable, object, say, a snowy owl, in terms of a specific combination of previously sensed qualities or objects. Again, one may think of another human mind as much like but different from oneself. It is not obvious that for Berkeley a representative model is required for such conceptualizing, but if it is, it can be provided both for thinking of sensibles and thinking of minds.

Not all conceptualizing is adequate. In some cases, one can think of an item not as what it is, but only as that which stands in a known relation to an adequately conceived item. One might know, for example, that a sensible object, O, must have a cause, yet not know that cause. One could conceive of an item, the cause of O, without having any further nonrelational content in one's conception of it or only such content as is implied by the relationship in terms of which the conception is provided. The key condition for this form of conceptualization is that no inconsistency be involved in the characterization of the item so conceived.[9] Berkeley argued, of course, that matter can be conceived in none of the ways mentioned. He stated,

> For you neither perceive matter objectively, as you do an inactive being or idea, nor know it, as you do your self by a reflex act: neither do you mediately apprehend it by similitude of the one or the other: nor yet collect it by reasoning from that which you know immediately. All which makes the case of *matter* widely different from that of *Deity*. (*Works*, p. 232)

One can conceive minds without employing ideas of them, but one cannot conceive of matter either with or without ideas. There is, then, no parity of cases.

So far, the first part of Berkeley's reply to the inconceivability argument. The other corrects Hylas' portrayal of the argument against matter. Philonous is made to say,

> . . . I do not deny the existence of material substance, merely because I have no notion of it, but because the notion of it is inconsistent, or in other words, because it is repugnant that there should be a notion of it. Many things, for aught I know, may exist, whereof neither I nor any other man hath or can have any idea or notion whatsoever. But then those things must be possible, that is, nothing inconsistent must be included in their definition. (pp. 232-33)[10]

In short, Berkeley maintains, the second presupposition of the inconceivability argument cannot be attributed to him. The problem for defenders of matter is not lack of images of it; rather, it is that attempts to define it as an unperceiving extended substance yield contradiction not intelligibility.

Some might dismiss as relatively insignificant Berkeley's refutation of the inconceivability and nescience arguments on the ground that the only important parity argument is the substance argument. On this view, what is inconsistent with the attack on material substance is not the assertion of knowledge of mental entities, it is the defense of mental substance.[11] The arguments used to dispatch matter also banish not mind, as such, but mental substance. A defender of this point of view might add that one can grant direct experience of sensibles and conscious activities without thereby granting the existence of substances, mental or physical. The category of substance can be invoked, if at all, in the systematic analysis of experience, not in the description of it. Berkeley seemingly abides by the last point, since in his reply to the substance argument he first insists upon consciousness of self, then proceeds to attack Hylas' characterization of it as a system of momentary states. The latter is clearly a separate line of argument. Here is the crucial passage.

> How often must I repeat, that I know or am conscious of my own being; and that I my self am not my ideas, but somewhat else, a thinking active principle that perceives, knows, wills, and operates about ideas. I know that I, one and the same self, perceive both colours and sounds; that a colour cannot perceive a sound, nor a sound a colour; that I am therefore one individual principle, distinct from colour and sound; and, for the same reason, from all other sensible things and inert ideas. (*Works*, II, pp. 233-34)

Berkeley has Philonous make a further point. "Material substance" is unintelligible not because "substance" is as such meaningless, but because no gloss on the latter yields consistency and sense to the former. In contrast, one can replace the metaphors in the case of mental substance. Philonous says,

> I know what I mean, when I affirm that there is a spiritual substance or support of ideas, that is, that a spirit knows and perceives ideas. But I do not know what is meant, when it is said, that an unperceiving substance hath inherent in it and supports either ideas or the archetypes of ideas. (p. 234)

The argument against material substance does not involve a rejection of the category of substance or a denial of all grounds for analyzing experience in terms of substance. The problem is material substance, not substance as such. There is then no parity between the case of matter and that of spirit.

One might come to Hylas' aid at this point and insist that the argument for substance offered by Philonous cannot be allowed within Berkeley's empiricist epistemology. Note that Philonous argues from what is experienced (the empirical self and its ideas) to an unexperienced entity (the individual active principle or substance) on the basis of a premise (one idea cannot perceive another) whose truth cannot be established from the data of experience. The criticism made is that such "metaphysical" premises were not allowed in support of material substance, so cannot be permitted on behalf of spiritual substance.

This criticism cannot be accepted. It involves a serious distortion of Berkeley's theory of knowledge. It is a profound mistake to represent Berkeley as permitting no metaphysical premises. To realize this, one need only recall the argument of sect. 26 of the *Principles*. It reads:

> We perceive a continual succession of ideas, some are anew excited, others are changed or totally disappear. There is therefore some cause of these ideas whereon they depend, and which produces and changes them. That this cause cannot be any quality or idea or combination of ideas, is clear from the preceding section. It must therefore be a substance; but it has been shewn that there is no corporeal or material substance: it remains therefore that the cause of ideas is an incorporeal active substance or spirit. (*Works*, II, p. 52)

Here Berkeley subscribes to a causal axiom, and, as the preceding section makes plain, to the further axiom that causes must be active. Notice, too, how Berkeley argues in developing his account of knowledge of minds or spirits other than his own. Both God and other finite spirits are inferred, but notice the difference in the way the inferences are characterized. Of the inference to God, Philonous says,

> Farther, from my own being, and from the dependency I find in my self and my ideas, I do by an act of reason, necessarily infer the existence of a God, and of all created things in the mind of God. (*Works*, II, p. 232)

Of other finite spirits he says,

> It is granted we have neither an immediate evidence nor a demonstrative knowledge of the existence of other finite spirits; but it will not thence follow that such spirits are on a foot with material substances: if to suppose the one be inconsistent, and it be not inconcsistent to suppose the other; if the one can be inferred by no argument, and there is a probability for the other; if we see signs and effects indicating distinct finite agents like our selves, and see no sign or symptom whatever that leads to a rational belief of matter. (p. 233)

As did many of his contemporaries, Berkeley distinguished between demonstrative inferences based on self-evident or necessary truths and merely probable inferences based on empirical data or analogies. Both permit us to infer one existent from another.[12]

There is a tendency to attribute to Berkeley the Humean principle that between two wholly distinct things there can be no necessary connection. On this view, premises upon which to build inferences from one existent to another are contingent, so must be founded, directly or analogically, on experience. Such inferences, therefore, are never demonstrative arguments. On this view, one may justly harbor grave doubts about inferences from experienced items to putative entities, which cannot in principle be experienced and which are altogether different from experienced items. At least one premise in such an inference must be without foundation. So much for the familiar Humean position. There is considerable evidence in both the *Principles* and the *Three Dialogues* that Berkeley did *not* accept it. Notice, first, the rhetorical development of sects. 18 and 19 of the *Principles*. Berkeley there denies that there is any evidence from which to infer material substance. His first point is that well-known facts show that there is no necessary connection between what is sensed (ideas) and matter. A necessary connection would indeed found an inference from ideas to imperceptible matter, but in the case at hand such a connection can be dismissed. In sect. 19, Berkeley goes on to deny probable grounds for inferring matter from ideas. Probable premises must be founded on experience, but matter is imperceptible. It is obvious that in these sections Berkeley recognizes two types of inference from one existent to another. He introduces specific reasons for denying that material substance can be inferred by either route. It does not follow that spiritual substance cannot be inferred by a demonstrative inference on the basis of necessary metaphysical premises.

Once one begins to think of Berkeley in Humean terms, his defense of mental substance becomes suspect. In characterizing the data of consciousness in terms of a single active principle, spirit or mental substance, Berkeley is seen as inconsistent, since such an analysis involves an exploded concept, substance, and premises banished as illegitimate. But the moral, I want to suggest, is not that Berkeley was an incomplete or veiled Humean, but rather that we too easily assimilate one philosopher to another. Berkeley is Berkeley and not another soul.

Notes

1. George Berkeley, *The Works of George Berkeley, Bishop of Cloyne* (hereafter referred to as *Works*), 9 vols., ed. A. A. Luce and T. E. Jessop (London: Thomas Nelson and

sons, 1948-57, 1964), vol. II, pp. 231-34; See, too, *Works*, II, p. 152. The additions may have resulted from Berkeley's correspondence with Samuel Johnson in 1729-1730. See *Works*, II, pp. 267-94. On the other hand, Berkeley had anticipated, indeed entertained, the arguments assigned to Hylas as early as 1710-1712. See *Works*, I, p. 72 (*Philosophical Commentaries*, entry 579), for example. I. C. Tipton offers a careful and thorough analysis of this material in his *The Philosophy of Immaterialism* (London: Methuen, 1974), pp. 257-69.

2. In his *Principles of Human Knowledge*, sect. 135-40 and 142, Berkeley discusses the view that humans are ignorant of the nature of spirits through want of ideas of them. See, especially, sect. 135. *Works*, II, pp. 103-06. The nescience argument is more sweeping, denying knowledge of both the existence and the nature of spirits.

3. *Principles of Human Knowledge*, sects. 2-8 and 27 (*Works*, II, pp. 41-44 and 52-53). Categorically considered, the contrasts work this way. Ideas are unperceiving entities that are perceived (sensed) and must be perceived. Spirits are unperceived (unsensed) entities that perceive and must perceive. Material substances, as defined by philosophers, are unperceiving entities that are capable of unperceived existence. (Whether or not they are perceived in some manner or other is examined by Berkeley in detail.) For Berkeley, material substances are impossible, because in his view the detailed descriptions given of them as extended, moving, etc., are inevitably formulated in the vocabulary of ideas, thereby implying the categorical sameness of the two classes.

4. Compare *Principles*, sects. 16 and 17 (*Works*, II, pp. 47-48).

5. Thomas Reid, *Essays on the Intellectual Powers of Man* (Cambridge, Mass.: M.I.T. Press, pp. 167-97. See, especially, pp. 186-97.

6. Edwin B. Allaire, "The Attack on Substance: Descartes to Hume," *Dialogue* 3 (1964): 284-87.

7. Colin M. Turbayne, "Berkeley's Two Concepts of Mind," *Philosophy and Phenomenological Research* 20 (1959-60): 85-92, and ibid. 22 (1961-62).: 383-86.

8. John Locke, *An Essay Concerning Human Understanding*, ed. P. H. Nidditch (Oxford: Clarendon Press, 1975). See, especially, bk. I, chap. i, sects. 1-2; II, i, 1 and 4; II, vi, 1-2; and II, ix, 1-10.

9. See *Works*, II, pp. 197 and 223. Philonous distinguishes between having a "direct and positive notion" and having a "relative notion." Hylas is said to have neither with respect to matter. Compare *Works*, II, pp. 47 and 75 (*Principles*, sects. 16 and 80), where Berkeley distinguishes among a positive notion, a relative notion, and a mere negative definition. The last he rejects as an implicit admission of incomprehensibility. Reid, *Essays*, essay II, chap. 17, pp. 252-55, distinguishes direct and distinct notions from relative notions. A relative notion is inadequate for Reid, who says at 253, "A relative notion of a thing, is, strictly speaking, no notion of the thing at all, but only of some relation which it bears to something else."

10. For an account of Berkeley's argument against matter and its basis, see my "Berkeley's Ideas of Sense," *Noûs* 9 (1975): 55-72.

11. It might seem plausible to argue that Berkeley defended spirit (mind, soul, consciousness, person), but rejected substance. Admittedly, Berkeley denied Locke's view that, in the expressions, "material substance" and "spiritual substance," "substance" has a univocal, but obscure, sense. Nevertheless, Philonous' response to the substance argument of Hylas would be all but inexplicable on the supposition that Berkeley rejected the category of substance altogether. (Minimally considered, a substance is an individual enduring being that is distinct from though in some manner connected with its changing states.) For the distinction between persons and substances, see I. C. Tipton, "Berkeley's View of Spirits," in *New Studies in Berkeley's Philosophy*, ed. W. E. Steinkraus (New York: Holt, Rinehart and Winston, 1966), pp. 59-71. Compare Tipton, *The Philosophy of Immaterialism*, chap. VII.

12. Locke, *Essay*, bk. IV, chaps. i, ii, vi, and xv. Compare Berkeley, *Principles*, sects. 30-31, 101-09, and 118-22 (*Works*, II, pp. 53-54, 85-89, and 94-97). See, too, *Principles*, Introduction, sects. 15-16 (*Works*, II, pp. 33-34). Compare David Hume, *A Treatise of Human Nature*, ed. L. A. Selby-Bigge (Oxford: Clarendon Press, 1967), bk. I, pt. ii, sect. 2; and I, iii, 1, 3, and 11.

20

Lending a Hand to Philonous:
The Berkeley, Plato, Aristotle Connection

Colin M. Turbayne

Modern philosophy is sometimes characterized as a gradual abandoning of the metaphysics of substance. In this scenario, we begin with Descartes, who set down two distinct substances and formulated the traditional mind/body dichotomy. With Hume we reach a logical conclusion in the disappearance of the two substances and, *a fortiori*, the disappearance of a metaphysic of substance.

Berkeley occupies an interesting position in this "history of substance" because, while he has at heart Descartes' ulterior motive to keep mind as a substance, he shares Hume's desire to drop matter as substance. And since Anglo-American philosophy sees Hume as one of its great forbears at the same time as it regards Descartes as the father of modern philosophy, Berkeley is commonly regarded as either a half-hearted Humean or, what may be worse, a "castrated Cartesian."[1]

This middle stance of Berkeley with its apparent inconsistencies is made all the more untenable because of the noticeably brief treatment he gives mind substance and mind's relation to ideas. As a result of the cursory mention of mind in Berkeley's extant works (a treatise on the mind was lost during his travels), it remains to sympathetic commentators to fill in the gaps, to reconcile the seeming contradictions, and to recreate a more complete picture than Berkeley himself left.

My belief is that Berkeley's half-hidden doctrine of mind substance belongs to an ancient tradition often overlooked, and that, if it is restored to this tradition, many of the issues that surround his present account of mind substance may be illuminated and the problems solved. It is not a Cartesian tradition; its roots are different. It begins with Plato and Aristotle, who formulated the notion of a substance entirely distinct from its qualities yet capable of supporting those qualities in itself.

Problems

Some of the main difficulties in the interpretation of Berkeley's account of the mind and its relations to ideas appear in his very first statements on these topics early in the *Principles*.[2] In sect. 2 he asserts:

> This perceiving, active being is what I call "mind", "spirit", "soul", or "myself". By which words I do not denote any one of my ideas, but a thing *entirely distinct from* them, *wherein they exist* or, which is the same thing, whereby they are perceived—for the existence of an idea consists in being perceived.

These are statements, not arguments[3] —suggesting that Berkeley is introducing axioms or principles referring to primitive entities that explain other things while remaining themselves unexplained. The mind is one of these primitive entities. It is "a thing," a substance, but is not called so until several sections later. It is a "perceiving active being," suggesting that it is a substance that is both passive and active, although that is not clearly indicated until much later in the book. In the second sentence, Berkeley introduces two important principles, one of which I call the "Distinction Principle":[4] The mind is *entirely distinct from* ideas; and the other, the "Inherence Principle": Ideas *exist only in* the mind. Although Berkeley begins to clarify the meaning of the latter, he leaves the relationship between the two begging for clarification, for the two principles are apparently inconsistent. How can ideas be *entirely distinct from* the mind and yet not *exist* unless they are *in* it? A little later, in sect. 5, Berkeley introduces a third principle and, in doing so, appears to contradict himself once more. He asserts that it is impossible to conceive "any sensible thing or object *distinct from* the sensation or perception of it." In the same section, he asks and answers the question: "Is it possible to *separate*, even in thought, any of these [ideas or impressions] *from* perception? For my part, I might as easily divide a thing from itself." I call this the "Identity Principle": The perceiving of an idea is *not distinct from* the idea perceived. The Identity Principle appears to contradict the Distinction Principle because we have been told, so it seems, that perceiving is part of the mind itself. How can ideas be *entirely distinct from* the mind although they are *not distinct from* their being perceived by the mind?

Solutions

These passages have been much discussed and given diverse interpretations in recent years. Of the Distinction Principle, A. A. Luce says, "This distinction is in the ground-plan of the book, in its very fabric. . . ."[5] But Luce's stance is shared by few. In the traditional view, as we shall see, the Distinction Principle must be dropped in order to make Berkeley's system consistent.

The Inherence Principle has always been near the forefront of discussion about Berkeley, from his day to ours. Lately, however, it has received more critical attention from several scholars. Edwin B. Allaire, who revived this discussion, claims that Berkeley's idealism rests upon the Inherence Principle, and that "Berkeley's rather simple mistake . . . is that he persists in claiming that qualities must inhere in a substance, even though he insists that they are not predicated of a substance."[6] Presumably, Allaire holds that if Berkeley corrects his mistake, he will claim that qualities inhere in mind substance *and* are predicated of that substance. But then, if they are predicated of mind substance, such qualities become parts of mind. If this is so, then mind substance collapses into its qualities in the same way as material substance collapses into *its* qualities, as Berkeley himself shows. Thus Berkeley is forced to drop his Distinction Principle and to hold that the mind is a collection of qualities or ideas; this is to adopt a Humean view of the mind.

The Identity Principle has been attacked throughout the century, beginning with G. E. Moore's celebrated attack on idealism.[7] Moore claims that Berkeley's idealism rests ultimately upon this principle. He argues that Berkeley contradicts himself within the Identity Principle. More recently, S. A. Grave and George Pitcher have drawn attention to the apparent inconsistency between the Distinction Principle and the Identity Principle; although, of course, they regard the apparent inconsistency as a real one. Grave says: "Nothing would be more valuable in Berkeleyan commentary than a reconciliation of these principles," and admits: "I regret having no suggestions to offer. The positions seem to be quite irreconcilable." Grave asks which of the two principles Berkeley "really held," and answers: "Berkeley did not hold two sets of conflicting opinions . . . ; he held the opinions prescribed by the identity principle." If this is so, then Berkeley must drop the Distinction Principle, "and the mind is thought of not as a substance but as a system"; and if this is so, "ideas will have to become 'part of the mind',"[8] Pitcher notes the same "serious inconsistency," and argues that "the simplest and best way to preserve the largest bulk of Berkeley's central philosophical doctrines is to have him abandon [the Distinction Principle]." Pitcher has Berkeley adopt instead the view that ideas are "only weakly distinct from the mind," and, instead of the act-object analysis required by the Distinction Principle, has him adopt the adverbial analysis.[9]

Thus, in the traditional view, Berkeley's principles are irreconcilable. Neither the Inherence Principle nor the Identity Principle is consistent with the Distinction Principle (the last being close to common sense). Berkeley's system can be made consistent only if he drops the Distinction Principle and adopts a phenomenalist account of the mind paralleling his phenomenalist account of matter, which is to adopt a Humean view of the mind. A. J. Ayer, looking at Berkeley through Humean spectacles, states his logical decline succinctly: "The considerations which make it necessary, as Berkeley saw, to give a phenomenalist account of material things, make it necessary, as Berkeley did not see, to give a phenomenalist account of the self."[10]

It is not, I think, generally realized that Berkeley was fully aware of this apparent inconsistency in his system and, at the same time, fully aware of the theory of mind that, according to posterity, he is forced by his own principles to hold. Berkeley in fact anticipated this objection in 1734. Hylas, the materialist, says: "You must either admit matter or reject spirit." Since Philonous, the "mind lover," refuses to admit matter, Hylas administers the apparent *coup de grace*. "In consequence of your own principles it should follow that you are only *a system of floating ideas* . . ." (*Dialogues*, III, sect. 4). Using principles like Berkeley's as well as words like Berkeley's, Hume reached the same conclusion in 1739: "The mind," he claimed, "is *a system of different perceptions*."[11] Unlike Berkeley, however, Hume accepted this conclusion, and thus, according to posterity, made Berkeley consistent.

Firmly entrenched as it is, the traditional view is an unsatisfactory interpretation of Berkeley's philosophy. This is so because subscribers to it must discard some fundamental facts, where the facts are Berkeley's "singular tenets," thus giving us an "emasculated Berkeley." In the following pages, as an alternative to the traditional view, I try to show that Berkeley's system is indeed consistent; thus enabling him, in accord with what he intended, to retain the Distinction Principle and to refrain from adopting the Humean theory of mind.

"Act" and Object

I shall consider first Berkeley's apparent contradiction between the Distinction and the Identity Principles. I shall begin with the Identity Principle, in which he asserts that perceiving an idea and the idea perceived are the same thing.

Most of us try to make a distinction between what has been called in philosophy "the act" and "the object." Certainly we can find words to suit such a distinction: for example, between having a toothache and the toothache itself, or between hearing a sound and the sound we hear. Early in this century, however, G. E. Moore, in his famous article, "The Refutation of Idealism" (1903), found it necessary to defend this distinction against its contrary notion: "To identify 'blue' or any other of what I have called 'objects' of sensation with the corresponding sensation is, in every case, a self-contradictory error."[12] Bertrand Russell, in his equally famous work, the *Problems of Philosophy* (1912), tried also to defend it: "This question of the distinction between *act* and *object* in our apprehending of things is vitally important, since our whole power of acquiring knowledge is bound up with it."[13]

Berkeley, as we have seen, holds a position contrary to that of Moore and Russell. Perhaps he expressed it most succinctly in sect. 5 of the first edition of the *Principles*: "In truth the object and the sensation are the same thing and cannot, therefore, be abstracted from each other." This is one half, and perhaps the more important half, of Berkeley's *esse-percipi* principle, the other half being the Inherence Principle.

Let us see where the principle fits within Berkeley's conception of the structure and functions of the mind. The mind (or spirit) he tells us, is "one, simple, undivided, active being." Nevertheless, it is "passive as well as active," as defined by its "two principal powers." "As it perceives ideas it is called 'the Understanding', and as it produces or otherwise operates about them it is called 'the Will'" (*Principles*, sect. 27; *Correspondence*, IV, sect. 3). What are powers? Here Berkeley subscribes to an ancient tradition, begun by Plato, of distinguishing passive and active powers—otherwise called faculties or capacities. Since a faculty (*dynamis*) cannot be perceived, it is identified by its *activities* and *objects* (*Republic* 477d). Sensation, for example, is a passive capacity. Whenever there is intercourse between any sense organ possessing this passive capacity and any appropriate external object possessing an active power, "there arise offspring, endless in number but in pairs of twins. One twin is the perceiving [for example, the activity of seeing or hearing], whose birth always coincides with that of the other twin, the thing perceived [i.e., the object; for example, a color or a sound] (*Theaetetus* 156). Aristotle goes further: "When that which can hear is actually hearing, and when that which can sound is sounding, then the *actual hearing* and the *actual sound* are merged in one"; and "The activity (*energeia*) of the [external] object and that of the sense faculty is the same" (*De Anima* 425b, 426a).

These features of passive and active powers and their twin activities reappear in Berkeley's concept of mind. Thus the Understanding (i.e., the thing *standing under*, as its synonyms indicate) is the passive capacity of supporting ideas, or of being a *substance* or *subject* in the sense of *"substratum,"* while the Will is an active power of making or creating ideas, or of being a substance in the sense of *"essence"* or *"ousia."* In "acts of imagination," so called, my will acts upon my understanding to produce ideas of imagination, which are creations or "creatures of my will." In sensation, a will external to mine (cf. Plato's and Aristotle's external object) acts upon my understanding to produce ideas of sense (colors, sounds, smells, tastes, and feels), which are *"not* creatures of my will" but are creations of "some *other* will." In perception, the two wills—God's and mine—are at work to produce "collections of ideas constitut[ing] a stone, a tree, a book, and the like sensible things," my will doing the collecting and combining, since "number is entirely the creature of the mind" (*Principles*, sects., 1, 12, 28, 29). It is the second of these unions of Understanding and Will, specifically in sensation, which concerns the Principle of Identity. Berkeley considers here only the second of Plato's twins—the object or the idea perceived (for example, a color or a sound), the merger of the *object* with the *activity* having been argued for at *Principles*, sect. 5.

How do we decide between the position held by Moore and Russell and its contrary held by Berkeley, Plato, and Aristotle? We do so, I think, partly by introspection. Berkeley asks us, in effect, to carry out the *Gedankenexperimente* of trying to abstract, for example, my having a toothache from the toothache I have, or my seeing a color from the color I see (*Principles*, sect. 5). He thinks that it cannot be done, and that in thinking we *can* achieve this feat we are the victims of words. Moreover, while Moore and Russell hold that, in the "act" or "activity" of perceiving percepts or of sensing sensa, we are active, Berkeley, Plato, and Aristotle hold that we are entirely passive. This issue also, Berkeley thinks, is resolved by engaging in introspection. At *Dialogues* I, sect. 9, Berkeley makes Philonous argue convincingly that while sniffing a rose I am active, in smelling it I am passive. He says that the sniffing cannot be called "smelling," "for if it were I should smell every time I breathed in that manner." Lending a hand to Philonous, one can see that Moore and Russell are victims of word magic. Aristotle's *"energeia"* is often translated in the present context as "activity," thus erroneously suggesting to readers the notions of "act" and "agency." Thus the mind has been regarded mistakenly as "active" or as an "agent" in having sensations. Aristotle's *energeia* is often translated also as "actuality," referring to the opposite of potentiality. This is the way Berkeley takes it in *Principles*, sect. 5, where he uses such phrases as "actually perceived" and "actual sensation."

Moore and Russell subsequently reversed their views and adopted this part of Berkeley's *esse-percipi* principle. Russell was the first to change, writing in 1921: "The possibility of distinguishing the sensation from the sense datum vanishes. . . . Accordingly, the sensation that we have when we see a patch of colour simply *is* that patch of colour, an actual constituent of the physical world, and a part of what physics is concerned with."[14] Moore's change of view, made in 1941, is certain but not so definite: "A toothache certainly cannot exist without being felt, but . . . on the other hand, the moon certainly can exist without being perceived."[15] In his original refutation, Moore intended to show that Berkeley's mistake lay in the identification of sensations with their objects, as in the toothache example and Russell's color example. Accordingly, his retraction, following Russell's, indicates his withdrawal of the charge that Berkeley's Identity Principle contained a "self-contradictory error."

We are more concerned, however, with the supposed contradiction between this principle and the Distinction Principle. It was necessary to examine the Identity Principle in order to find out whether it could possibly conflict with the Distinction Principle. From the preceding account it is obvious that the two principles are perfectly compatible: In his Distinction Principle, Berkeley states that the mind is entirely distinct from ideas. We now see that, in terms of faculties or capacities and their actualities, or powers and their effects, Berkeley is claiming that the mind with its capacities belongs to an entirely different category from its actualities or effects.

This interpretation opposes that of Grave and Pitcher, stated on p. 297. They maintain that Berkeley contradicts himself in holding both of these principles. Although the issue is now fairly clearly defined, it is helpful to summarize the main points:

First: From *Principles*, sects. 2 and 27, it is clear that the mind or spirit is not the same as its two principal powers or faculties or capacities, viz., the Understanding and the Will. Rather the mind *has* or *possesses* these powers. This view of Berkeley differs from the view of Gilbert Ryle who, in his *Concept of Mind*,[16] holds that the mind *is* (i.e., *is nothing but*) its powers, "abilities," or "dispositions," and that it is the person, or perhaps the body, that has or possesses them.

MIND
(A)

PASSIVE POWER   ACTIVE POWER
The Understanding   The Will
(B)   ACTUALITIES
Sensing an object—An object sensed
(X)   (Y)

The Distinction Principle: A or B is entirely distinct from X and Y
The Identity Principle: X = Y

Second: According to the *Distinction* Principle, the mind with its powers or faculties is specifically distinct or heterogeneous from its actualities or activities (i.e., from its ideas "actually perceived" or its "actual sensations[s]" (*Principles*, sect. 5). In the phrase "This perceiving, active being" of *Principles*, sect. 2, the words "perceiving" and "active" refer to powers or faculties; while the words "being perceived," "actually perceived," etc., of *Principles*, sect. 5, refer to activities or actualities. The two sorts or kinds are "more distant and heterogeneous from [each other] than light is from darkness" (*Principles*, sect. 141); they are what we might call nowadays different logical types or categories.

Third: According to the *Identity* Principle, the so-called "act" and object—the supposedly different actualities or "activities"—are identical when the mind is actually *undergoing* or *receiving* them. They are passive "activities."

Fourth: In the light of the second and third points just made, it is obvious that Berkeley can hold consistently both the Distinction and the Identity Principles. This is so because in the former he is distinguishing "heterogeneous" items (items from two different categories), while in the latter he is identifying items within one category. It is true that Berkeley, to some extent, invites the charge of inconsistency; for he does not clearly indicate in *Principles*, sect. 2, that he uses the words "perceiving" to refer to a *power or faculty*, nor in *Principles*, sect. 5, that he uses the words "being perceived," "perception," etc., to refer to the *exercise or actuality* of that power or faculty. But when we consider all his utterances, especially those of *Principles*, sect. 27, his meaning becomes clear.

Plato's Receptacle and Berkeley's Mind

Let me now consider the other apparent inconsistency in Berkeley's system, supposed to exist between the Distinction and Inherence Principles. I shall use two well-known methods for testing the consistency of a theory. The first is to reduce it to another, more firmly established theory—one whose consistency, though not necessarily whose content, is generally accepted. The second is to find a familiar interpretation of the structure of the theory in which the commonplace statements are true; in effect, to find a model. Since a model is nothing but an alternative interpretation of the calculus of a theory, both these methods involve the use of models.

I shall present Berkeley's account in terms of an account of a wholly different subject given by Plato in the second part of the *Timaeus*.[17] This subject is the Receptacle[18] "and, as it were, the Nurse of all Becoming and change" (49a), which Plato later calls "space." Since the things that enter the Receptacle (images of the Forms) are "fleeting, changeable entities, they cannot be designated as 'this thing' or 'that thing' but only as 'of a certain quality' (49d, e)." Only the Receptacle itself "wherein all of these qualities come to exist . . . deserves the name 'this thing' and 'that thing' (49e, 50a). "The Receptacle, with its features of stability and receptivity, models Berkeley's mind substance, while the fleeting and changeable qualities within the Receptacle model Berkeley's ideas. This distinction enables me to clarify the puzzling relationship between Berkeley's two principles:

Plato	*Berkeley*
The things entering [the Receptacle] . . . are of an *entirely distinct* kind (*parapan alles physeos*) (*Timaeus* 50e).	[A mind] is a thing *entirely distinct* from [its ideas] wherein they exist (*Principles*, sect. 2).
It is proper that an image . . . should come into *existence in something else*, clinging to existence as best it may, on pain of being nothing at all (*Timaeus* 52c).	[Ideas] are . . . fleeting, dependent beings which subsist not by themselves, but are supported by or *exist in minds* or spiritual substances (*Principles*, sect. 89).

In *Principles*, sect. 89, Berkeley's statement of the Distinction Principle is even more emphatic. He distinguishes "two kinds entirely distinct and heterogeneous, . . . to wit, *spirits* and *ideas*." Just as there is no contradiction in holding that physical qualities must exist in space although they are not a part of space, so there is none in holding that ideas can exist only in a mind although they are not a part of mind.

Since I have assumed in using this method that Plato's account is consistent, it is advisable to go farther back to a more concrete and familiar model against which we can test both Plato's and Berkeley's theories. Fortunately, Plato himself provides the model. He likens the Receptacle and the Becoming (i.e., any of the phenomena) to a mother and her child, respectively; and probably also to their essential biological features, the womb and the embryo (*Timaeus* 50d, 91d). Just as the embryo is entirely distinct from the womb in which it exists, but cannot exist without it, so the ideas are entirely distinct from the mind in which they exist although they cannot exist without it.

The solution just given is independent of whether Berkeley himself was aware of the parallel between Plato's Receptacle and his own concept of mind. Other parallels, however, confirm the view of Berkeley's first biographer, Joseph Stock: "His favourite author from whom many of his notions were borrowed was Plato."[19] They confirm the view also that Berkeley was familiar with the *Timaeus*.

Aristotle's Subject and Berkeley's Mind

The apparent inconsistency of *Principles*, sect. 2, recurs in the famous Fifth Objection of *Principles*, sect. 49. On the latter occasion, however, Berkeley assumes the first of his suspect principles, "Mind is entirely distinct from ideas," and tries to anticipate an objection to his second suspect principle, "Ideas exist only in the mind:"

> It may perhaps be objected that if extension and figure exist only in the mind, it follows that the mind is extended and figured, since extension is a mode or attribute which (to speak with the Schools) is predicated of the subject in which it exists.

Here Berkeley deduces an apparent but, to him, mistaken consequence from his Inherence Principle: Largeness and squareness, for example, being ideas, exist only in the mind; therefore the mind is large and square. It has been customary for posterity to accept Berkeley's objection against himself as his real view, since the consequences he deduces from his Inherence Principle look irresistible. Bertrand Russell, for example, sustains Berkeley's objection against himself and comments: "This confusion may seem to gross to have been really committed by any competent philosopher."[20] In the same sect. 49, Berkeley begins his defence:

> I answer, those qualities are in the mind only as they are perceived by it — that is, not by way of *mode* or *attribute*, but only by way of *idea*.

This answer appears inadequate where it stands, but not so when it is moved to the conclusion of the following argument, in which Berkeley sets up rival interpretations of the simple proposition.

A die is hard, extended, and square.

First, the interpretation of the "philosophers":

> They will have it that the word "die" denotes a *subject* or *substance* distinct from the hardness, extension, and figure which are *predicated of* it, and *in which* they exist.

Berkeley here sketches a traditional doctrine of Western philosophy, according to which the subject-predicate distinction in logic and grammar parallels the substance-attribute dichotomy in ontology. Thus the subject "die" and the substance *die* are "distinct from" their predicates and attributes, respectively; they are "complete," "self-subsistent" entities that can "stand alone," while the corresponding predicates and attributes are "incomplete," "dependent" entities.[21] Berkeley calls this interpretation "groundless and unintelligible." It is easy to see why he must reject it. First, if it is true, then materialism is true, for the die is an instance of material substance; it is "an inert, senseless substance *in which* extension, figure, and motion do actually subsist" (*Principles*, sect. 9). Second, to use the substance *die* as a model for the substance *mind* would be disastrous. Certainly Berkeley holds of the word "mind," just as the philosophers hold of the word "die," that it "denotes a subject or substance *distinct from* the hardness, extension, and figure . . . and *in which* they exist." But he cannot hold that these qualities are *predicated of* the subject mind. If he does, then he will be forced, as many think he is, to adopt a Humean view of mind or to commit the gross confusion noted by Russell.

Accordingly, Berkeley gives a different interpretation of the proposition:

> To me a die seems to be nothing distinct from those things which are termed its modes or accidents. And to say a die is hard, extended, and square is not to attribute those qualities to a subject distinct from and supporting them, but only an explication of the meaning of the word "die."

In this short passage, which concludes sect. 49, Berkeley sketches a new theory of predication or, since he drops the subject-predicate distinction, a rival to the subject-predicate theory itself, which I have called the "*Definiendum-Definiens* Theory."[22] He dispenses with the "is" of predication and replaces it with the "is" of identity, thus interpreting the proposition not as a subject-predicate proposition but as a *definiendum-definientes* expression. He is aware that a *definiendum* names no new entity distinct from those entities named by the *definientes*. By discarding the subject-predicate logic, Berkeley also drops the parallel substance-attribute ontology, and adopts a "no-substance" theory. He does this by claiming that a die is the same as "its qualities," that a die can be analysed into "its qualities."

On the face of it, as an argument for a new theory of mind, the preceding argument of *Principles*, sect. 49, achieves the opposite of what Berkeley intends. By showing how the subject "die" collapses into its predicates or the substance *die* into its attributes, Berkeley appears to reinforce the objection against himself. If this argument demolishes material substance, then it should demolish mind substance as well, and Berkeley should end once again with a phenomenalist theory of mind. He appears to give the game away to Hume. Berkeley has to show that sensible qualities, although they are mind-dependent, are not attributes of mind. Thus his overall problem is the same as before: If fleeting sensible qualities must cling to existence in the mind on pain of being nothing at all, how can they remain entirely distinct from it? What this amounts to is perhaps the major problem of Berkeley's philosophy in his defense against Humean skepticism: How, in answer to Hylas of *Dialogues*, III, sect. 4, can he consistently reject matter and admit spirit? Although Berkeley concludes the debate on this subject between Hylas and Philonous with the words, "there is, therefore, upon the whole, no parity[23] of case between spirit and matter," hardly anyone has accepted this conclusion.

In order to see whether Berkeley can hold consistently that mind substance does not collapse into the sensible qualities that exist in it while material substance does collapse into the qualities that exist in it, let us consider Berkeley's startling paradox in the light of Aristotle's account of predication and inherence in *Categories* II. Here I notice another remarkable recurrence of the juxtaposition of the Distinction and Inherence Principles which we found occurring in Berkeley's *Principles*, sect. 2. It is to be expected, I suppose, that this peculiar marriage of two such apparently incompatible relations as *entire distinction* and *"complete" inherence*, which occurs in Plato's cosmology and cosmogony and recurs in Berkeley's psychology and ontology, should appear also in the logic and ontology of Plato's own student. At the start of his fourfold classification of "the things there are," Aristotle defines "in a subject":

> By "in a subject" (*en hypokeimeno*) I mean what is in something *not as a part* but which *cannot exist apart from* what it is in.[24]

As we have seen with the help of Plato's account of the things in the Receptacle, this is precisely the conjunction of relations that Berkeley needs to model the peculiar relation that sensible ideas have to minds.

But if Aristotle's "in a subject" captures all that Berkeley needs (i.e., if the inherence relation has already built into it the distinction relation), is not Berkeley's assertion of the Distinction Principle redundant? The answer, I believe, is that Berkeley wants to stress the distinction relation. As we have seen, the ideas *in the mind* belong to a different category from the mind, and, as Aristotle holds, the things *in a subject* belong to a category other than substance.

Aristotle now appears to complicate the matter unnecessarily, however, by conjoining the inherence relation with a new relation—that of predication. He classifies all existing things into those that are:

a) predicated of some subject, but are in no subject;
b) predicated of no subject, but are in some subject;
c) predicated of some subject, and also are in a subject;
d) neither predicated of a subject, nor are in a subject.

The class of existing things into which "the philosophers" put the qualities of material substances, as reported by Berkeley, is readily apparent. This class is defined by Aristotle's (c), for the philosophers hold that the qualities of the subject *die* are *predicated of* it *and exist in* it. Descartes, as one of "the philosophers," subscribes to this view: "When we say that any attribute is contained in the nature or concept of anything, that is precisely the same as saying that it is true of that thing or can be affirmed of it."[25] But the philosophers only appear to subscribe to (c), for they deviate from Aristotle in holding that if something exists in a subject, then it is predicated of that same subject. Aristotle does not say this. His example, "Knowledge is in a subject, the soul, and is also predicated of a subject, knowledge-of-grammar," indicates that two different subjects are involved. Moreover, Aristotle holds, as in (b), that some things are in a subject although they are not predicated of any subject.

The class of existing things into which Berkeley himself puts sensible qualities is equally apparent. This is defined by Aristotle's (b), for Berkeley holds that sensible qualities "are predicated of no subject but are in some subject [the mind]." Each of them is in such a subject "not as a part, but [as that] which cannot exist apart from what it is in"; or, as Berkeley concludes his defence, they are in a subject, the mind, "not by way of *mode* or *attribute* but only by way of idea." Aristotle's examples of the members of class (b) are "some particular grammatical knowledge" and "a particular white." Because these are particular or individual, they cannot be predicated, and they cling to existence only in something else. It is precisely these atomic particulars of Aristotle's second example that constitute Berkeley's simple ideas or sensible qualities. Both Aristotle and

Berkeley leave it unclear as to whether such atomic simples are non-recurrent particulars or whether they are particular in being determinate in kind (e.g., in being determinate shades of color, etc., which are recurrent and can exist in more than one mind). It is likely, however, that Berkeley intends the latter, that his "certain colour, taste, smell, figure, and consistence" of *Principles*, sect. 1, can occur in several minds and not just in "this or that particular mind" (*Principles*, sect. 48).

But whether these qualities are recurrent or nonrecurrent is beside our main question of the consistency of the Distinction and Identity Principles. This question has been largely answered. We have seen that Berkeley's two principles can be regarded as a direct application of Aristotle's Inherence theory, a theory whose consistency, though not perhaps whose entire contents, would be generally accepted. We have seen that Berkeley's attempted demolition of material substance by showing that the substance *die* collapses into its "predicates" does not demolish mind substance as well. This is so because the things that exist in the subject [mind] are not predicated of any subject. It is now generally accepted that such entities, being individuals, can never be predicated. We have seen that Berkeley's two principles of *Principles*, sect. 2, as well as the two corresponding relations present in Aristotle's and Plato's theory, can be further tested for consistency by using Plato's Procreation model of the *Timaeus*. We have seen that Berkeley, while he used some of Aristotle's notions effectively, differed from him in a fundamental respect. He was ahead of his time in attempting to explode the Subject-Predicate Myth.

Finally, and most significant for my purposes, we have seen that, since Berkeley can hold consistently his three important principles of Distinction, Inherence, and Identity, he can refrain from adopting the Humean theory of mind, which, according to the traditional view of Berkeley, he is forced to accept.

Notes

1. Willis Doney, "Is Berkeley's a Cartesian Mind?", this volume, p. 274.

2. Citations from Berkeley's *A Treatise Concerning the Principles of Human Knowledge, Three Dialogues Between Hylas and Philonous*, and *Philosophical Correspondence Between Berkeley and Samuel Johnson* are from C. M. Turbayne, ed., *Principles, Dialogues and Correspondence* (Indianapolis: Bobbs-Merrill, 1965). Some words I have italicized for emphasis. References are by section numbers. In my edition I have sectioned the *Dialogues* in conformity with Berkeley's other works.

3. Cf. the first words of *Principles*, sect. 1, "It is evident to anyone . . . ," also his references in sect. 34 to "the principles hitherto *laid down*" and to "the principles *premised*."

4. For the names "Distinction Principle" and "Identity Principle," I am indebted to S. A. Grave, "The Mind and Its Ideas: Some Problems in the Interpretation of Berkeley," in C. B. Martin and D. M. Armstrong, eds., *Locke and Berkeley, A Collection of Critical Essays* (New York: Doubleday, 1968), p. 298.

5. *Berkeley's Immaterialism* (London: Thomas Nelson and Sons, 1946), p. 51.

6. "Berkeley's Idealism," *Theoria* 29 (1963): 229, 231; and his "Berkeley's Idealism Revisited," this volume, pp. 197-206. Other recent contributors are R. Watson, "The Breakdown of Cartesian Metaphysics," *Journal of the History of Philosophy* 1, 2 (1963): 177-97; Phillip Cummins, "Perceptual Relativity and Ideas in the Mind," *Philosophy and Phenomenological Research* 24 (1963): 202-14; Harry M. Bracken, "Substance in Berkeley," in Warren E. Steinkraus, ed., *New Studies in Berkeley's Philosophy* (New York: Holt, Rinehart and Winston, 1966), pp. 85-97; L. N. Oaklander, "The Inherence Interpretation of Berkeley: A Critique," *Modern Schoolman* 54 (1977): 261-69; George S. Pappas, "Ideas, Minds, and Berkeley," *American Philosophical Quarterly* 17, 3 (1980): 181-94.

7. "The Refutation of Idealism," in C. M. Turbayne, ed., *Berkeley: Principles, Text and Critical Essays* (Indianapolis: Bobbs-Merrill, 1970), pp. 57-84. Originally published in *Mind* 12, 48 (1903): 433-53.

8. "Mind and Its Ideas," p. 298.

9. George Pitcher, *Berkeley* (London: Routledge and Kegan Paul, 1977), pp. 192-201.

10. *Language, Truth and Logic* (1936; repr. New York: Dover, 1946), p. 126.

11. David Hume, *A Treatise of Human Nature* (London, 1739), bk. I, pt. IV, sect. 6.

12. "Refutation of Idealism," p. 73. Moore's "most famous criticism" and rejoinders by C. J. Ducasse and E. E. Harris are illuminatingly discussed by Steinkraus, "Berkeley and His Modern Critics," in his *New Studies*, pp. 159-62.

13. New York: Oxford University Press, 1959, p. 42.

14. *Analysis of Mind* (London: Allen and Unwin, 1921), p. 142.

15. P. A. Schilpp, ed., *The Philosophy of G. E. Moore* (Evanston: Library of Living Philosophers, 1942), p. 653.

16. London: Hutchinson, 1949, pp. 168-198.

17. See Robert Blanché, *Axiomatics* (London: Routledge and Kegan Paul, 1962), pp. 38-41.

18. I have discussed the Receptacle and the model Plato uses for it in more detail in "Plato's 'Fantastic Appendix': The Procreation Model of the *Timaeus*," *Paideia. Special Plato Issue* (1976): 125-40.

19. *Life of the Author*, included in G. N. Wright, ed., *Works of George Berkeley* (London, 1843), p. x. Originally published separately in 1776.

One likely borrowing is Philonous' statement at *Dialogues*, I, sect. 10, "I am not for imposing any sense on your words: you are at liberty to explain them as you please. Only, I beseech you make me understand something by them." This echoes the remark of Socrates at *Charmides* 163, "I have no objection to your giving names any signification which you please, if you will only tell me what you mean by them." This parallel was first noticed by D. S. Robinson in his "The Platonic Model of *Hylas* and *Philonous*," *Philosophical Review* 29, 5 (1920): 484-87.

Another parallel suggests that Berkeley was familiar with the *Timaeus* long before he became Junior Greek Lecturer at Trinity College in 1712. At *Principles*, sect. 32, Berkeley says that "the consistent uniform working" that we observe in nature" is so far from leading our thoughts to [the First Cause] that it rather sends them *awandering* after *second causes*." In the last phrase, Berkeley plays with two of Plato's titles for the same thing, "The Wandering Cause" (*he planomeni aitia*) of *Timaeus* 48a, and "Second Causes" (*sunaitias*) of *Timaeus* 46e.

20. *Problems of Philosophy*, p. 40.

21. The adjectives "complete" and "incomplete" are used by more recent defenders of the traditional doctrine. See P. F. Strawson, *Individuals* (London: Methuen, 1959), pp. 152ff. For an analysis of the traditional doctrine, see my "The Subject-Predicate Myth," *Studies in the Twentieth Century* 1, 1 (1968): 8-20.

22. In "Berkeley's Metaphysical Grammar," in *Berkeley: Principles, Text, and Critical Essays* (cited in n. 7), p. 34.

23. See text to n. 17. Phillip Cummins explores this topic from a different approach in his "Hylas' Parity Argument," this volume, pp. 283-94.

24. I have shown Aristotle's use of this relation in his psychology in my "Aristotle's Androgynous Mind," *Paideia: Special Aristotle Issue* (1978): 30-49.

25. "Arguments . . . Drawn Up In Geometrical Fashion," Definition IX.

A Bibliography of George Berkeley 1963-1979

A Bibliography
of George Berkeley 1963-1979

Colin M. Turbayne

This bibliography incorporates C. M. Turbayne and R. Appelbaum, "A Bibliography of George Berkeley, 1963-1974," *Journal of the History of Philosophy* 15, 1 (1977).

Entries in Part I, *Berkeley's Writings*, are ordered chronologically, while those in Part II, *Writings on Berkeley*, are ordered alphabetically by the author's name. There are some double entries that occur mainly in Part I. It is hoped that such duplication will facilitate reference.

I wish to record my gratitude to Leon Creek, Helen Powers, and Robert Compton, of Rush Rhees Library, and to Shari Elliott, for help in research.

I. BERKELEY'S WRITINGS

i. Collections

1. *Works on Vision: An Essay towards a New Theory of Vision, The Theory of Vision or Visual Language Vindicated and Explained*, and selections from *Alciphron* and *Principles*, with a commentary and notes, ed. C. M. Turbayne. Indianapolis: Bobbs-Merrill, 1963.

2. *Principles, Dialogues, and Philosophical Correspondence*, ed. C. M. Turbayne. Indianapolis: Bobbs-Merrill, 1965.

3. *Berkeley's Philosophical Writings*, ed. D. M. Armstrong. New York: Collier-Macmillan, 1965. Selected works.

4. *Présentation, choix de textes, . . . bibliographie*, ed. Jean Pucelle. Paris: Seghers, 1967. (*Philosophes de tous les temps*, 35.)

5. *Berkeley. Antologia degli scritti filosofici*, ed. T. E. Jessop, tr. Cordelia Guzzo. Florence: La Nuova Italia, 1967. Selections.

6. *Grande antologia filosofica*. Vol. 13, ed. A. Guzzo. Milan, 1969. Selections.

7. *Schriften über die Grundlagen der Mathematik und Physik*, ed. W. Breidert. Frankfurt a.M.: Suhrkamp Verlag, 1969.

8. *Philosophical Works*, ed. M. R. Ayers. London: Dent (Everyman), 1973. Selected works.

9. *Tratado Sobre os Principios do Conhecimento Humano. Três Diálogos entre Hilas e Filonous*, tr. Antonio Sérgio. São Paulo: Abril Cultural, 1973.

10. *The Works of George Berkeley, Bishop of Cloyne*, ed. A. A. Luce and T. E. Jessop. Repr. of the 1948-57 ed. in 3 vols. by Kraus Reprint, Milwood, N. Y., 1979, with Supplement to vol. 1 by Désirée Park.

ii. Individual Works

Of Infinites, 1707

11. *Of Infinites*, ed. W. Breidert. 1969. See 7.

Philosophical Commentaries, 1707-1708

12. *Philosophical Commentaries*, transcribed from the manuscript by G. Thomas. Mount Union College, 1976. With notes by A. A. Luce.

13. *Philosophisches Tagebuch*, tr. W. Breidert. Hamburg: Felix Miner Verlag, 1979. (*Philosophische Bibliothek* 318.)

An Essay towards a New Theory of Vision, 1709

14. In *Works on Vision*, ed. C. M. Turbayne. 1963. See 1.

15. In *Berkeley's Philosophical Writings*, ed. D. M. Armstrong. 1965. See 3.

16. *Ensayo de una nueva teoria de la vision*, tr. F. Benot (Bibl. de Iniciacion Filosofica). Buenos Aires: Aguilar, 1965.

17. In *Philosophical Works*, ed. M. R. Ayers. 1973. See 8.

A Treatise Concerning the Principles of Human Knowledge, 1710

18. In *Principles, Dialogues, and Philosophical Correspondence*, ed. C. M. Turbayne. 1965. See 2.

19. In *Berkeley's Philosophical Writings*, ed. D. M. Armstrong. 1965. See 3.

20. In *Berkeley: Principles . . . Text and Critical Essays*, ed. C. M. Turbayne. 1970. See 372.

21. In *Philosophical Works*, ed. M. R. Ayers. 1973. See 8.

22. *Tratado Sobre os Princípios do Conhecimento Humano*, tr. A. Sérgio. 1973. See 9.

Three Dialogues between Hylas and Philonous, 1713

23. *Tre dialoghi fra Hylas e Philonous*, tr. E. Riverso. Torino, 1964.

24. In *Principles, Dialogues, and Philosophical Correspondence*, ed. C. M. Turbayne. 1965. See 2.

25. In *Berkeley's Philosophical Writings*, ed. D. M. Armstrong. 1965. See 3.

26. *Trois Dialogues entre Hylas et Philonous*, ed. Michel Ambacher. Paris: Varii, Aubier-Montaigue, 1970. See 49.

27. In *Philosophical Works*, ed. M. R. Ayers. 1973. See 8.

28. *Três Diálogos entre Hilas e Filonous*, tr. A. Sérgio. 1973. See 22.

29. *Three Dialogues Between Hylas and Philonous*, ed. R. M. Adams. Indianapolis: Hackett Publ. Co., 1979.

De Motu, 1721

30. In *Berkeley's Philosophical Writings*, ed. D. M. Armstrong. 1965. (Tr. A. A. Luce.) See 3.

31. *De Motu*, ed. W. Breidert. 1969. See 7.

A Proposal for the Better Supplying of Churches . . . 1724

32. *A Proposal for the Better Supplying of Churches in our Foreign Plantations and for Converting the Savage Americans to Christianity*. Louisville, Ky.: Lost Cause Press, Misc. Pamphlets, 442, 4, 1969.

Alciphron: or the Minute Philosopher, 1732

33. *Alcifrone*, tr. A. and C. Guzzo. Bologna, 1963.

The Theory of Vision, or Visual Language . . . Vindicated and Explained, 1733

34. In *Works on Vision*, ed. C. M. Turbayne. 1963. See 1.

The Analyst, 1734

35. *Analyst,* ed. W. Breidert. 1969. See 7.

36. *L'Analista. Discorso indirizzato a un matematico infedele,* in *Atti della Fondazione Giorgio Ronchi* 26, Florence (1971): 213-37, 301-33, 457-97.

Defense of Free-Thinking in Mathematics, 1735

37. *Defense of Free-Thinking in Mathematics,* ed. W. Breidert. 1969. See 7.

Reasons for not Replying, 1735

38. *Reasons for not Replying,* ed. W. Breidert. 1969. See 7.

The Querist, 1735-1737

39. *The Querist,* Wakefield, Eng: S. R. Publishers; New York: Johnson Reprint Corp., 1970.

40. In Johnston, J., *Bishop Berkeley's* Querist *in Historical Perspective.* Dundalk, Ireland: Dundalgan Press, 1970. Contains also "Project of a National Bank" and "The Irish Patriot."

Maxims Concerning Patriotism, 1750

41. *Maxims Concerning Patriotism.* Dublin, Ireland: Trinity Closet Press, 1979.

II. WRITINGS ON BERKELEY

42. Abelove, H. "George Berkeley's Attitude to John Wesley: The Evidence of a Lost Letter." *Harvard Theological Review* 70 (1977): 175-76.

43. Acton, H. B. "George Berkeley." *The Encyclopedia of Philosophy,* ed. Paul Edwards, vol. 1, pp. 295-304. New York: Collier Macmillan, 1967.

44. Adams, Robert M. "Berkeley's 'Notion' of Spiritual Substance." *Archiv für Geschichte der Philosophie* 55, 1 (1973): 47-69.

45. Agassi, Joseph. "The Future of Berkeley's Instrumentalism." *International Studies in Philosophy* 7 (1975): 167-78. See 103.

46. Allaire, Edwin B. "Berkeley's Idealism." *Theoria* 29 (1963): 229-44. Repr. in Allaire. *Essays in Ontology. Iowa Publications in Philosophy* 1 (1963):92-105.

47. Allen, Harold J. "Berkeley's Notions and Hume's Problems." *Philosophical Forum,* New Series, 2 (1971):371-83.

48. Allison, Henry E. "Bishop Berkeley's Petitio." *Personalist* 54 (1973): 232-45.

49. Allison, Henry E. "Kant's Critique of Berkeley." *Journal of the History of Philosophy* 11 (1963).43-63. See 187, 231, 268, 269, 293, 350, 391, 393, 400.

50. Ambacher, Michel. "Le langage de la Nature." In *Trois Dialogues entre Hylas et Philonous,* ed. Michel Ambacher. 1970. See 26.

51. Anderson, J. C. "What There Might Be After All." *Mind* 87 (1978): 588-94.

52. Archibald, Douglas N. "W. B. Yeats's Encounter with Swift, Berkeley, and Burke." Doctoral dissertation, University of Michigan. Ann Arbor, Mich.: University Microfilms, 1966.

53. Ardley, G. W. R. "Berkeley's Philosophy of Nature." *University of Auckland Bulletin* (Auckland, N. Z.) 63, Phil. Series No. 3, (1962).

54. Ardley, G. W. R. *Berkeley's Renovation of Philosophy.* The Hague: Martinus Nijhoff, 1968.

55. Armstrong, David M., ed., with C. B. Martin. *Locke and Berkeley. A Collection of Critical Essays.* 1968. See 261.

56. Armstrong, Robert L., "Berkeley's Theory of Signification." *Journal of the History of Philosophy* 7 (1969):163-76.

57. Armstrong, Robert L. *Metaphysics and British Empiricism.* Lincoln, Nebraska: University of Nebraska Press, 1970.

58. Attfield, R. "Berkeley and Imagination." *Philosophy* 45 (1970):237-39. A discussion of 397.

59. Ayers, Michael R. "Substance, Reality, and the Great Dead Philosophers." *American Philosophical Quarterly* 7 (1970):38-49.

60. Baier, Annette. "The Intentionality of Intentions." *Review of Metaphysics* 30 (1977): 389-414.

61. Barber, Kenneth. "Gruner on Berkeley on General Ideas." *Dialogue* 10 (1971):337-41. On 197.

62. Baum, Robert J. "Berkeley's Philosophy of Mathematics." Doctoral dissertation, Ohio State University. Ann Arbor, Mich.: University Microfilms, 1969.

63. Baum, Robert J. *Philosophy and Mathematics: From Plato to the Present*. San Francisco: Freeman, Cooper & Co., 1973. Chap. 8 on Berkeley.

64. Beal, Melvin W. "Berkeley's Linguistic Criterion." *Personalist* 52 (1971):499-514.

65. Beal, Melvin W. "Universality without Universals: A Deleted Argument from Berkeley's Introduction to the *Principles*." *Modern Schoolman* 50 (1973):301-10.

66. Beal, M. W. "Berkeley's Deletions." *Canadian Journal of Philosophy* 6 (1976):455-78.

67. Belfrage, Bertil. "George Berkeley's *Philosophical Commentaries*." In *Logik Rätt och Moral*, ed. Sören Halldén *et al.* Lund: Studentlitteratur, 1969. pp. 19-34. See 255.

68. Belfrage, Bertil. "Did Berkeley Become Certain of the Existence of Matter?" Lund: The Mattias Fremling Society, 1973. Pamphlet. 16 pp.

69. Belfrage, Bertil. "A New Dating of Berkeley's Draft Introduction." *Berkeley Newsletter* 1 (1977):10-11.

70. Belfrage, Bertil. "Notes By Berkeley On Moral Philosophy." *Berkeley Newsletter* 2 (1978):4-5.

71. Belfrage, Bertil. "A Summary of Berkeley's Metaphysics in a Hitherto Unpublished Berkeleian Manuscript." *Berkeley Newsletter* 3 (1979): 1-4.

72. Belfrage, Bertil. "The Bond of Society: Berkeley's Theory of Social Reality." *Berkeley Newsletter* 3 (1979):16-19.

73. Bender, Franz. *George Berkeley*. Baarn: Het Wereldvenster, 1965.

74. Bennett, Jonathan. "Substance, Reality, and Primary Qualities." *American Philosophical Quarterly* 2 (1965):1-17. Repr. in Engle and Taylor (160).

75. Bennett, Jonathan. "Berkeley and God." *Philosophy* 40 (1965):207-21. Repr. in Martin and Armstrong (261) and in Engle and Taylor (160).

76. Bennett, Jonathan. *Locke, Berkeley, Hume: Central Themes*. Oxford: Clarendon Press, 1971. Reviewed by: W. Gietz. *Archiv für Geschichte der Philosophie* 56 (1974):109-14; E. J. Furlong. *Hermathena* 117 (1974): 100-01; C. E. Marks. *Philosophical Review* 83 (1974):126-31; D. Berman (82).

77. Berman, David. "A New Letter by Berkeley on Tar-Water." *Hermathena* 107 (1968): 45-48.

78. Berman, David. "An Early Essay Concerning Berkeley's Immaterialism." *Hermathena* 109 (1969):37-43.

79. Berman, David, and J. P. Pittion. "A New Letter by Berkeley to Browne on Divine Analogy." *Mind* 78 (1969):375-92.

80. Berman, David. "Some New Bermuda Berkeleiana." *Hermathena* 110 (1970):24-31.

81. Berman, David. "Berkeley, Clayton, and an 'Essay on Spirit'." *Journal of the History of Ideas* 32 (1971):367-78.

82. Berman, David. "On Missing the Wrong Target: A Criticism of Some Chapters in Jonathan Bennett's *Locke, Berkeley, Hume: Central Themes*." *Hermathena* 113 (1972):54-67. On 76.

83. Berman, David. "Francis Hutcheson on Berkeley and the Molyneux Problem." *Proceedings of the Royal Irish Academy* 74, 8 (1974):259-65.

84. Berman, D. "Anthony Collins: Aspects of His Thought and Writings." *Hermathena* 119 (1975):49-68.

85. Berman, D. "A Bibliography of the Published Writings of Dr. A. A. Luce." *Hermathena* 123 (1977):11-18.

86. Berman, D. "Mrs. Berkeley's Annotations in her Interleaved Copies of *An Account of the Life of Berkeley* (1776)." *Hermathena* 122 (1977):15-28.

87. Berman, D. "Berkeley's Letter to H. Clarke." *Berkeley Newsletter* 1 (1977):9.

88. Berman, D. "A Note on Berkeley and his Catholic Countrymen." *Long Room* 16-17 (1978):26-28.

89. Berman, D. "Berkeley's Letter to Lord Orrery." *Berkeley Newsletter* 3 (1979):12-13.

90. Best, A. E. "Misleading Questions and Irrelevant Answers in Berkeley's *Theory of Vision*." *Philosophy* 43 (1968):138-51.

90a. Blake, J. B. "Addenda to Keynes: *Bibliography of Berkeley*." *Bibliographical Society of America Papers* 73 (1979):337-40. See 234.

91. Borges, Jorge Luis. "Tlön, Uqbar, Orbis Tertius." In J. L. Borges. *Ficciones*, ed. Anthony Kerrigan. New York: Grove Press, 1962. pp. 17-35.

92. Bourdillon, Philip. "Berkeley and Reid: An Analysis of Reid's Reaction to Berkeley's Rejection of Material Substance." Doctoral dissertation, University of Rochester. Ann Arbor, Mich.: University Microfilms, 1972.

93. Bower, T. G. R. "Object Perception in Infants." *Perception* 1 (1972):15-30.

94. Bracken, Harry M. "Berkeley and Malebranche on Ideas." *Modern Schoolman* 41 (1963-64):1-15.

95. Bracken, Harry M. *The Early Reception of Berkeley's Immaterialism.* The Hague: Martinus Nijoff, 1965. Revision of the 1959 ed. Reviewed by D. B. Heron. *Australian Journal of Philosophy* 44 (1966):269-70.

96. Bracken, Harry M. "Substance in Berkeley." In Steinkraus. *New Studies.* 1966. pp. 85-97. See 343.

97. Bracken, Harry M. *Berkeley.* New York: St. Martin's Press, 1974.

98. Bracken, H. M. "Berkeley: Irish Cartesian." *Philosophical Studies* 24 (1976):39-51.

99. Brandt, Reinhard. "Historical Observations on the Genesis of the Three-Dimensional Optical Picture." *Ratio* 17 (1975):176-90.

100. Breidert, Wolfgang. "'Momentum' und 'Minimum', Zwei Notizen in Berkeleys *Philosophischen Kommentaren*." *Archiv Begriffsgeschichte* 13 (1969):76-78.

101. Broad, C. D. *Berkeley's Argument about Material Substance.* New York: Haskell House, 1975. Repr. of the 1942 ed. publ. by the British Academy, London.

102. Brook, Richard J. "Berkeley's Philosophy of Science." Doctoral dissertation, New School for Social Research. Ann Arbor, Mich.: University Microfilms, 1972.

103. Brook, Richard J. *Berkeley's Philosophy of Science.* The Hague: Martinus Nijhoff, 1973. See 44.

104. Brown, Stuart C. *Realism and Logical Analysis.* Milton Keynes: Open University Press, 1976.

105. Brown, S. C. "Berkeley on the Unity of the Self." In *Reason and Reality*, Royal Institute of Philosophy Lectures, vol. 5, 1970-1971.

106. Browne, J. W. "Berkeley and Scholasticism." *Modern Schoolman* 49 (1972):113-23.

107. Browne, J. W. *Berkeley's Intellectualism.* Jamaica, N. Y.: St. John's University Press, 1975.

108. Brykman, G. "Berkeley: Sa Lecture de Malebranche à travers le Dictionnaire de Bayle." *Revue internationale philosophique* 29 (1975):496-514; also in *Recherches sur le XVIIᵉ Siècle* 2 (1976):125-27.

109. Brykman, G. "Berkeley, Lecteur et Critique de Spinoza." *Recherches sur le XVIIᵉ Siècle* 2 (1978):173-92.

110. Brykman, G. "The Close Inspection of Words and Ideas in Berkeley's Writings." *Berkeley Newsletter* 3 (1979):9-10.

111. Brykman, G. "Berkeley à Newport. 1729-1979." *Recherches sur le XVIIe Siècle* 4 (1979).

112. Brykman, G. "Le Modèle Visuel de la Connaissance chez Berkeley." *Recherches sur le XVIIe Siècle* 4 (1979).

113. Brykman, G. "Berkeley et le Désir de Voir." *Revue Philosophique de la France et de l'Étranger* 163 (1973):206-13.

114. Bruner, J. S., and Barbara Koslowski. "Visually Preadapted Constituents of Manipulatory Action." *Perception* 1 (1972):3-14.

115. Brunton, J. A. "The Absolute Existence of Unthinking Things." *Philosophy* 45 (1970): 267-80.

116. Buchdahl, Gerd. *Metaphysics and the Philosophy of Science*. Oxford: Blackwell, 1969. Chap. 5.

117. Bush, Eric. "Berkeley, Truth and the World." *Inquiry* 20 (1977):205-25.

118. Cantor, G. N. "Berkeley, Reid and the Mathematization of Mideighteenth-century Optics." *Journal of the History of Ideas* 38 (1977):429-48.

119. Carter, Kay C. "George Berkeley's Views on Linguistic Meaning." Doctoral dissertation, Cornell University. Ann Arbor, Mich.: University Microfilms, 1968.

120. Carter, W. B. "Some Problems of the Relation between Berkeley's *New Theory of Vision* and his *Principles*." *Ratio* 3 (1961):174-92.

121. Casini, Paolo. *L'universo macchina—Origini della filosofia newtoniana*. Bari: Laterza, 1969. Chap. 8, "Berkeley e Newton."

122. Cathcart, H. R. "Berkeley's Philosophy through Soviet Eyes." *Hermathena* 98 (1964): 33-42.

123. Catir, J. "Berkeley's Successful Failure. A Study of George Berkeley's Contribution to American Education." *Historical Magazine of the Protestant Episcopal Church* 33 (1964): 65-82.

124. Chachkievitch, P. D. *Empirisme et Rationalisme dans la Philosophie des Temps Nouveaux*. Moscow: Mysl, 1976. Discusses the doctrines of "l'empirisme idéaliste" of Berkeley and Hume.

125. Collins, James D. *The British Empiricists: Locke, Berkeley, Hume*. Milwaukee, Wis.: Bruce Publ. Co., 1967.

126. Collins, James D. *Interpreting Modern Philosophy*. Princeton: Princeton University Press, 1972. Discusses some recent interpretations of Berkeley, pp. 252-55.

127. Collingridge, D. G. "Berkeley on Space, Sight, and Touch." *Philosophy* 53 (1978): 102-05.

128. Conroy, Graham P. "Language and Morals in Berkeley's Philosophy." Doctoral dissertation, University of California at Berkeley. Ann Arbor, Mich.: University Microfilms, 1957.

129. Conroy, Graham P. "Did Hume Really Follow Berkeley?" *Philosophy* 44 (1969): 238-42. See 201, also 202, 203, 308.

130. Cornman, James W. "Theoretical Terms, Berkeleian Notions, and Minds." In Turbayne, ed. *Berkeley: Principles . . . Text and Critical Essays*. 1970. pp. 161-81. See 372.

131. Cornman, James W. "A Reconstruction of Berkeley: Minds and Physical Objects as Theoretical Entities." *Ratio* 13 (1971):76-87.

132. Cornman, James W. "On Direct Perception." *Review of Metaphysics* 26 (1972):38-56.

133. Cornman, James W. "Theoretical Phenomenalism." *Nous* 7 (1973):120-38. Discusses a major problem for Berkeley as a theoretical phenomenalist. See 372.

134. Cornman, J. W. *Perception, Common Sense and Science*. New Haven: Yale University Press, 1975.

135. Craig, E. J. "Berkeley's Attack on Abstract Ideas." *Philosophical Review* 77 (1968): 425-37.

136. Creery, Walter E. "Berkeley's Argument for a Divine Visual Language." *International Journal of the Philosophy of Religion* 3 (1973):212-22. Contains discussion of 395.

137. Cross, C. B. "Berkeley on Other Minds." *Auslegung* 6 (1978):45-50.

138. Cummins, Phillip D. "Perceptual Relativity and Ideas in the Mind." *Philosophy and Phenomenological Research* 24 (1963):202-14.

139. Cummins, Phillip D. "Berkeley's Likeness Principle." *Journal of the History of Philosophy* 4 (1966):63-69. Reprinted in Martin and Armstrong (261).

140. Cummins, Phillip. "Berkeley's Ideas of Sense." *Nous* 9 (1975):55-72.

141. Czarnecki, Z. J. "Historical Premises and Theoretical Aims of Berkeley's Immaterialistic Metaphysics." *Annalis Universitatis Mariae Curie-Sklodowska Philosophia-Sociologia. Lublin* (1976):123-35.

142. Daniels, Norman. *Thomas Reid's* Inquiry, *the Geometry of Visibles and the Case for Realism*. New York: Burt Franklin, 1974.

143. Dascal, M., and Adi Parush. "On New Aspects in George Berkeley's Philosophy of Nature in *Siris*." In *The Rational and the Irrational: A Collection of Papers*. Beersheba, Israel: The Ben Gurion University of the Negev, 1975.

144. Datta, D. M. "Berkeley's Objective Idealism: An Indian View." In Steinkraus. *New Studies*. 1966. pp. 110-22. See 343.

145. Davie, Donald. *The Language of Science and the Language of Literature, 1709-1740*. London: Sheed and Ward, 1963. On *Siris*, pp. 49-58, and *Alciphron*, pp. 80-85.

146. Davie, Donald. "Berkeley and the Style of Dialogue." In *The English Mind*, ed. H. S. Davies and G. Watson. Cambridge: Cambridge University Press, 1964. pp. 90-106.

147. Davie, Donald. "Yeats, Berkeley, and Romanticism." In *English Literature and British Philosophy*, ed. S. P. Rosenbaum. Chicago: University of Chicago Press, 1971. pp. 278-84.

148. Davie, G. E. "Berkeley's Impact on Scottish Philosophers." *Philosophy* 40 (1965): 222-34.

149. Davis, John W. "Berkeley and Newton on Space." In R. E. Butts and John W. Davis. *The Methodological Heritage of Newton*. Oxford: Blackwell, 1970.

150. Davis, Martin, and Reuben Hersh. "Nonstandard Analysis." *Scientific American* (June, 1972):78-86. Contains discussion of Berkeley's critique of the infinitesimal in *The Analyst*.

151. De Alejandro, J. M. "El Atomismo Gnoseologico de David Hume (1711-1776)." *Pensamiento* 32 (1976):383-403.

152. Delkeskamp, C. "La Temporalité et l'Etat d'Aliénation chez G. Berkeley." In Enrico Castelli. *Temporalité et Alienation*. Paris: Aubier-Montaigne, 1975.

153. De Stasio, Clotilde. "Pope, Berkeley e il *Guardian*." *Acme* 3 (1966):341-58.

154. Dicker, Georges. "Primary and Secondary Qualities: A Proposed Modification of the Lockean Account." *Southern Journal of Philosophy* 15 (1977):457-68.

155. Dilman, Ilham. *Matter and Mind: Two Essays in Epistemology*. London: Macmillan, 1975.

156. Donagan, Alan. "Berkeley's Theory of the Immediate Objects of Vision." In *Studies in Perception*. Columbus: Ohio State University Press, 1978. See 257.

157. Downey, James. *The Eighteenth-Century Pulpit*. London: Clarendon Press, 1969.

158. Duchesneau, F. "Semiotique et Abstraction: De Locke à Condillac." *Philosophiques* 3 (1976):147-66.

159. Earman, John. "Who's Afraid of Absolute Space?" *Australian Journal of Philosophy* 48 (1970):287-319.

160. Engle, Gale, and Gabriele Taylor. *Berkeley's Principles of Human Knowledge: Critical Studies*. Belmont, Cal.: Wadsworth, 1968. Repr. of essays by S. A. Grave (190), C. M. Turbayne, M. C. Beardsley, K. Marc-Wogau, K. R. Popper, T. E. Jessop (222), J. Bennett (74,

75), and E. J. Furlong (178) and extracts from Mill (on Hamilton), Hume (*Treatise*), Reid (*Intellectual Powers*), and Chisholm (*Perceiving*).

161. Ewing, A. C. "The Significance of Idealism for the Present Day." *Idealistic Studies* 1 (1971):1-12.

162. Ewing, A. C. "The Problem of Universals." *Philosophical Quarterly* 21 (1971):207-16.

163. Fabro, Cornelio. *God in Exile: A Study of the Internal Dynamic of Modern Atheism, from Its Roots in the Cartesian 'Cogito' to the Present Day*, tr. and ed. Arthur Gibson. New York: Newman Press, 1968. See pt. II, sect. 4.

164. Faggiotti, Pietro. *Il Problema della Metafisica nel Pensiero Moderno, II: Leibniz, Berkeley, Hume*. Padua: Cedam, 1975.

165. Farooqi, Waheed Ali. "An Ontological Construction of Berkeley's Idealism." *Pakistan Philosophical Journal* 8 (1964):14-20.

166. Farooqi, Waheed Ali. "A Spiritual Interpretation of Reality in the Light of Berkeley's Immaterialism." Doctoral dissertation, Michigan State University. Ann Arbor, Mich.: University Microfilms, 1966.

167. Farooqi, Waheed Ali. "Berkeley's Ontology and Islamic Mysticism." In Steinkraus. *New Studies*. 1966. pp. 123-33. See 343.

168. Farooqi, Waheed Ali. "The Physical World as a Spiritual Order." *Pakistan Philosophical Journal* 10 (1971):49-72.

169. Finiano, Mariapaolo. "Soggetivita e Communicazione in George Berkeley." *Atti dell' Accademia di Scienze ed Arti in Napoli* 77 (1966):68ff.

170. Flew, Antony. "Was Berkeley a Precursor of Wittgenstein?" In *Hume and the Enlightenment: Essays Presented to Ernest Campbell Mossner*, ed. William T. Todd. Austin: Humanities Research Center, University of Texas, 1974. pp. 153-63.

171. Forth, David S. "Berkeley and Buber: An Epistemological Comparison." *Dialogue* 10 (1971):690-707.

172. Frankel, Henry. "Berkeley's Concept of Mind as presented in Book II of the *Principles*." *Southern Journal of Philosophy* 15 (1977):37-51.

173. Fulton, James S. "Whitehead's 'Footnote' to Berkeley." *Rice University Studies* 50 (1964):13-22.

174. Furlong, E. J. "Berkeley and the Knot About Inverted Images." *Australian Journal of Philosophy* 41 (1963):306-16.

175. Furlong, E. J. "An Ambiguity in Berkeley's *Principles*." *Philosophical Quarterly* 14 (1964):334-44.

176. Furlong, E. J. "Berkeley's Theory of Meaning." *Mind* 73 (1964):437-38.

177. Furlong, E. J., with I. C. Tipton. "Mrs. George Berkeley and Her Washing Machine." *Hermathena* 101 (1965):38-47.

178. Furlong, E. J. "Berkeley and the Tree in the Quad." *Philosophy* 41 (1966):169-73. Repr. in Martin and Armstrong (261) and in Engle and Taylor (160).

179. Furlong, E. J. "Berkeley on Relations, Spirits, and Notions." *Hermathena* 106 (1968): 60-66.

180. Furlong, E. J. "The Berkeley Window in Trinity College, with an Account of Berkeleian Studies in the College, 1830-1900." *Hermathena* 114 (1972): 70-87.

181. Furlong, E. J. "Some Puzzles in Berkeley's Writings." *Hermathena* 120 (1976):63-73.

182. Furlong, E. J. "A Berkeleian Nod?" *Berkeley Newsletter* 2 (1978):3.

183. Gallois, André. "Berkeley's Master Argument." *Philosophical Review* 83 (1974):55-69.

183a. Gaustad, Edwin S. *George Berkeley in America*. New Haven and London: Yale University Press, 1979.

183b. Gaustad, Edwin S. "George Berkeley and the New World Community." *Church History* 48 (1979):5-17.

184. Gawlick, Günter. "Menschheitsglück und Wille Gottes: Neues Licht auf Berkeleys

Ethik." *Philosophische Rundschau* 1-2 (January 1973):24-42. On Olscamp (289).

185. Gibbens, Helen. "Berkeley and Wittgenstein—Some Correlations." Doctoral dissertation, University of Oklahoma. Ann Arbor, Mich.: University Microfilms, 1970.

186. Givner, David. "Berkeley's Ambiguity." *Dialogue* 8 (1970):646-62.

187. Gochnauer, Myron. "Kant's Refutation of Idealism." *Journal of the History of Philosophy* 12 (1974):195-207. See 49, 231, 268, 293, 350, 391, 393, 400.

188. Gotternbarn, D. "Berkeley: God's Pain." *Philosophical Studies* 28 (1975):245-54.

189. Gouhier, Henri. "La Signification Historique de la Pensée de Berkeley." In *Mélanges Alexandre Koyré*. Paris: Hermann, 1964. pp. 225-31. (*Histoire de la Pensée*, 12-13.)

190. Grave, S. A. "The Mind and Its Ideas: Some Problems in the Interpretation of Berkeley." *Australian Journal of Philosophy* 42 (1964):199-210. Repr. in Martin and Armstrong (261) and in Engle and Taylor (160).

191. Gray, R. "Berkeley's Theory of Space." *Journal of the History of Ideas* 16 (1978): 415-34.

192. Greenberg, A. R. "Reid, Berkeley, and Notional Knowledge." *Monist* 61 (1978):271-81.

193. Gregory, R. L., and J. G. Wallace. *Recovery from Early Blindness: A Case Study.* Experimental Psychology Society Monograph, No. 2, Cambridge (1963).

194. Gregory, R. L. "The Scientific Past and the Practising Scientist." *Times Literary Supplement* 3, 764 (26 April 1974):429-30. Includes discussion of the Molyneux Problem. Followed by replies by: J. L. Mackie (3 May), Gregory (17 May), Désirée Park (31 May), and D. Berman (21 June).

195. Griffen-Collart, E. "Perception et Sens Commun. L'Immatérialisme de Berkeley et le Réalisme de Reid." *Annales de l'Institut de Philosophie*. Bruxelles (1977):63-85.

196. Grossman, Reinhardt. "Structures Versus Sets: The Philosophical Background of Gestalt Psychology." *Critica* 9 (1977):3-21.

197. Gruner, Rolf. "Berkeley on General Ideas." *Dialogue* 8 (1969):481-85. See 61.

198. Gunderson, Martin L. "Berkeley's Idealism." Doctoral dissertation, Cornell University. Ann Arbor, Mich.: University Microfilms, 1974.

199. Guzzo, Augusto. "Berkeley and 'Things'." In Steinkraus. *New Studies*. 1966. pp. 72-84. See 343.

200. Hacking, Ian. *Why Does Language Matter to Philosophy?* London: Cambridge University Press, 1975. Discusses Berkeley on abstract ideas.

201. Hall, Roland. "Did Hume Read Some Berkeley Unawares?" *Philosophy* 42 (1967): 276-77. See 129, 202, 203, 308.

202. Hall, Roland. "Hume's Actual Use of Berkeley's *Principles*." *Philosophy* 43 (1968): 278-80. See 201.

203. Hall, Roland. "Yes, Hume Did Use Berkeley." *Philosophy* 45 (1970):152-53. See 201.

204. Hall, Roland. "New Words in Berkeley's Writings." *Berkeley Newsletter* 1 (1977):4-8.

205. Hall, Roland. *Fifty Years of Hume Scholarship* Edinburgh: University Press, 1978. Touches on Humes's knowledge of Berkeley's "Principles."

206. Harrison, Frank R., III. "Metaphysics and Common Sense." *Philosophy Today* 45 (1970):33-37.

207. Hausman, Alan. "Solipsism and Berkeley's Alleged Realism." *Revue internationale philosophique* 22 (1968):403-12. See 376, 378.

208. Henze, D. F. "Berkeley on Sensations and Qualities." *Theoria* 31, 3 (1965):174-80.

209. Henze, D. F. "Descartes vs. Berkeley: A Study in Early Modern Metaphilosophy." *Metaphilosophy* 8 (1977):147-63.

210. Hersh, Reuben, with Martin Davis. "Nonstandard Analysis." *Scientific American* (June 1972):78-86. Contains discussion of Berkeley's critique of the infinitesimal in *The Analyst*.

211. Hershbell, Jackson P. "Berkeley and the Problem of Evil." *Journal of the History of Ideas* 31 (1970):543-54.

212. Hicks, George Dawes. *Berkeley*. New York: Russell and Russell, 1968. Repr. of 1932 ed.

213. Hobbs, A. Hoyt. "Sensory Integration in Aristotle and Berkeley." Doctoral dissertation, Brandeis University. Ann Arbor, Mich.: University Microfilms, 1971.

214. Huber, D. E. "Der Englische Empirismus als Bewusstseinsphilosophie: Seine Eigenart und das Problem der Geltung von Bewusstseinsinhalten in Ihm." *Gregorianum* 58 (1977): 641-74.

215. Huber, C. E. "Die Vollendung des Englischen Empirismus als Bewusstseinphilosophie." *Gregorianum* 59 (1978):129-74.

216. Hungerman, Sister Marie B. "Berkeley and Newtonian Natural Philosophy." Doctoral dissertation, St. Louis University. Ann Arbor, Mich.: University Microfilms, 1960.

217. Hurley, Michael. "Berkeley and Methodism: A New Letter." *Berkeley Newsletter* 2 (1978):1-2.

218. Immerwahr, John. "Berkeley's Causal Thesis." *New Scholasticism* 48, 2 (1974):153-70.

219. Imlay, Robert A. "Berkeley on Abstract General Ideas." *Journal of the History of Philosophy* 9 (1971):321-28.

220. Jessop, T. E. *A Bibliography of George Berkeley*. With an inventory of Berkeley's manuscript remains by A. A. Luce. 2nd ed. The Hague: Martinus Nijhoff, 1973.

221. Jessop, T. E. *Berkeley e l'Italia (Quaderni della Biblioteca Filosofica di Torino*, no. 10). Turin: Edizioni di Filosofia, 1965.

222. Jessop, T. E. "Berkeley's Philosophy of Science." *Hermathena* 97 (1963):23-35. Repr. in Engle and Taylor (160).

223. Jessop, T. E. "Berkeley as Religious Apologist." In Steinkraus. *New Studies*. 1966. pp. 98-109. See 343.

224. Jessop, T. E., and Mariapaola Fimiani, eds. *George Berkeley: Viaggio in Italia*. Naples: Bibliopolis, 1979.

225. Johnston, G. A. *The Development of Berkeley's Philosophy*. New York: Russell and Russell, 1965. Repr. of 1923 ed.

226. Johnston, J. "The Relevance of a Berkeleian Theory of Credit to the Problem of Today." *Irish Press*. Dublin, April 20, 1965.

227. Johnston, J. "Monetary Manipulation: Berkeleian and Otherwise." *Hermathena* 110 (1970):32-36.

228. Johnston, J. *Bishop Berkeley's 'Querist' in Historical Perspective*. Dundalk, Ireland: Dundalgan Press, 1970. Text and commentary. Reviewed by: L. M. Cullin. *Hermathena* 113 (1972):78-79; D. Berman. *Hibernia*, April 16, 1971, p. 11.

229. Joseph, Horace W. B. *A Comparison of Kant's Idealism with That of Berkeley*. New York: Haskell House, 1975. Repr. of 1929 ed.

230. Joske, W. D. *Material Objects*. London: Macmillan; New York: St. Martin's Press, 1967.

231. Justin, Gale D. "On Kant's Analysis of Berkeley." *Kant-Studien* 65 (1974):20-33. See 49, 187, 268, 269, 293, 350, 391, 400.

232. Justin, G. D. "Re-relating Kant and Berkeley." *Kant-Studien* (1977):77-89.

233. Kearney, John. "Thought, Language and Meaning in Berkeley's Philosophy." *The New Scholasticism* 49 (1975):480-94.

234. Keynes, Geoffrey Langdon. *A Bibliography of George Berkeley, Bishop of Cloyne: His Works and His Critics in the Eighteenth Century*. Oxford: Clarendon Press, 1976. See 90a.

235. King, Edward G. "The Concept of Spiritual Substance in the Empiricist Philosophy

of George Berkeley." Doctoral dissertation, University of Notre Dame. Ann Arbor, Mich.: University Microfilms, 1965.

236. King, Edward G. "Language, Berkeley and God." *International Journal of the Philosophy of Religion* 1 (1970):112-13.

237. Kivy, Peter. *The Seventh Sense: A Study of Francis Hutcheson's Aesthetics and Its Influence in Eighteenth Century Britain.* New York: Burt Franklin, 1976.

238. Klein, D. B. *A History of Scientific Psychology — Its Origins and Philosophical Background.* London: Routledge and Kegan Paul, 1970.

239. Koicke, H. *Haikaisonyai no Mondai* [The Problem of the Outer World in British Empiricism]. Tokyo: Miraisha, 1967.

240. Koslowski, Barbara, with J. S. Bruner. "Visually Preadapted Constituents of Manipulatory Action." *Perception* 1 (1972):3-14.

241. Kupfer, Joseph H. "Bishop Berkeley's Rule — Utilitarianism." Doctoral dissertation, University of Rochester. Ann Arbor, Mich.: University Microfilms, 1971.

242. Kupfer, Joseph H. "A Note on Berkeley's Linguistic Criterion." *Personalist* 54 (1973): 227-31.

243. Kupfer, Joseph. "Universalization in Berkeley's Rule — Utilitarianism." *Revue internationale philosophique* 28 (1974):511-31.

244. Kupperman, Joel. "Realism vs. Idealism." *American Philosophical Quarterly* 12 (1975):199-210.

245. Kuzminski, Adrian. "The Languages of the World: The Dilemmas of Rationalist Thought and the Linguistic Metaphysics of George Berkeley." Doctoral dissertation, University of Rochester. Ann Arbor, Mich.: University Microfilms, 1970.

246. Lascola, R. A. "The Role of Relativity in Berkeley's Philosophy." Doctoral dissertation, University of Southern California. Ann Arbor, Mich.: University Microfilms, 1970.

247. Lascola, R. A. "Ideas and Archetypes: Appearance and Reality in Berkeley's Philosophy." *Personalist* 54 (1973):42-59.

248. Leroy, André-Louis. "Was Berkeley an Idealist?" In Steinkraus. *New Studies.* 1966. pp. 134-47. See 343.

249. Lewis, Douglas. "Some Problems of Perceptions." *Philosophy of Science* 37 (1970): 100-13.

249a. Lord, S. K. "Berkeleian Linguistics." *Linguistics* 213 (1978):5-28.

250. Luce, A. A. *The Dialectic of Immaterialism.* London: Hodder & Stoughton, 1963.

251. Luce, A. A. "Berkeley's New Principle Completed." In Steinkraus. *New Studies.* 1966. pp. 1-12. See 343.

252. Luce, A. A. "Sensible Ideas and Sensations." *Hermathena* 105 (1967):74-83.

253. Luce, A. A. *Berkeley and Malebranche. A Study in the Origins of Berkeley's Thought.* New York: Oxford, 1967. Repr. of 1934 ed. with new Preface.

254. Luce, A. A. *Berkeley's Immaterialism. A Commentary on His "A Treatise Concerning the Principles of Human Knowledge."* New York: Russell and Russell, 1968. Repr. of 1945 ed.

255. Luce, A. A. "Another Look at Berkeley's Notebooks." *Hermathena* 110 (1970):5-23. Reply to 67.

256. Luce, A. A. "Berkeley and the Living Thing." *Hermathena* 123 (1977):19-25.

257. Machamer, Peter, and R. G. Turnbull, eds. *Studies in Perception: Interrelations in the History of Philosophy and Science.* Columbus: Ohio State University Press, 1978. Includes essays by A. Donagan (156) and W. Sellars (320).

258. Macintosh, J. J. "Leibniz and Berkeley." *Proceedings of the Aristotelian Society* 71 (1970-71):147-63.

259. Mackie, J. L. *Problems from Locke.* Oxford: Clarendon Press, 1976.

260. Margolis, Joseph. "*Esse est percipi* Once Again." *Dialogue* 5 (1967):516-24.

261. Martin, C. B., and D. M. Armstrong, eds. *Locke and Berkeley: A Collection of Critical Essays*. New York: Doubleday Anchor, 1968. Includes repr. of essays by C. D. Broad, A. A. Luce, K. Marc-Wogau, P. D. Cummins (139), S. A. Grave (190), J. D. Mabbott, J. Bennett (75), E. J. Furlong (178), M. C. Beardsley, J. F. Thomson, and K. R. Popper.

262. Maull, N. "Cartesian Optics and Geometrization of Nature." *Review of Metaphysics* 32 (1978):253-73.

263. McConnell, F. W. "Berkeley and Scepticism." In Steinkraus. *New Studies*. 1966. pp. 43-58. See 343.

264. McGuire, J. E. "Boyle's Conception of Nature." *Journal of the History of Ideas* 33 (1972):523-41.

265. McNeill, D. *The Acquisition of Language: The Study of Developmental Psycholinguistics*. New York: Harper and Row, 1970. Defends Bailey's nativism against Berkeley's empiricism, pp. 74-79.

266. Metz, Rudolph. *George Berkeley. Leben und Lehre*. Stuttgart: Faks-Nevdr. d. Ausg., 1925. Phototype repr., 1968.

267. Miller, George W. "*The Commonplace Book* and Berkeley's Concept of the Self." *Southern Journal of Philosophy* 2 (1965):23-32.

268. Miller, George W. "Kant's First Edition Refutation of Dogmatic Idealism." *Kant-Studien* 62 (1971):298-313. See 49, 187, 269, 293, 350, 391, 393, 400.

269. Miller, George W. "Kant and Berkeley: Alternative Theories." *Kant-Studien* 64 (1973):315-35. See 268.

270. Miller, E. F. "Hume's Reduction of Cause to Sign." *New Scholasticism* 53 (1979): 42-75.

271. Mirarchi, L. A. "Force and Absolute Motion in Berkeley's Philosophy of Physics." *Journal of the History of Ideas* 38 (1977):705-13. See 325, 272.

272. Mirarchi, L. A. "A Rejoinder to Bruce Silver's Reply." *Journal of the History of Ideas* 38 (1977):716-18. See 271, 325.

273. Moked, Gabriel. "A Note on Berkeley's Corpuscularian Theories in *Siris*." *Studies in the History of the Philosophy of Science* 2 (1971):257-71.

274. Mourant, John A. "Some Unresolved Issues in Berkeley's Natural Theology." *Philosophical Studies* 15 (1966):58-75.

275. Moreau, A. "Merleau-Ponty et Berkeley." *Dialogue* 5 (1966):418-24.

276. Moreau, A. "Le problème de la raison chez Berkeley." *Dialogue* 5 (1966):154-83.

277. Moreau, A. "La conception berkeleyenne de l'évidence." *Proceedings, 8th Inter-American Congress of Philosophy* 2 (1967):288-98.

278. Morgan, M. J. *Molyneux's Question*. Cambridge: Cambridge University Press, 1977.

279. Muehlmann, R. "Berkeley's Ontology and the Epistemology of Idealism." *Canadian Journal of Philosophy* 8 (1978):89-111.

279a. Mugnai, Paolo F. *Segno e Linguaggio in George Berkeley*. Florence: Leo S. Olschki, 1979.

280. Murphy, Jeffrie G. "Berkeley and the Metaphor of Mental Substance." *Ratio* 7 (1965):170-79.

281. Najm, S. M. "Knowledge of the Self in Berkeley's Philosophy." *International Philosophical Quarterly* 6 (1966):248-69.

282. Najm, S. M. "Knowledge of Other Selves in Berkeley's Philosophy." *Personalist* 49 (1968):370-98.

282a. Oakes, Robert A. "God and Physical Objects." *International Journal of the Philosophy of Religion* 9 (1978):16-29.

283. Oaklander, L. N. "The Inherence Interpretation of Berkeley: A Critique." *Modern Schoolman* 54 (1977):261-69.

284. Odegard, D. "Berkeley and the Perception of Ideas." *Canadian Journal of Philosophy* 7 (1971):155-72.

285. Olscamp, Paul J. "Wittgenstein's Refutation of Skepticism." *Philosophy and Phenomenological Research* 26, 2 (1965):239-47.

286. Olscamp, Paul J. "The Philosophical Importance of C. M. Turbayne's *The Myth of Metaphor*." *International Philosophical Quarterly* 6 (1966):110-31. See 374.

287. Olscamp, Paul J. "Some Suggestions About the Moral Philosophy of George Berkeley." *Journal of the History of Philosophy* 6 (1968):147-56.

288. Olscamp, Paul J. "Does Berkeley Have an Ethical Theory?" In Turbayne. *Berkeley, Principles . . . Text and Critical Essays*. 1970. pp. 182-200. See 372.

289. Olscamp, Paul J. *The Moral Philosophy of George Berkeley*. The Hague: Martinus Nijhoff, 1970. Reviewed by: Désirée Park. *Studi internazionali filosofici* 3 (1971):228-30; G. J. Warnock. *Journal of Philosophy* 69, 15 (1972):460-62; Günter Gawlick (127); H. M. Bracken. *Eighteenth-Century Studies* 3 (1973):396-97; and Stanley Green. *Journal of the History of Philosophy* 12, 3 (1974):398-403.

290. Olscamp, Paul J. "George Berkeley's Unique Arguments About God." *Studi internazionali filosofici* 2 (1970):29-48.

291. Park, Désirée. "Berkeley's Theory of Notions." Doctoral dissertation, Indiana University. Ann Arbor, Mich.: University Microfilms, 1968.

292. Park, Désirée. "Locke and Berkeley on the Molyneux Problem." *Journal of the History of Ideas* 30 (1969):253-60.

293. Park, Désirée. "Kant and Berkeley's 'Idealism'." *Studi internazionali filosofici* 2 (1970):3-10. See 49, 187, 231, 268, 269, 350, 391, 393, 400.

294. Park, Désirée. "Lenin and Berkeley: Origins of a Contemporary Myth." *Studi internazionali filosofici* 2 (1970):11-28.

295. Park, Désirée. *Complementary Notions: A Critical Study of Berkeley's Theory of Concepts*. The Hague: Martinus Nijhoff, 1972. Reviewed by A. A. Luce. *Hermathena* 116 (1973):111.

296. Parkinson, G. H. R. "From Descartes to Collingwood: Recent Work on the History of Philosophy." *Philosophy* 50 (1975):205-20.

297. Parush, Adi, and M. Dascal. "On New Aspects in George Berkeley's Philosophy of Nature in *Siris*." See 143.

298. Pastore, Nicholas. "Samuel Bailey's Critique of Berkeley's Theory of Vision." *Journal of the History of the Behavioral Sciences* 1 (1965):321-37.

299. Pastore, Nicholas. "Condillac's Phenomenological Rejection of Locke and Berkeley." *Philosophy and Phenomenological Research* 27 (1967):429-31.

300. Perkins, Moreland. "Sentience." *Journal of Philosophy* 68 (1971):329-37.

301. Petrella, F. "George Berkeley's Theory of Economic Policy and Classical Economic Liberalism." *Southern Economics Journal* 32 (1966):275-84.

302. Phillips, Robert L. "Austin and Berkeley on Perception." *Philosophy* 39 (1964):161-63.

303. Piquet, Jean-Claude. "Kunst und Philosophie." *Studi internazionali filosofici* 2 (1970):49-63.

304. Pitcher, George. "Minds and Ideas in Berkeley." *American Philosophical Quarterly* 6 (1969):198-207.

305. Pitcher, George. "Thomson's Problem." *Journal of Philosophy* 71 (1974):651-52.

306. Pitcher, G. *Berkeley (Arguments of the Philosophers)*. London: Routledge and Kegan Paul, 1977.

307. Pittion, J. P., and D. Berman. "A New Letter by Berkeley to Browne on Divine Analogy." *Mind* 78 (1969):375-92.

308. Popkin, Richard H. "So, Hume Did Read Berkeley." *Journal of Philosophy* 61 (1964): 773-78. See 129, 201, 202, 203.

309. Raine, Kathleen. "Berkeley, Blake and the New Age." *Thought* 51 (1976):356-77. Repr. by Golgonooza Press, 1977.

310. Ramsey, Ian T. "Berkeley and the Possibility of an Empirical Metaphysics." In Steinkraus. *New Studies*. 1966. pp. 13-30. See 343.

311. Rauter, H. "The Veil of Words: Sprachauffassung und Dialogform bei George Berkeley." *Anglia* (Tübingen) 79 (1962):378-404.

312. Ritchie, Arthur D. *George Berkeley: A Reappraisal*, ed., and with preface, by G. E. Davie. Manchester: Manchester University Press; New York: Barnes and Noble, 1967. Reviewed by C. M. Turbayne. *Journal of Philosophy* 66 (1969):113-16, H. M. Bracken. *Dialogue* 7 (1968-69):674-75.

313. Rollin, B. E. *Natural and Conventional Meaning: An Examination of the Distinction*. The Hague: Mouton, 1976.

314. Rossi, Mario M. *Introduzione a Berkeley*. Bari: Laterza, 1970.

315. Sartorius, Rolf. "A Neglected Aspect of the Relationship Between Berkeley's Theory of Vision and his Immaterialism." *American Philosophical Quarterly* 6 (1969):318-23.

316. Scallet, Jeffrey. "A Sequel to Berkeley's *Dialogues*: Excerpts." *Dialogue* 17 (1974): 1-6.

317. Scott, Ulric C., Jr. "The Philosophical Notebooks of George Berkeley: An Historical, Structural, Textual, and Interpretive Analysis." Doctoral dissertation, University of Minnesota. Ann Arbor, Mich.: University Microfilms, 1970.

318. Sellars, Roy Wood. *Lending a Hand to Hylas*. Ann Arbor, Mich.: Edwards Bros., 1968.

319. Sellars, Wilfred. *Science, Perception and Reality*. New York: Routledge and Kegan Paul, 1963. Contains chapter "Phenomenalism." See 133.

320. Sellars, Wilfred. "Berkeley and Descartes: Reflections on the Theory of Ideas." In Machamer and Turnbull. *Studies in Perception*. 1978. pp. 259-311. See 257.

321. Shimony, Abner. "Perception From an Evolutionary Point of View." *Journal of Philosophy* 68 (1971):571-83.

322. Silver, Bruce. "The Status of the Sciences in the Philosophy of George Berkeley." Doctoral dissertation, University of Colorado. Ann Arbor, Mich.: University Microfilms, 1971.

323. Silver, Bruce. "Berkeley and the Mathematics of Materialism." *New Scholasticism* 46 (1972):427-38.

324. Silver, Bruce. "Berkeley and the Principle of Inertia." *Journal of the History of Ideas* 34, 4 (1973):599-608.

325. Silver, Bruce. "Reply to Professor Mirarchi's 'Force and Absolute Motion . . . '." *Journal of the History of Ideas* 38 (1977):714-15. See 271, 272.

326. Silver, Bruce. "The Invisible World of Berkeley's *New Theory of Vision*." *New Scholasticism* 51 (1977):142-61.

327. Silver, Bruce. "The Conflicting Microscopic Worlds of Berkeley's *Three Dialogues*." *Journal of the History of Ideas* 37 (1976):343-49.

328. Sinha, C. P. "Berkeley's Learning Theory of Perception." *Darshana International* 10 (1970):19-21.

329. Sinha, L. P. N. "The Sign Theories of Perception." *Darshana International* 7 (1967): 90-94.

330. Sosa, Ernesto. "Russell, Berkeley y la Materia Objectivo." *Critica* 7 (1975):35-41.

331. Sousa e Silva, A. A. "Motivos do imaterialismo de Berkeley." *Lumen* (Lisbon) 27 (1963):159-64.

332. Stack, George J. "Berkeley's Theory of Perception." Doctoral dissertation, Pennsylvania State University. Ann Arbor, Mich.: University Microfilms, 1964.

333. Stack, George J. "Berkeley's Conception of Object." *Modern Schoolman* 45 (1967): 1-27.

334. Stack, George J. "Berkeley's Phenomenalism." *Personalist* 50 (1969):335-59.

335. Stack, George J. *Berkeley's Analysis of Perception.* The Hague: Mouton, 1970. Reviewed by H. M. Bracken. *Journal of the History of Philosophy* 10 (1972):480-81.

336. Stack, George J. "Berkeley and Phenomenalism." *Modern Schoolman* 47 (1970): 391-422.

337. Stack, George J. "Berkeley's New Theory of Vision." *Personalist* 51 (1970):106-38.

338. Stack, George. "Berkeley's Concept of Existence." *Modern Schoolman* 53 (1976): 281-89.

339. Stainsby, H. V. "Sight and Sense Data." *Mind* 79 (1970):170-87.

340. Steinkraus, Warren E. "Two Philosopher-Bishops." *Journal of Bible and Religion* (January 1957):24-29.

341. Steinkraus, Warren E. "Berkeley's Wisdom on Other Minds." *Philosophical Forum*, Old Series, 15 (1957-58):3-24.

342. Steinkraus, Warren E. "On Defending Idealism." *Philosophical Quarterly* (India) 34, 4 (1962):261-67.

343. Steinkraus, Warren E., ed. *New Studies in Berkeley's Philosophy.* New York: Holt, Rinehart and Winston, 1966. Foreword by Brand Blanshard. New essays by Luce (251), Ramsey (310), Turbayne (370), McConnell (263), Tipton (365), Guzzo (199), Bracken (96), Jessop (223), Datta (144), Farooqi (167), Leroy (248), Steinkraus (344), and Werkmeister (391). Reviewed by George J. Stack. *Journal of the History of Ideas* 5 (1967):178-80.

344. Steinkraus, Warren E. "Berkeley and His Modern Critics." In Steinkraus. *New Studies.* 1966. pp. 148-62. See 343.

345. Steinkraus, Warren E. "Is Berkeley a Subjective Idealist?" *Personalist* 48 (1967):103-18.

346. Steinkraus, Warren E. "A Note on Gladstone and Berkeley." *Journal of the History of Philosophy* 9 (1971):372-74.

347. Steinkraus, Warren E. "Berkeley and Inferred Friends." *Dialogue* 11 (1972):592-95.

348. Steinkraus, W. E. "A Piece of Sensible Bread." *Indian Philosophical Quarterly* 5 (1978):619-25.

349. Sterling, M. C. "Berkeley Contra el Realismo." *Sapienta* 33 (1978):153-55.

350. Stuart, James D. "Kant's Refutation of Berkeley's Idealism." Doctoral dissertation, University of Cincinnati. Ann Arbor, Mich.: University Microfilms, 1970. See 49, 187, 231, 268, 269, 293, 391, 393, 400.

351. Stuart, James. "Berkeley's Appearance/Reality Distinction." *Southwestern Journal of Philosophy* 8 (1977):119-30.

352. Suchting, W. A. "Berkeley's Criticism of Newton on Space and Time." *Isis* 58 (1967): 186-97.

353. Sullivan, Timothy D. "Berkeley's Moral Philosophy." *Philosophical Studies of Ireland* 19 (1970):193-201.

354. Taylor, C. C. W. "Berkeley's Theory of Abstract Ideas." *Philosophical Quarterly* 28 (1978):97-115.

355. Taylor, Gabriele, with Gale Engel, eds. *Berkeley's Principles . . . Critical Studies.* 1968. See 160.

356. Testa, Aldo. *Meditazioni su Berkeley.* Bologna: Capelli, 1965. (*Biblioteca di cultura filosofica,* 36.)

357. Thayer, H. S. "Berkeley and Some Anticipations of Pragmatism." In his *Meaning and Action: A Critical History of Pragmatism.* New York: Bobbs-Merrill, 1968. pp. 499-507.

358. Theau, Jean. "Comment on est passé de l'idée cartésienne à l'idée berkleyenne de la matière." *Dialogue* 11 (1972):509-34.

359. Thomas, George H. "The Implications of Berkeley's Earliest Philosophy Concerning Things." *Journal of the History of Philosophy* 10 (1972):425-30.

360. Thomas, George. "Berkeley's God Does Not Perceive." *Journal of the History of Philosophy* 14 (1976):163-68.

361. Thomson, James F. "Berkeley." In *A Critical History of Western Philosophy*, ed. D. J. O'Connor. New York: Free Press, 1964. pp. 236-53.

362. Thomson, Judith J. "Molyneux's Problem." *Journal of Philosophy* 71 (1974):637-51.

363. Thrane, Gary. "Berkeley's Proper Objects of Vision." *Journal of the History of Ideas* 38 (1977):243-60.

364. Tipton, I. C., and E. J. Furlong. "Mrs. George Berkeley and Her Washing Machine." *Hermathena* 101 (1965):38-47.

365. Tipton, I. C. "Berkeley's View of Spirit." In Steinkraus. *New Studies*. 1966. pp. 59-71. See 343.

366. Tipton, I. C. "Two Questions on Bishop Berkeley's Panacea." *Journal of the History of Ideas* 30 (1969):203-24.

367. Tipton, I. C. *Berkeley, The Philosophy of Immaterialism*. London: Methuen, 1974. Reviewed by E. J. Furlong. *Hermathena* 117 (1974):100-01.

368. Trejo, Wonfilic. "Sobre la Definicion de Fenomenalismo." *Dianoia* 27 (1971):62-88.

369. Turbayne, Colin Murray, and Robert Ware. "A Bibliography of George Berkeley, 1933-1962." *Journal of Philosophy* 60 (1963):93-112.

370. Turbayne, Colin Murray. "The Origin of Berkeley's Paradoxes." In Steinkraus. *New Studies*. 1966. pp. 31-42. See 343.

371. Turbayne, Colin Murray. "Visual Language from the Verbal Model." *Visible Language* 3 (1969):345-70; and *Luce e Immagini* 24, 5, 6 (1970):137-50, 180-85, tr. Lucia Ronchi; and *Proceedings, First National Conference on Visual Literacy*. New York: Pitman, 1970. pp. 17-27; modified with title "Visual Language." *ETC* 28 (1971):51-58.

372. Turbayne, Colin Murray, ed. *Berkeley: Principles of Human Knowledge, Text and Critical Essays*. Indianapolis: Bobbs-Merrill, 1970. New essays by Turbayne (373), Cornman (133), Olscamp (288): reprints of essays by W. H. Hay, R. J. Van Iten (376), G. E. Moore, W. T. Stace, R. H. Popkin, K. R. Popper, C. M. Turbayne, J. D. Mabbott. Reviewed by G. P. Conroy. *Journal of the History of Philosophy* 9 (1971):510-12; J. M. Beyssade. *Études Philosophiques* 4 (1970):523-26.

373. Turbayne, Colin Murray. "Berkeley's Metaphysical Grammar." In Turbayne. *Berkeley, Principles . . . Text and Critical Essays*. 1970. pp. 3-36. See 372, 136.

374. Turbayne, Colin Murray. *The Myth of Metaphor*. With forewords by Morse Peckham and Foster Tait and appendix by Rolf Eberle. Columbia, S. C.: University of South Carolina Press, 1970. Rev. of 1962 ed. Spanish ed., Fondo de Cultura Economica, Mexico, 1974. Reviewed by Paul J. Olscamp (286).

375. Turbayne, C. M., and R. Appelbaum. "A Bibliography of George Berkeley, 1963-1974." *Journal of the History of Philosophy* 15 (1977):83-95.

376. Van Iten, Richard J. "Berkeley's Alleged Solipsism." *Revue internationale philosophique* 16 (1962):447-52. Repr. in Turbayne (372). See 207, 378.

377. Van Iten, Richard J. "Berkeley's Analysis of Mind." *Philosophy and Phenomenological Research* 24 (1963-64):375-82.

378. Van Iten, Richard J. "Berkeley's Realism and His Alleged Solipsism Re-examined." *Revue internationale philosophique* 22 (1968):413-22. See 207, 376.

379. Van Steenburgh, E. W. "Berkeley Revisited." *Journal of Philosophy* 60 (1963):85-89.

380. Varnedoe, Samuel L. "A Critical Examination of Berkeley's Doctrine of Ideas and its

Role in His Philosophy." Doctoral dissertation, University of Pennsylvania. Ann Arbor, Mich.: University Microfilms, 1966.

381. Wagner, Jennie, and Ron Brooks. *The Bunyip of Berkeley's Creek*. Melbourne: Longman, 1974.

382. Wallace, J. G., with R. L. Gregory. *Recovery from Early Blindness: A Case Study*. *Experimental Psychology Society Monographs* No. 2. Cambridge, 1963.

383. Ware, Robert, with C. M. Turbayne. "A Bibliography of George Berkeley, 1933-1962." *Journal of Philosophy* 60 (1963):93-112.

384. Watson, Richard A. "Berkeley in a Cartesian Context." *Revue international philosophique* 17 (1963):381-94.

385. Watson, Richard A. "Berkeley in the Cartesian Tradition." *Papers of the Michigan Academy of Science, Arts and Letters* 48 (1963):587-97.

386. Watson, Richard A. "The Breakdown of Cartesian Metaphysics." *Journal of the History of Philosophy* 1 (1963):177-97.

387. Watson, Richard A. *The Downfall of Cartesianism*. The Hague: Martinus Nijhoff, 1966. Contains section on Berkeley.

388. Wenz, Peter S. "George Berkeley's Attack on the Doctrine of Abstract Ideas." Doctoral dissertation, University of Wisconsin. Ann Arbor, Mich.: University Microfilms, 1971.

389. Wenz, Peter. "Berkeley's Christian Neo-Platonism." *Journal of the History of Ideas* 37 (1976):537-46.

390. Weir, Winfried. "Logical Problems of Epistemological Immanentism." *Ratio* 14 (1972):59-73.

391. Werkmeister, W. H. "Notes to an Interpretation of Berkeley." In Steinkraus. *New Studies*. 1966. pp. 163-72. See 343, also 49, 187, 231, 268, 269, 293, 350, 393, 400.

392. Willard, Dallas. "Perceptual Realism." *Southwestern Journal of Philosophy* 1 (1970): 75-84.

393. Wilson, Margaret D. "Kant and 'The Dogmatic Idealism of Berkeley'." *Journal of the History of Philosophy* 9 (1971):459-76. See 49, 187, 231, 268, 293, 350, 391, 400.

394. Wilson, Fred. "The Role of a Principle of Acquaintance in Ontology." *Modern Schoolman* 47 (1969):37-56.

395. Wilson, Fred. "Acquaintance, Ontology, and Knowledge." *New Scholasticism* 44 (1970):1-48.

396. Wimmer, Hans Alfred. *Neue Dialoge zwischen Hylas und Philonous*. Heidelberg: Carl Winters Universitäts Buchhandlung, 1938.

397. Woolhouse, Roger. "Berkeley, The Sun that I see by day and that which I imagine by night." *Philosophy* 43 (1968):152-60. See 61.

398. Woolhouse, R. S. "Berkeley and a Famous Man of Modern Times." *Berkeley Newsletter* 3 (1979):5-7.

399. Woozley, A. D. "Berkeley's Doctrine of Notions and Theory of Meaning." *Journal of the History of Philosophy* 14 (1976):427-34.

400. Workman, Rollin W. "Kant's Refutation of Idealism." *Philosophical Forum*, New Series, 1 (1969):332-51. See 49, 187, 231, 268, 269, 293, 350, 391, 393.

401. Yolton, John. "As in a Looking-Glass: Perceptual Acquaintance in Eighteenth-Century Britain." *Journal of the History of Ideas* 40 (1979):207-34.

402. Ziedan, M. F. "The Development of Berkeley's Philosophy, 1708-1710." *Hermathena* 97 (1963):36-56.

Indexes

Name Index

Subject Index

Colin M. Turbayne is professor of philosophy, emeritus, at the University of Rochester. He is the author of *The Myth of Metaphor* and has edited several of Berkeley's works.